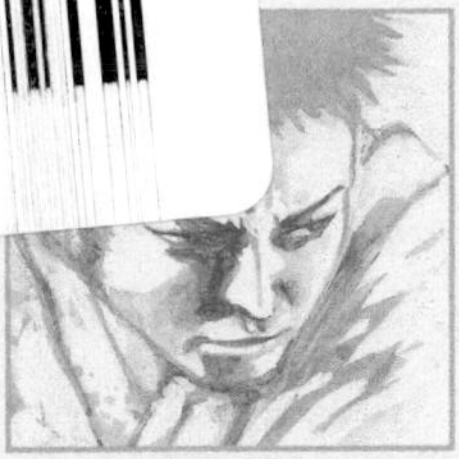

尾田栄一郎

The following saying is often held to be male chauvinistic: "A wife should follow three steps behind her husband." This actually stems from an old samurai custom. If you were a samurai carrying around a dreadfully long katana, never knowing when you might need to use it, could you really let the most important person in your world walk next to you? The three steps are a distance meant to keep womankind safe!! So a real man should propose by saying, "Do me the honor of following three steps behind me for the rest of our lives!!"
Now let's start three steps behind Volume 79. It's Volume 76!!!

-Eiichiro Oda, 2014

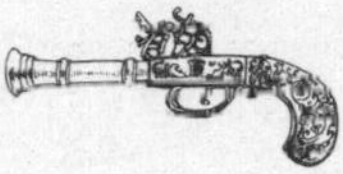

Eiichiro Oda began his manga career at the age of 17, when his one-shot cowboy manga **Wanted!** won second place in the coveted Tezuka manga awards. Oda went on to work as an assistant to some of the biggest manga artists in the industry, including Nobuhiro Watsuki, before winning the Hop Step Award for new artists. His pirate adventure **One Piece**, which debuted in **Weekly Shonen Jump** in 1997, quickly became one of the most popular manga in Japan.

ONE PIECE VOL. 76
NEW WORLD PART 16

SHONEN JUMP Manga Edition

STORY AND ART BY EIICHIRO ODA

Translation/Stephen Paul
Touch-up Art & Lettering/Vanessa Satone
Design/Fawn Lau
Editor/Alexis Kirsch

Printed in the U.S.A.

Published by VIZ Media, LLC
P.O. Box 77010
San Francisco, CA 94107

10 9 8 7
First printing, November 2015
Seventh printing, July 2022

viz.com

PARENTAL ADVISORY
ONE PIECE is rated T for Teen and is recommended for ages 13 and up. This volume contains fantasy violence and tobacco usage.

ratings.viz.com RATED T TEEN

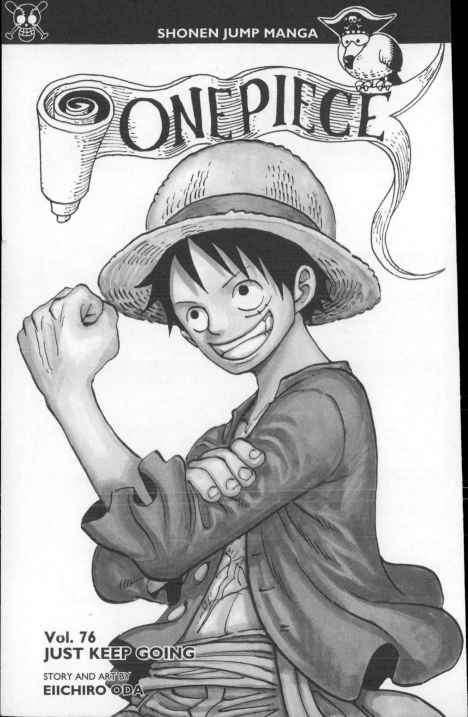

ONE PIECE

Vol. 76
JUST KEEP GOING

STORY AND ART BY
EIICHIRO ODA

The Straw Hat Crew

Monkey D. Luffy

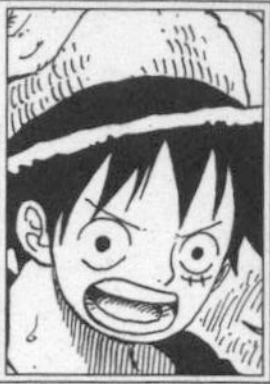

A young man who dreams of becoming the Pirate King. After training with Rayleigh, he and his crew head for the New World!

Captain, Bounty: 400 million berries

Tony Tony Chopper

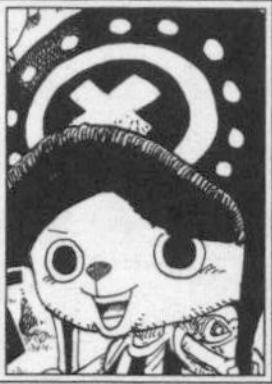

After researching powerful medicine in Birdie Kingdom, he reunites with the rest of the crew.

Ship's Doctor, Bounty: 50 berries

Roronoa Zolo

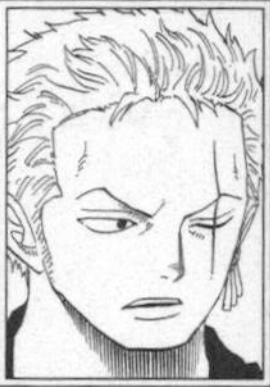

He swallowed his pride and asked to be trained by Mihawk on Gloom Island before reuniting with the rest of the crew.

Fighter, Bounty: 120 million berries

Nico Robin

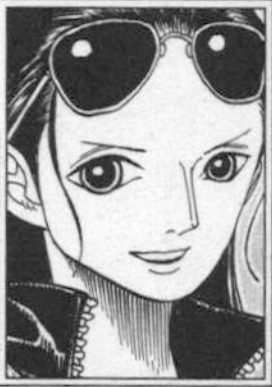

She spent her time in Baltigo with the leader of the Revolutionary Army: Luffy's father, Dragon.

Archeologist, Bounty: 80 million berries

Nami

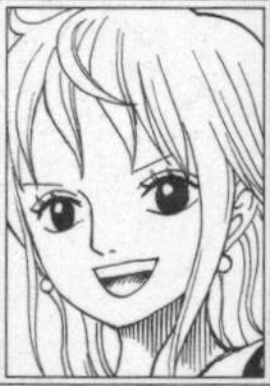

She studied the weather of the New World on the small Sky Island Weatheria, a place where weather is studied as a science.

Navigator, Bounty: 16 million berries

Franky

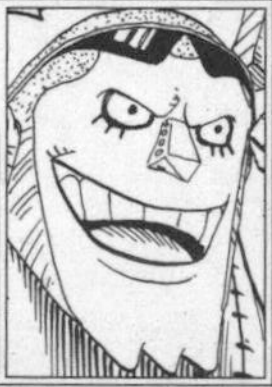

He modified himself in Future Land Baldimore and turned himself into Armored Franky before reuniting with the rest of the crew.

Shipwright, Bounty: 44 million berries

Usopp

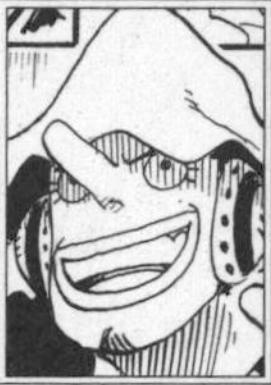

He trained under Heracles at the Bowin Islands to become the King of Snipers.

Sniper, Bounty: 30 million berries

Brook

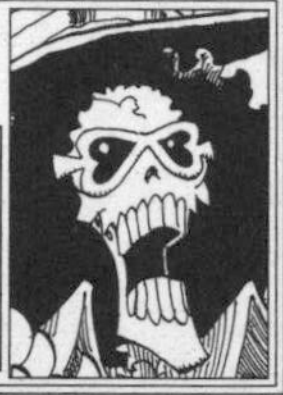

After being captured and used as a freak show by the Longarm Tribe, he became a famous rock star called "Soul King" Brook.

Musician, Bounty: 33 million berries

Sanji

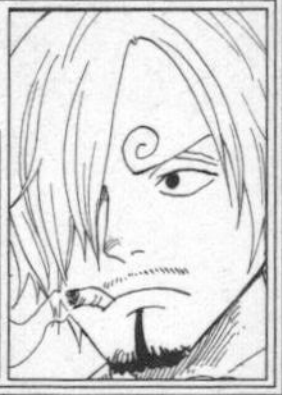

After fighting the New Kama Karate masters in the Kamabakka Kingdom, he returned to the crew.

Cook, Bounty: 77 million berries

Shanks

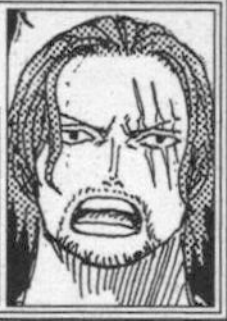

One of the Four Emperors. Waits for Luffy in the "New World," the second half of the Grand Line.

Captain of the Red-Haired Pirates

the crew meets a one-legged toy soldier who informs them of the nation's hidden darkness, and they decide to help the little Tontattas in their fight for freedom. Luffy rescues Law from captivity, and Usopp succeeds in freeing those who have been turned into toys. Furious, Doflamingo covers the island in a giant birdcage and puts bounties on our heroes' heads!! Now on the run from Dressrosa's citizens, Luffy heads for Doflamingo in the palace on the fourth step to rescue the kingdom, but...

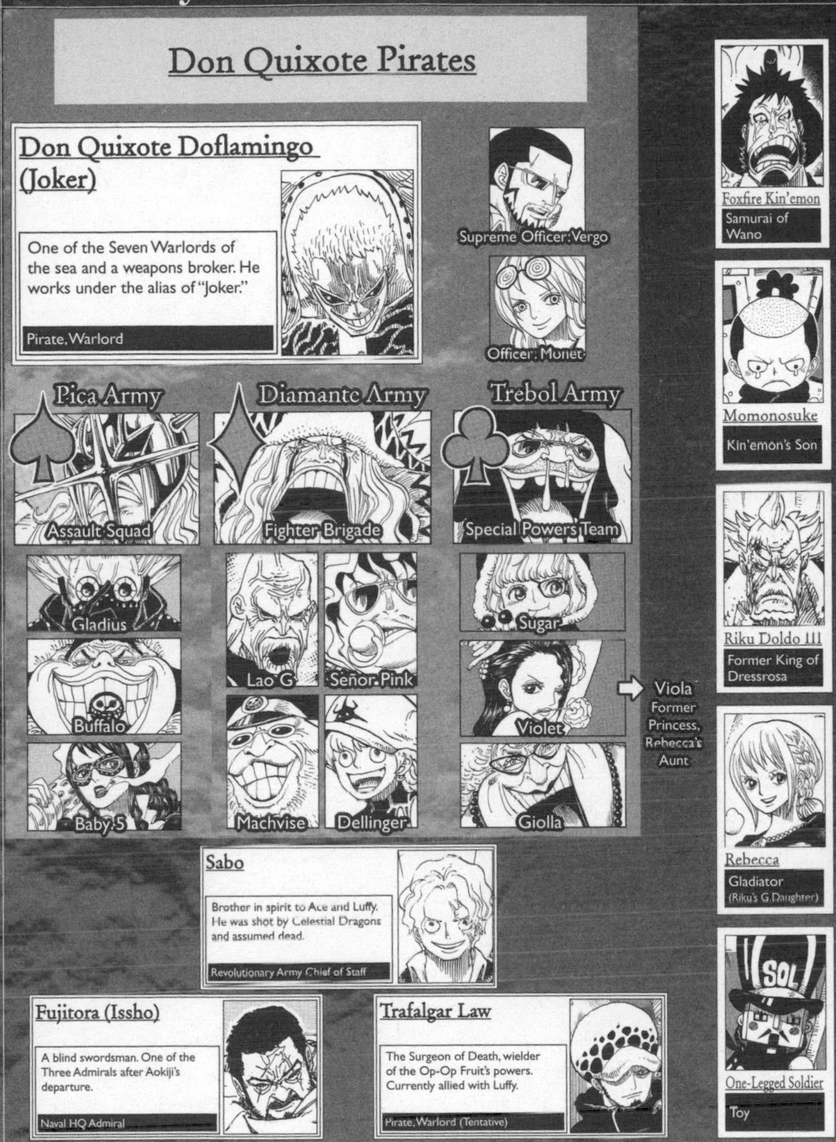
Don Quixote Pirates
Don Quixote Doflamingo (Joker)
One of the Seven Warlords of the sea and a weapons broker. He works under the alias of "Joker."
Pirate, Warlord
Supreme Officer: Vergo
Officer: Monet
Pica Army
Assault Squad
Gladius
Buffalo
Baby 5
Diamante Army
Fighter Brigade
Lao G
Señor Pink
Machvise
Dellinger
Trebol Army
Special Powers Team
Sugar
Violet
Giolla
Viola
Former Princess, Rebecca's Aunt
Foxfire Kin'emon
Samurai of Wano
Momonosuke
Kin'emon's Son
Riku Doldo III
Former King of Dressrosa
Rebecca
Gladiator
(Riku's G.Daughter)
One-Legged Soldier
Toy
Sabo
Brother in spirit to Ace and Luffy. He was shot by Celestial Dragons and assumed dead.
Revolutionary Army Chief of Staff
Fujitora (Issho)
A blind swordsman. One of the Three Admirals after Aokiji's departure.
Naval HQ Admiral
Trafalgar Law
The Surgeon of Death, wielder of the Op-Op Fruit's powers. Currently allied with Luffy.
Pirate, Warlord (Tentative)

Story

After two years of hard training, the Straw Hat pirates are back together, first at the Sabaody Archipelago and then through Fish-Man Island to their next stage: the New World!!

The crew happens across Trafalgar Law on the island of Punk Hazard. At his suggestion, they form a new pirate alliance that seeks to take down one of the Four Emperors. The group infiltrates the kingdom of Dressrosa in an attempt to set up Doflamingo, but Law is abducted after falling into a trap. The rest of

NEW WORLD ONE PIECE

Vol. 76
Just Keep Going

CONTENTS

Chapter 753:
BATTLE

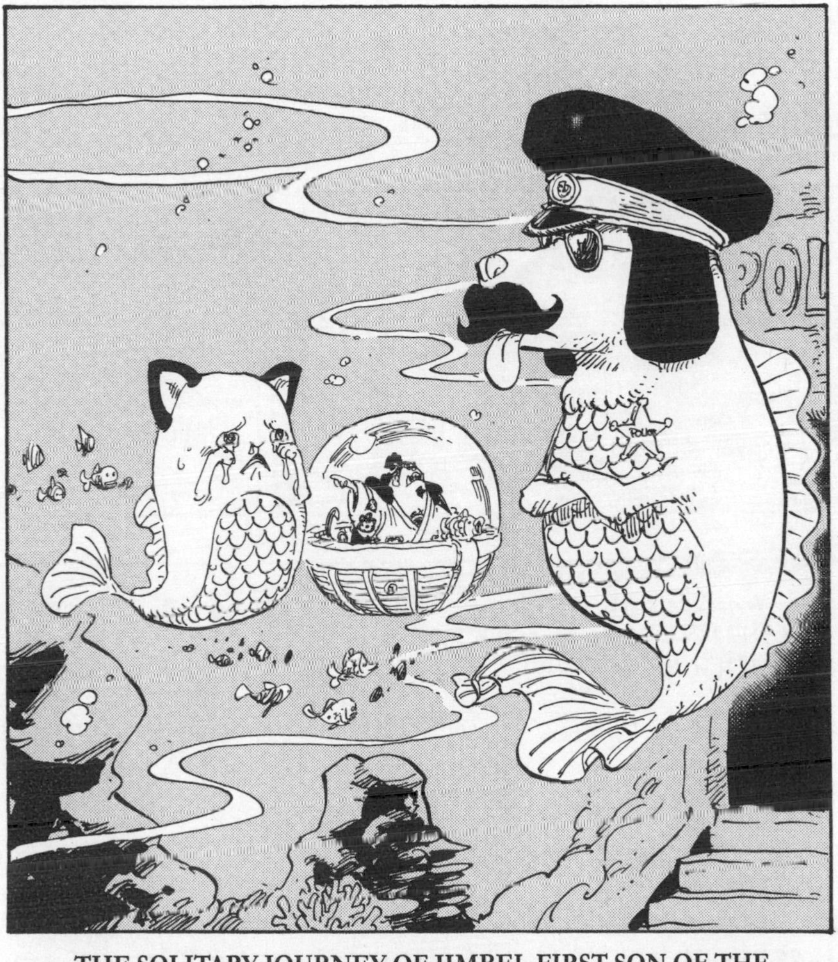
POL
POLICE

THE SOLITARY JOURNEY OF JIMBEI, FIRST SON OF THE SEA, VOL. 3: "LOOKS LIKE TROUBLE FOR THIS SEA-DOG OFFICER (SEA ANIMAL SHERIFF)"

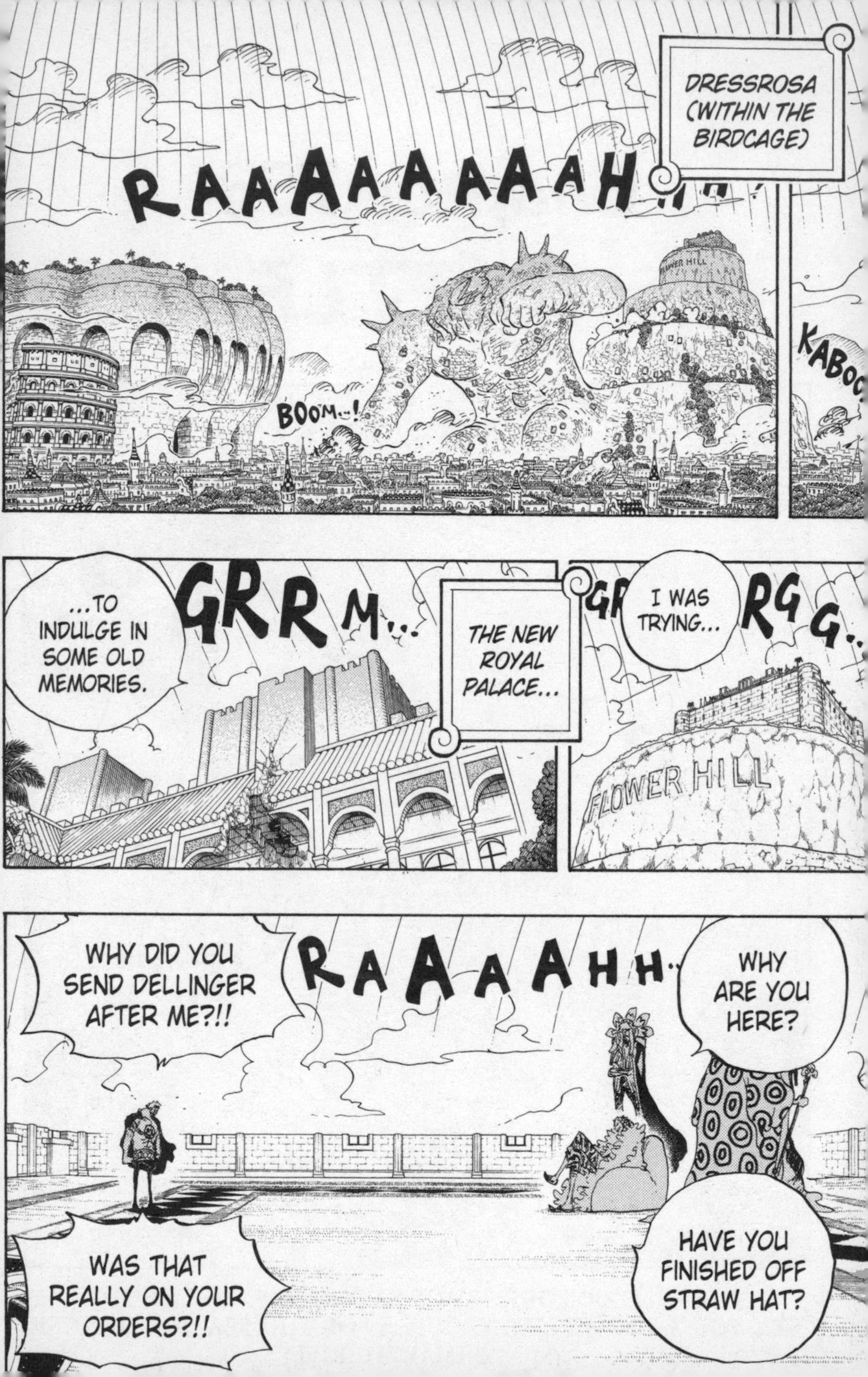

KABOO
DRESSROSA (WITHIN THE BIRDCAGE)
RAAAAAAAAH
FLOWER HILL
BOOM...!
GR
I WAS TRYING...
RGG...
FLOWER HILL
THE NEW ROYAL PALACE...
GRRM...
...TO INDULGE IN SOME OLD MEMORIES.
WHY ARE YOU HERE?
RAAAAHH...
WHY DID YOU SEND DELLINGER AFTER ME?!!
HAVE YOU FINISHED OFF STRAW HAT?
WAS THAT REALLY ON YOUR ORDERS?!!

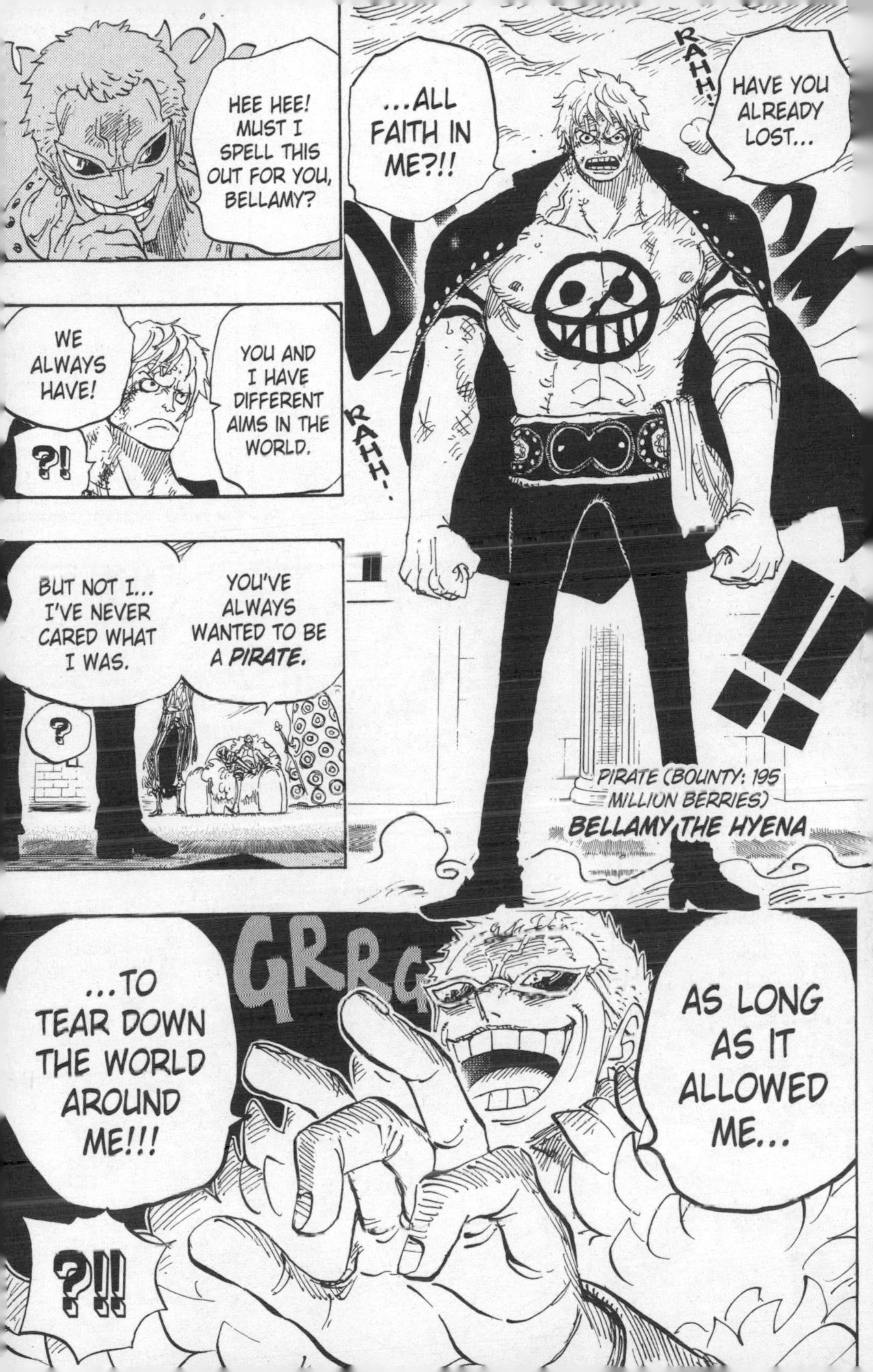
RAHH!
HAVE YOU ALREADY LOST...
...ALL FAITH IN ME?!!
DOM!!
RAHH!
PIRATE (BOUNTY: 195 MILLION BERRIES)
BELLAMY THE HYENA
HEE HEE! MUST I SPELL THIS OUT FOR YOU, BELLAMY?
YOU AND I HAVE DIFFERENT AIMS IN THE WORLD.
WE ALWAYS HAVE!
?!
YOU'VE ALWAYS WANTED TO BE A *PIRATE.*
BUT NOT I... I'VE NEVER CARED WHAT I WAS.
?
AS LONG AS IT ALLOWED ME...
GRRG
...TO TEAR DOWN THE WORLD AROUND ME!!!
?!!

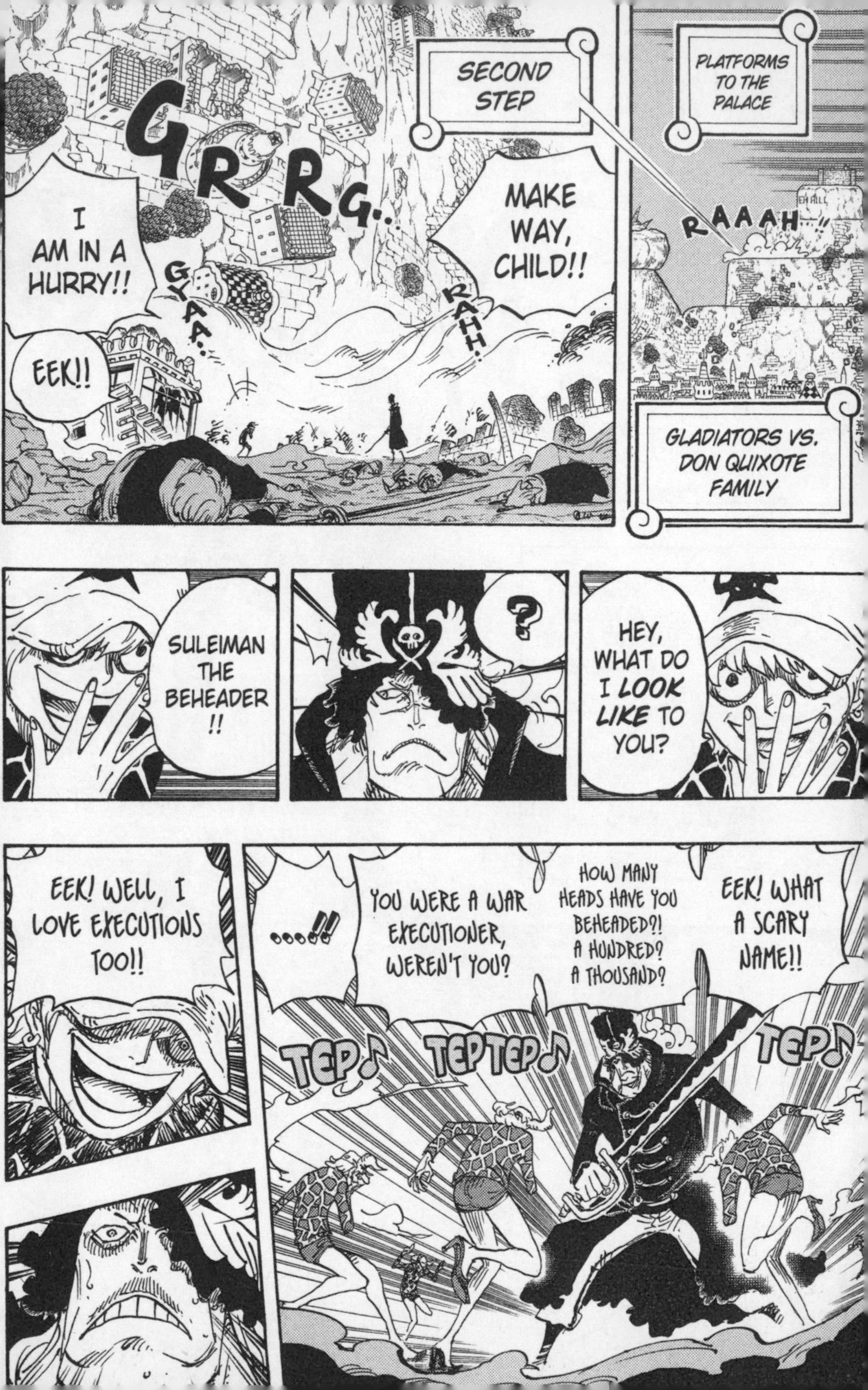
PLATFORMS TO THE PALACE
GLADIATORS VS. DON QUIXOTE FAMILY
RAAAH...!!
SECOND STEP
GRRRG...
MAKE WAY, CHILD!!
RAHH...
GYAA...
I AM IN A HURRY!!
EEK!!
HEY, WHAT DO I LOOK LIKE TO YOU?
?
SULEIMAN THE BEHEADER!!
EEK! WHAT A SCARY NAME!!
HOW MANY HEADS HAVE YOU BEHEADED?! A HUNDRED? A THOUSAND?
YOU WERE A WAR EXECUTIONER, WEREN'T YOU?
....!!
TEP♪
TEPTEP♪
TEP♪
EEK! WELL, I LOVE EXECUTIONS TOO!!

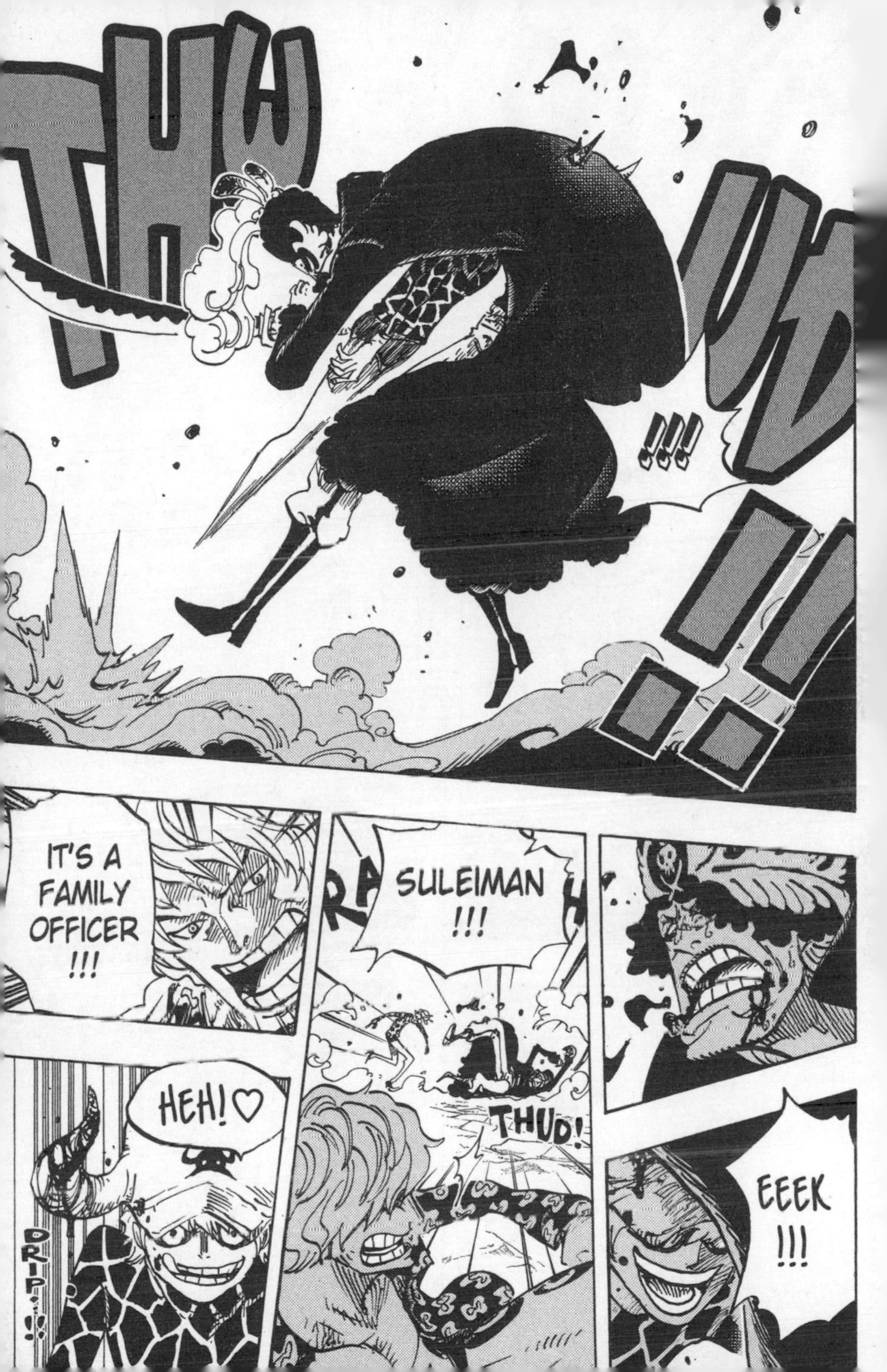
THWUD
!!!
EEEK !!!
SULEIMAN !!!
THUD!
IT'S A FAMILY OFFICER !!!
HEH!♡
DRIP...

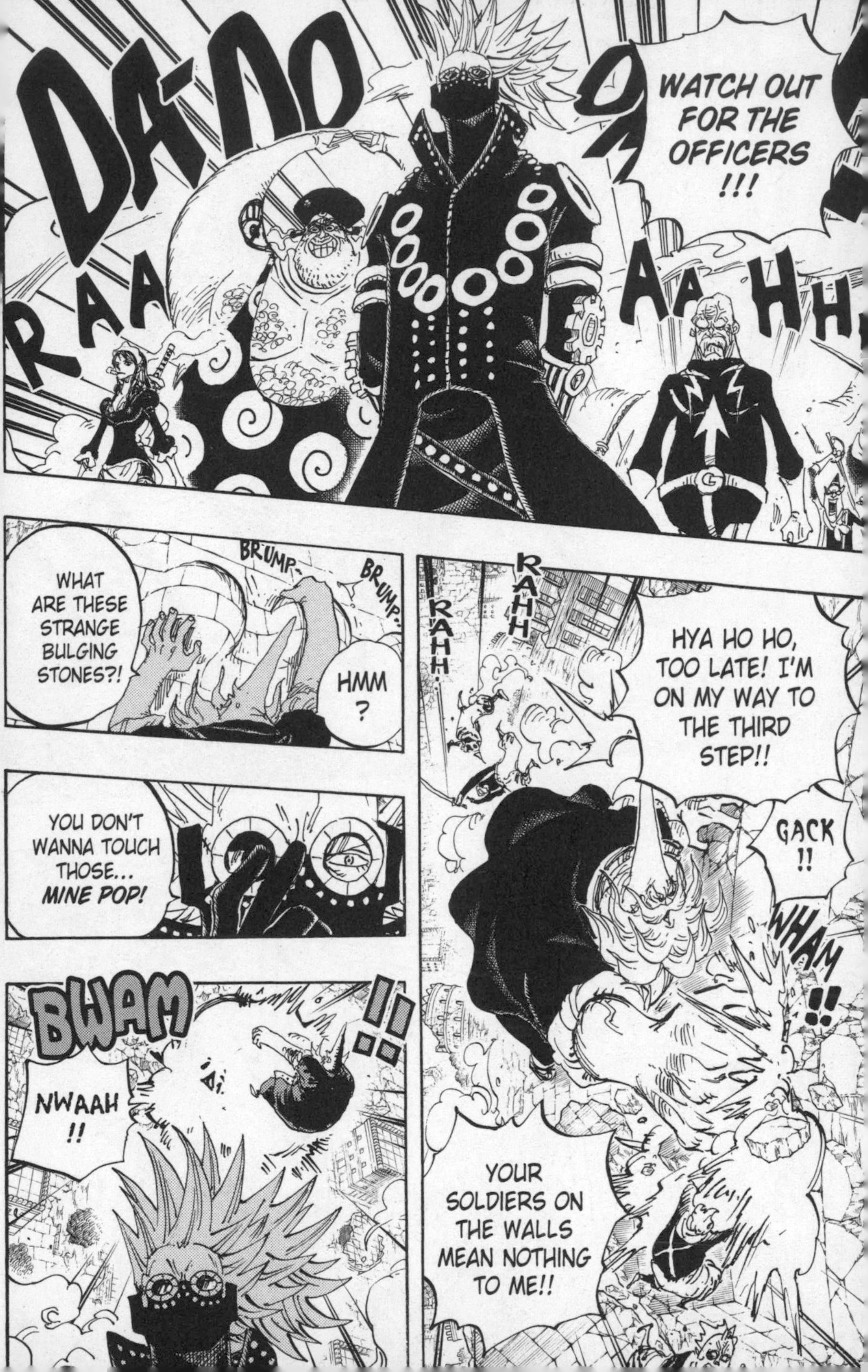
WATCH OUT FOR THE OFFICERS !!!
DA-DO
AAHH
RAA
RAHH
RAHH
HYA HO HO, TOO LATE! I'M ON MY WAY TO THE THIRD STEP!!
GACK !!
WHAM !!
YOUR SOLDIERS ON THE WALLS MEAN NOTHING TO ME!!
BRUMP
BRUMP
HMM ?
WHAT ARE THESE STRANGE BULGING STONES?!
YOU DON'T WANNA TOUCH THOSE... *MINE POP!*
BWAM !!
NWAAH !!

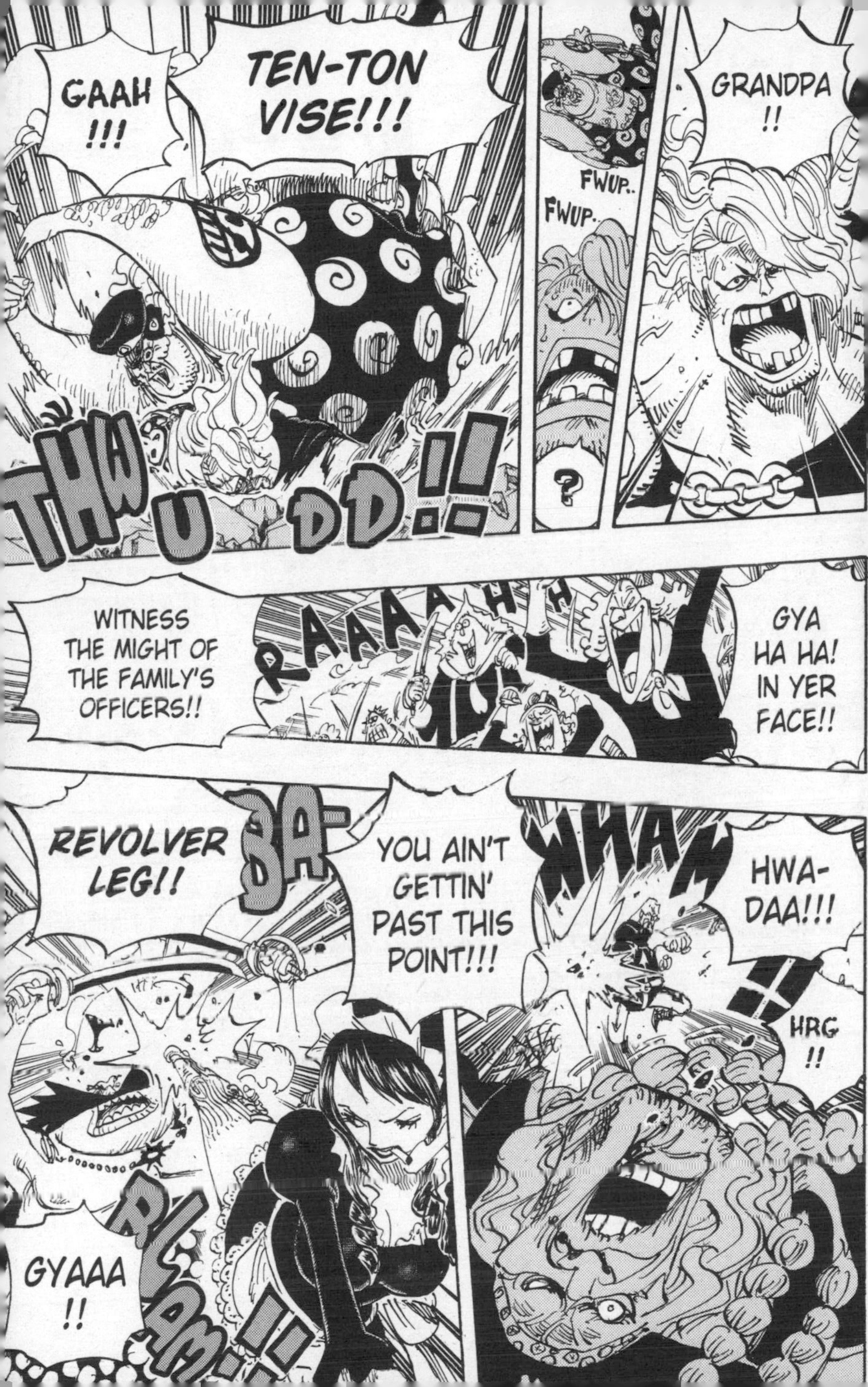
GRANDPA !!
FWUP..
FWUP..
?
TEN-TON VISE!!!
GAAH !!!
THWUDD!!
GYA HA HA! IN YER FACE!!
RAAAAHH
WITNESS THE MIGHT OF THE FAMILY'S OFFICERS!!
HWA-DAA!!!
WHAM
HRG !!
YOU AIN'T GETTIN' PAST THIS POINT!!!
BA-
REVOLVER LEG!!
BLAM!!
GYAAA !!

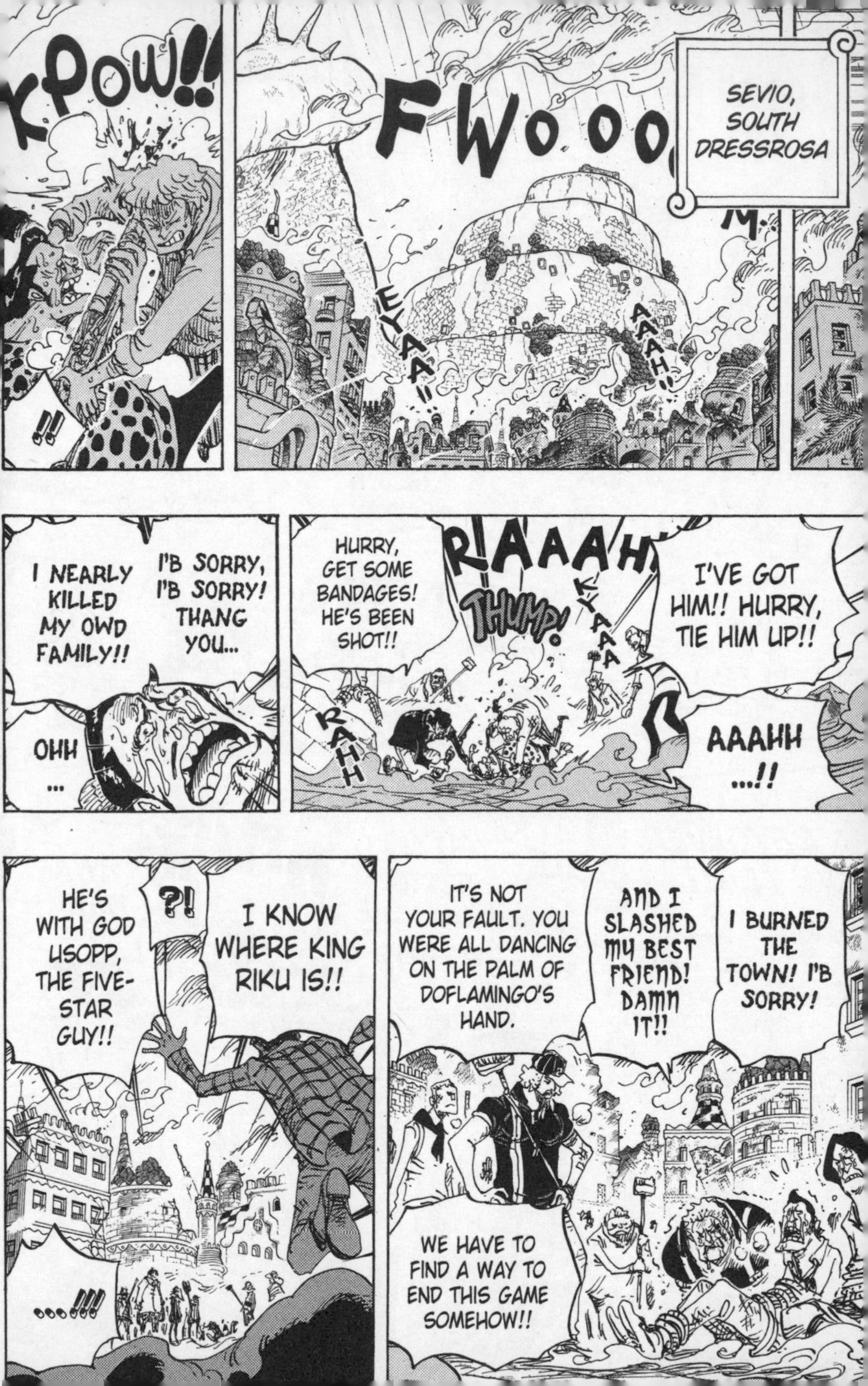
SEVIO, SOUTH DRESSROSA
FWOOOOM
EYAAA!!
AAAAH!!
KPOW!!
!!
I'VE GOT HIM!! HURRY, TIE HIM UP!!
RAAAAH
HURRY, GET SOME BANDAGES! HE'S BEEN SHOT!!
THUMP!
KYAAAA
RAHH
AAAHH ...!!
I'B SORRY, I'B SORRY! THANG YOU...
I NEARLY KILLED MY OWD FAMILY!!
OHH ...
I BURNED THE TOWN! I'B SORRY!
AND I SLASHED MY BEST FRIEND! DAMN IT!!
IT'S NOT YOUR FAULT. YOU WERE ALL DANCING ON THE PALM OF DOFLAMINGO'S HAND.
WE HAVE TO FIND A WAY TO END THIS GAME SOMEHOW!!
I KNOW WHERE KING RIKU IS!!
?!
HE'S WITH GOD USOPP, THE FIVE-STAR GUY!!
...!!!

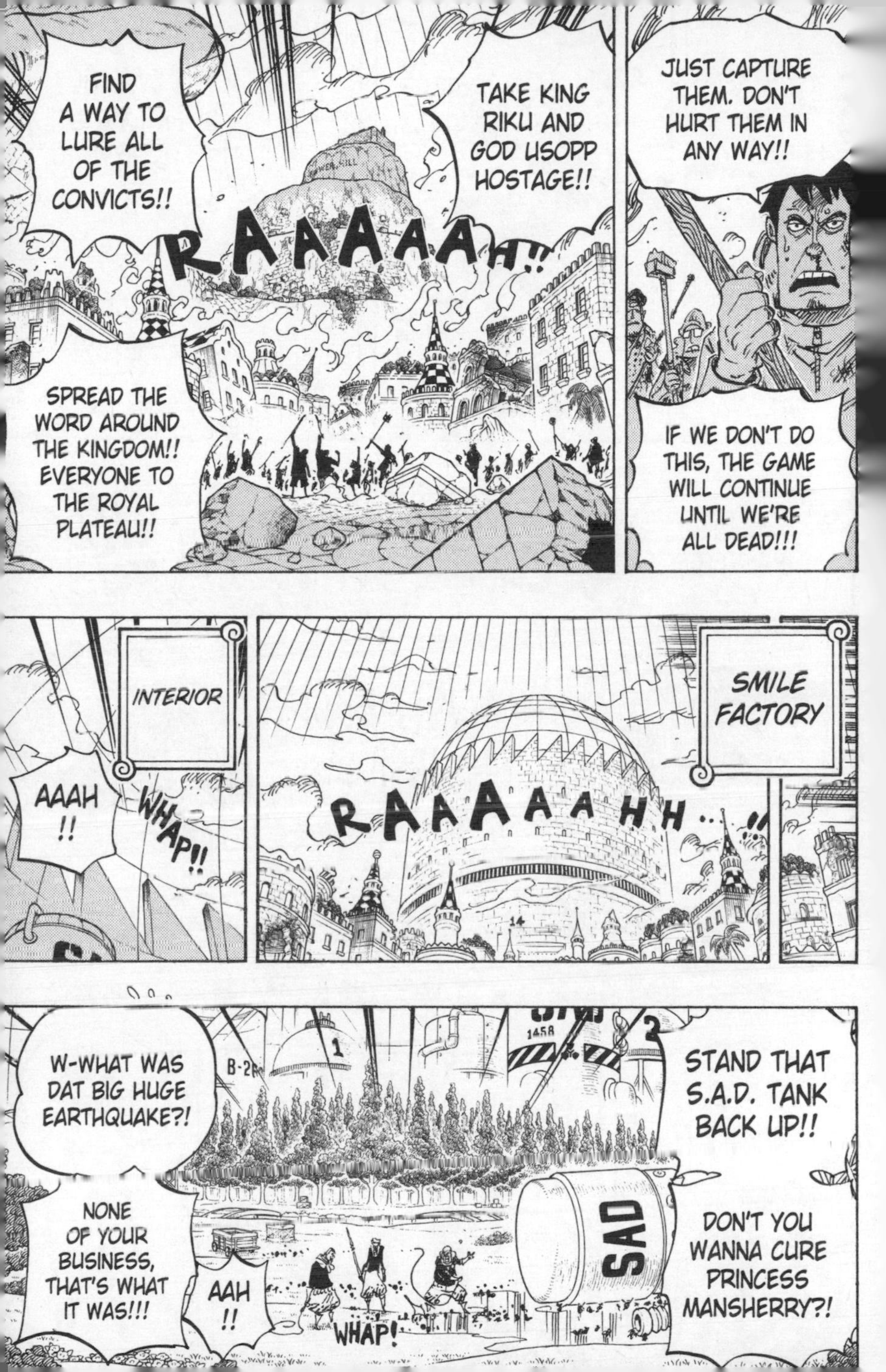
JUST CAPTURE THEM. DON'T HURT THEM IN ANY WAY!!
IF WE DON'T DO THIS, THE GAME WILL CONTINUE UNTIL WE'RE ALL DEAD!!!
TAKE KING RIKU AND GOD USOPP HOSTAGE!!
FIND A WAY TO LURE ALL OF THE CONVICTS!!
RAAAAAH!!
SPREAD THE WORD AROUND THE KINGDOM!! EVERYONE TO THE ROYAL PLATEAU!!
SMILE FACTORY
RAAAAAHH...!!
INTERIOR
AAAH !!
WHAP!!
STAND THAT S.A.D. TANK BACK UP!!
DON'T YOU WANNA CURE PRINCESS MANSHERRY?!
W-WHAT WAS DAT BIG HUGE EARTHQUAKE?!
NONE OF YOUR BUSINESS, THAT'S WHAT IT WAS!!!
SAD
AAH !!
WHAP!

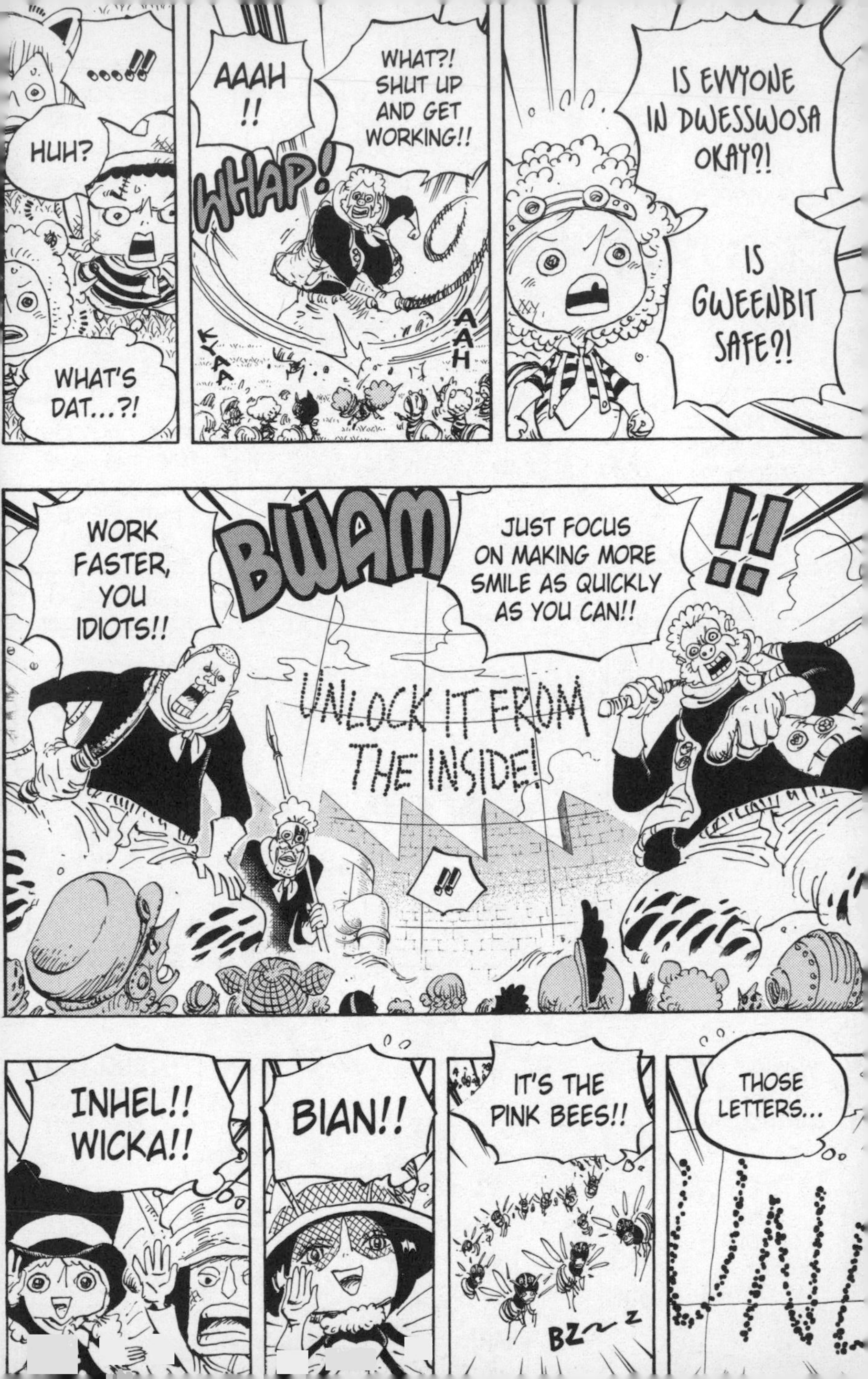
IS EVVYONE IN DWESSWOSA OKAY?!
IS GWEENBIT SAFE?!
WHAT?! SHUT UP AND GET WORKING!!
AAAH !!
WHAP!
AAH
KYAA
....!!
HUH?
WHAT'S DAT...?!
!!
JUST FOCUS ON MAKING MORE SMILE AS QUICKLY AS YOU CAN!!
BWAM
WORK FASTER, YOU IDIOTS!!
UNLOCK IT FROM THE INSIDE!
!!
THOSE LETTERS...
IT'S THE PINK BEES!!
BZ~~z
BIAN!!
INHEL!! WICKA!!

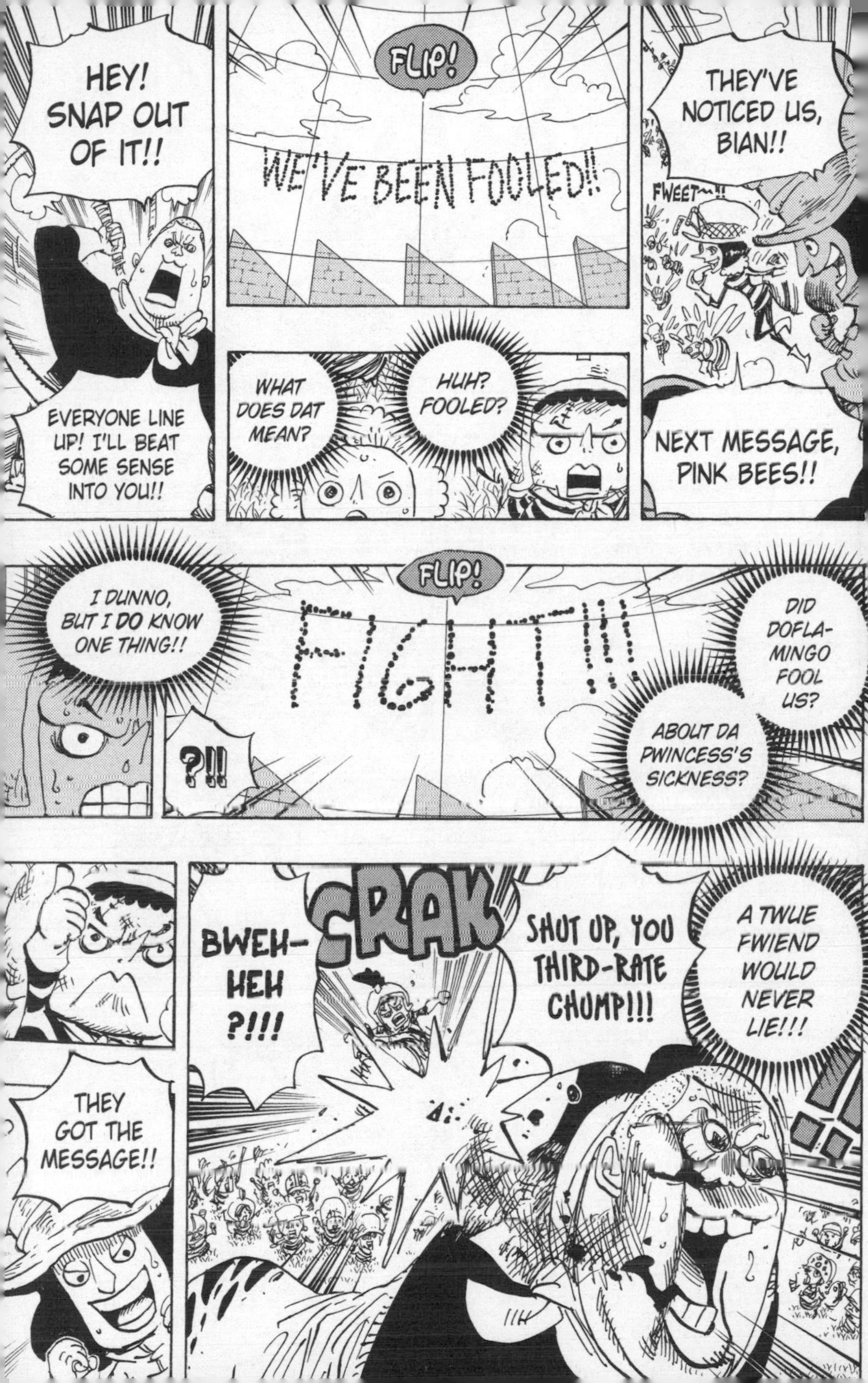
THEY'VE NOTICED US, BIAN!!
FWEET~!!
NEXT MESSAGE, PINK BEES!!
FLIP!
WE'VE BEEN FOOLED!!
HUH? FOOLED?
WHAT DOES DAT MEAN?
HEY! SNAP OUT OF IT!!
EVERYONE LINE UP! I'LL BEAT SOME SENSE INTO YOU!!
DID DOFLA-MINGO FOOL US?
ABOUT DA PWINCESS'S SICKNESS?
FLIP!
FIGHT!!!
?!!
I DUNNO, BUT I DO KNOW ONE THING!!
A TWUE FWIEND WOULD NEVER LIE!!!
SHUT UP, YOU THIRD-RATE CHUMP!!!
CRAK
BWEH-HEH ?!!!
THEY GOT THE MESSAGE!!

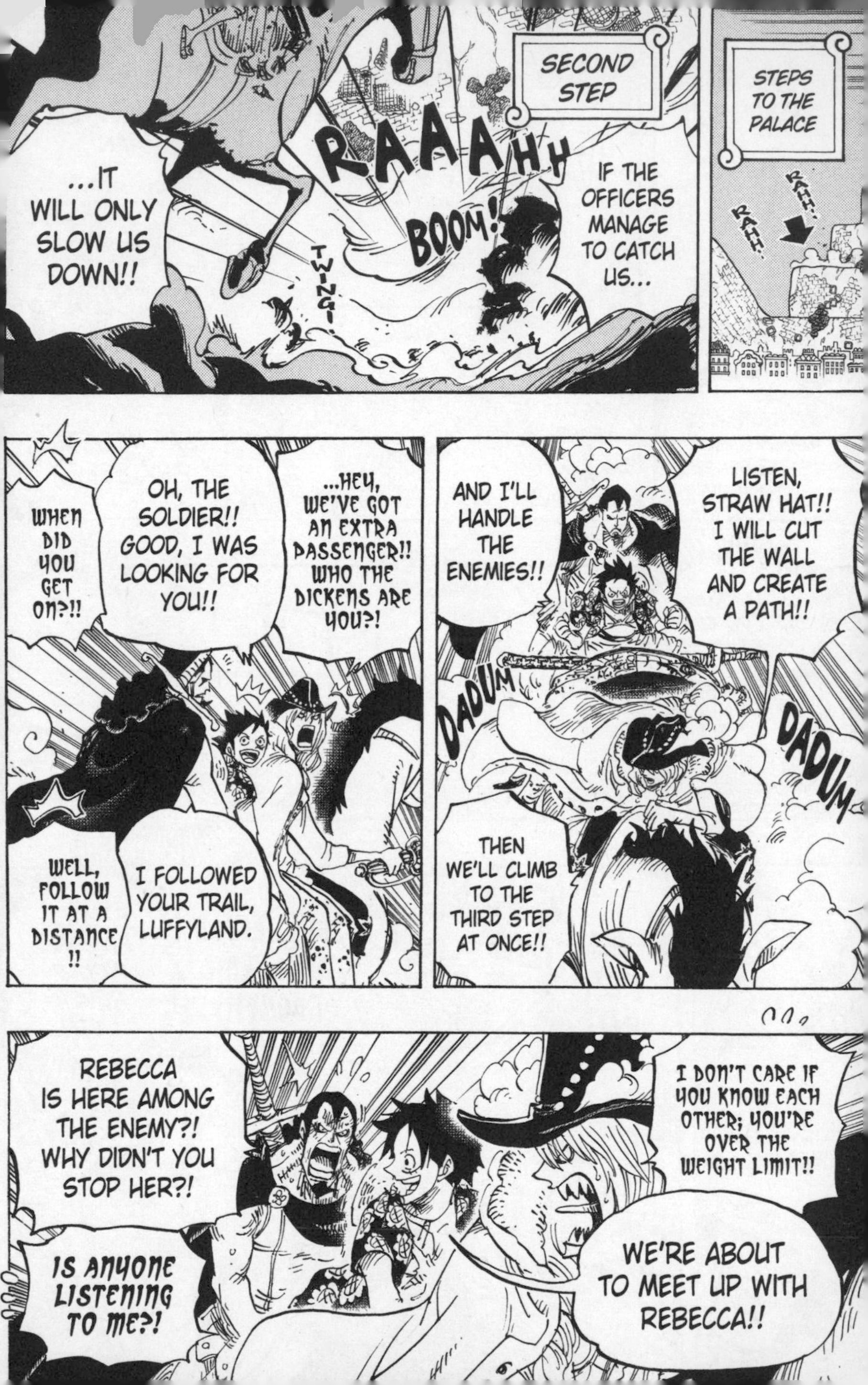
STEPS TO THE PALACE
RAHH!
RAHH!
SECOND STEP
IF THE OFFICERS MANAGE TO CATCH US...
RAAAHH
BOOM!
TWING!
...IT WILL ONLY SLOW US DOWN!!
LISTEN, STRAW HAT!! I WILL CUT THE WALL AND CREATE A PATH!!
AND I'LL HANDLE THE ENEMIES!!
DADUM
DADUM
THEN WE'LL CLIMB TO THE THIRD STEP AT ONCE!!
...HEY, WE'VE GOT AN EXTRA PASSENGER!! WHO THE DICKENS ARE YOU?!
OH, THE SOLDIER!! GOOD, I WAS LOOKING FOR YOU!!
WHEN DID YOU GET ON?!!
I FOLLOWED YOUR TRAIL, LUFFYLAND.
WELL, FOLLOW IT AT A DISTANCE!!
I DON'T CARE IF YOU KNOW EACH OTHER; YOU'RE OVER THE WEIGHT LIMIT!!
WE'RE ABOUT TO MEET UP WITH REBECCA!!
REBECCA IS HERE AMONG THE ENEMY?! WHY DIDN'T YOU STOP HER?!
IS ANYONE LISTENING TO ME?!

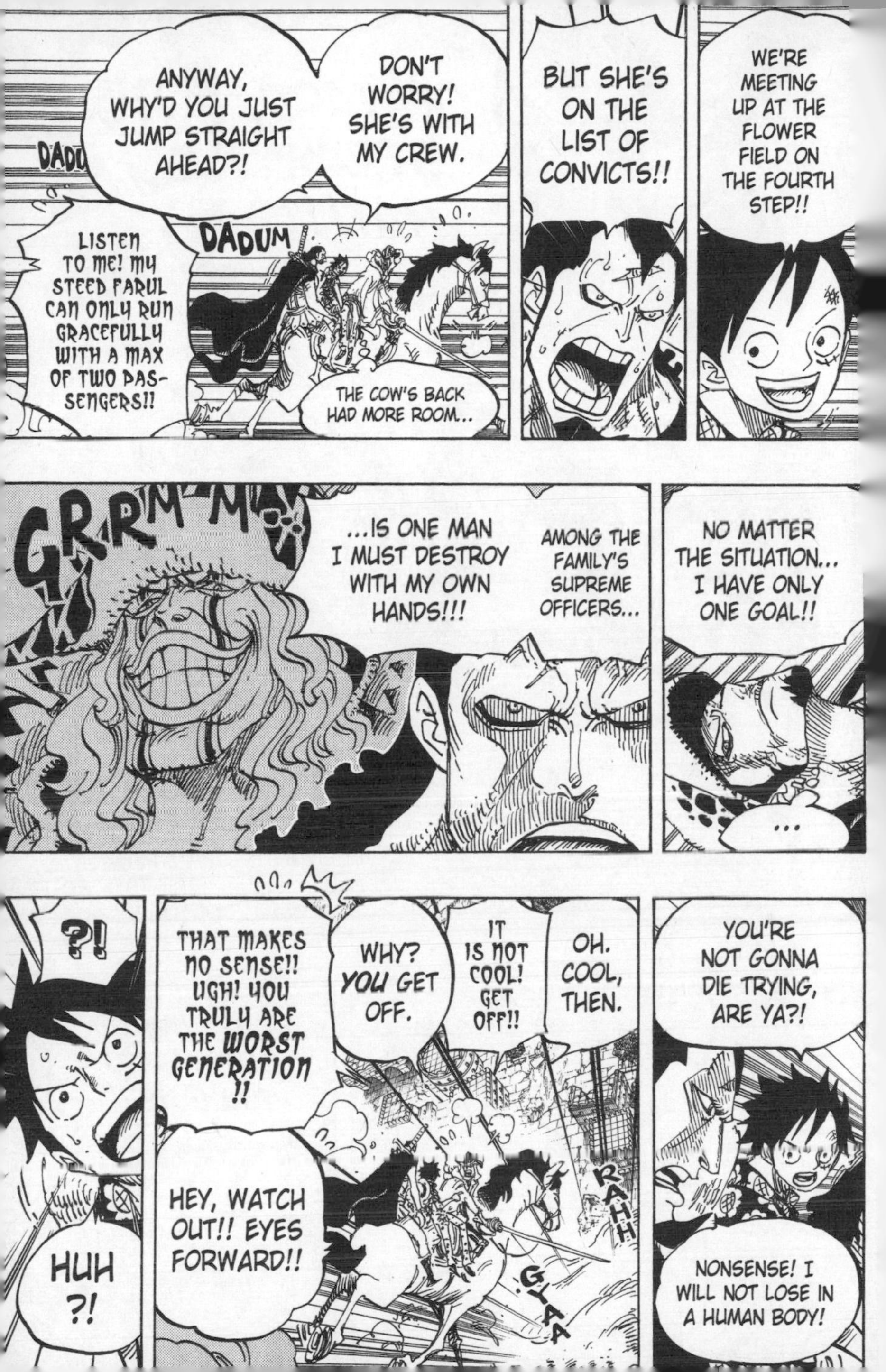
WE'RE MEETING UP AT THE FLOWER FIELD ON THE FOURTH STEP!!
BUT SHE'S ON THE LIST OF CONVICTS!!
DON'T WORRY! SHE'S WITH MY CREW.
ANYWAY, WHY'D YOU JUST JUMP STRAIGHT AHEAD?!
DADO
DADUM
LISTEN TO ME! MY STEED FARUL CAN ONLY RUN GRACEFULLY WITH A MAX OF TWO PAS-SENGERS!!
THE COW'S BACK HAD MORE ROOM...
NO MATTER THE SITUATION... I HAVE ONLY ONE GOAL!!
...
AMONG THE FAMILY'S SUPREME OFFICERS...
...IS ONE MAN I MUST DESTROY WITH MY OWN HANDS!!!
YOU'RE NOT GONNA DIE TRYING, ARE YA?!
NONSENSE! I WILL NOT LOSE IN A HUMAN BODY!
OH. COOL, THEN.
IT IS NOT COOL! GET OFF!!
WHY? YOU GET OFF.
THAT MAKES NO SENSE!! UGH! YOU TRULY ARE THE WORST GENERATION!!
RAHH
HEY, WATCH OUT!! EYES FORWARD!!
GYAA
?!
HUH ?!

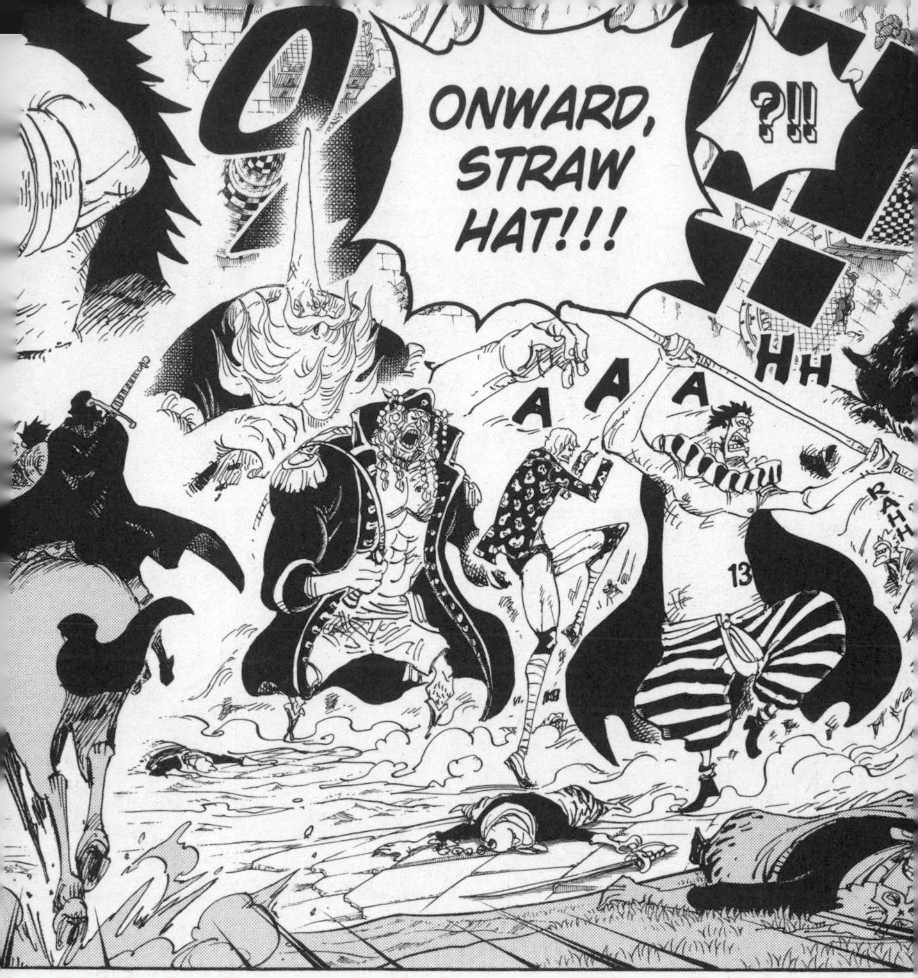
?!!
ONWARD, STRAW HAT!!!
AAAHH

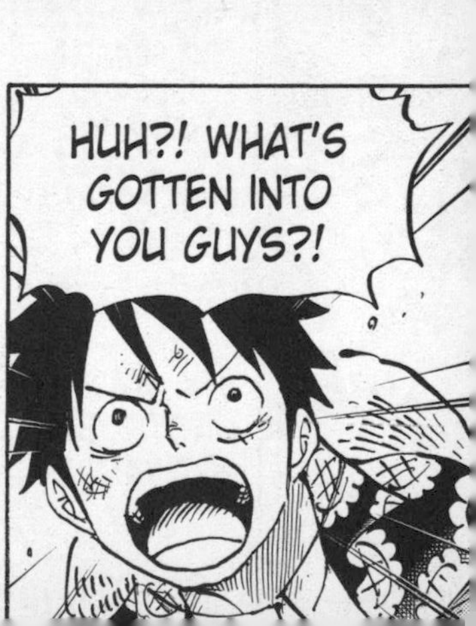
HUH?! WHAT'S GOTTEN INTO YOU GUYS?!

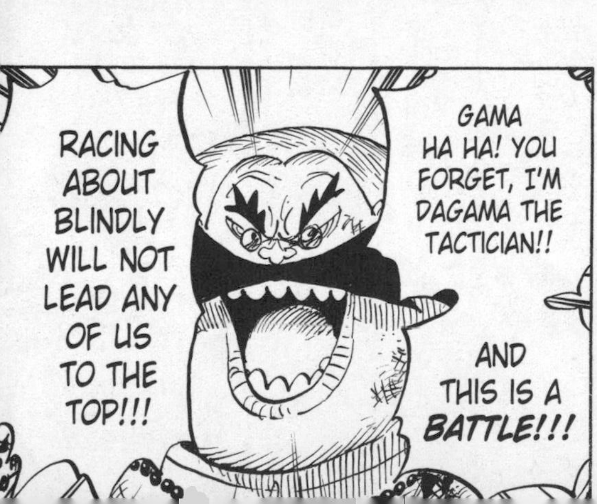
GAMA HA HA! YOU FORGET, I'M DAGAMA THE TACTICIAN!!
RACING ABOUT BLINDLY WILL NOT LEAD ANY OF US TO THE TOP!!!
AND THIS IS A BATTLE!!!

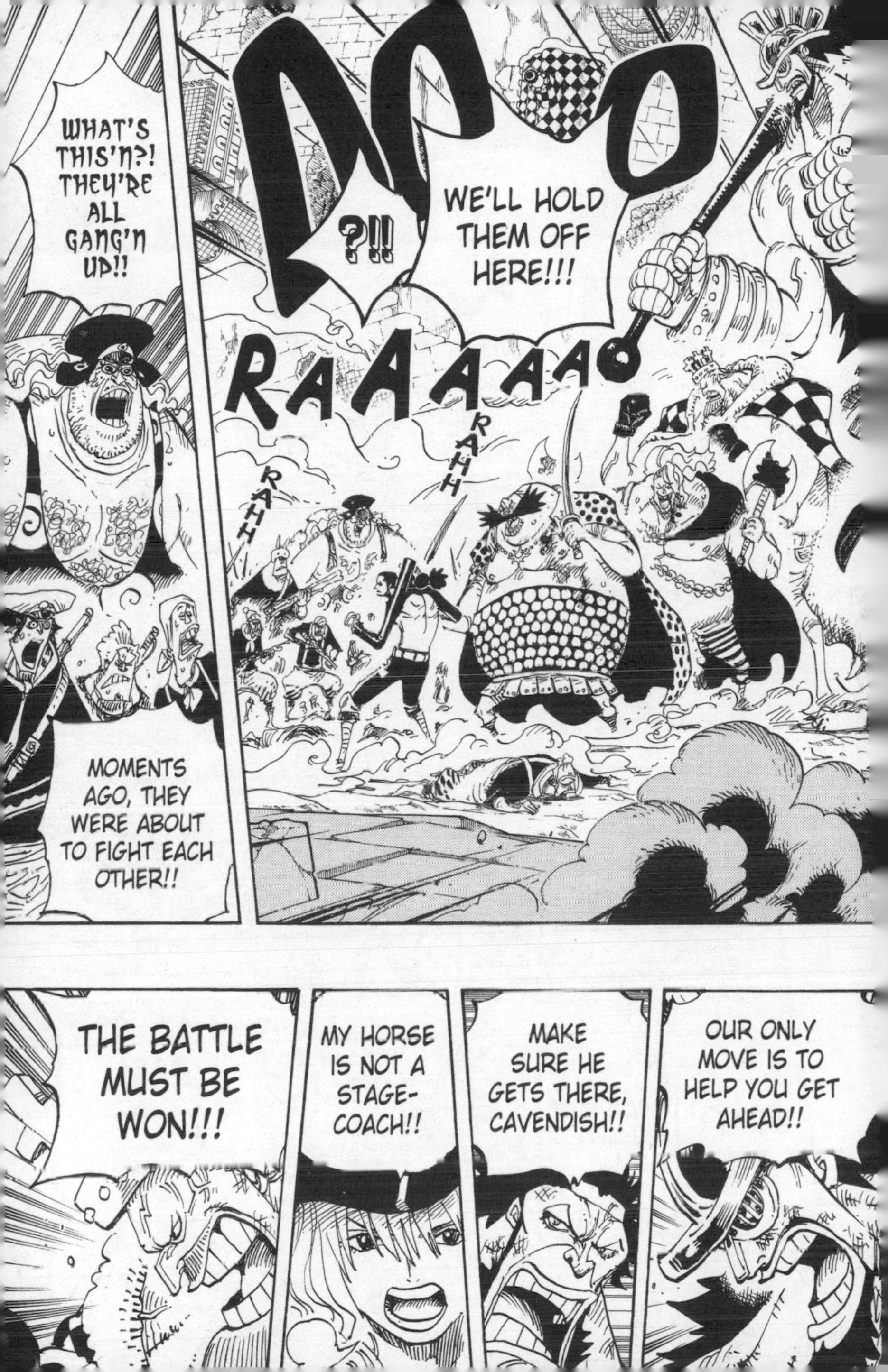
DOO
?!!
WE'LL HOLD THEM OFF HERE!!!
RAAAAA
RAHH
RAHH
WHAT'S THIS'N?! THEY'RE ALL GANG'N UP!!
MOMENTS AGO, THEY WERE ABOUT TO FIGHT EACH OTHER!!
OUR ONLY MOVE IS TO HELP YOU GET AHEAD!!
MAKE SURE HE GETS THERE, CAVENDISH!!
MY HORSE IS NOT A STAGE-COACH!!
THE BATTLE MUST BE WON!!!

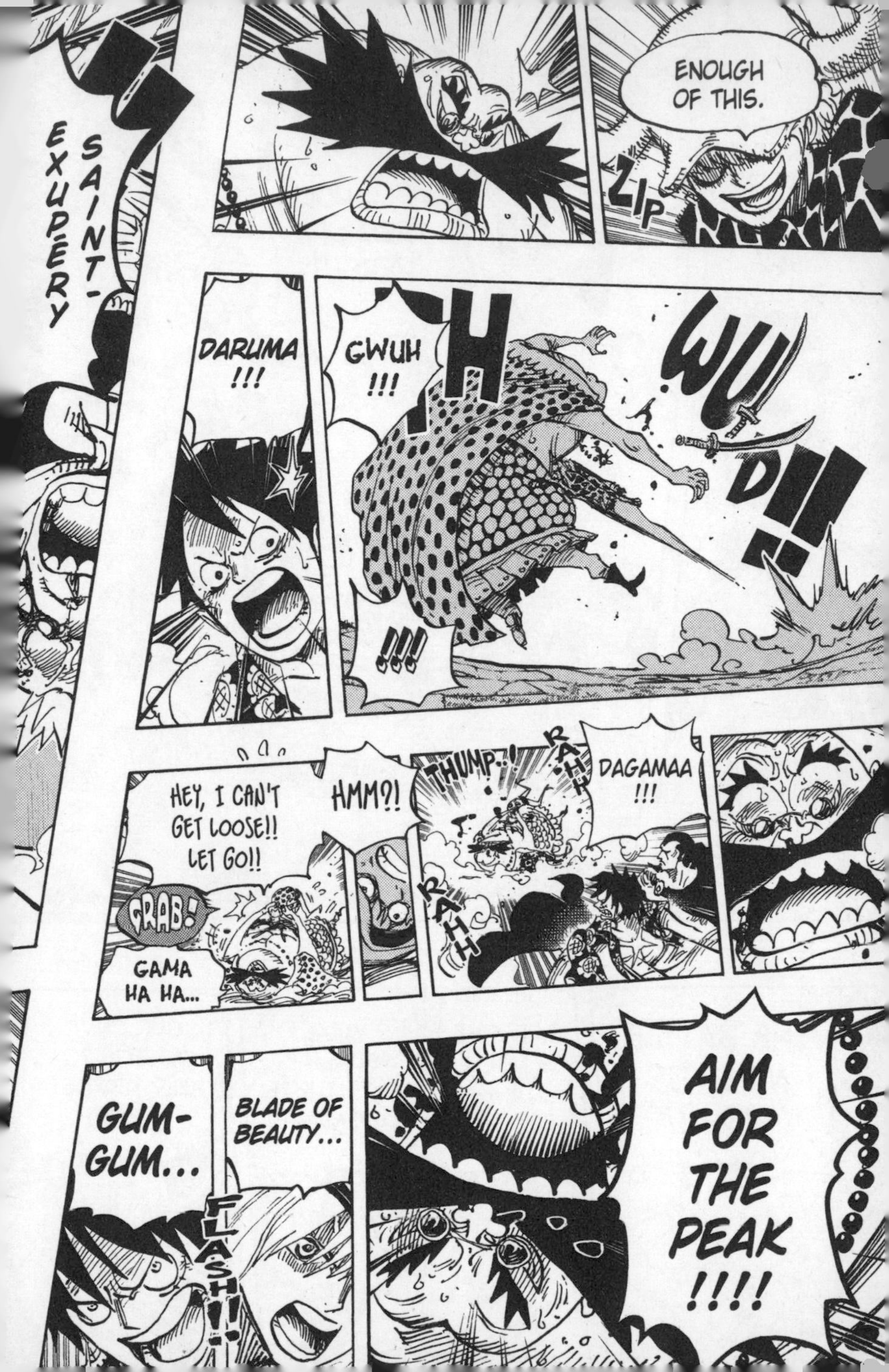
ENOUGH OF THIS.
ZIP
WUD!!
H
GWUH !!!
!!!
DARUMA !!!
DAGAMAA !!!
THUMP..!!
RAHH
RAHH
HMM?!
HEY, I CAN'T GET LOOSE!! LET GO!!
GRAB!
GAMA HA HA...
AIM FOR THE PEAK !!!!
BLADE OF BEAUTY...
FLASH!!
GUM-GUM...
SAINT-EXUPÉRY

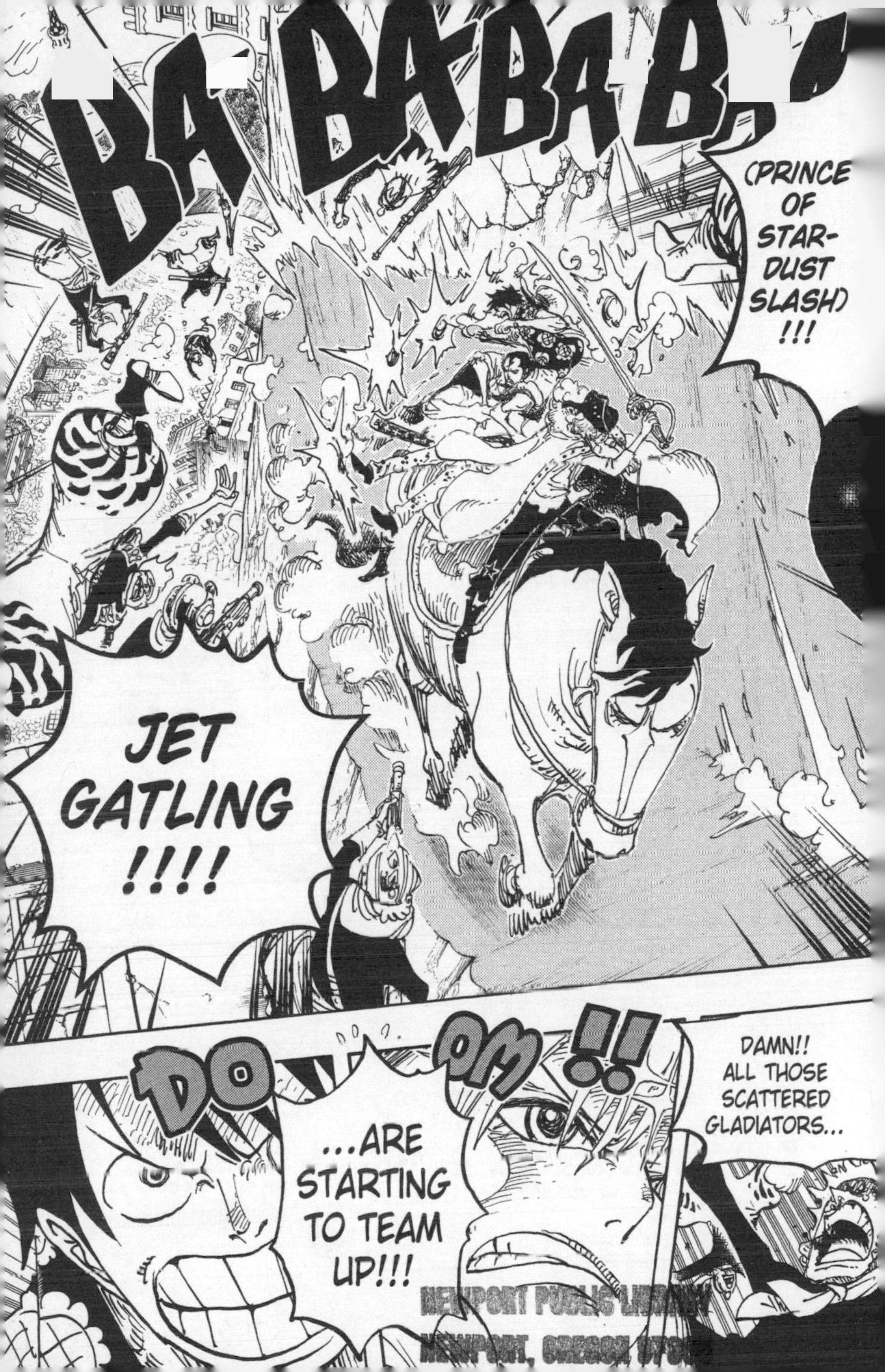
BA BA BA B
(PRINCE OF STAR-DUST SLASH)!!!
JET GATLING!!!!
DAMN!! ALL THOSE SCATTERED GLADIATORS...
DO OM!!
...ARE STARTING TO TEAM UP!!!

SBS Question Corner

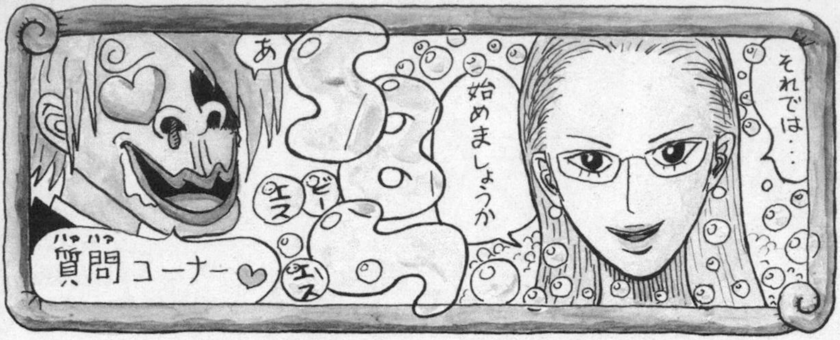
それでは・・・
始めましょうか
あ
エス
ビー
エス
の
質問コーナー♥

(In My 50s, Oita)

Q: I'm sorry to have kept you waiting for ten long years!!!
Let the SBS begin!!!!

--Spartacos

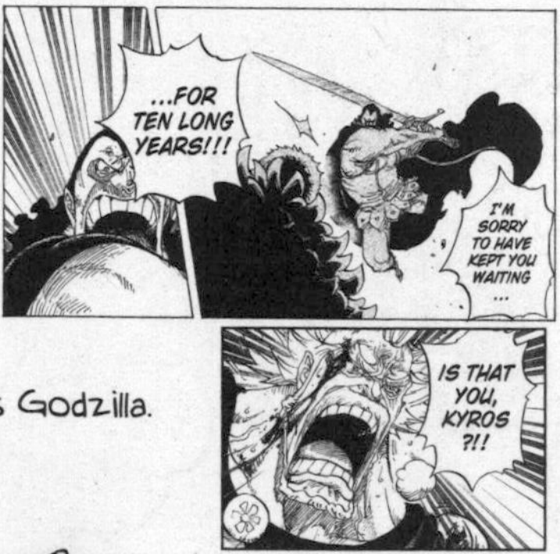
I'M SORRY TO HAVE KEPT YOU WAITING...
...FOR TEN LONG YEARS!!!
IS THAT YOU, KYROS?!!

A: Is that you, Kyros?!! (cries)
My goodness, what a touching start to this segment!
A letter from Kyros himself...
wait, it's just Spartacos.

Q: Odacchi, draw Godzilla.

--Yukidama

A: Here's Godzilla.

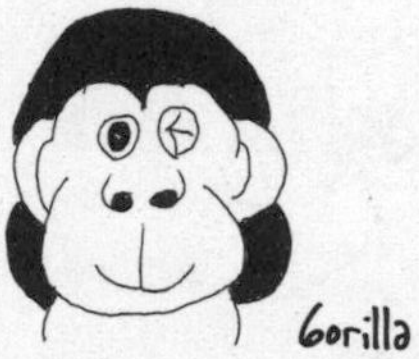
Gorilla

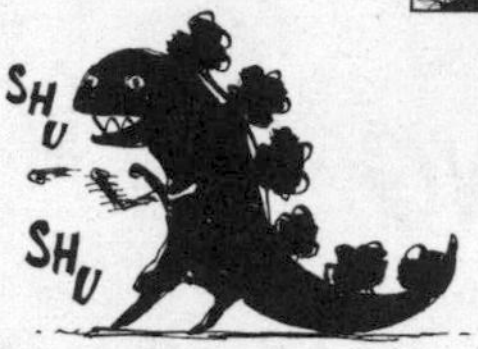
SHU
SHU

Q: Here's a question. Out of all the many characters who have appeared in the story, only Vivi has been accepted by the Straw Hats as one of the crew while remaining separate. Can you tell us her number, color, animal, likes and dislikes, and so on, the same way you told us those details for the main crew?

--Rei Hoshino

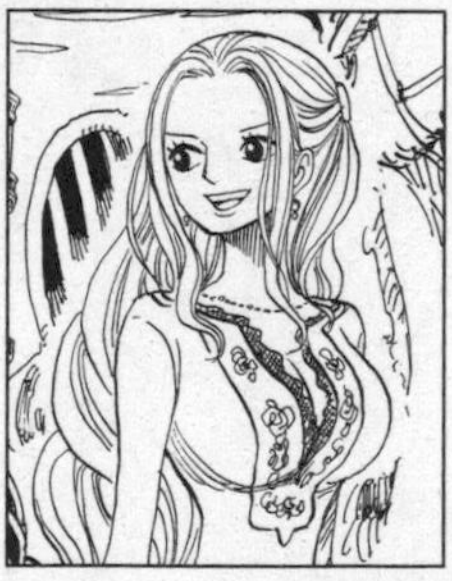

A: Sure. Vivi's always been very popular.

- Number: 5.5
- Color: White (and Gold)
- Animal: Pigeon (according to V.A. Misa Watanabe)
- Blood Type: F
- Likes: Curry, Pudding
- Dislikes: Dried Squid

Chapter 754: MAKING ACQUAINTANCE

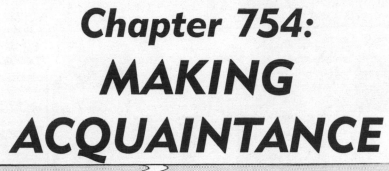

THE SOLITARY JOURNEY OF JIMBEI, FIRST SON OF THE SEA, VOL. 4: "WELL, GOOD THING THIS SEA KITTEN HAPPENS TO LIVE IN MY TOWN"

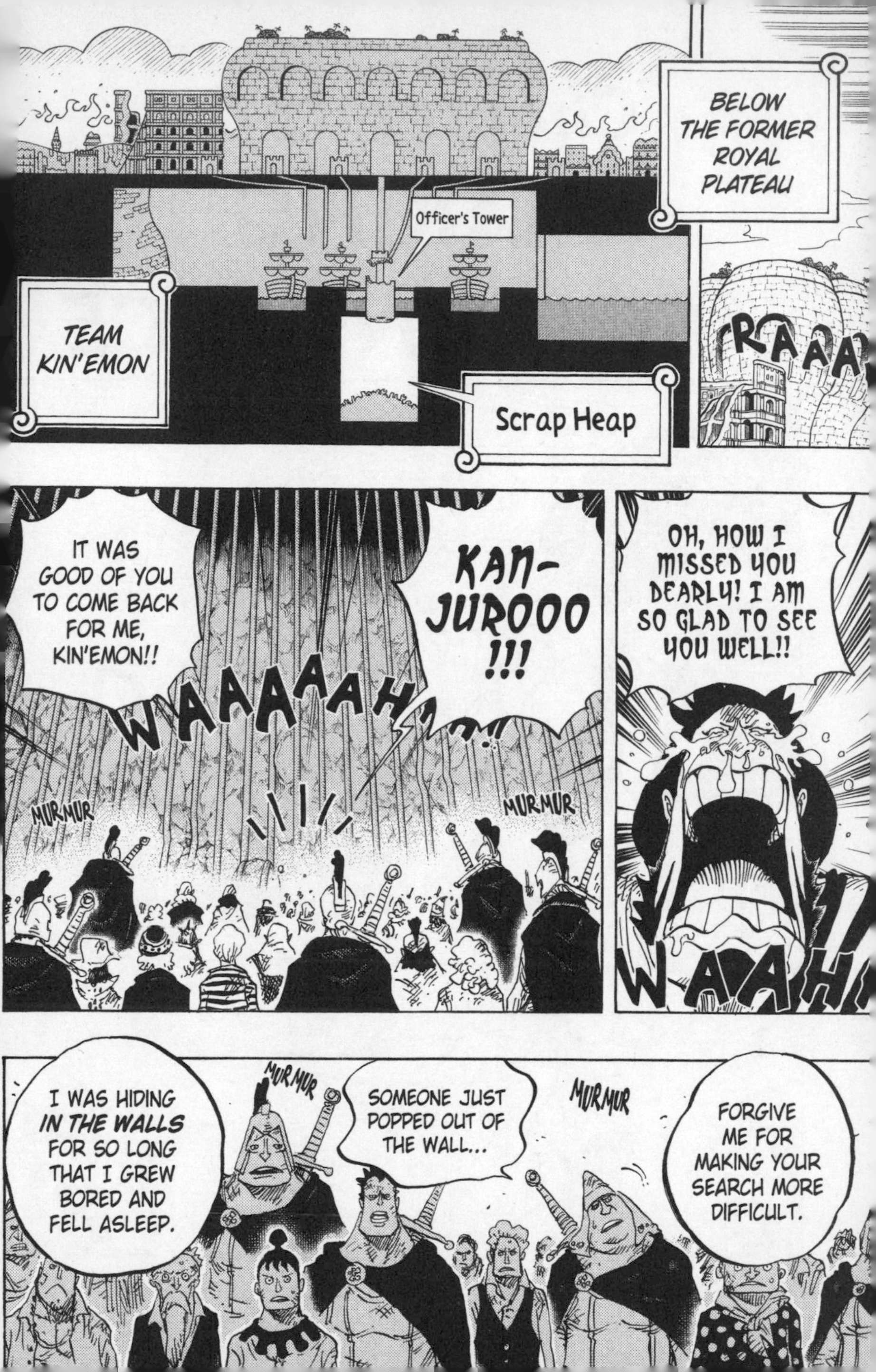
RAAAA
BELOW THE FORMER ROYAL PLATEAU
Officer's Tower
TEAM KIN'EMON
Scrap Heap
OH, HOW I MISSED YOU DEARLY! I AM SO GLAD TO SEE YOU WELL!!
WAAH
KAN-JUROOO!!!
IT WAS GOOD OF YOU TO COME BACK FOR ME, KIN'EMON!!
WAAAAAH
MURMUR
MURMUR
FORGIVE ME FOR MAKING YOUR SEARCH MORE DIFFICULT.
MURMUR
SOMEONE JUST POPPED OUT OF THE WALL...
MURMUR
I WAS HIDING ***IN THE WALLS*** FOR SO LONG THAT I GREW BORED AND FELL ASLEEP.

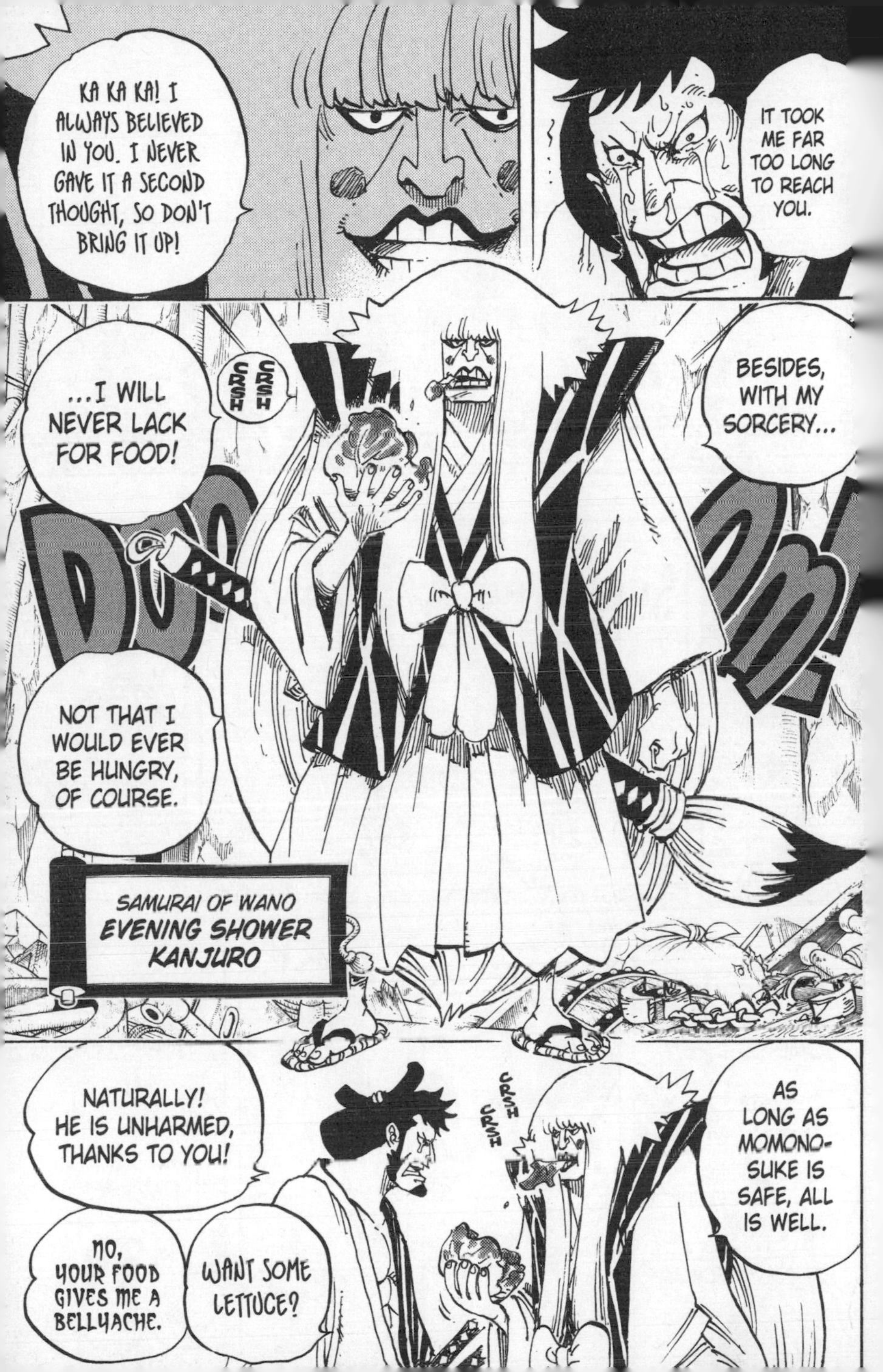
IT TOOK ME FAR TOO LONG TO REACH YOU.
KA KA KA! I ALWAYS BELIEVED IN YOU. I NEVER GAVE IT A SECOND THOUGHT, SO DON'T BRING IT UP!
BESIDES, WITH MY SORCERY...
CRSH CRSH
...I WILL NEVER LACK FOR FOOD!
DOOM!
NOT THAT I WOULD EVER BE HUNGRY, OF COURSE.
SAMURAI OF WANO
EVENING SHOWER KANJURO
AS LONG AS MOMONOSUKE IS SAFE, ALL IS WELL.
CRSH CRSH
NATURALLY! HE IS UNHARMED, THANKS TO YOU!
WANT SOME LETTUCE?
NO, YOUR FOOD GIVES ME A BELLYACHE.

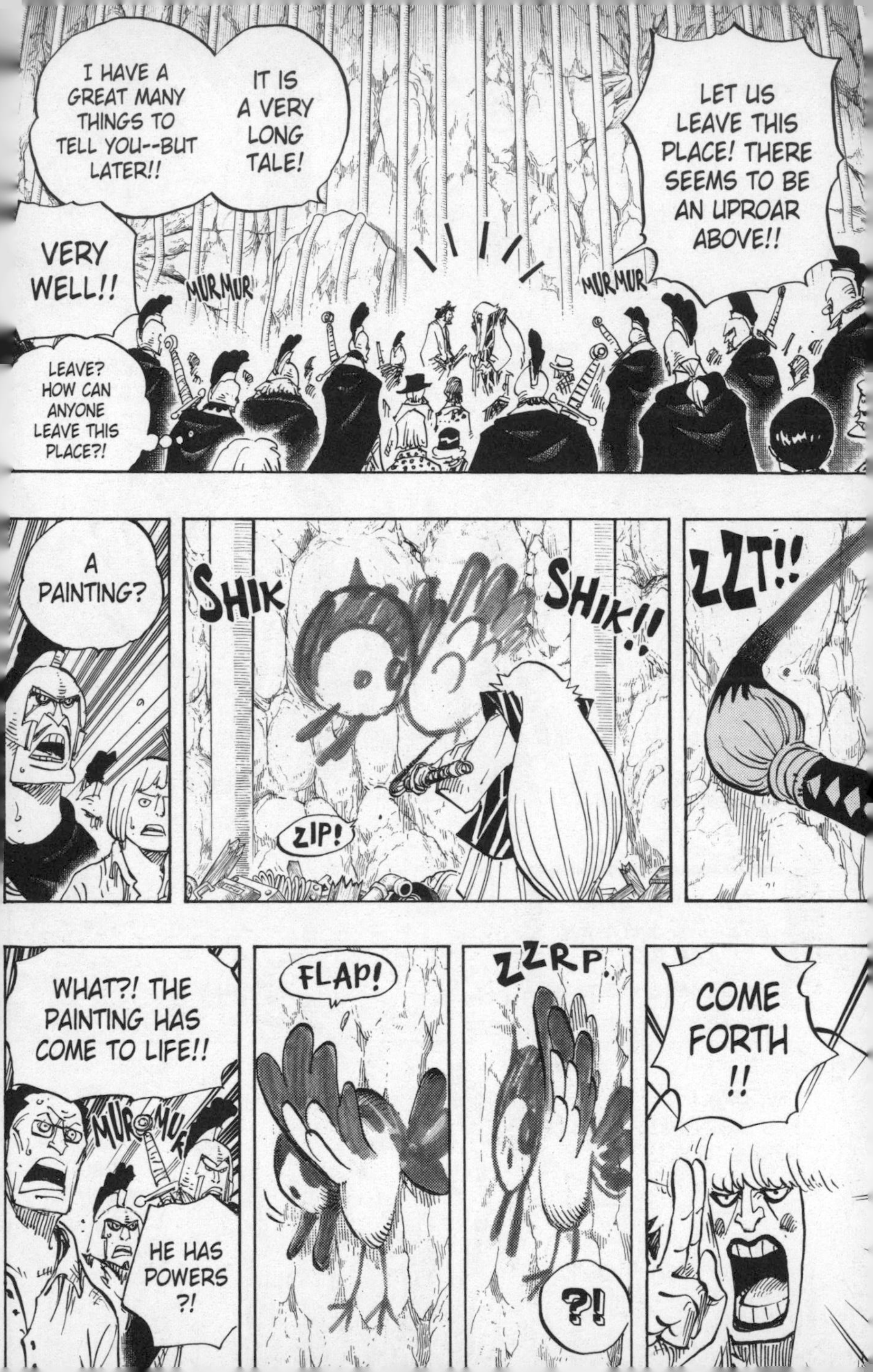
LET US LEAVE THIS PLACE! THERE SEEMS TO BE AN UPROAR ABOVE!!
IT IS A VERY LONG TALE!
I HAVE A GREAT MANY THINGS TO TELL YOU--BUT LATER!!
MURMUR
MURMUR
VERY WELL!!
LEAVE? HOW CAN ANYONE LEAVE THIS PLACE?!
ZZT!!
SHIK!!
SHIK
ZIP!
A PAINTING?
COME FORTH!!
ZZRP
?!
FLAP!
WHAT?! THE PAINTING HAS COME TO LIFE!!
MURMUR
HE HAS POWERS?!

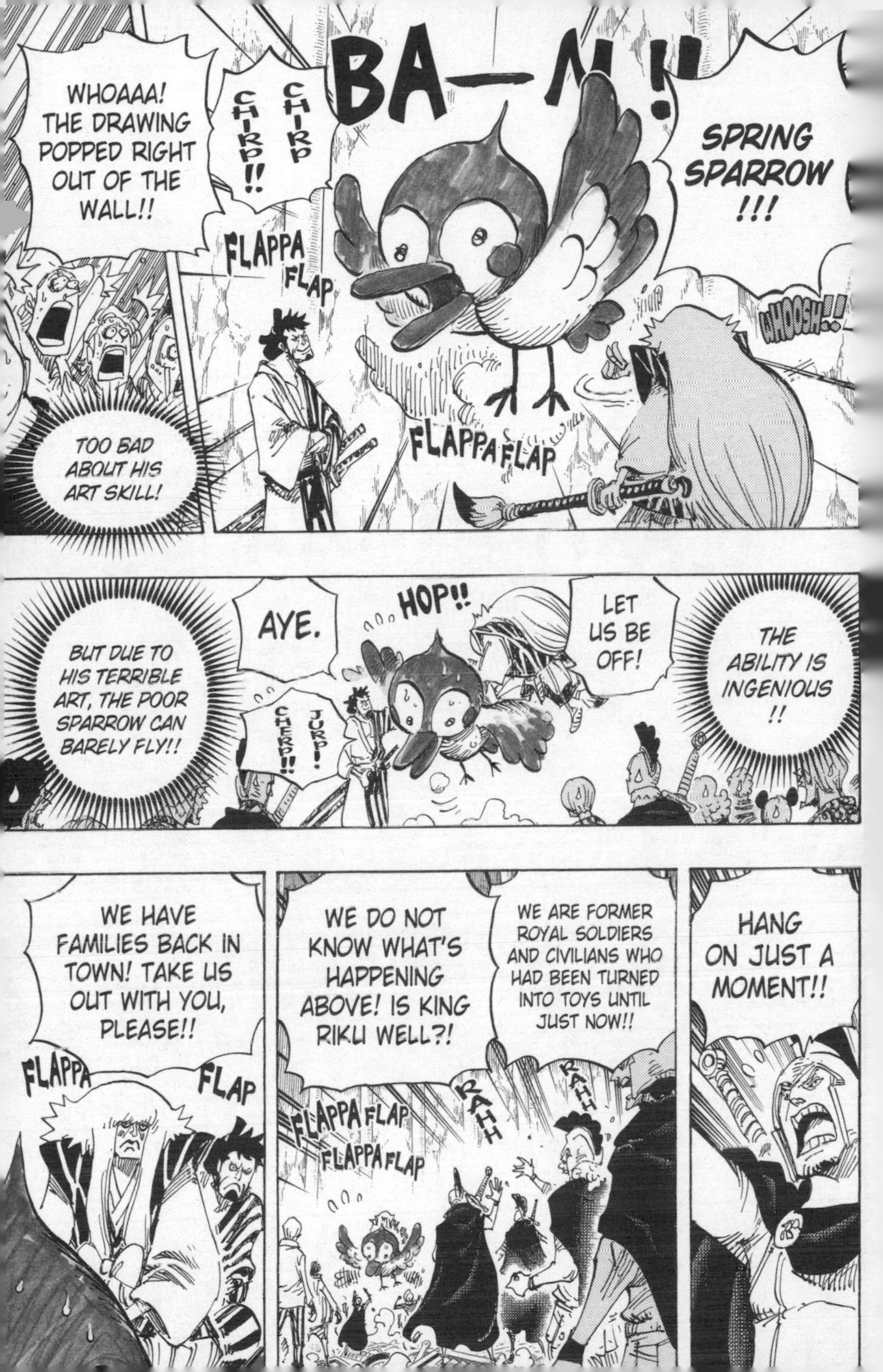
BA—N!!
SPRING SPARROW!!!
WHOOSH!!
CHIRP
CHIRP!!
WHOAAA! THE DRAWING POPPED RIGHT OUT OF THE WALL!!
FLAPPA FLAP
FLAPPA FLAP
TOO BAD ABOUT HIS ART SKILL!
THE ABILITY IS INGENIOUS!!
LET US BE OFF!
HOP!!
AYE.
JURP!
CHERP!!
BUT DUE TO HIS TERRIBLE ART, THE POOR SPARROW CAN BARELY FLY!!
HANG ON JUST A MOMENT!!
WE ARE FORMER ROYAL SOLDIERS AND CIVILIANS WHO HAD BEEN TURNED INTO TOYS UNTIL JUST NOW!!
WE DO NOT KNOW WHAT'S HAPPENING ABOVE! IS KING RIKU WELL?!
RAHH
RAHH
FLAPPA FLAP
FLAPPA FLAP
WE HAVE FAMILIES BACK IN TOWN! TAKE US OUT WITH YOU, PLEASE!!
FLAPPA FLAP

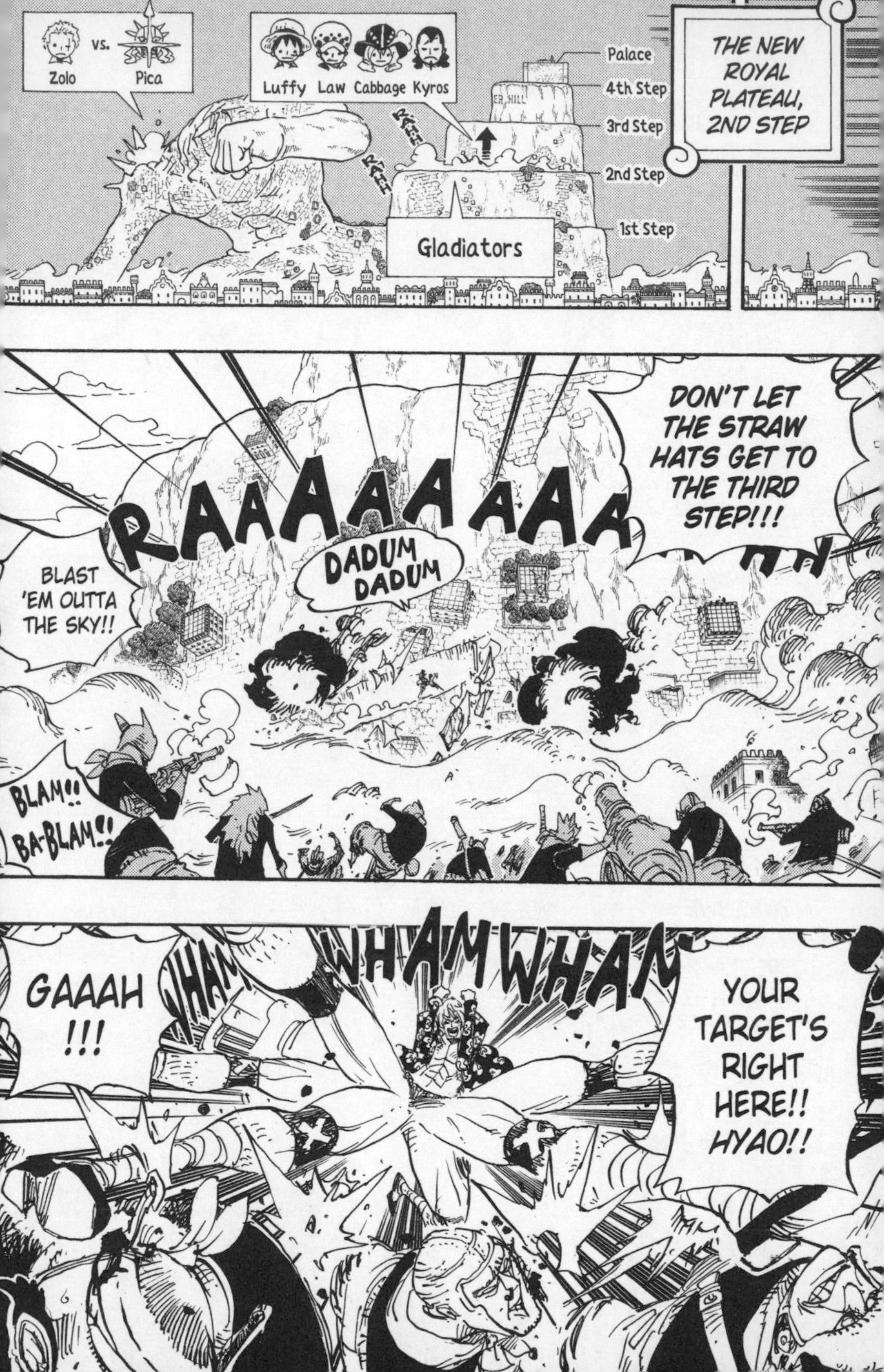
THE NEW ROYAL PLATEAU, 2ND STEP
Palace
4th Step
3rd Step
2nd Step
1st Step
Luffy Law Cabbage Kyros
RAHH
RAHH
Zolo vs. Pica
Gladiators
DON'T LET THE STRAW HATS GET TO THE THIRD STEP!!!
RAAAAAAAAHH
DADUM DADUM
BLAST 'EM OUTTA THE SKY!!
BLAM!!
BA-BLAM!!
YOUR TARGET'S RIGHT HERE!! HYAO!!
WHAM WHAM WHAM
GAAAH !!!

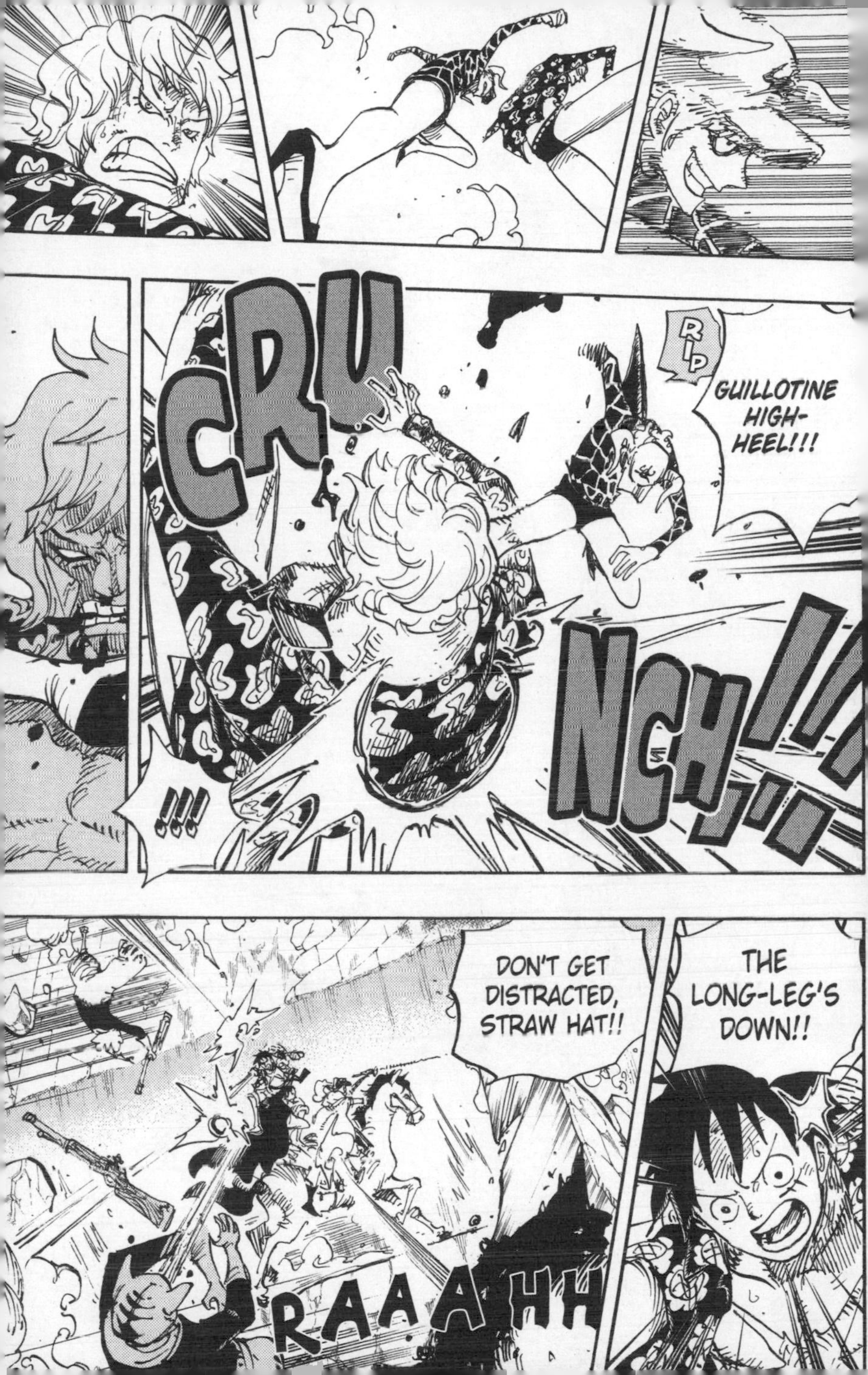

RIP
GUILLOTINE HIGH-HEEL!!!
CRUNCH!!!!
!!!
THE LONG-LEG'S DOWN!!
DON'T GET DISTRACTED, STRAW HAT!!
RAAAAHH

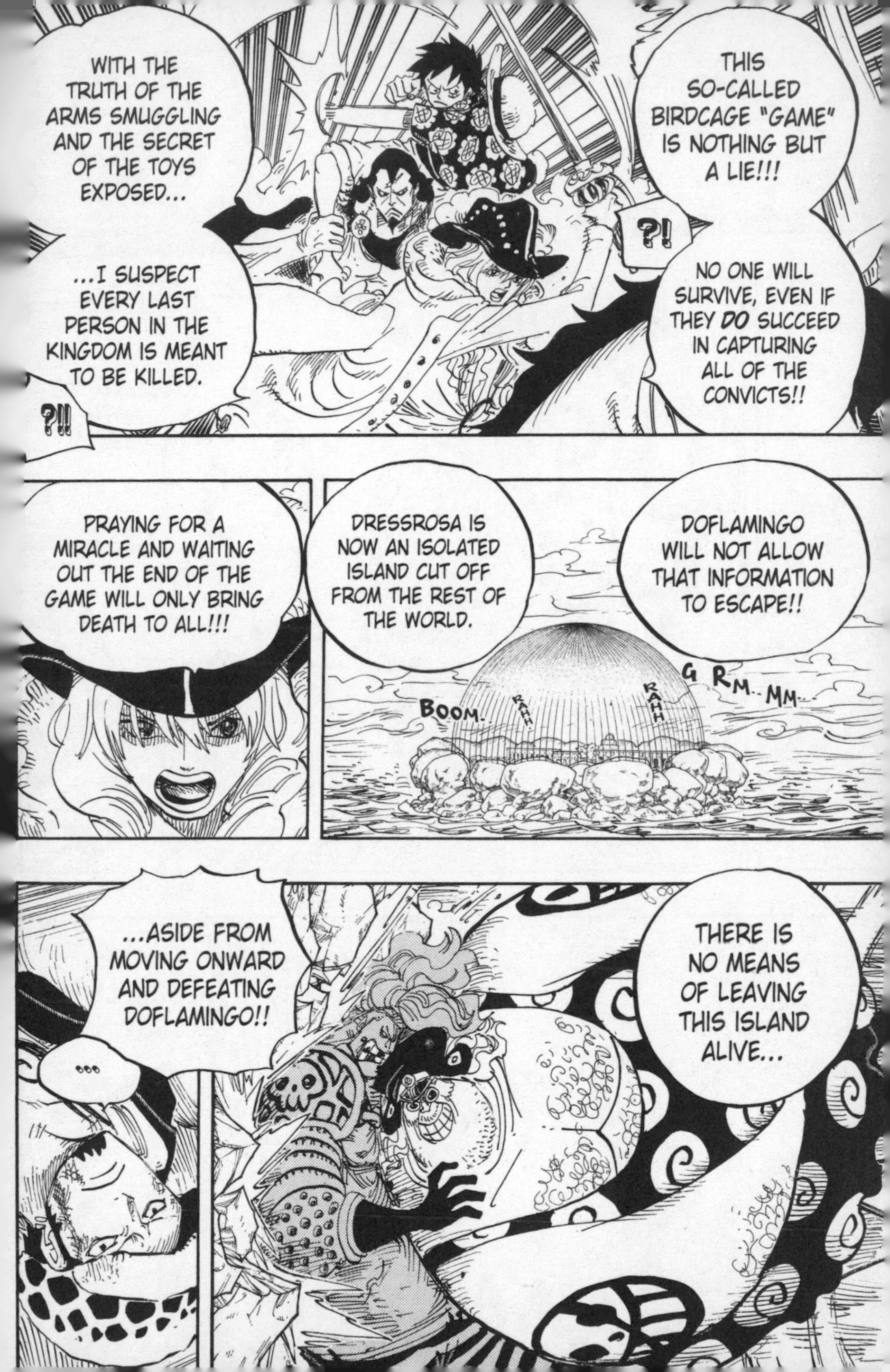
THIS SO-CALLED BIRDCAGE "GAME" IS NOTHING BUT A LIE!!!
?!
NO ONE WILL SURVIVE, EVEN IF THEY *DO* SUCCEED IN CAPTURING ALL OF THE CONVICTS!!
WITH THE TRUTH OF THE ARMS SMUGGLING AND THE SECRET OF THE TOYS EXPOSED...
...I SUSPECT EVERY LAST PERSON IN THE KINGDOM IS MEANT TO BE KILLED.
?!!
DOFLAMINGO WILL NOT ALLOW THAT INFORMATION TO ESCAPE!!
DRESSROSA IS NOW AN ISOLATED ISLAND CUT OFF FROM THE REST OF THE WORLD.
G RM.. MM..
RAHH
RAHH
BOOM
PRAYING FOR A MIRACLE AND WAITING OUT THE END OF THE GAME WILL ONLY BRING DEATH TO ALL!!!
THERE IS NO MEANS OF LEAVING THIS ISLAND ALIVE...
...ASIDE FROM MOVING ONWARD AND DEFEATING DOFLAMINGO!!
...

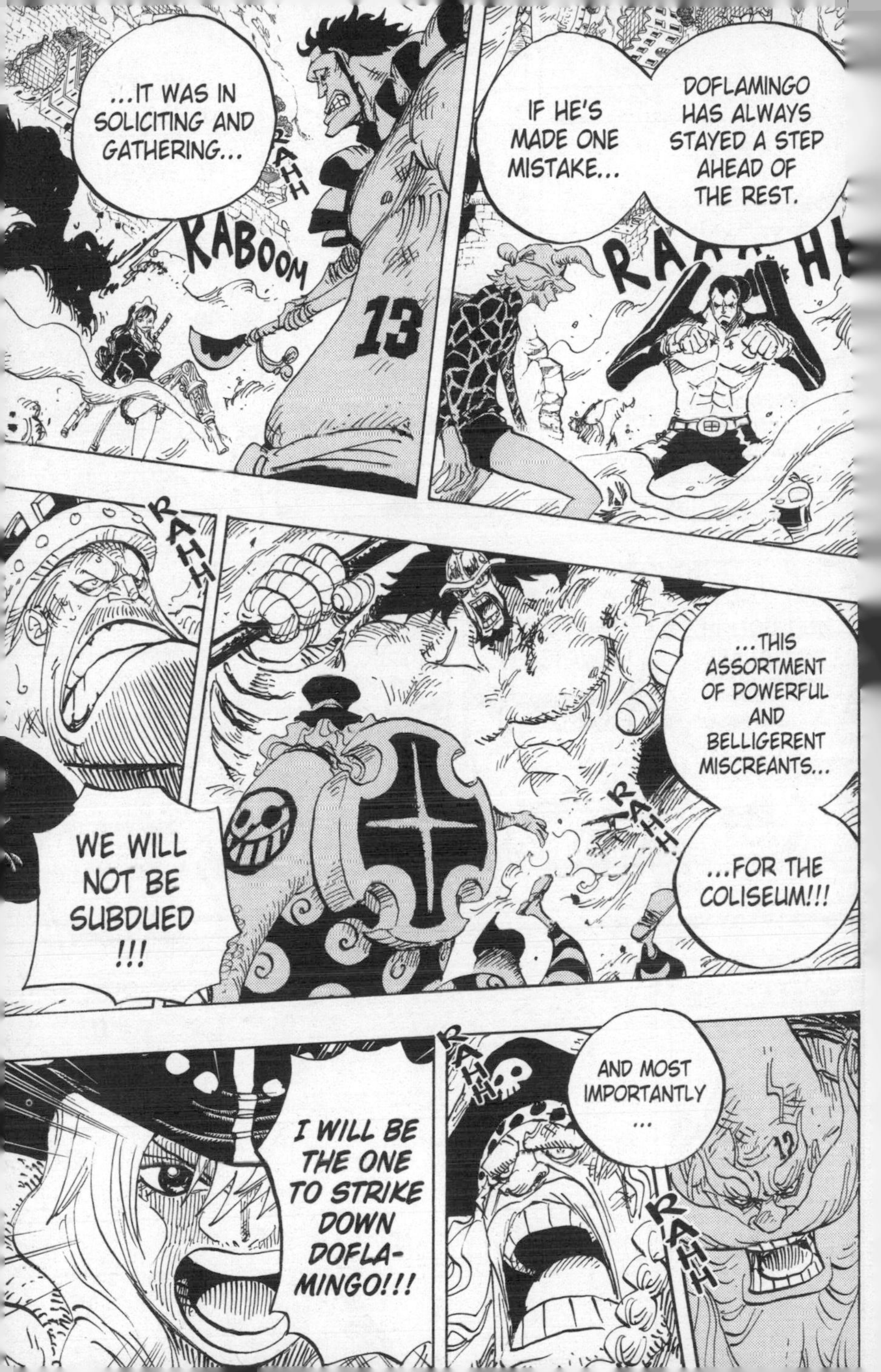
DOFLAMINGO HAS ALWAYS STAYED A STEP AHEAD OF THE REST.
IF HE'S MADE ONE MISTAKE...
...IT WAS IN SOLICITING AND GATHERING...
RAHH
KABOOM
...THIS ASSORTMENT OF POWERFUL AND BELLIGERENT MISCREANTS...
RAHH
...FOR THE COLISEUM!!!
RAHH
WE WILL NOT BE SUBDUED!!!
AND MOST IMPORTANTLY...
RAHH
RAHH
I WILL BE THE ONE TO STRIKE DOWN DOFLA-MINGO!!!

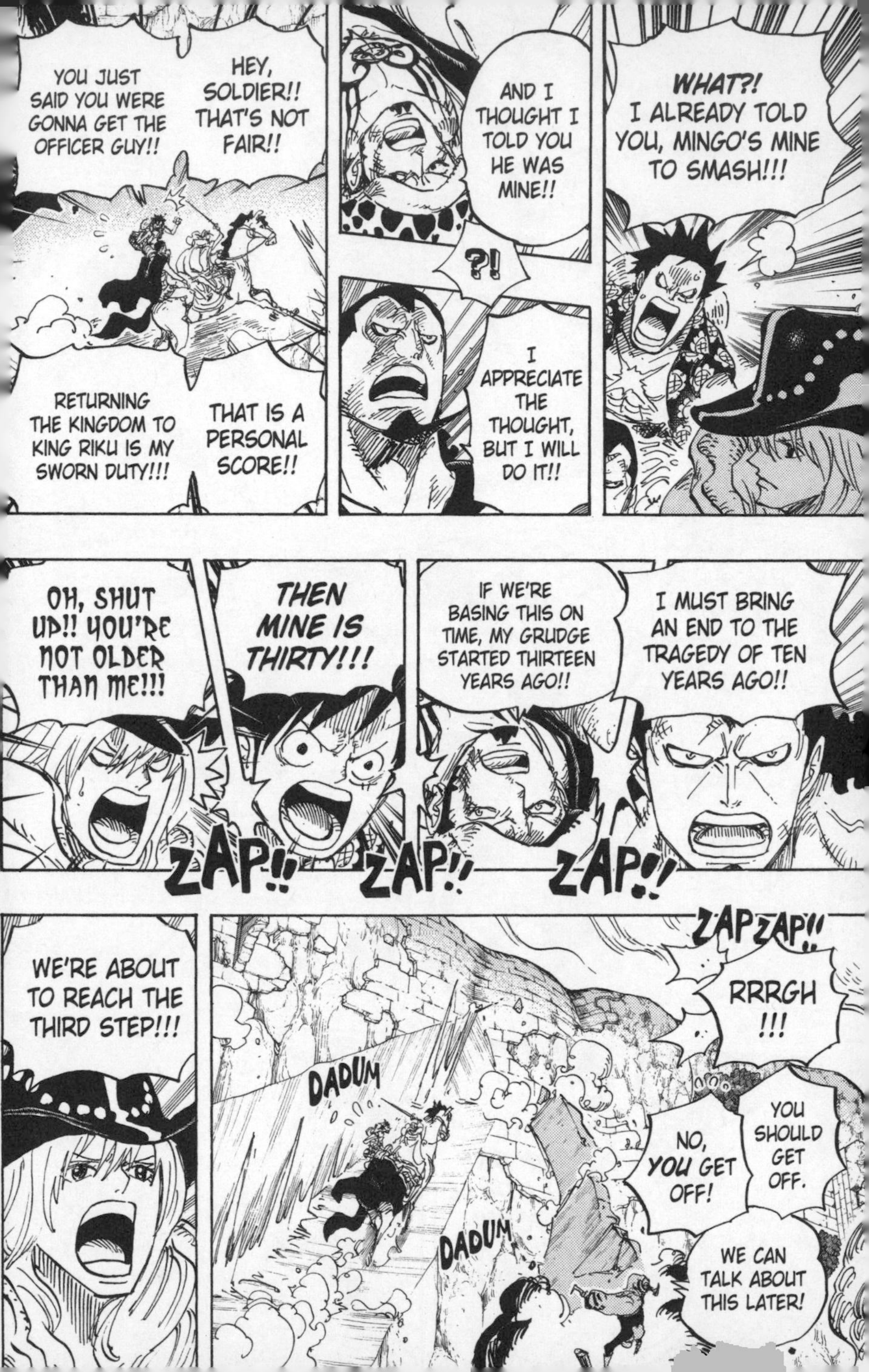
WHAT?! I ALREADY TOLD YOU, MINGO'S MINE TO SMASH!!!
AND I THOUGHT I TOLD YOU HE WAS MINE!!
?!
I APPRECIATE THE THOUGHT, BUT I WILL DO IT!!
HEY, SOLDIER!! THAT'S NOT FAIR!!
YOU JUST SAID YOU WERE GONNA GET THE OFFICER GUY!!
THAT IS A PERSONAL SCORE!!
RETURNING THE KINGDOM TO KING RIKU IS MY SWORN DUTY!!!
I MUST BRING AN END TO THE TRAGEDY OF TEN YEARS AGO!!
IF WE'RE BASING THIS ON TIME, MY GRUDGE STARTED THIRTEEN YEARS AGO!!
THEN MINE IS THIRTY!!!
OH, SHUT UP!! YOU'RE NOT OLDER THAN ME!!!
ZAP!!
ZAP!!
ZAP!!
ZAP ZAP!!
RRRGH!!!
YOU SHOULD GET OFF.
NO, YOU GET OFF!
WE CAN TALK ABOUT THIS LATER!
DADUM
DADUM
WE'RE ABOUT TO REACH THE THIRD STEP!!!

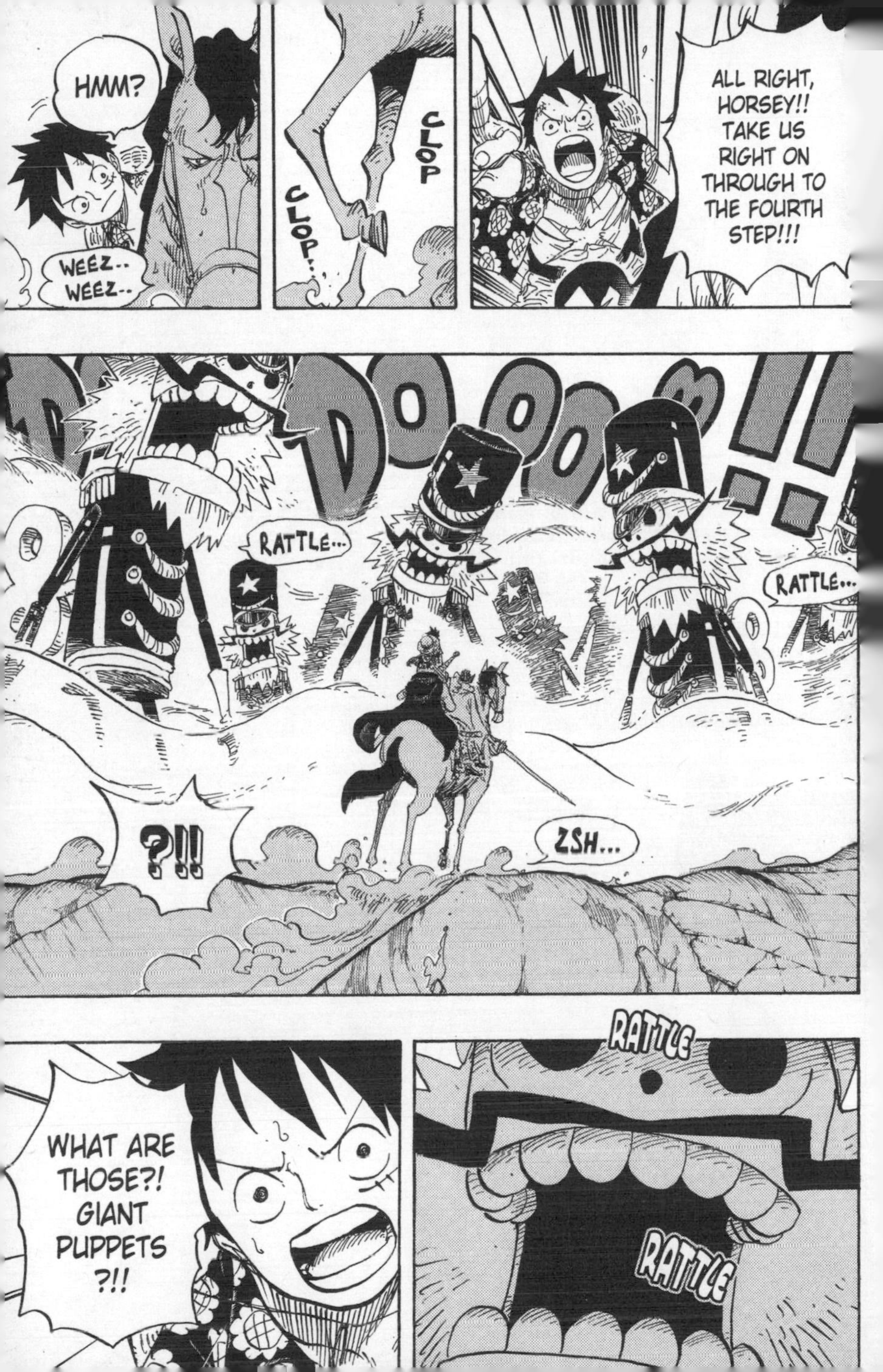

ALL RIGHT, HORSEY!! TAKE US RIGHT ON THROUGH TO THE FOURTH STEP!!!
CLOP
CLOP
CLOP...
HMM?
WEEZ.. WEEZ..
DOOOM!!!
RATTLE...
RATTLE...
ZSH...
?!!
RATTLE
RATTLE
WHAT ARE THOSE?! GIANT PUPPETS ?!!

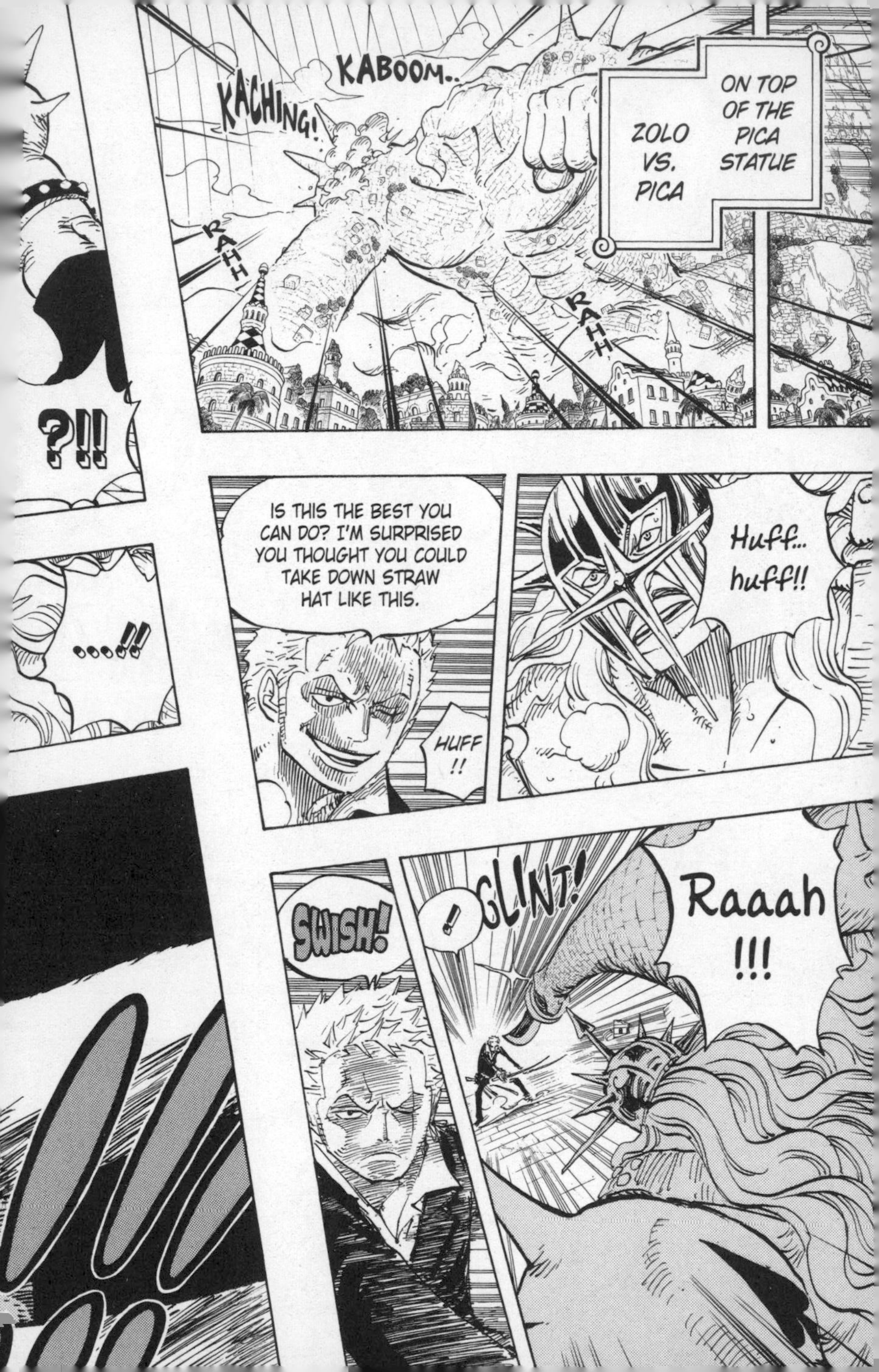
ON TOP OF THE PICA STATUE
ZOLO VS. PICA
KABOOM..
KACHING!
RAHH
RAHH
?!!
Huff... huff!!
IS THIS THE BEST YOU CAN DO? I'M SURPRISED YOU THOUGHT YOU COULD TAKE DOWN STRAW HAT LIKE THIS.
HUFF !!
...!!
Raaah !!!
GLINT!
!
SWISH!

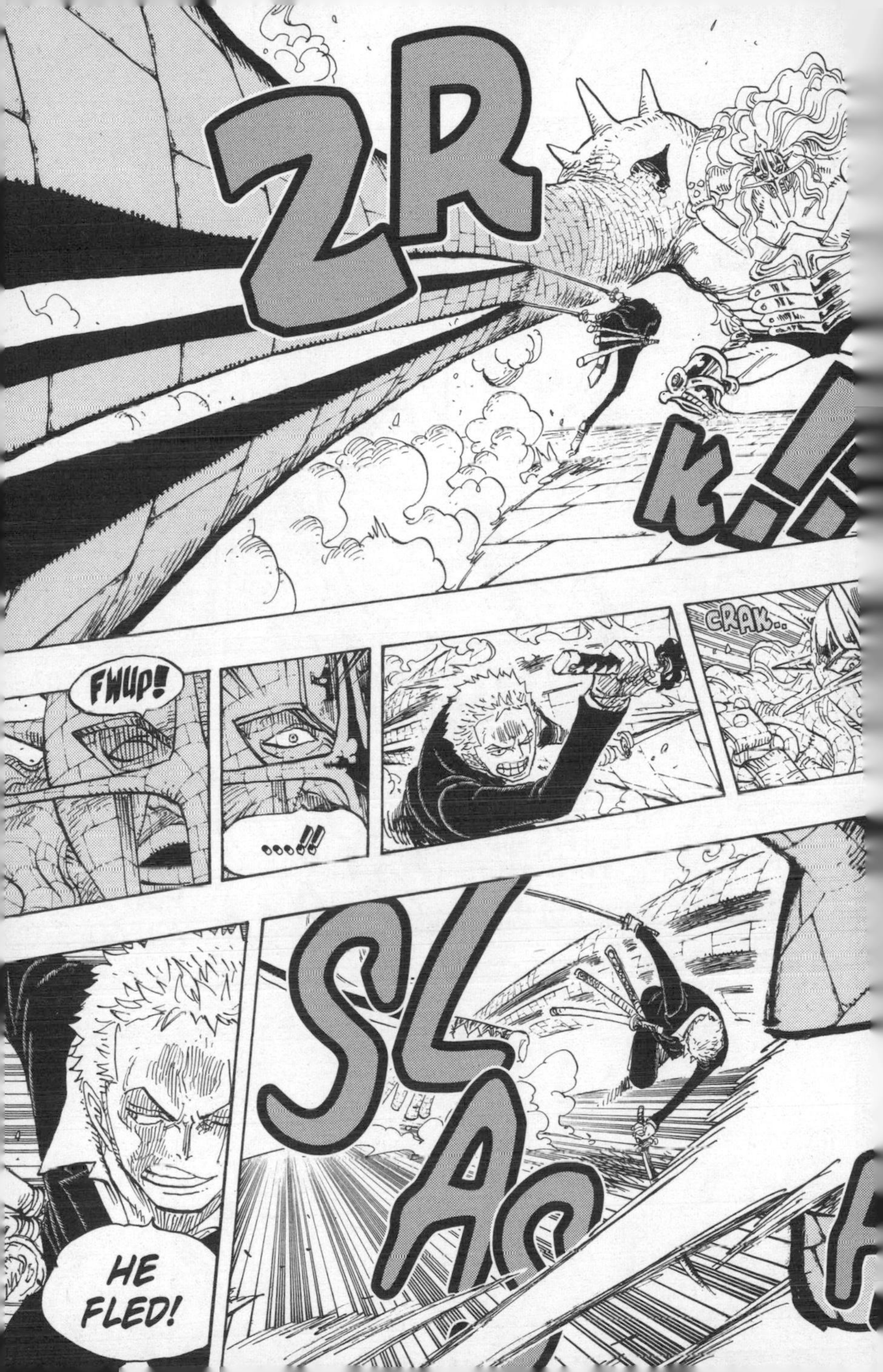

ZR
K..!!
CRAK..
....!!
FWUP!
SLA
HE FLED!

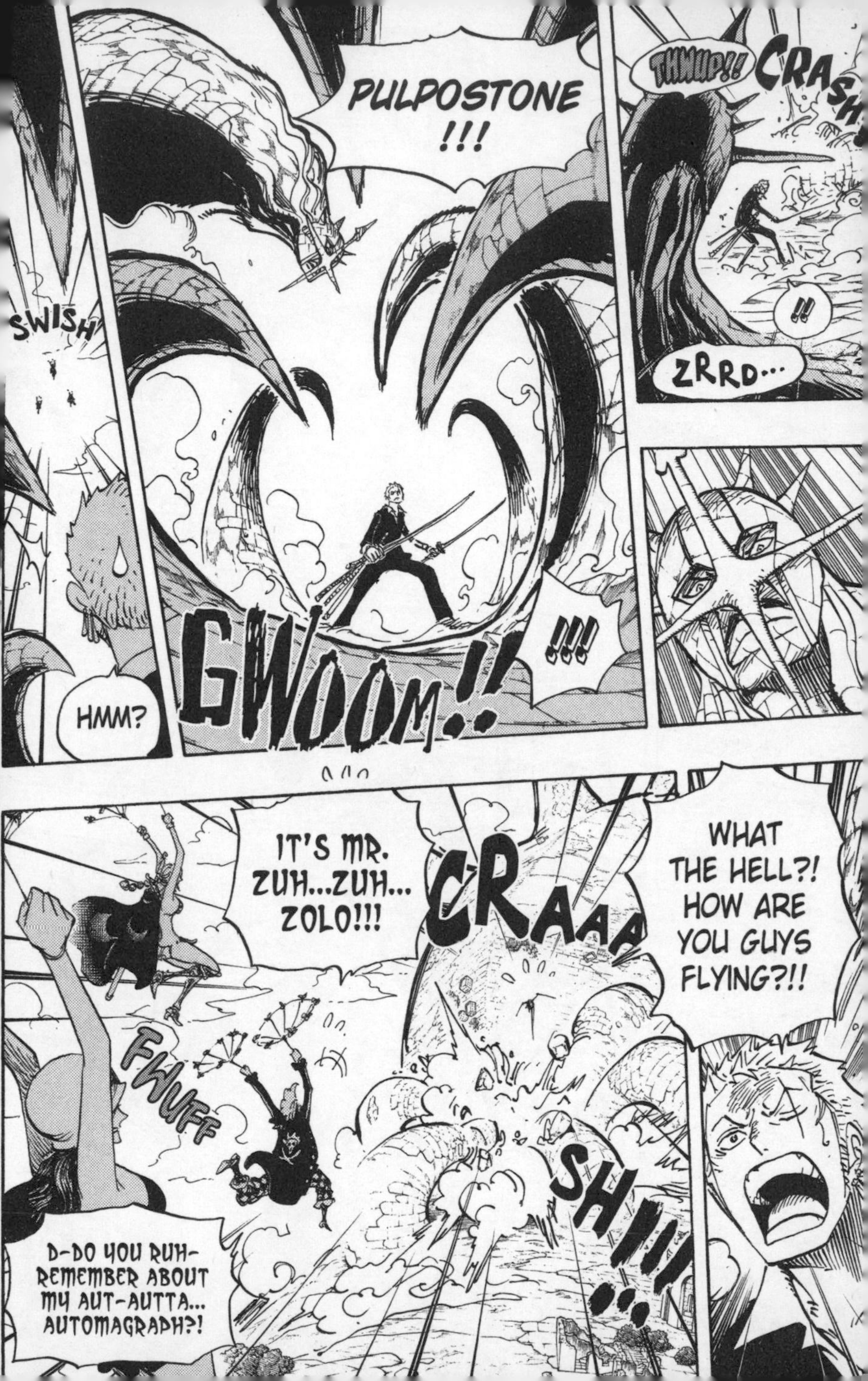
THWUP!!
CRASH
!!
ZRRD...
PULPOSTONE !!!
GWOOM!!
!!!
SWISH
HMM?
WHAT THE HELL?! HOW ARE YOU GUYS FLYING?!!
SHIII!!
CRAAA
IT'S MR. ZUH...ZUH... ZOLO!!!
FWUFF
D-DO YOU RUH-REMEMBER ABOUT MY AUT-AUTTA... AUTOMAGRAPH?!

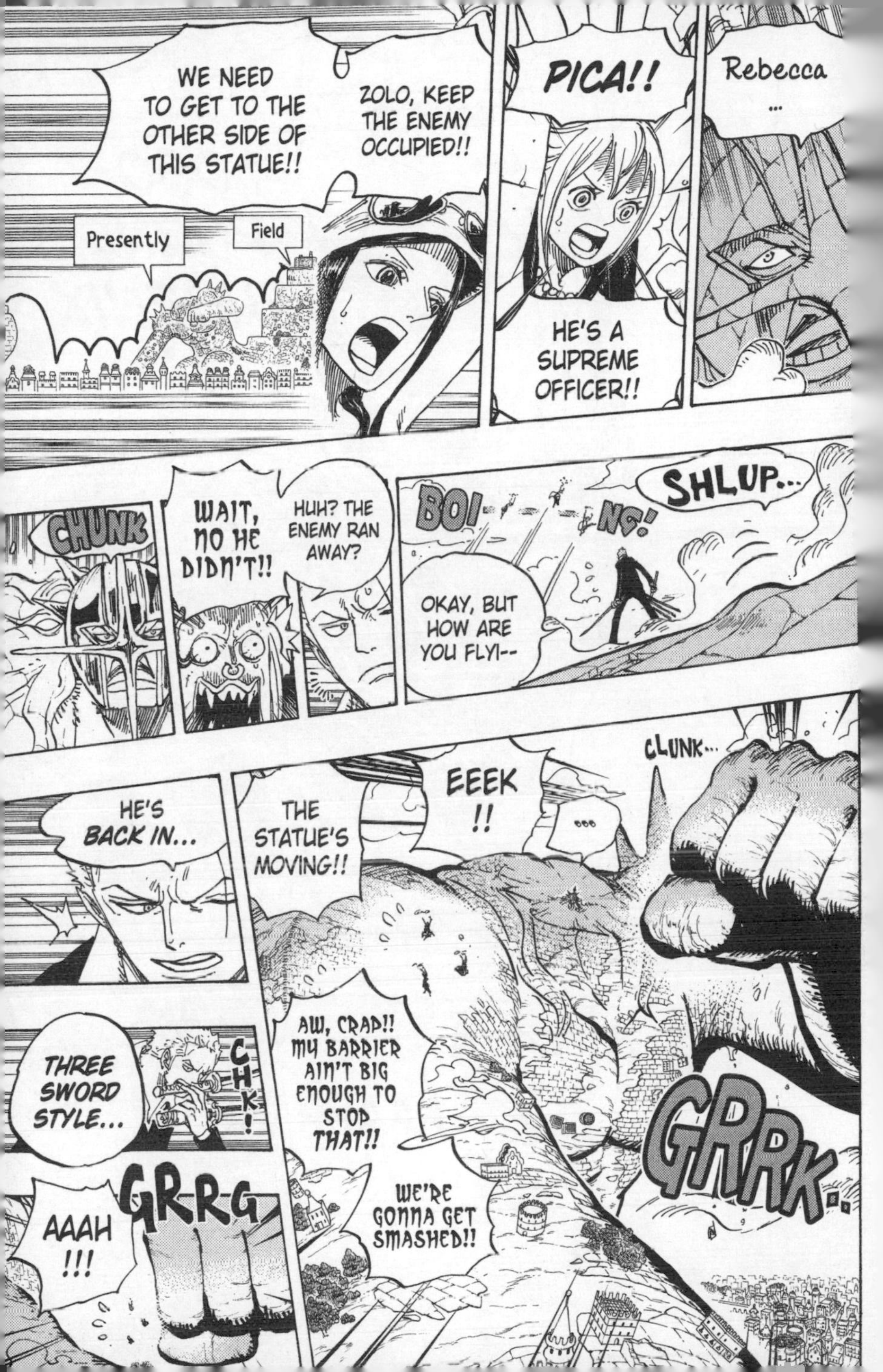

Rebecca ...
PICA!!
HE'S A SUPREME OFFICER!!
ZOLO, KEEP THE ENEMY OCCUPIED!!
WE NEED TO GET TO THE OTHER SIDE OF THIS STATUE!!
Field
Presently
SHLUP...
BOI-NG!
OKAY, BUT HOW ARE YOU FLYI--
HUH? THE ENEMY RAN AWAY?
WAIT, NO HE DIDN'T!!
CHUNK
CLUNK...
...
EEEK !!
THE STATUE'S MOVING!!
AW, CRAP!! MY BARRIER AIN'T BIG ENOUGH TO STOP THAT!!
WE'RE GONNA GET SMASHED!!
GRRK..
HE'S BACK IN...
THREE SWORD STYLE...
CHK!
AAAH !!!
GR-R-G

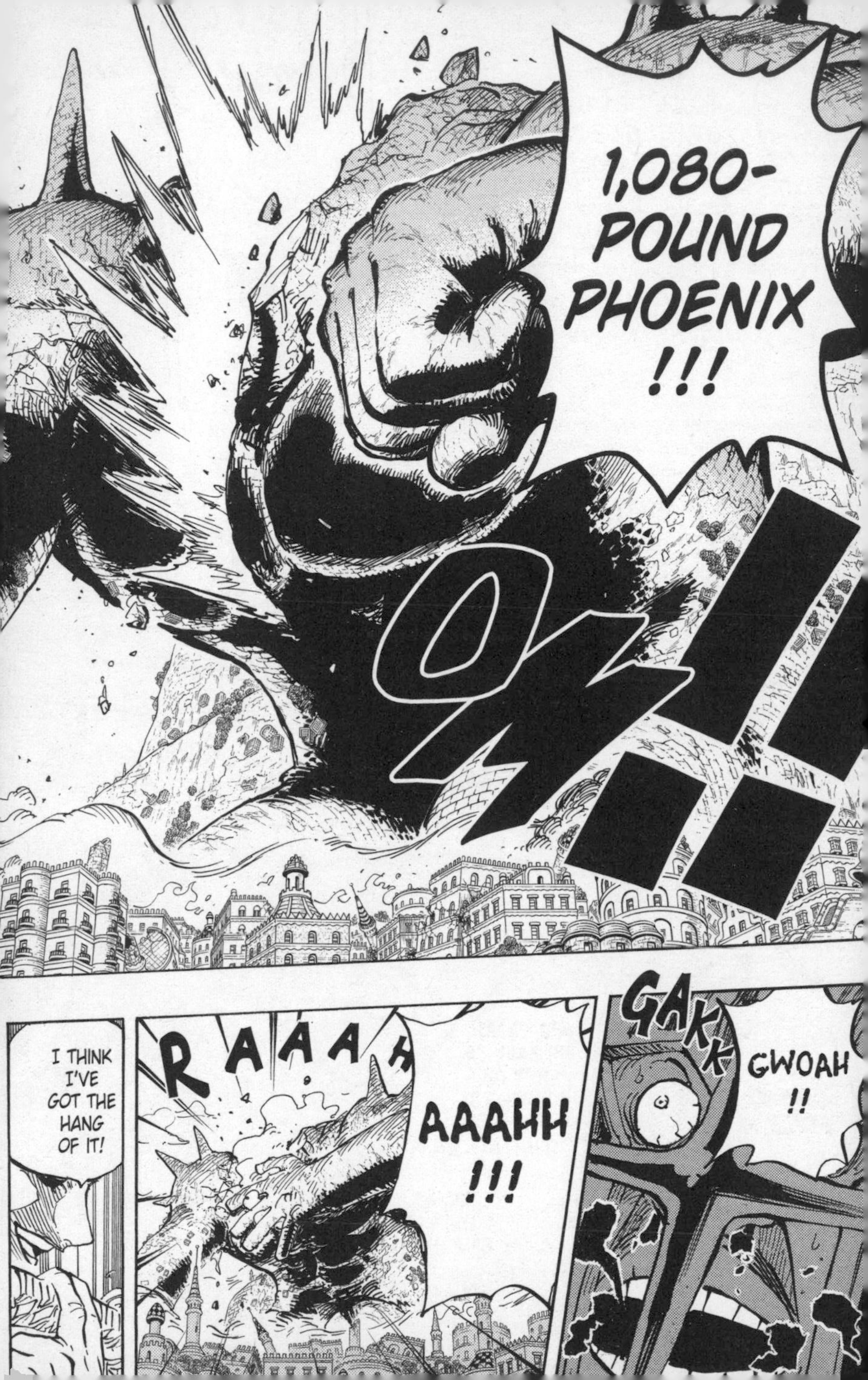
1,080-POUND PHOENIX !!!
GAKK
GWOAH !!
RAAAAH
AAAHH !!!
I THINK I'VE GOT THE HANG OF IT!

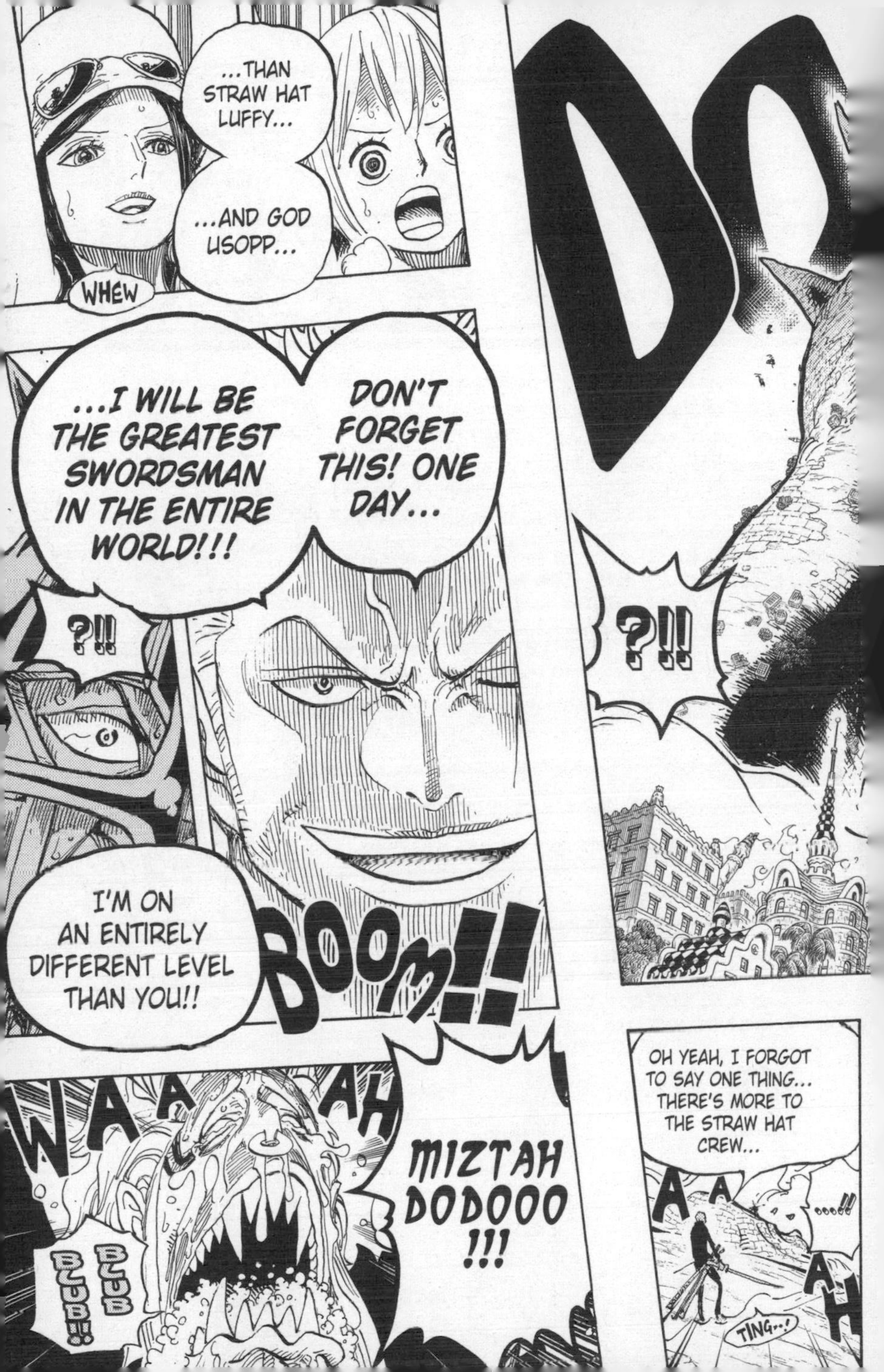

DO
?!!
...THAN STRAW HAT LUFFY...
...AND GOD USOPP...
WHEW
DON'T FORGET THIS! ONE DAY...
...I WILL BE THE GREATEST SWORDSMAN IN THE ENTIRE WORLD!!!
?!!
I'M ON AN ENTIRELY DIFFERENT LEVEL THAN YOU!!
BOOM!!
OH YEAH, I FORGOT TO SAY ONE THING... THERE'S MORE TO THE STRAW HAT CREW...
AAAH
...!!
TING..!
WAAAH
MIZTAH DODOOO!!!
BLUB BLUB!!

SBS Question Corner

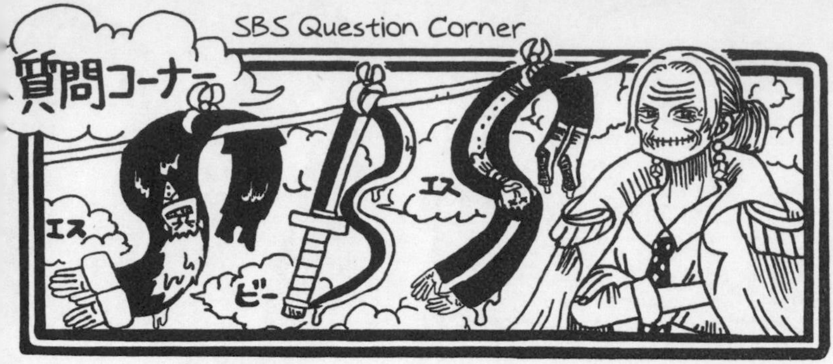
質問コーナー
エス
ビー
エス

(Fujima, Fukuoka)

Q: I was noticing that Law's crewmates are Penguin, Bepo, and Shachi, which means killer whale. Does that mean Law's supposed to be a spotted seal? I mean, that pattern on his hat is pretty suspicious… Explain!!

--I am the Walrus

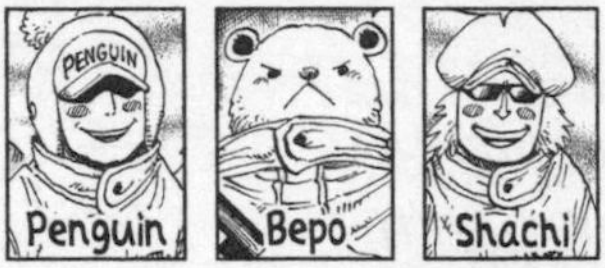
PENGUIN
Penguin
Bepo
Shachi

A: I see, ha ha. They're all Arctic animals, aren't they? His hat does look like a seal. Okay, let's go with that. By the way, when Mr. Toshio Asakuma created his One Piece x Animal mash-up figurines, he depicted Law as a snow leopard. So there you go, another cold-climate animal.

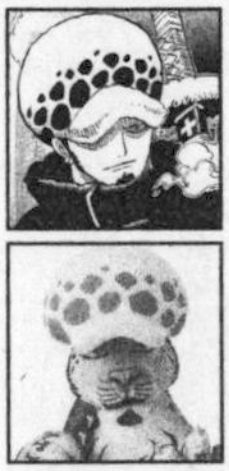

Q: Mr. Oda, draw Franky cute! What would happen if Franky was *kawaii?*

--Keisuke Igarashi, age 12, 7th grade

A: Here. I tried my best, but it didn't work...

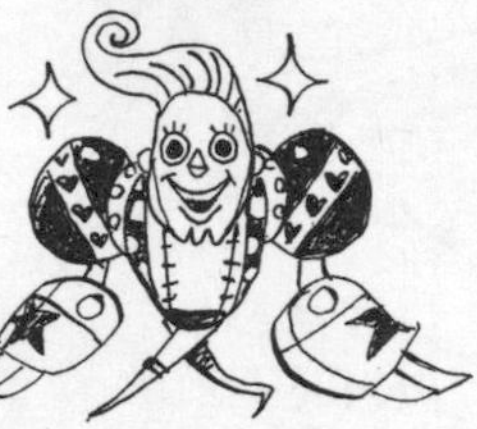

Q: If the Straw Hat Crew weren't pirates, what jobs would they have? Tell us! (I'm assuming Sanji is a cook…)

--H. Momo, age 9

A: Actually, I got the following answers from a different reader's suggestions. They asked the same thing and wrote their own ideas on the side, but they were so perfect that I agreed with all of them. So they have my stamp of approval.

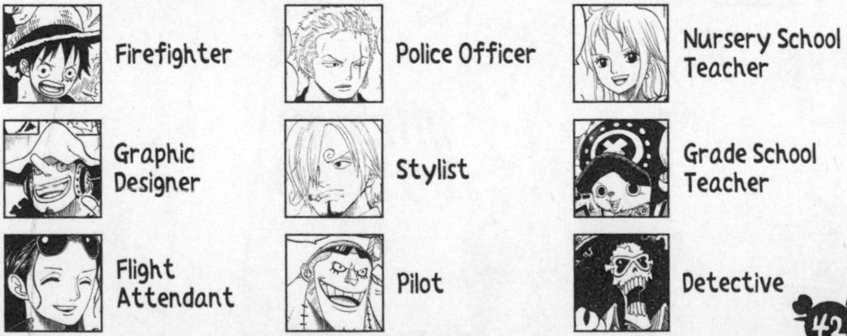
Firefighter
Police Officer
Nursery School Teacher
Graphic Designer
Stylist
Grade School Teacher
Flight Attendant
Pilot
Detective

Chapter 755:
A MAN'S WORLD

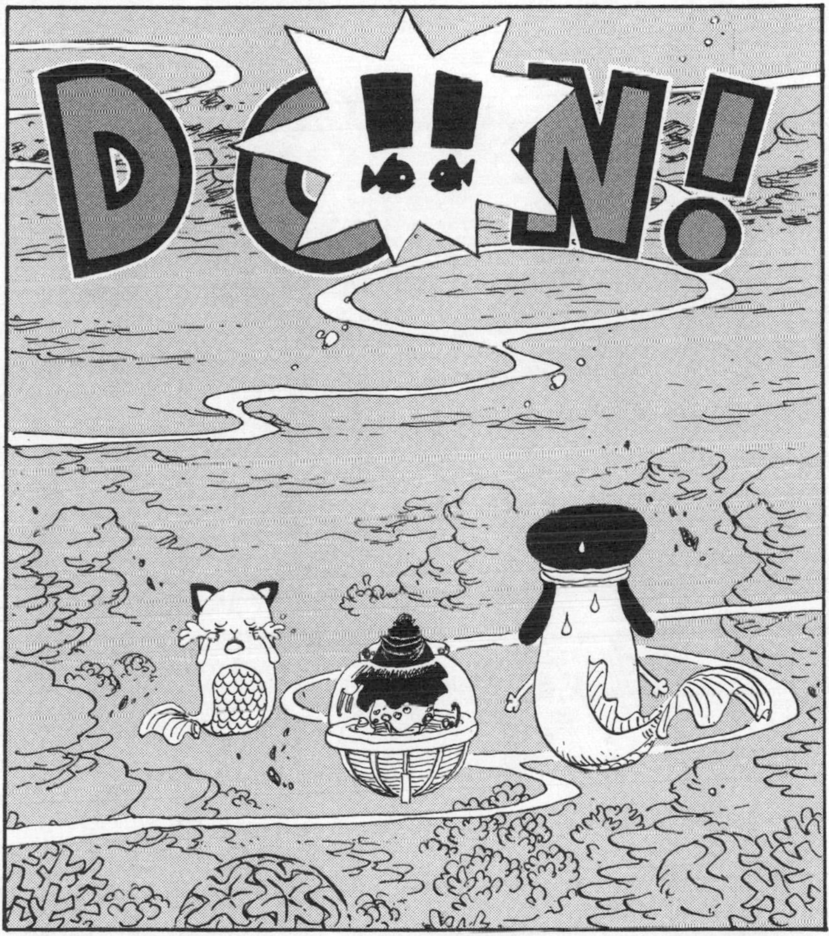
DON!!

THE SOLITARY JOURNEY OF JIMBEI, FIRST SON OF THE SEA, VOL. 5: "GOT AN INCIDENT ON OUR HANDS. TOWN'S GONE."

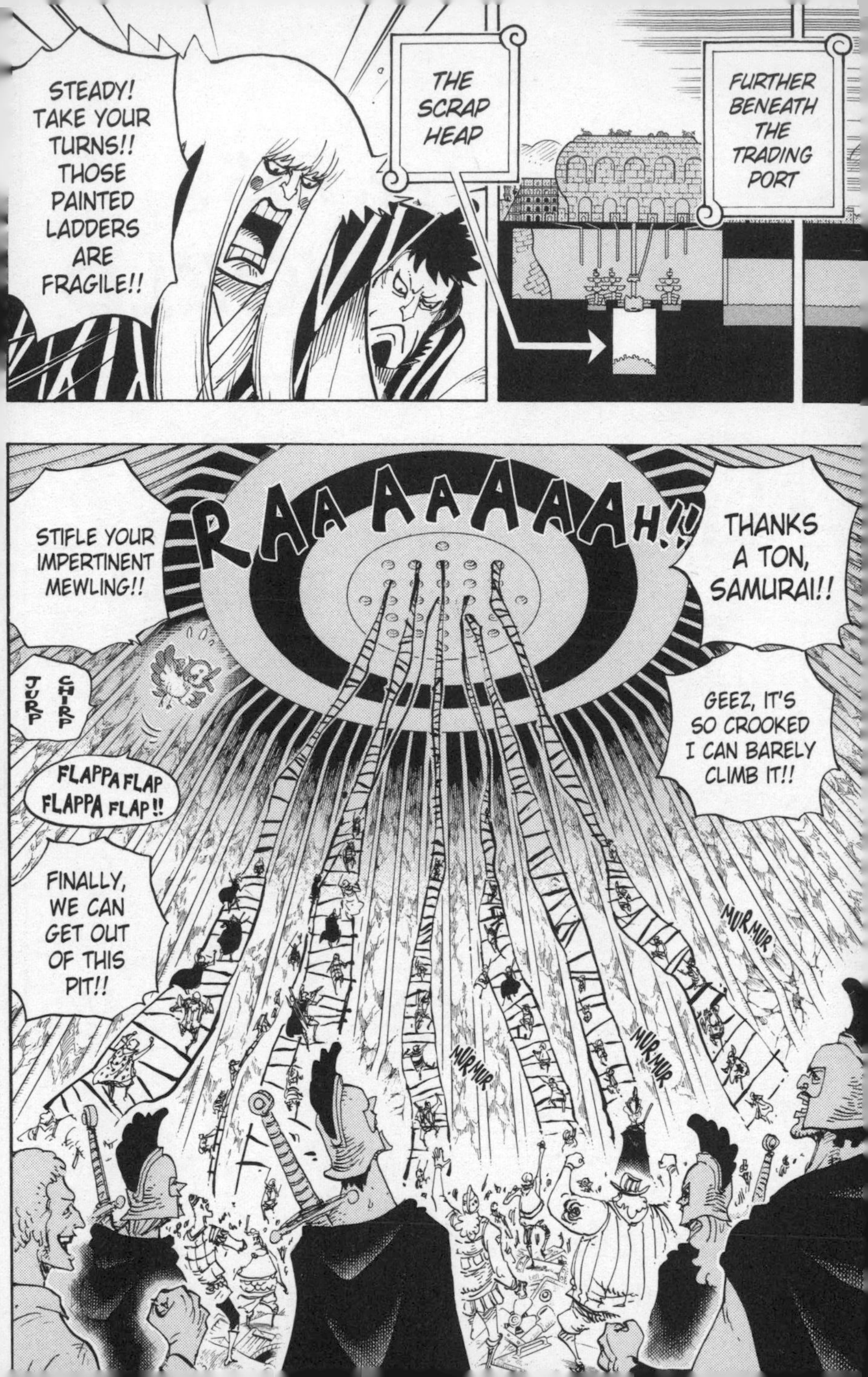
FURTHER BENEATH THE TRADING PORT
THE SCRAP HEAP
STEADY! TAKE YOUR TURNS!! THOSE PAINTED LADDERS ARE FRAGILE!!
THANKS A TON, SAMURAI!!
RAAAAAAH!!
STIFLE YOUR IMPERTINENT MEWLING!!
GEEZ, IT'S SO CROOKED I CAN BARELY CLIMB IT!!
CHIRP
JURP
FLAPPA FLAP FLAPPA FLAP!!
MUR MUR
MUR MUR
MUR MUR
FINALLY, WE CAN GET OUT OF THIS PIT!!

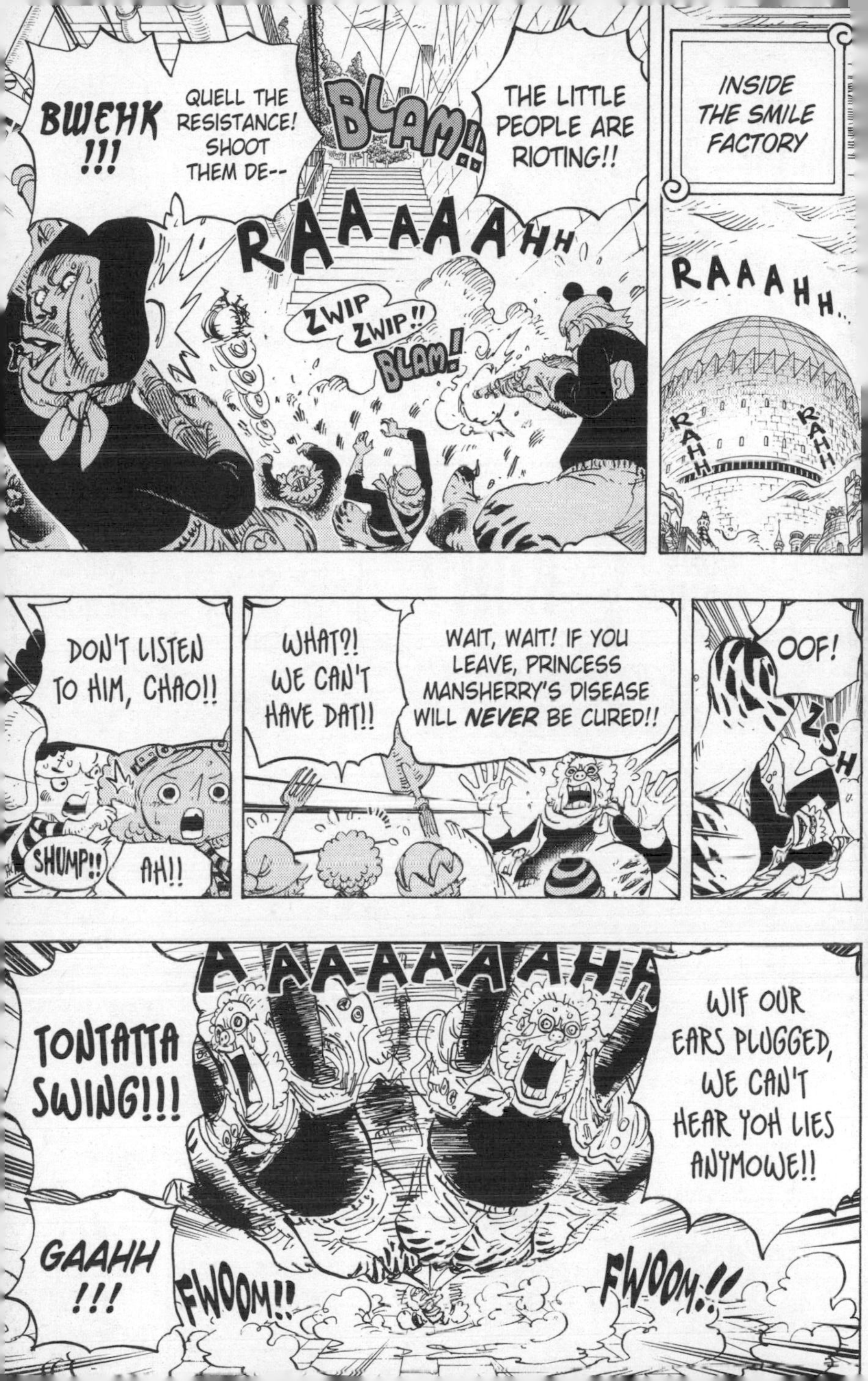
INSIDE THE SMILE FACTORY
RAAAHH...
RAHH
RAHH
THE LITTLE PEOPLE ARE RIOTING!!
BLAM!!
QUELL THE RESISTANCE! SHOOT THEM DE--
BWEHK!!!
RAAAAAHH
ZWIP ZWIP!!
BLAM!
OOF!
ZSH
WAIT, WAIT! IF YOU LEAVE, PRINCESS MANSHERRY'S DISEASE WILL NEVER BE CURED!!
WHAT?! WE CAN'T HAVE DAT!!
DON'T LISTEN TO HIM, CHAO!!
AH!!
SHUMP!!
AAAAAAAAHH
WIF OUR EARS PLUGGED, WE CAN'T HEAR YOH LIES ANYMOWE!!
TONTATTA SWING!!!
FWOOM!!
FWOOM!!
GAAHH!!!

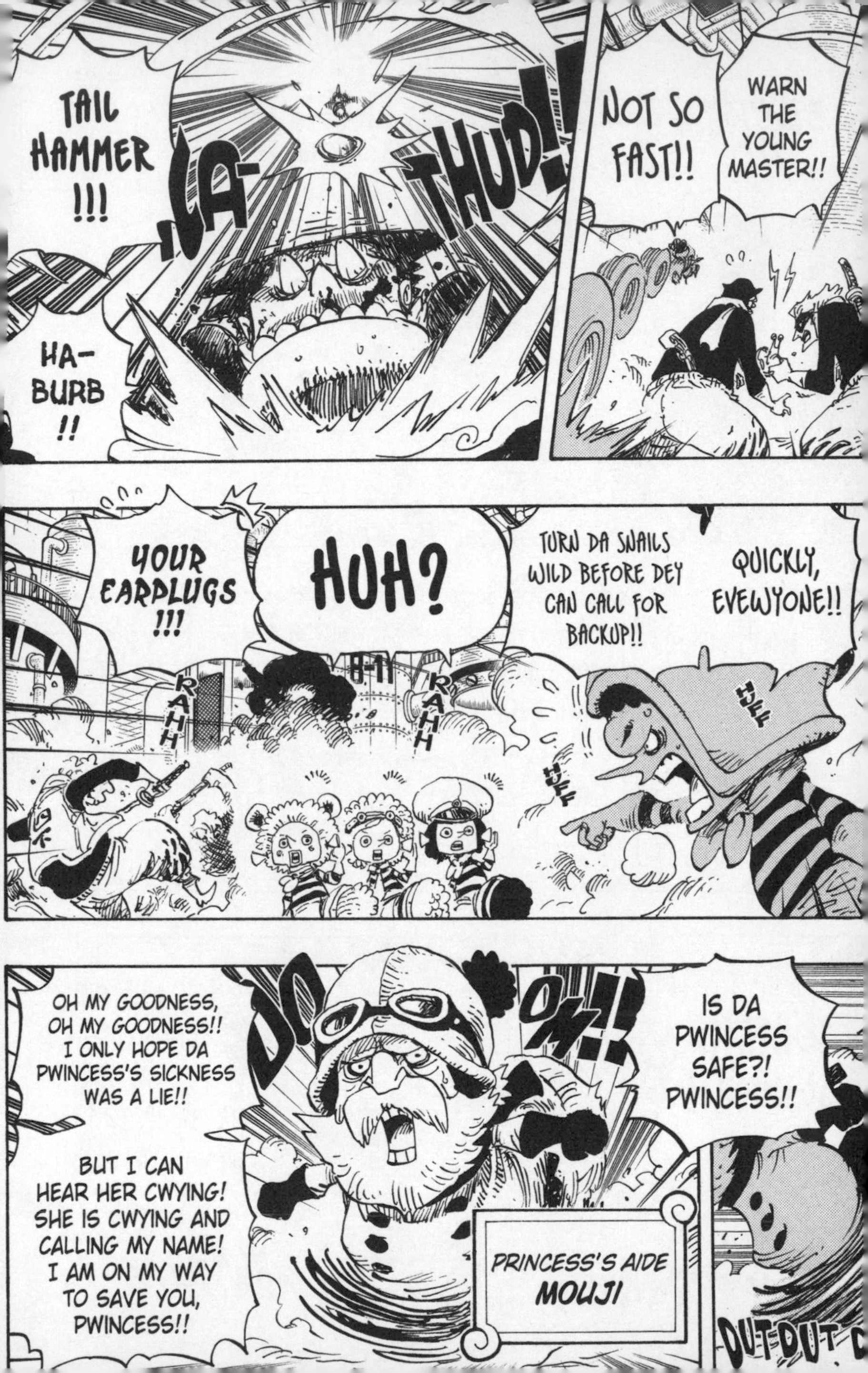
WARN THE YOUNG MASTER!!
NOT SO FAST!!
TAIL HAMMER!!!
KA-THUD!!
HA-BURB!!
QUICKLY, EVEWYONE!!
TURN DA SNAILS WILD BEFORE DEY CAN CALL FOR BACKUP!!
HUFF
HUFF
HUH?
YOUR EARPLUGS!!!
RAHH
RAHH
IS DA PWINCESS SAFE?! PWINCESS!!
DUT DUT D
DOOM!!
OH MY GOODNESS, OH MY GOODNESS!! I ONLY HOPE DA PWINCESS'S SICKNESS WAS A LIE!!
BUT I CAN HEAR HER CWYING! SHE IS CWYING AND CALLING MY NAME! I AM ON MY WAY TO SAVE YOU, PWINCESS!!
PRINCESS'S AIDE MOUJI

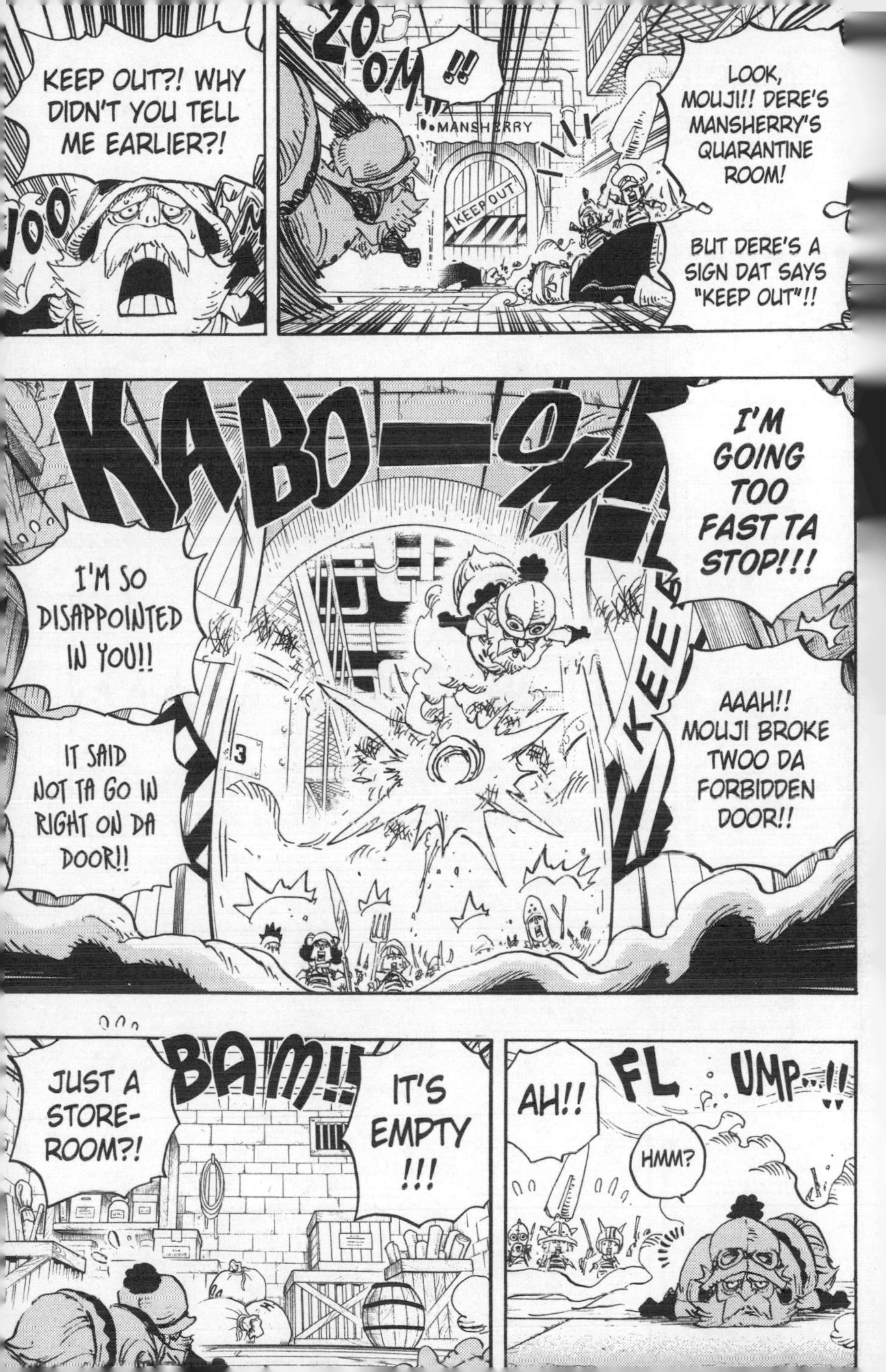
LOOK, MOUJI!! DERE'S MANSHERRY'S QUARANTINE ROOM!
BUT DERE'S A SIGN DAT SAYS "KEEP OUT"!!
ZOOM!!
MANSHERRY
KEEP OUT
KEEP OUT?! WHY DIDN'T YOU TELL ME EARLIER?!
I'M GOING TOO FAST TA STOP!!!
KABO—O
AAAH!! MOUJI BROKE TWOO DA FORBIDDEN DOOR!!
I'M SO DISAPPOINTED IN YOU!!
IT SAID NOT TA GO IN RIGHT ON DA DOOR!!
FL . . UMP...!!
AH!!
HMM?
BAM!!
IT'S EMPTY!!!
JUST A STORE-ROOM?!

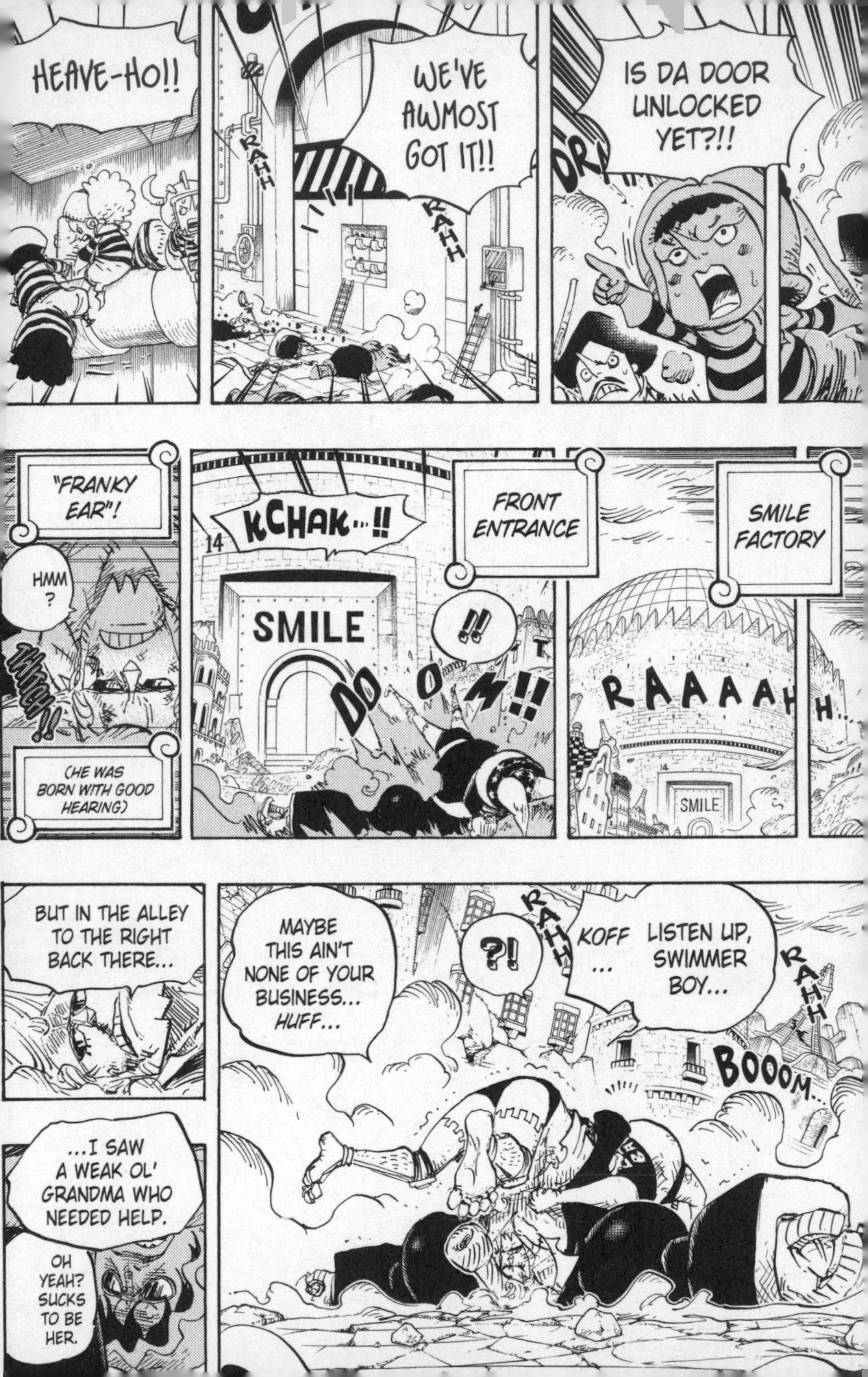
IS DA DOOR UNLOCKED YET?!!
WE'VE AWMOST GOT IT!!
RAHH
RAHH
HEAVE-HO!!
SMILE FACTORY
RAAAAHH...
14
SMILE
FRONT ENTRANCE
KCHAK...!!
14
SMILE
!!
DOOM!!
"FRANKY EAR"!
HMM?
(HE WAS BORN WITH GOOD HEARING)
RAHH
LISTEN UP, SWIMMER BOY...
KOFF...
RAHH
?!
MAYBE THIS AIN'T NONE OF YOUR BUSINESS... HUFF...
BOOOM...
BUT IN THE ALLEY TO THE RIGHT BACK THERE...
...I SAW A WEAK OL' GRANDMA WHO NEEDED HELP.
OH YEAH? SUCKS TO BE HER.

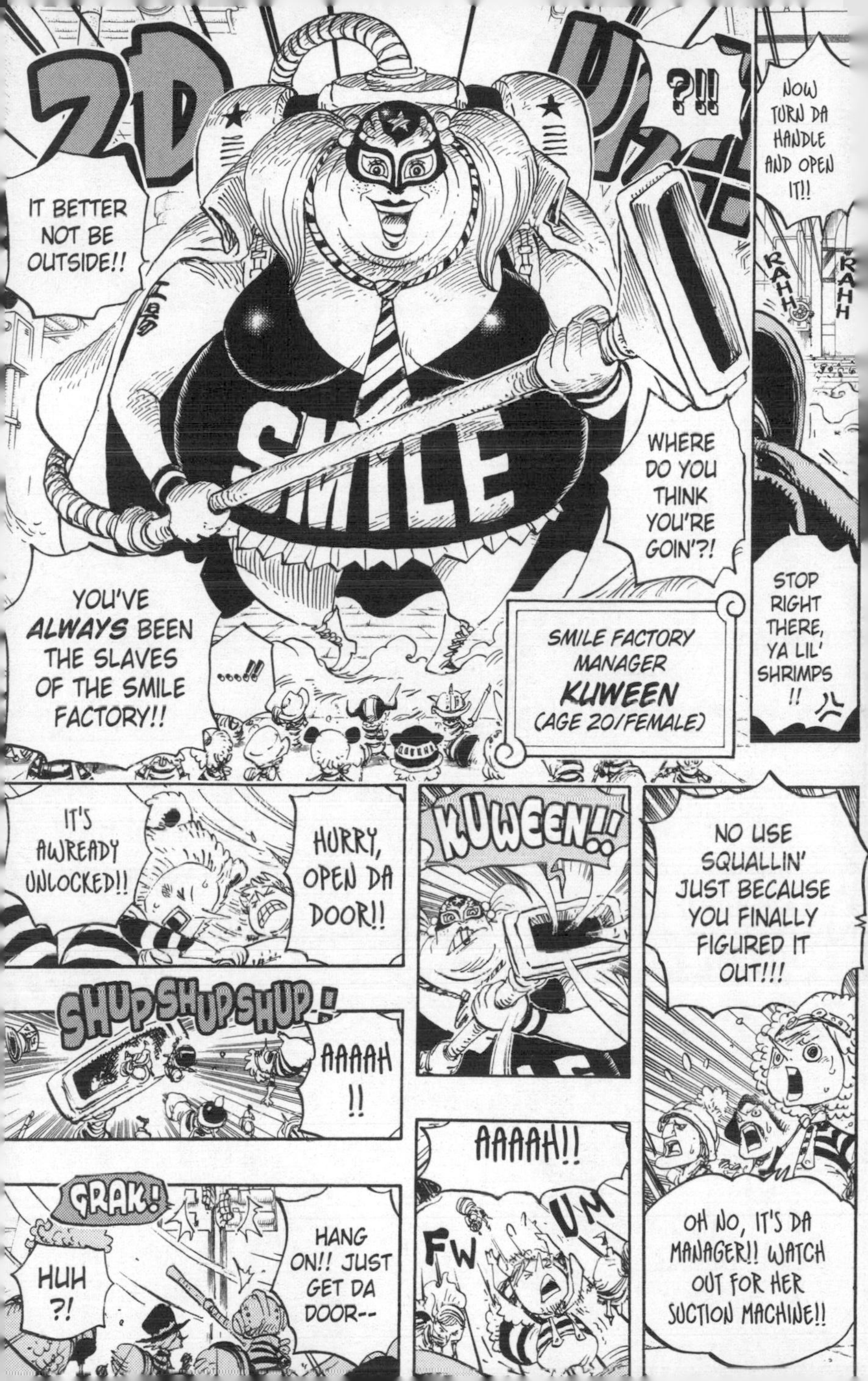
NOW TURN DA HANDLE AND OPEN IT!!
RAHH
RAHH
STOP RIGHT THERE, YA LIL' SHRIMPS!!
?!!
WHERE DO YOU THINK YOU'RE GOIN'?!
IT BETTER NOT BE OUTSIDE!!
SMILE
YOU'VE ALWAYS BEEN THE SLAVES OF THE SMILE FACTORY!!
....!!
SMILE FACTORY MANAGER KUWEEN (AGE 20/FEMALE)
NO USE SQUALLIN' JUST BECAUSE YOU FINALLY FIGURED IT OUT!!!
OH NO, IT'S DA MANAGER!! WATCH OUT FOR HER SUCTION MACHINE!!
KUWEEN!!
AAAAH!!
FW
UM
HURRY, OPEN DA DOOR!!
IT'S AWREADY UNLOCKED!!
SHUPSHUPSHUP..!
AAAAH!!
GRAK!
HANG ON!! JUST GET DA DOOR--
HUH ?!

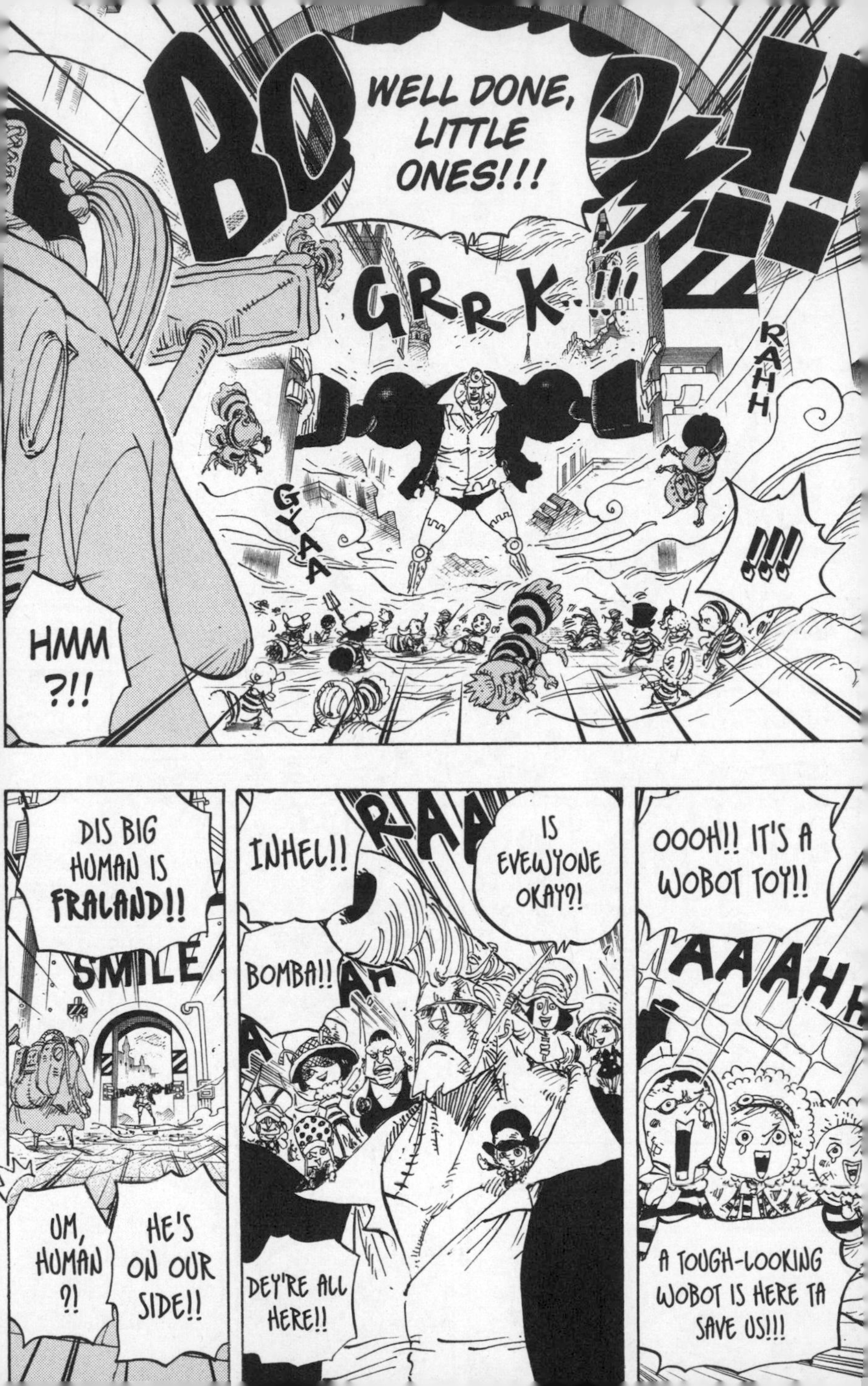
BO
WELL DONE, LITTLE ONES!!!
GRRK..!!!
RAHH
!!!
GYAA
HMM?!!
OOOH!! IT'S A WOBOT TOY!!
AAAAHH
A TOUGH-LOOKING WOBOT IS HERE TA SAVE US!!!
IS EVEWYONE OKAY?!
RAA
INHEL!!
BOMBA!!
AAH
DEY'RE ALL HERE!!
DIS BIG HUMAN IS FRALAND!!
SMILE
HE'S ON OUR SIDE!!
UM, HUMAN?!

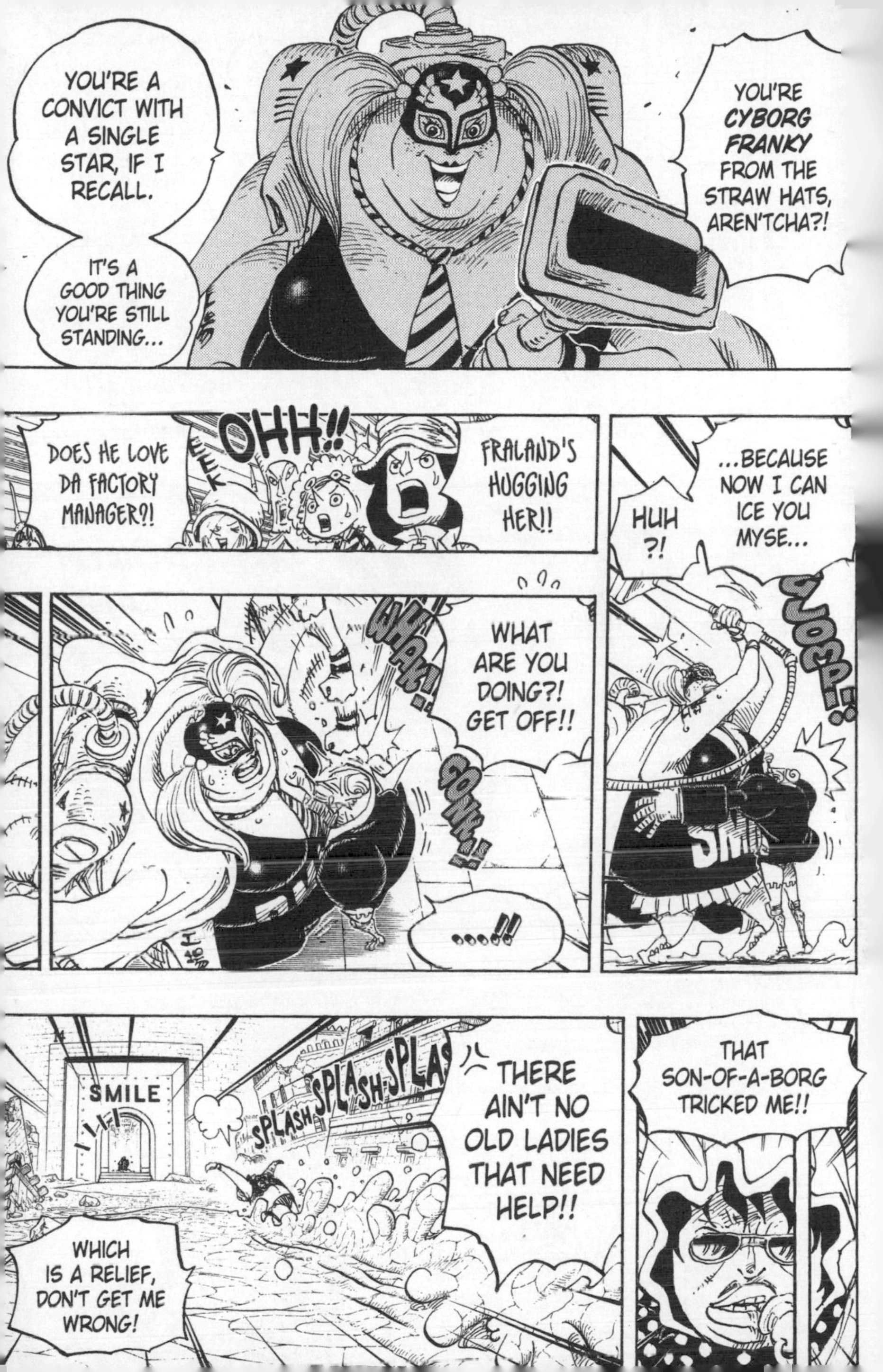
YOU'RE CYBORG FRANKY FROM THE STRAW HATS, AREN'TCHA?!
YOU'RE A CONVICT WITH A SINGLE STAR, IF I RECALL.
IT'S A GOOD THING YOU'RE STILL STANDING...
...BECAUSE NOW I CAN ICE YOU MYSE...
HUH?!
DJOMP!!
FRALAND'S HUGGING HER!!
OHH!!
DOES HE LOVE DA FACTORY MANAGER?!
WHAT ARE YOU DOING?! GET OFF!!
WHAK!!
GONK!!
.....!!
THAT SON-OF-A-BORG TRICKED ME!!
THERE AIN'T NO OLD LADIES THAT NEED HELP!!
SPLASH SPLASH SPLAS
SMILE
WHICH IS A RELIEF, DON'T GET ME WRONG!

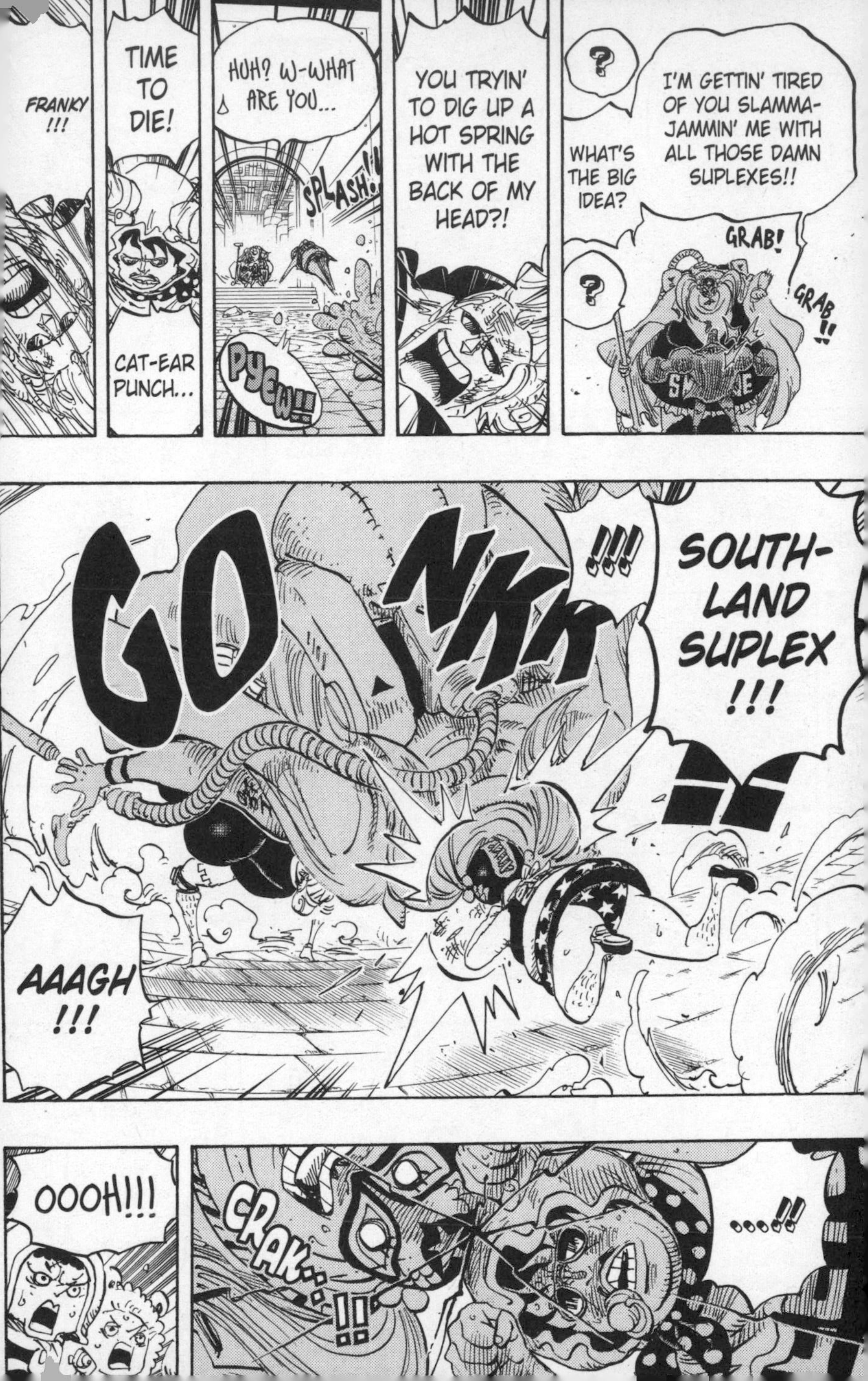
?
I'M GETTIN' TIRED OF YOU SLAMMA-JAMMIN' ME WITH ALL THOSE DAMN SUPLEXES!!
WHAT'S THE BIG IDEA?
?
GRAB!
GRAB!!
YOU TRYIN' TO DIG UP A HOT SPRING WITH THE BACK OF MY HEAD?!
HUH? W-WHAT ARE YOU...
SPLASH!!
PYEW!!
TIME TO DIE!
CAT-EAR PUNCH...
FRANKY!!!
SOUTH-LAND SUPLEX!!!
GONK!!!
AAAGH!!!
...!!
CRAK...!!
OOOH!!!

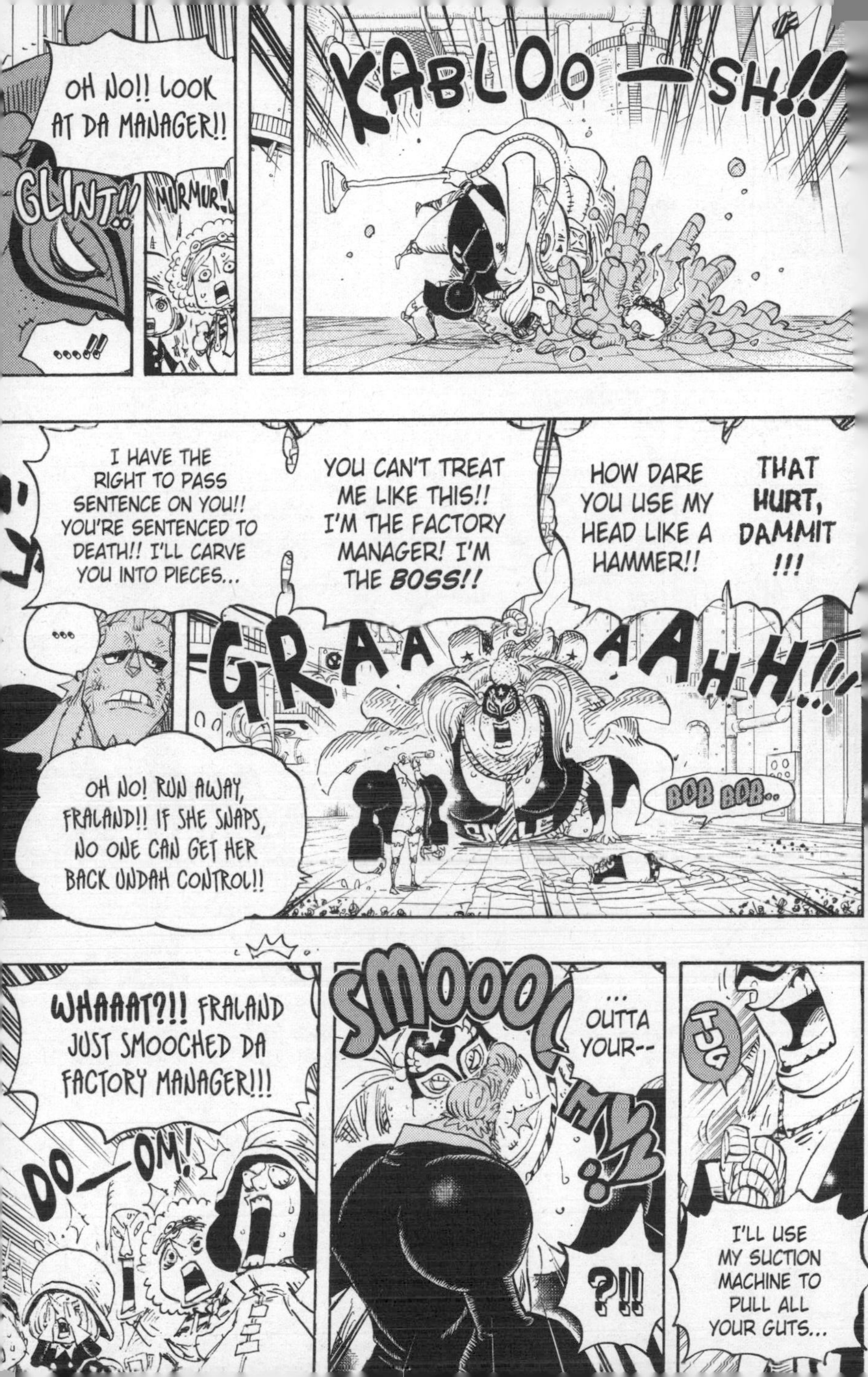
KABLOO—SH!!
MURMUR!
OH NO!! LOOK AT DA MANAGER!!
GLINT!!
....!!
THAT HURT, DAMMIT!!!
HOW DARE YOU USE MY HEAD LIKE A HAMMER!!
YOU CAN'T TREAT ME LIKE THIS!! I'M THE FACTORY MANAGER! I'M THE BOSS!!
I HAVE THE RIGHT TO PASS SENTENCE ON YOU!! YOU'RE SENTENCED TO DEATH!! I'LL CARVE YOU INTO PIECES...
GRAAAAHH!!
BOB BOB..
...
OH NO! RUN AWAY, FRALAND!! IF SHE SNAPS, NO ONE CAN GET HER BACK UNDAH CONTROL!!
TUG
I'LL USE MY SUCTION MACHINE TO PULL ALL YOUR GUTS...
... OUTTA YOUR--
SMOOOCH!!
?!!
WHAAAT?!! FRALAND JUST SMOOCHED DA FACTORY MANAGER!!!
DO—OM!

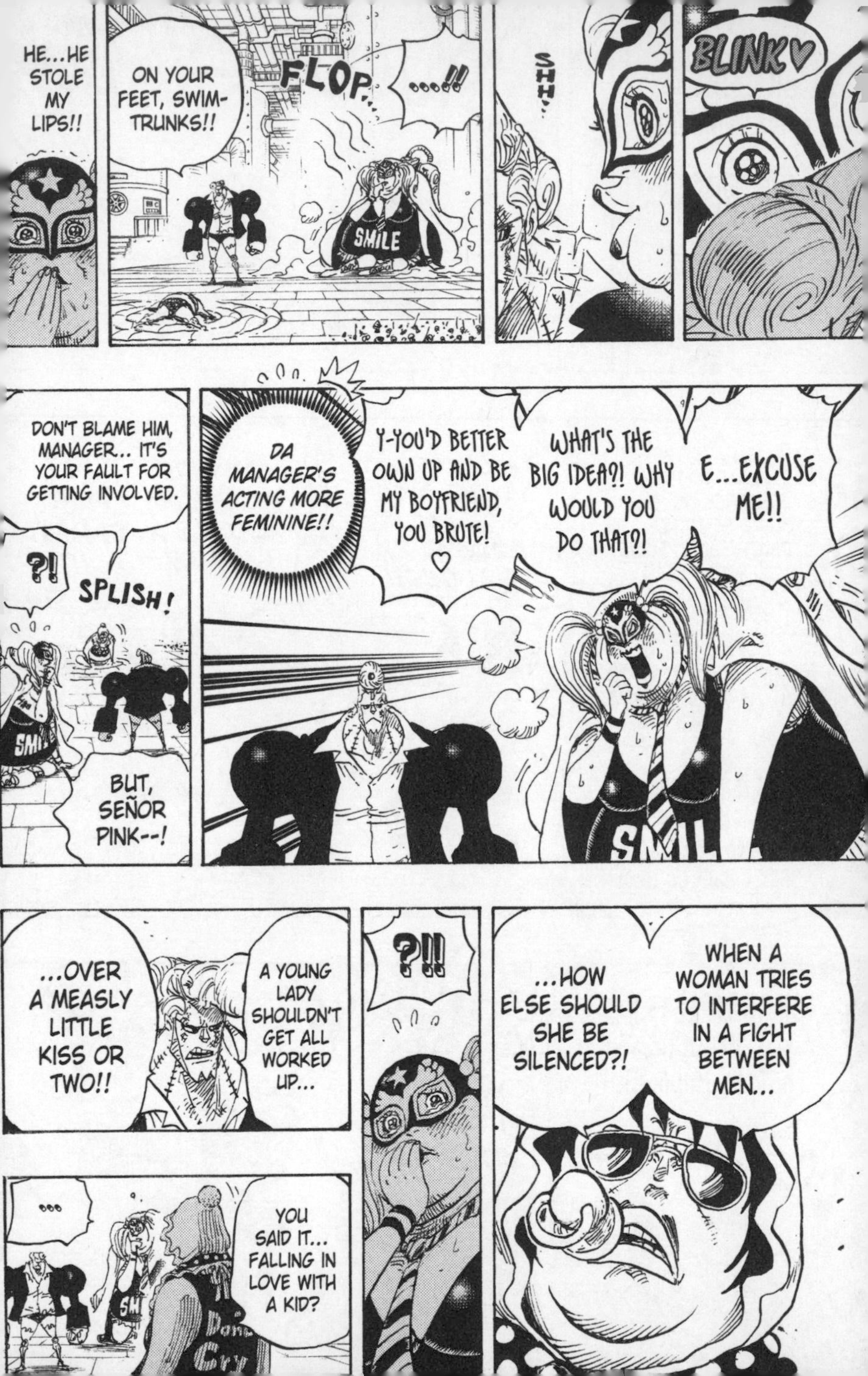
BLINK♥
SHH...
...!!
FLOP...
ON YOUR FEET, SWIM-TRUNKS!!
HE...HE STOLE MY LIPS!!
E...EXCUSE ME!!
WHAT'S THE BIG IDEA?! WHY WOULD YOU DO THAT?!
Y-YOU'D BETTER OWN UP AND BE MY BOYFRIEND, YOU BRUTE! ♥
DA MANAGER'S ACTING MORE FEMININE!!
DON'T BLAME HIM, MANAGER... IT'S YOUR FAULT FOR GETTING INVOLVED.
?!
SPLISH!
BUT, SEÑOR PINK--!
WHEN A WOMAN TRIES TO INTERFERE IN A FIGHT BETWEEN MEN...
...HOW ELSE SHOULD SHE BE SILENCED?!
?!!
A YOUNG LADY SHOULDN'T GET ALL WORKED UP...
...OVER A MEASLY LITTLE KISS OR TWO!!
YOU SAID IT... FALLING IN LOVE WITH A KID?
...

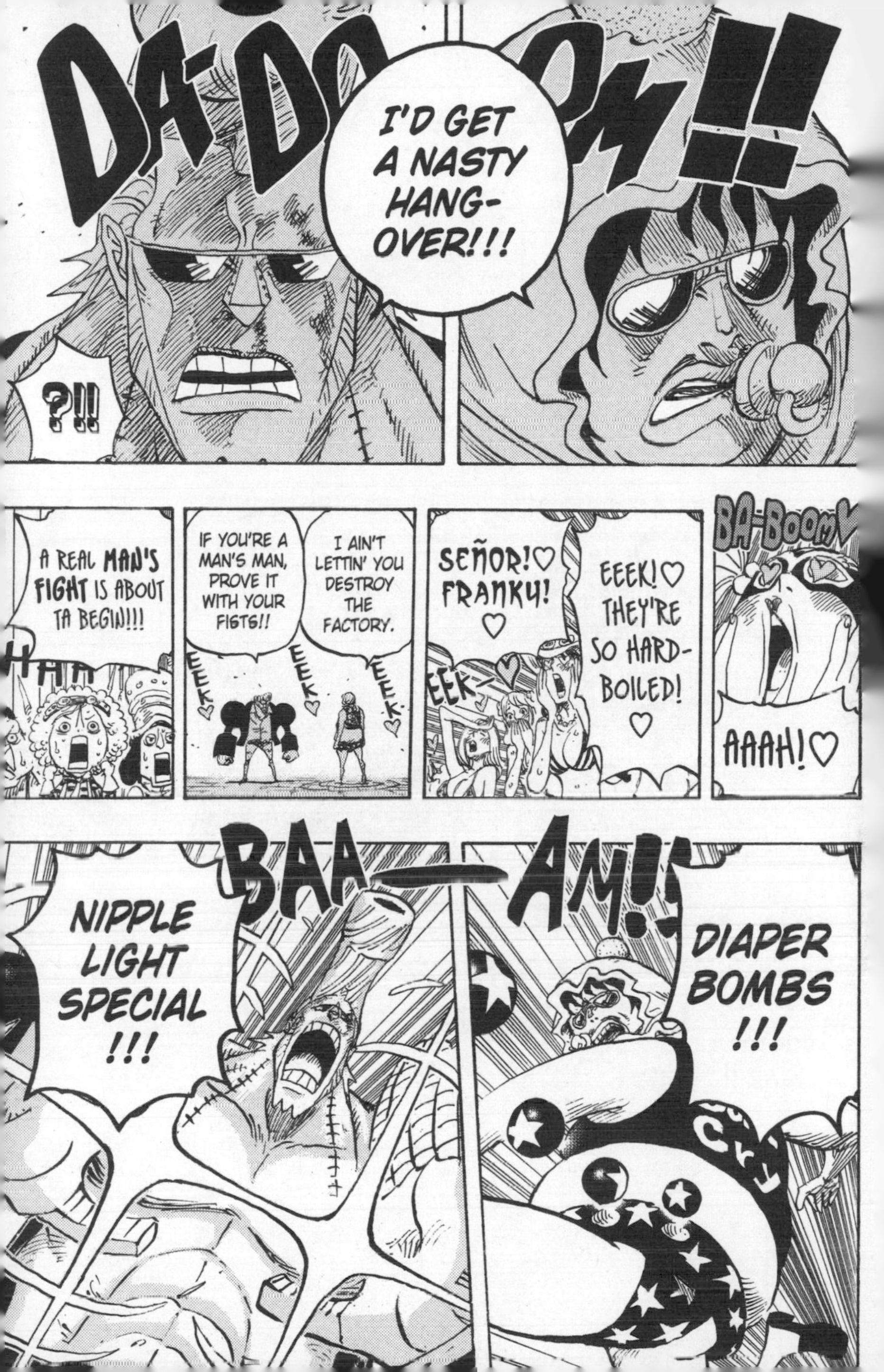
DA-DOOM!!
I'D GET A NASTY HANG-OVER!!!
?!!
BA-BOOM♥
AAAH!♡
EEEK!♡ THEY'RE SO HARD-BOILED! ♡
SEÑOR!♡ FRANKY! ♡
I AIN'T LETTIN' YOU DESTROY THE FACTORY.
IF YOU'RE A MAN'S MAN, PROVE IT WITH YOUR FISTS!!
A REAL MAN'S FIGHT IS ABOUT TA BEGIN!!!
BAA—AM!!
DIAPER BOMBS!!!
NIPPLE LIGHT SPECIAL!!!

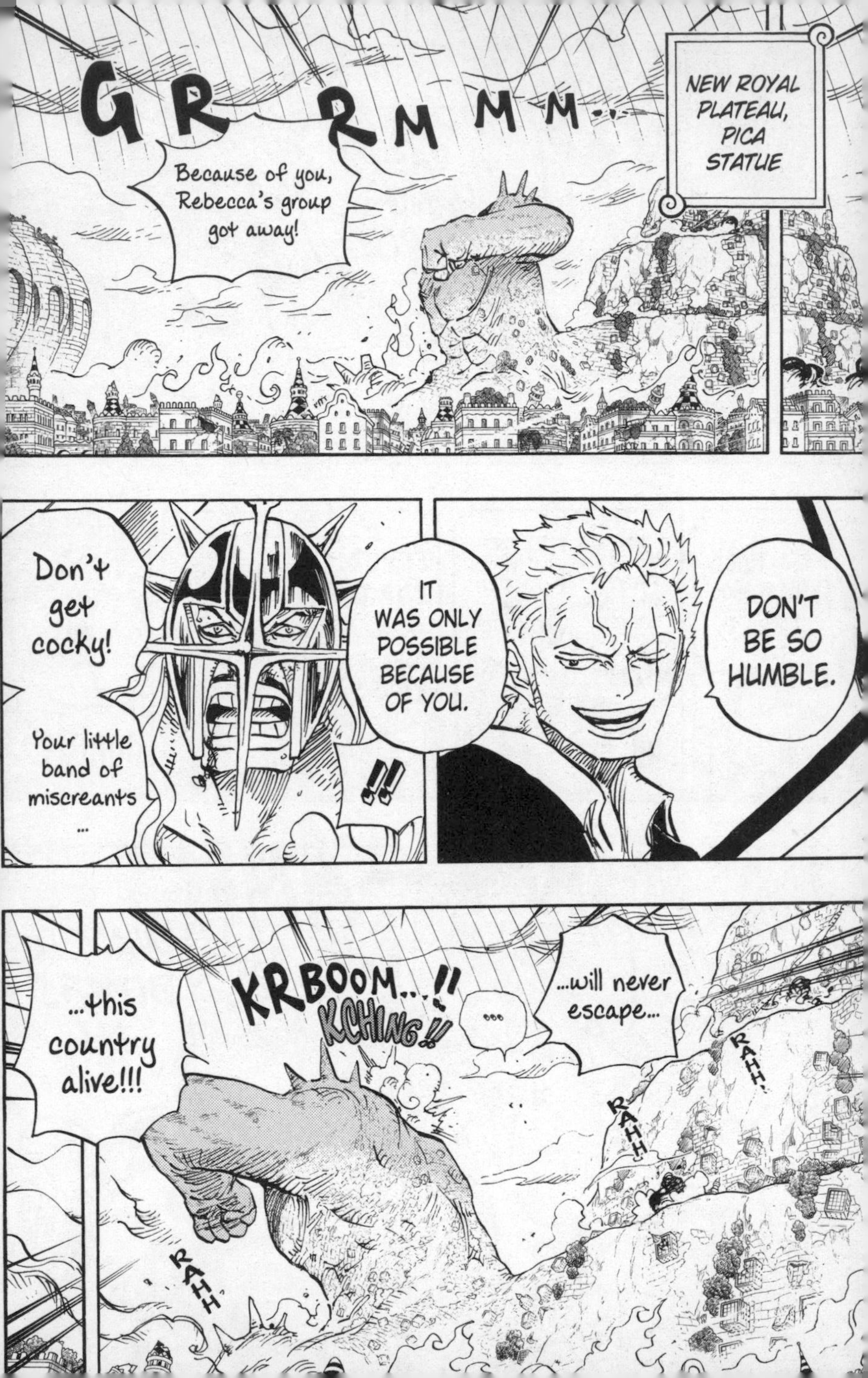
NEW ROYAL PLATEAU, PICA STATUE
GRRMMM...
Because of you, Rebecca's group got away!
DON'T BE SO HUMBLE.
IT WAS ONLY POSSIBLE BECAUSE OF YOU.
!!
Don't get cocky!
Your little band of miscreants ...
...will never escape...
...
KRBOOM...!!
KCHING!!
...this country alive!!!
RAHH
RAHH
RAHH

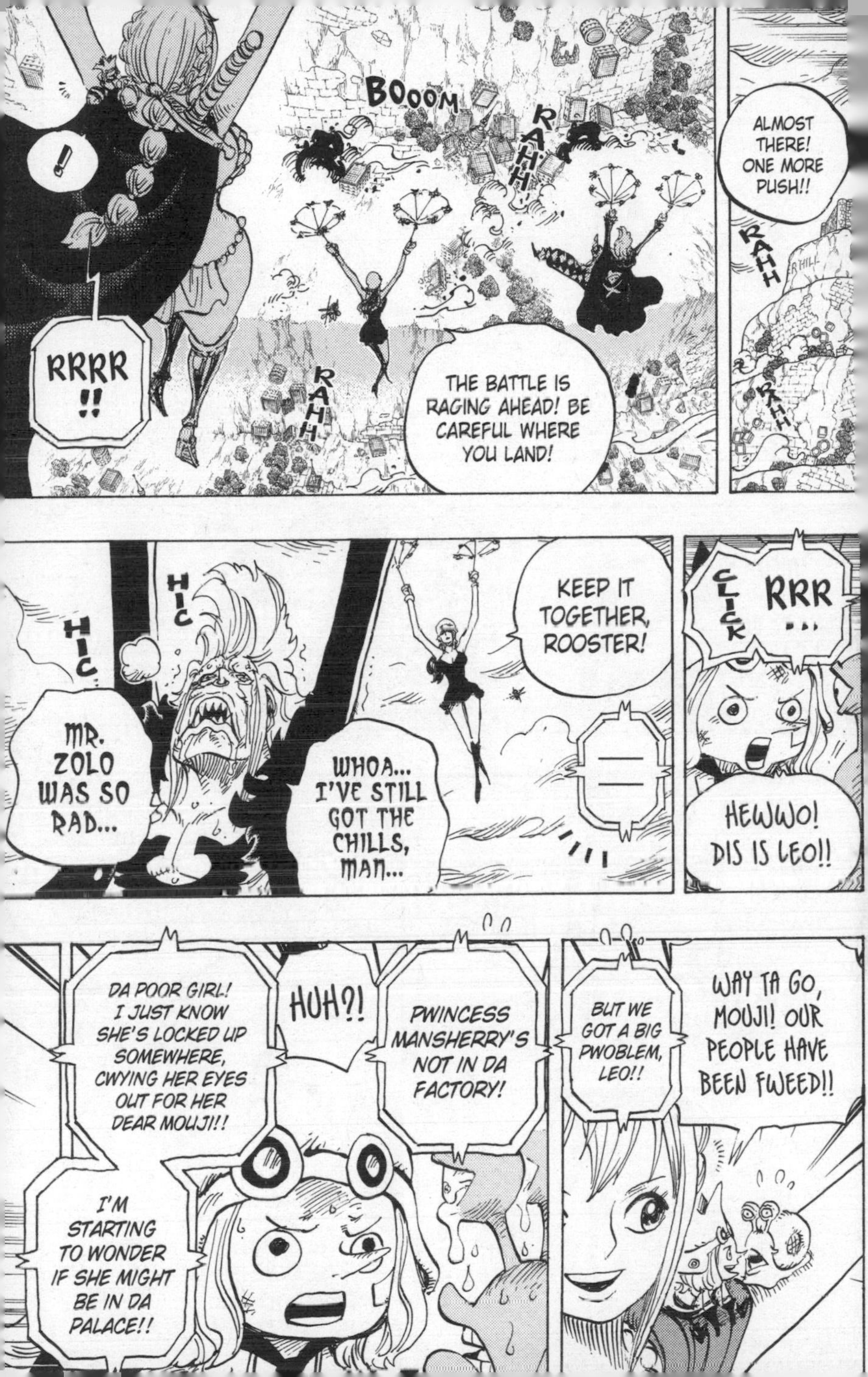

ALMOST THERE! ONE MORE PUSH!!
RAHH
RAHH
RAHHH
BOOOM
!
THE BATTLE IS RAGING AHEAD! BE CAREFUL WHERE YOU LAND!
RAHH
RRRR!!
CLICK
RRR...
HEWWO! DIS IS LEO!!
KEEP IT TOGETHER, ROOSTER!
——
WHOA... I'VE STILL GOT THE CHILLS, MAN...
HIC
HIC
MR. ZOLO WAS SO RAD...
WAY TA GO, MOUJI! OUR PEOPLE HAVE BEEN FWEED!!
BUT WE GOT A BIG PWOBLEM, LEO!!
PWINCESS MANSHERRY'S NOT IN DA FACTORY!
HUH?!
DA POOR GIRL! I JUST KNOW SHE'S LOCKED UP SOMEWHERE, CWYING HER EYES OUT FOR HER DEAR MOUJI!!
I'M STARTING TO WONDER IF SHE MIGHT BE IN DA PALACE!!

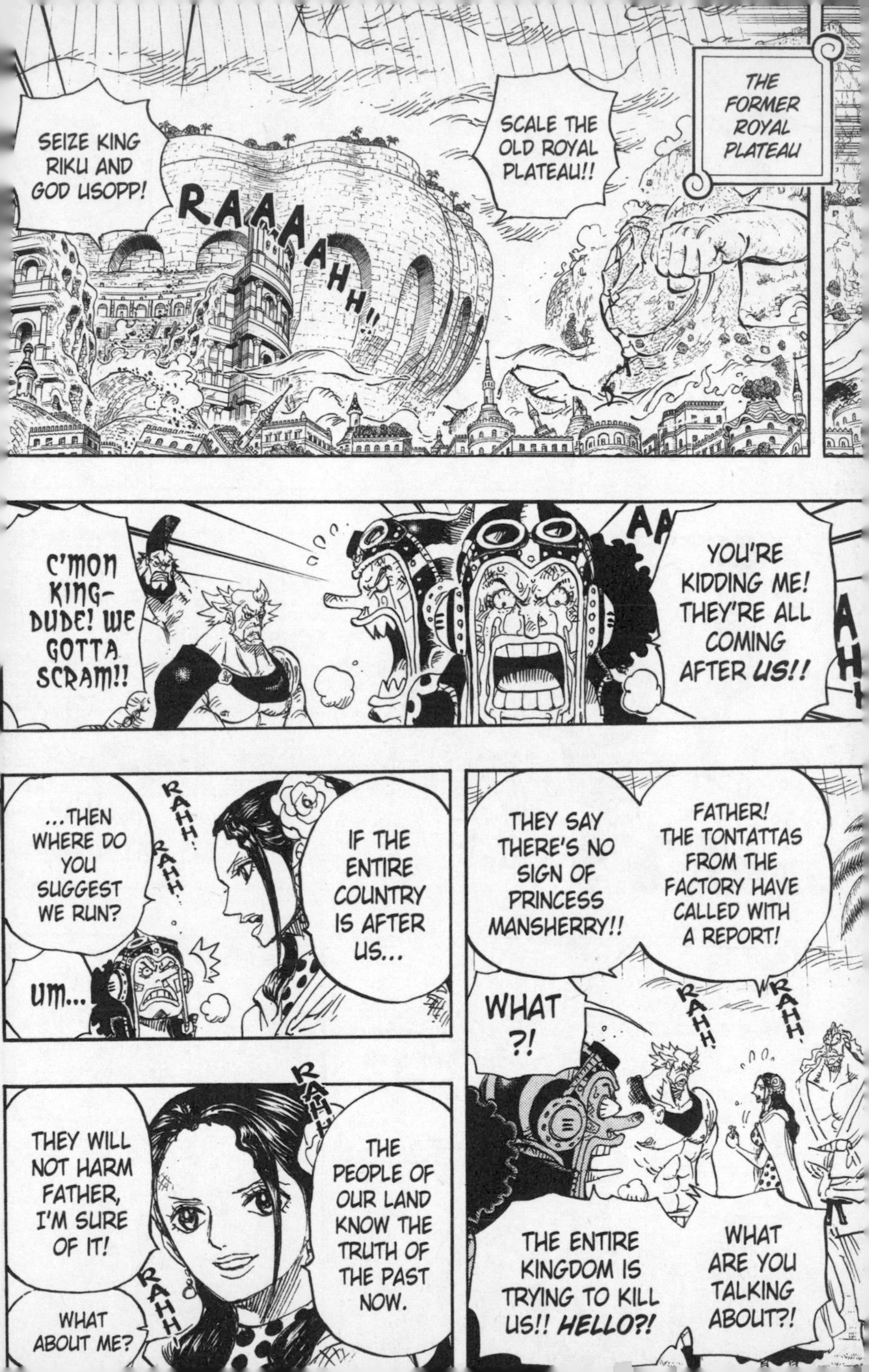
THE FORMER ROYAL PLATEAU
SCALE THE OLD ROYAL PLATEAU!!
RAAAAAHH!!
SEIZE KING RIKU AND GOD USOPP!
AA
YOU'RE KIDDING ME! THEY'RE ALL COMING AFTER US!!
C'MON KING-DUDE! WE GOTTA SCRAM!!
FATHER! THE TONTATTAS FROM THE FACTORY HAVE CALLED WITH A REPORT!
THEY SAY THERE'S NO SIGN OF PRINCESS MANSHERRY!!
RAHH
RAHH
WHAT?!
WHAT ARE YOU TALKING ABOUT?!
THE ENTIRE KINGDOM IS TRYING TO KILL US!! HELLO?!
IF THE ENTIRE COUNTRY IS AFTER US...
RAHH
RAHH
...THEN WHERE DO YOU SUGGEST WE RUN?
UM...
RAHH
THE PEOPLE OF OUR LAND KNOW THE TRUTH OF THE PAST NOW.
THEY WILL NOT HARM FATHER, I'M SURE OF IT!
RAHH
WHAT ABOUT ME?

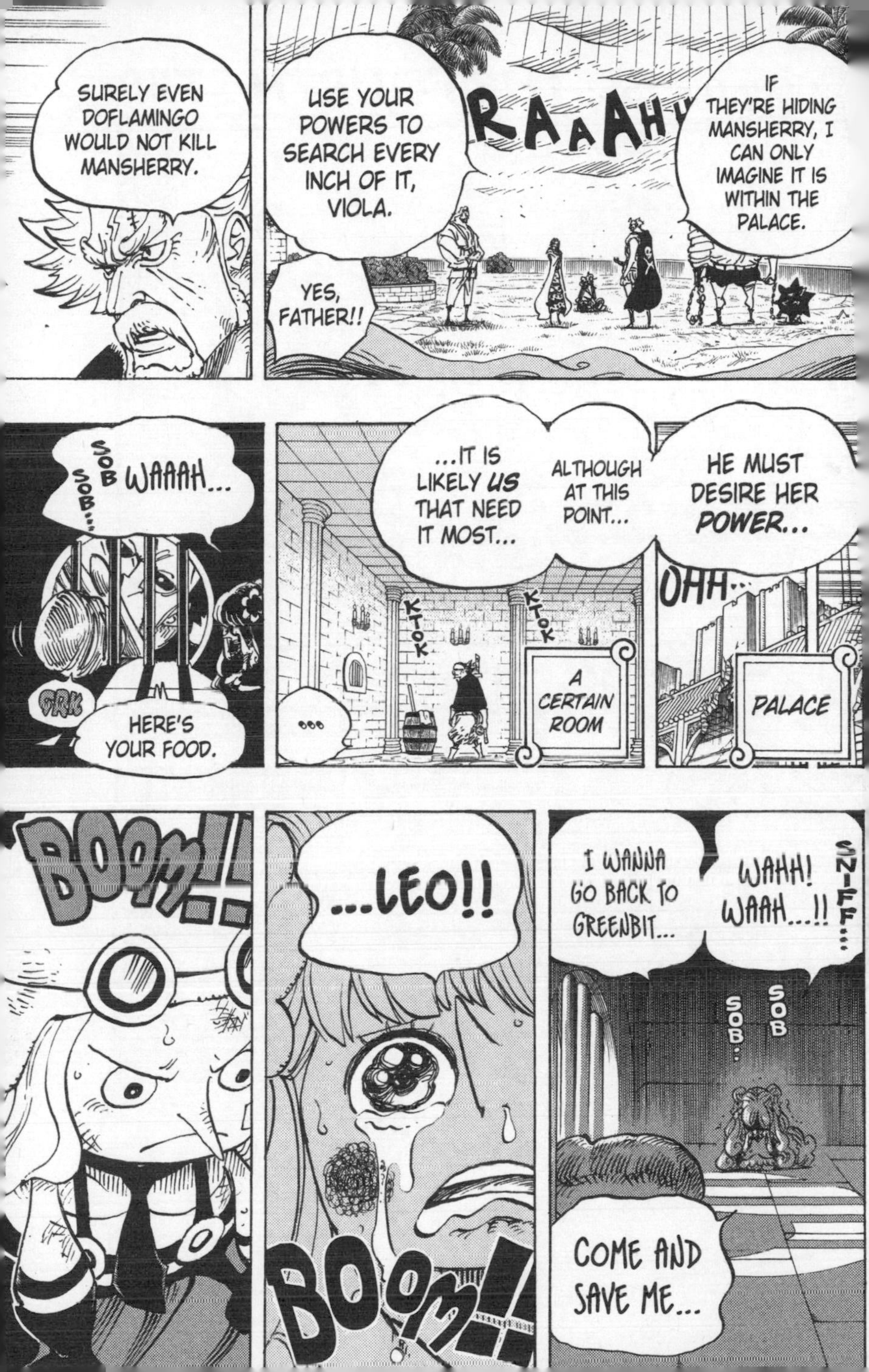
IF THEY'RE HIDING MANSHERRY, I CAN ONLY IMAGINE IT IS WITHIN THE PALACE.
RAAAHH
USE YOUR POWERS TO SEARCH EVERY INCH OF IT, VIOLA.
YES, FATHER!!
SURELY EVEN DOFLAMINGO WOULD NOT KILL MANSHERRY.
HE MUST DESIRE HER POWER...
OHH...
PALACE
ALTHOUGH AT THIS POINT...
...IT IS LIKELY US THAT NEED IT MOST...
KTOK
KTOK
A CERTAIN ROOM
...
SOB SOB... WAAAH...
GRK
HERE'S YOUR FOOD.
SNIFF...
WAHH! WAAH...!!
I WANNA GO BACK TO GREENBIT...
SOB SOB...
COME AND SAVE ME...
...LEO!!
BOOM!!
BOOM!!

Chapter 756: THE FOURTH STEP

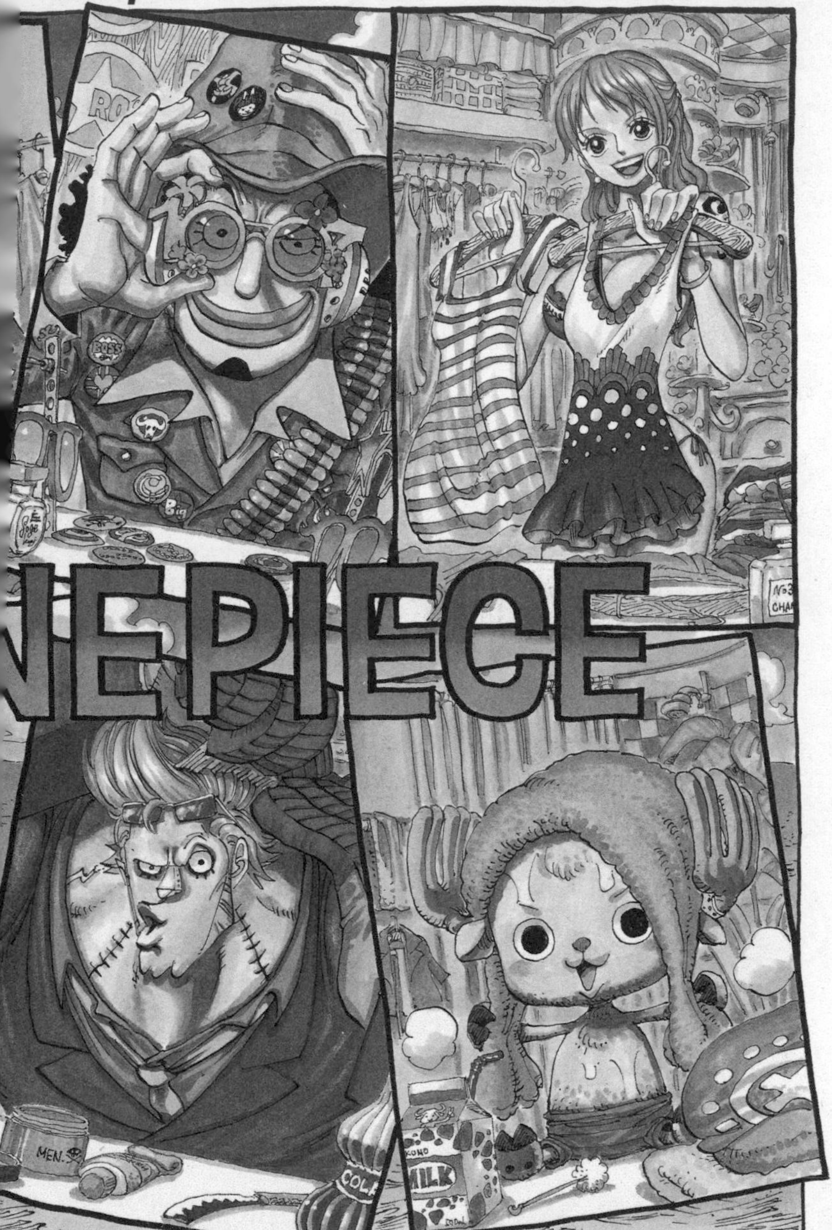
NEPIECE
BOSS
MEN.
COLA
MILK

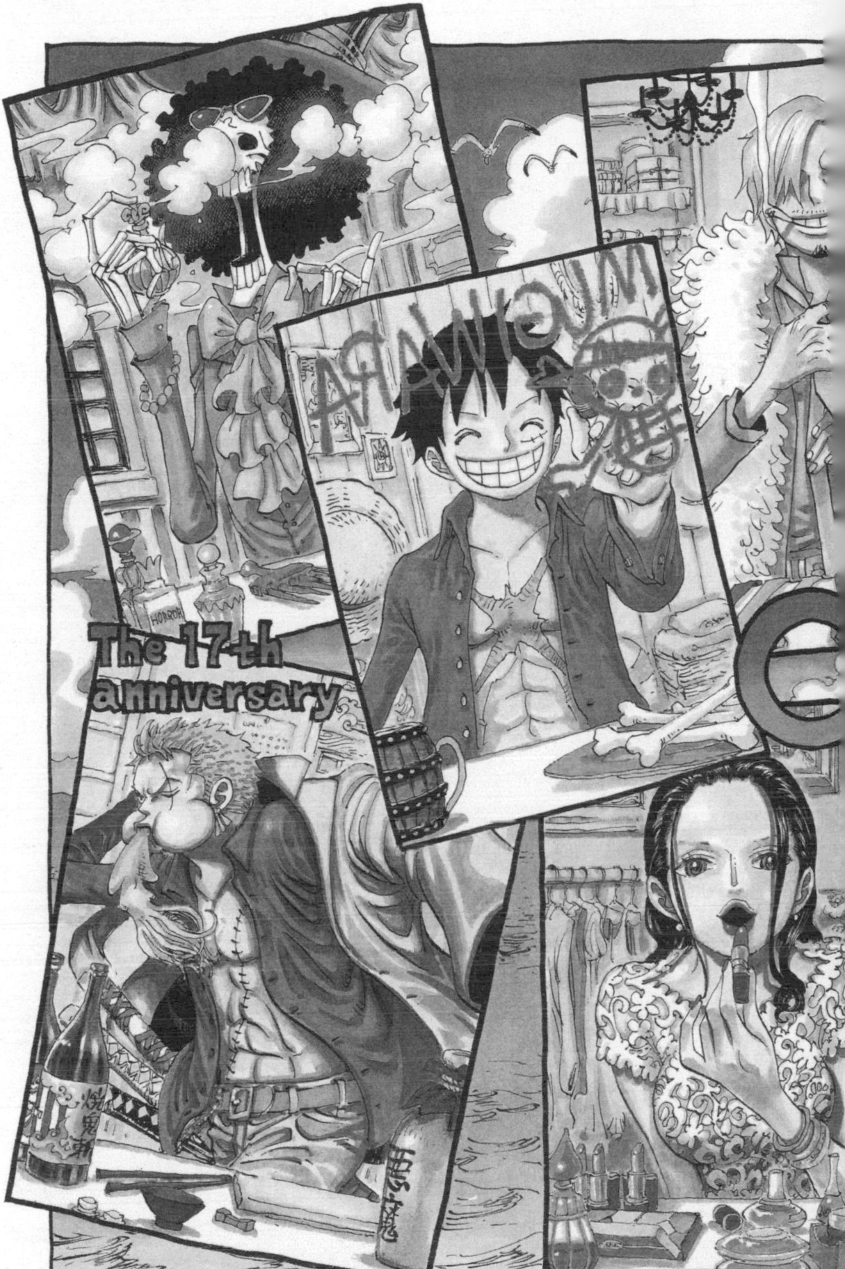
MUGIWARA
The 17th anniversary

vol. 76
ONE PIECE

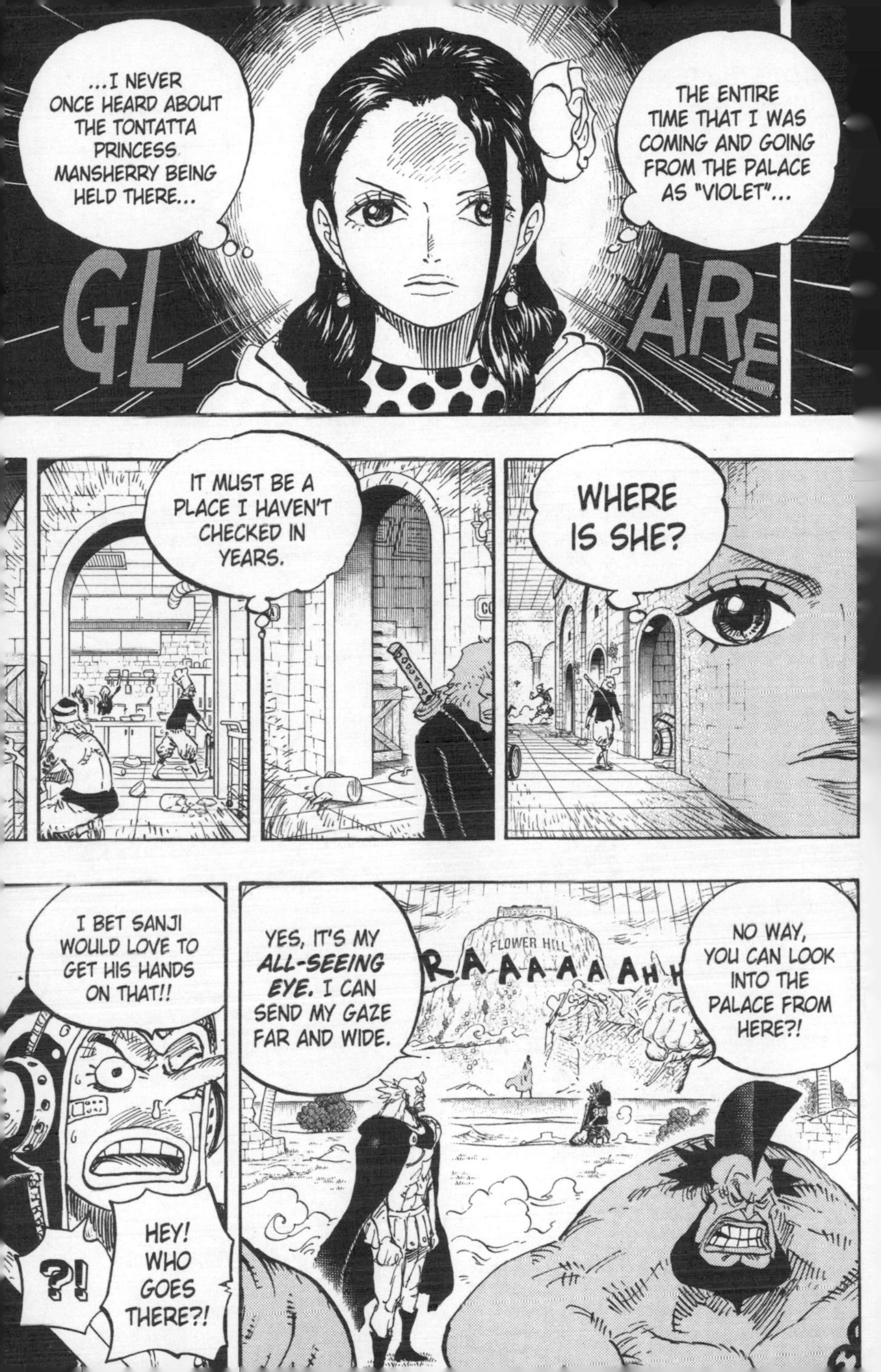
THE ENTIRE TIME THAT I WAS COMING AND GOING FROM THE PALACE AS "VIOLET"...
...I NEVER ONCE HEARD ABOUT THE TONTATTA PRINCESS MANSHERRY BEING HELD THERE...
GLARE
WHERE IS SHE?
IT MUST BE A PLACE I HAVEN'T CHECKED IN YEARS.
NO WAY, YOU CAN LOOK INTO THE PALACE FROM HERE?!
FLOWER HILL
RAAAAAAAHH
YES, IT'S MY ***ALL-SEEING EYE.*** I CAN SEND MY GAZE FAR AND WIDE.
I BET SANJI WOULD LOVE TO GET HIS HANDS ON THAT!!
HEY! WHO GOES THERE?!
?!

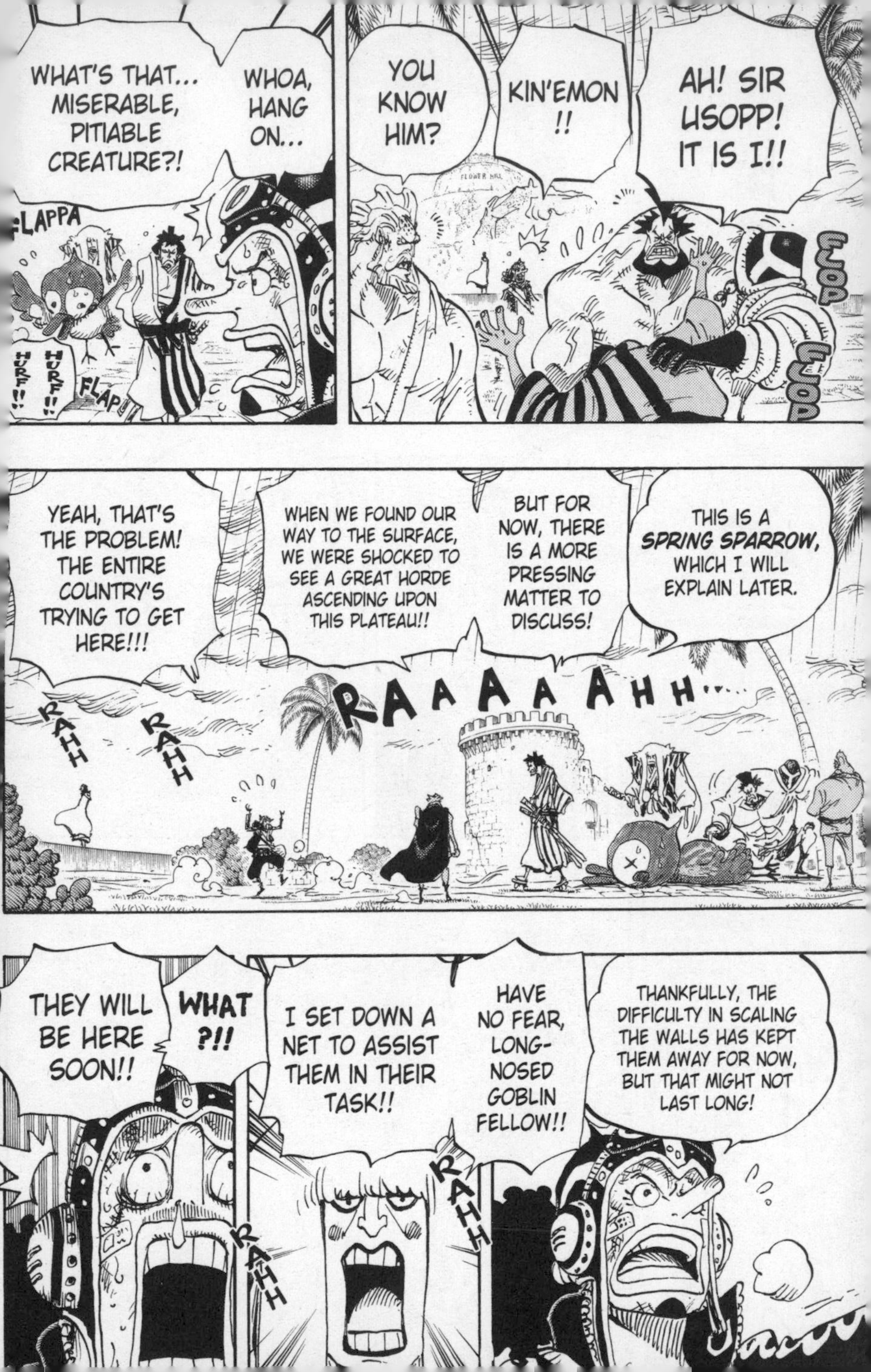

AH! SIR USOPP! IT IS I!!
KIN'EMON !!
YOU KNOW HIM?
FLOWER HILL
FLOP FLOP
WHOA, HANG ON...
WHAT'S THAT... MISERABLE, PITIABLE CREATURE?!
FLAPPA
HURF!! HURF!!
FLAP
THIS IS A *SPRING SPARROW*, WHICH I WILL EXPLAIN LATER.
BUT FOR NOW, THERE IS A MORE PRESSING MATTER TO DISCUSS!
WHEN WE FOUND OUR WAY TO THE SURFACE, WE WERE SHOCKED TO SEE A GREAT HORDE ASCENDING UPON THIS PLATEAU!!
YEAH, THAT'S THE PROBLEM! THE ENTIRE COUNTRY'S TRYING TO GET HERE!!!
RAAAAAHH...
RAHH
RAHH
THANKFULLY, THE DIFFICULTY IN SCALING THE WALLS HAS KEPT THEM AWAY FOR NOW, BUT THAT MIGHT NOT LAST LONG!
HAVE NO FEAR, LONG-NOSED GOBLIN FELLOW!!
I SET DOWN A NET TO ASSIST THEM IN THEIR TASK!!
RAHH
WHAT ?!!
THEY WILL BE HERE SOON!!
RAHH

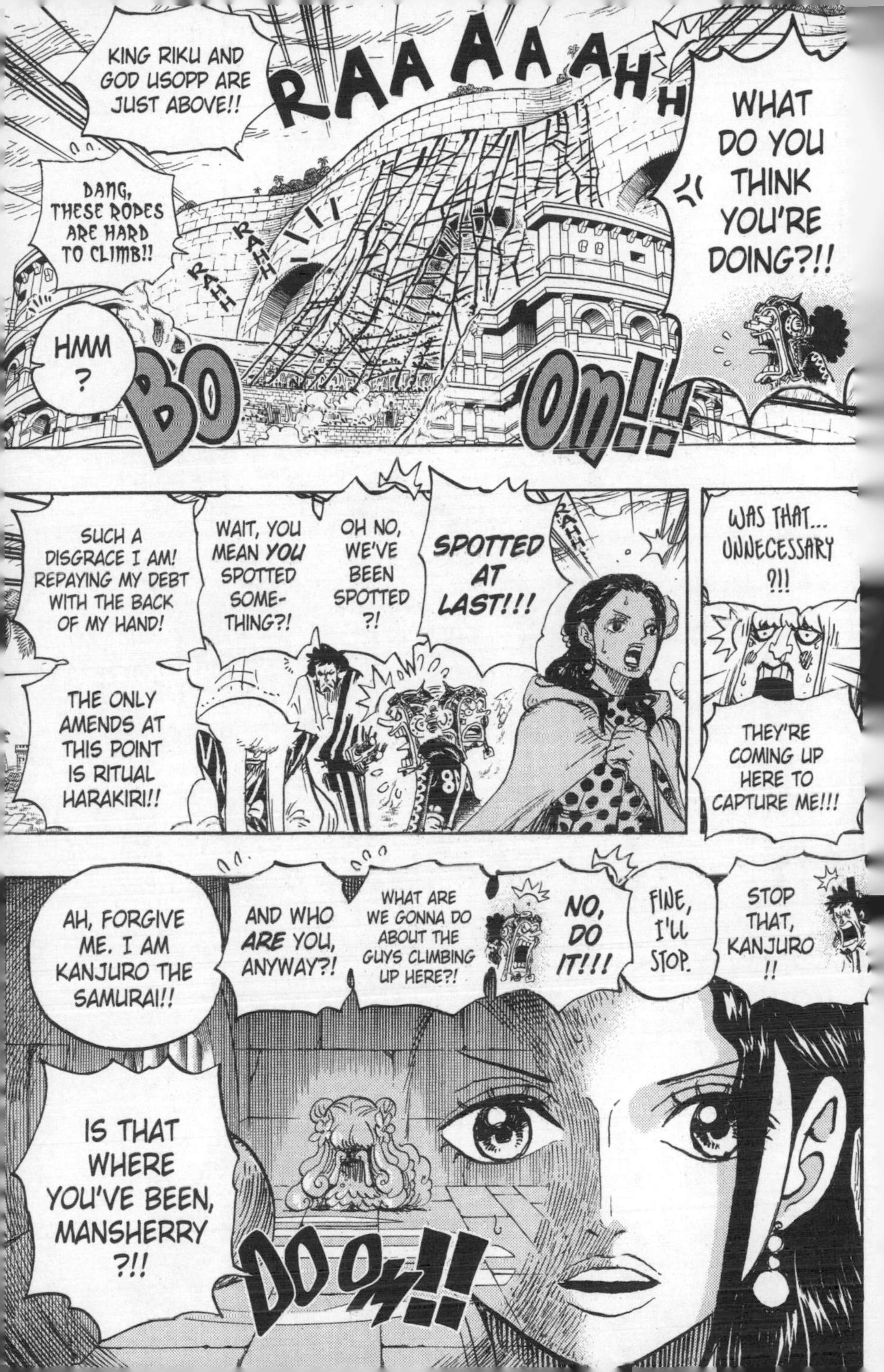
WHAT DO YOU THINK YOU'RE DOING?!!
RAAAAAHH
KING RIKU AND GOD USOPP ARE JUST ABOVE!!
DANG, THESE ROPES ARE HARD TO CLIMB!!
RAHH
RAHH
HMM ?
BOOM!!
WAS THAT... UNNECESSARY ?!!
THEY'RE COMING UP HERE TO CAPTURE ME!!!
RAHH
SPOTTED AT LAST!!!
OH NO, WE'VE BEEN SPOTTED ?!
WAIT, YOU MEAN *YOU* SPOTTED SOMETHING?!
SUCH A DISGRACE I AM! REPAYING MY DEBT WITH THE BACK OF MY HAND!
THE ONLY AMENDS AT THIS POINT IS RITUAL HARAKIRI!!
STOP THAT, KANJURO !!
FINE, I'LL STOP.
NO, DO IT!!!
WHAT ARE WE GONNA DO ABOUT THE GUYS CLIMBING UP HERE?!
AND WHO *ARE* YOU, ANYWAY?!
AH, FORGIVE ME. I AM KANJURO THE SAMURAI!!
IS THAT WHERE YOU'VE BEEN, MANSHERRY ?!!
DOON!!

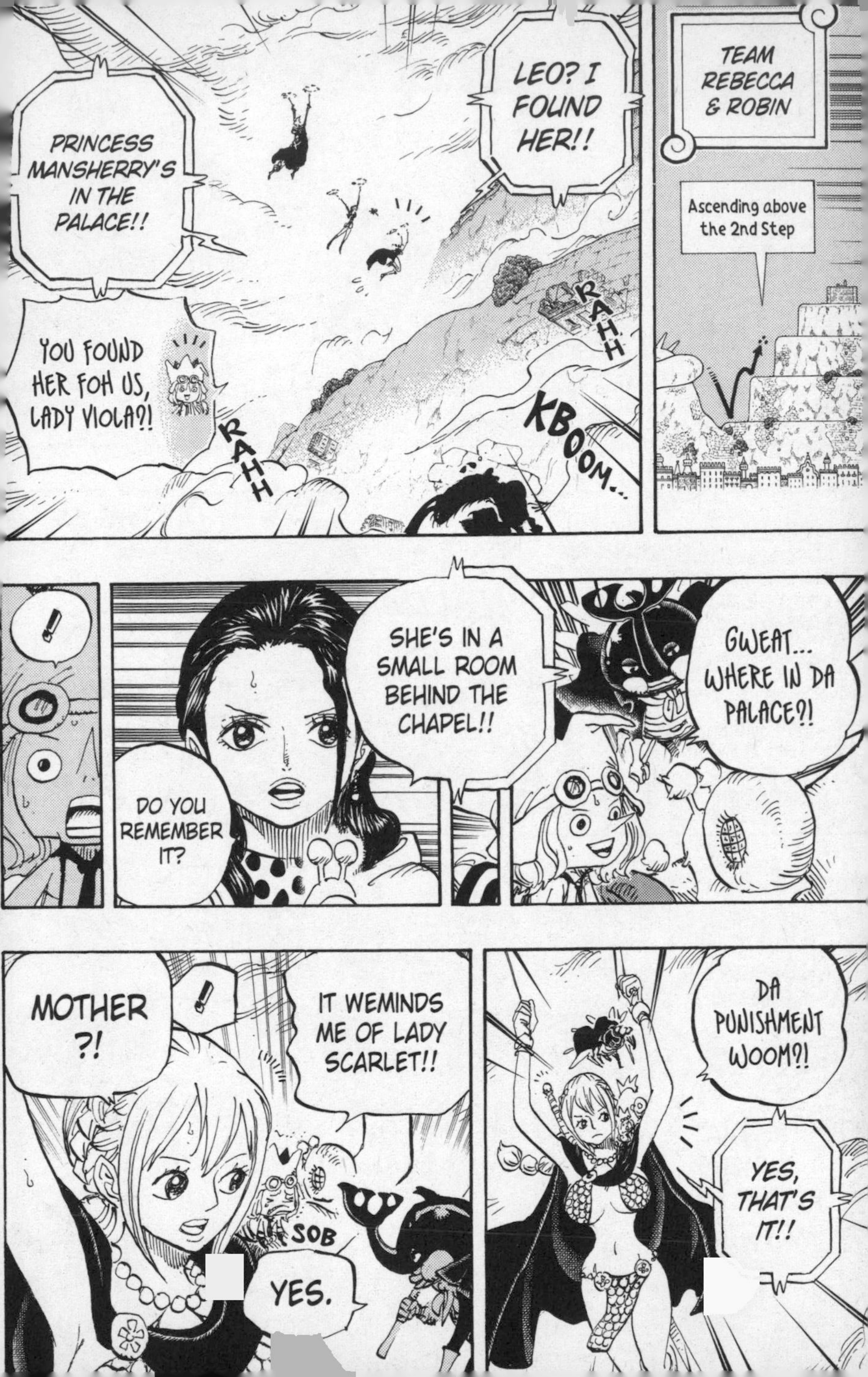
TEAM REBECCA & ROBIN
Ascending above the 2nd Step
LEO? I FOUND HER!!
RAHH
KBOOM...
PRINCESS MANSHERRY'S IN THE PALACE!!
YOU FOUND HER FOH US, LADY VIOLA?!
RAHH
GWEAT... WHERE IN DA PALACE?!
SHE'S IN A SMALL ROOM BEHIND THE CHAPEL!!
DO YOU REMEMBER IT?
!
DA PUNISHMENT WOOM?!
YES, THAT'S IT!!
IT WEMINDS ME OF LADY SCARLET!!
!
MOTHER?!
SOB
YES.

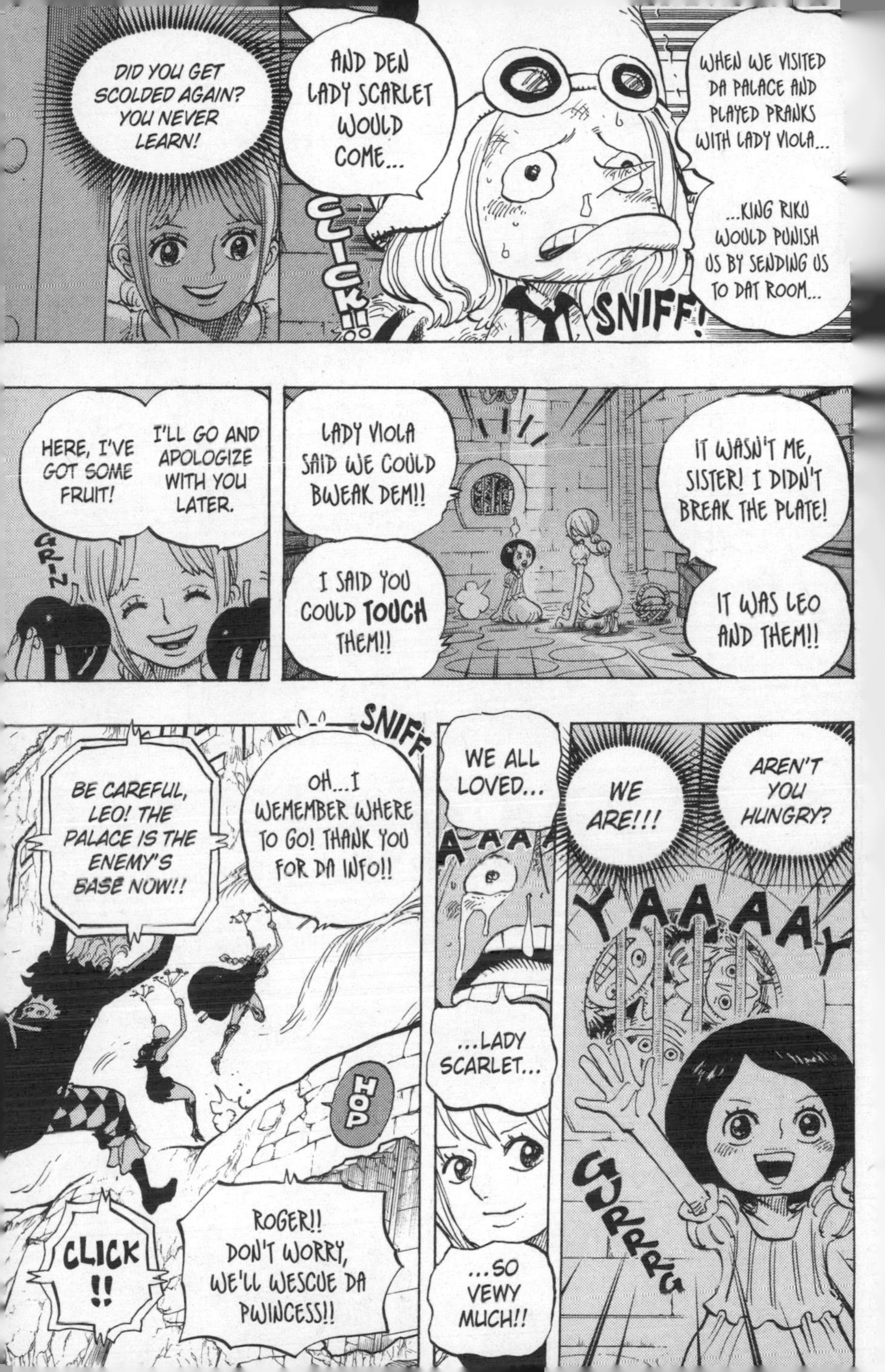
WHEN WE VISITED DA PALACE AND PLAYED PRANKS WITH LADY VIOLA...
...KING RIKU WOULD PUNISH US BY SENDING US TO DAT ROOM...
SNIFF!
AND DEN LADY SCARLET WOULD COME...
CLICK!!
DID YOU GET SCOLDED AGAIN? YOU NEVER LEARN!
IT WASN'T ME, SISTER! I DIDN'T BREAK THE PLATE!
IT WAS LEO AND THEM!!
LADY VIOLA SAID WE COULD BWEAK DEM!!
I SAID YOU COULD **TOUCH** THEM!!
I'LL GO AND APOLOGIZE WITH YOU LATER.
HERE, I'VE GOT SOME FRUIT!
GRIN
AREN'T YOU HUNGRY?
WE ARE!!!
YAAAAY
GURRRG
WE ALL LOVED...
AAAA
...LADY SCARLET...
...SO VEWY MUCH!!
SNIFF
OH...I WEMEMBER WHERE TO GO! THANK YOU FOR DA INFO!!
BE CAREFUL, LEO! THE PALACE IS THE ENEMY'S BASE NOW!!
HOP
ROGER!! DON'T WORRY, WE'LL WESCUE DA PWINCESS!!
CLICK!!

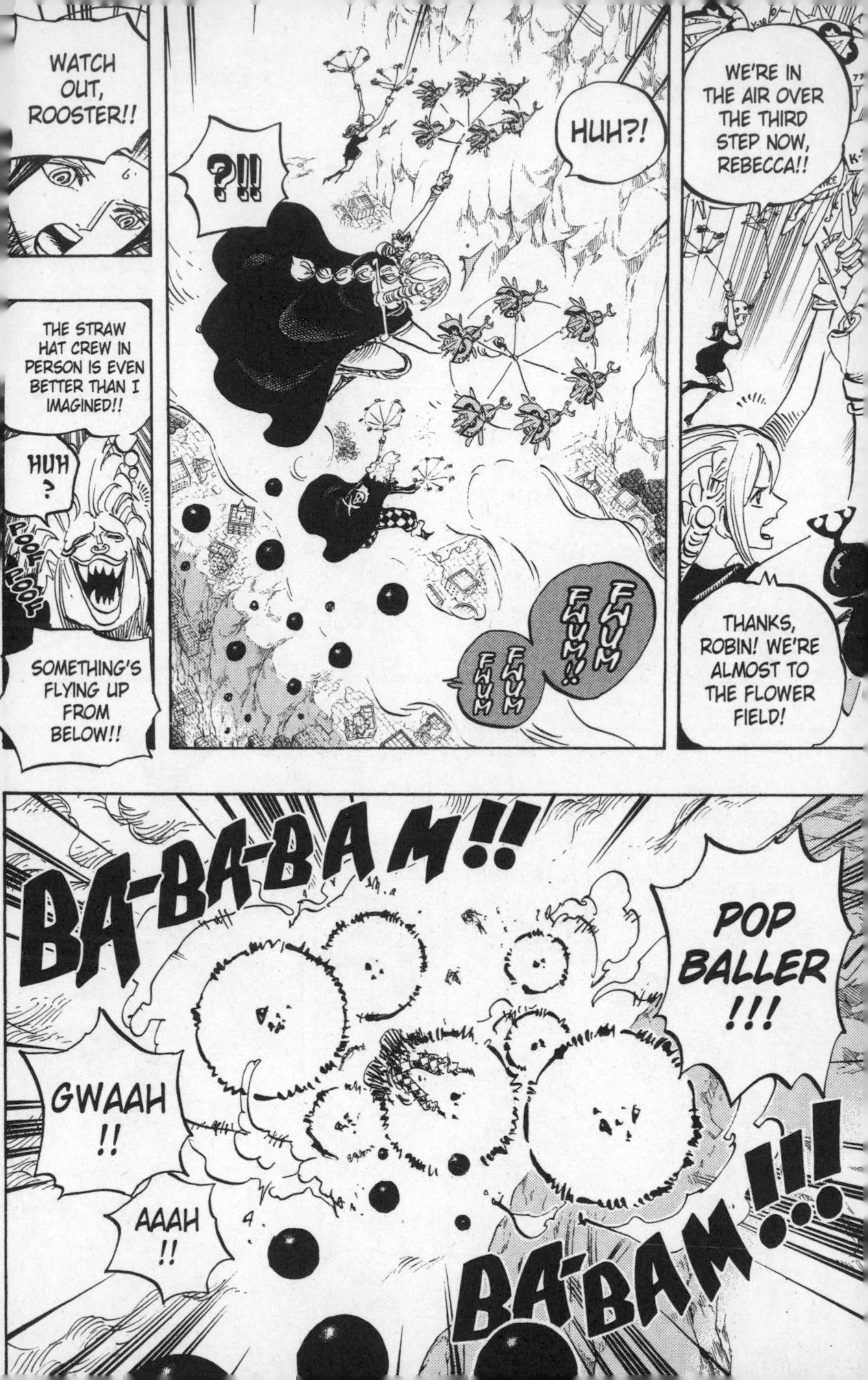
WE'RE IN THE AIR OVER THE THIRD STEP NOW, REBECCA!!
THANKS, ROBIN! WE'RE ALMOST TO THE FLOWER FIELD!
HUH?!
?!!
FWUM FWUM!!
FWUM FWUM
WATCH OUT, ROOSTER!!
THE STRAW HAT CREW IN PERSON IS EVEN BETTER THAN I IMAGINED!!
HUH ?
POOF POOF
SOMETHING'S FLYING UP FROM BELOW!!
POP BALLER !!!
BA-BA-BAM!!
GWAAH !!
BA-BAM!!!
AAAH !!

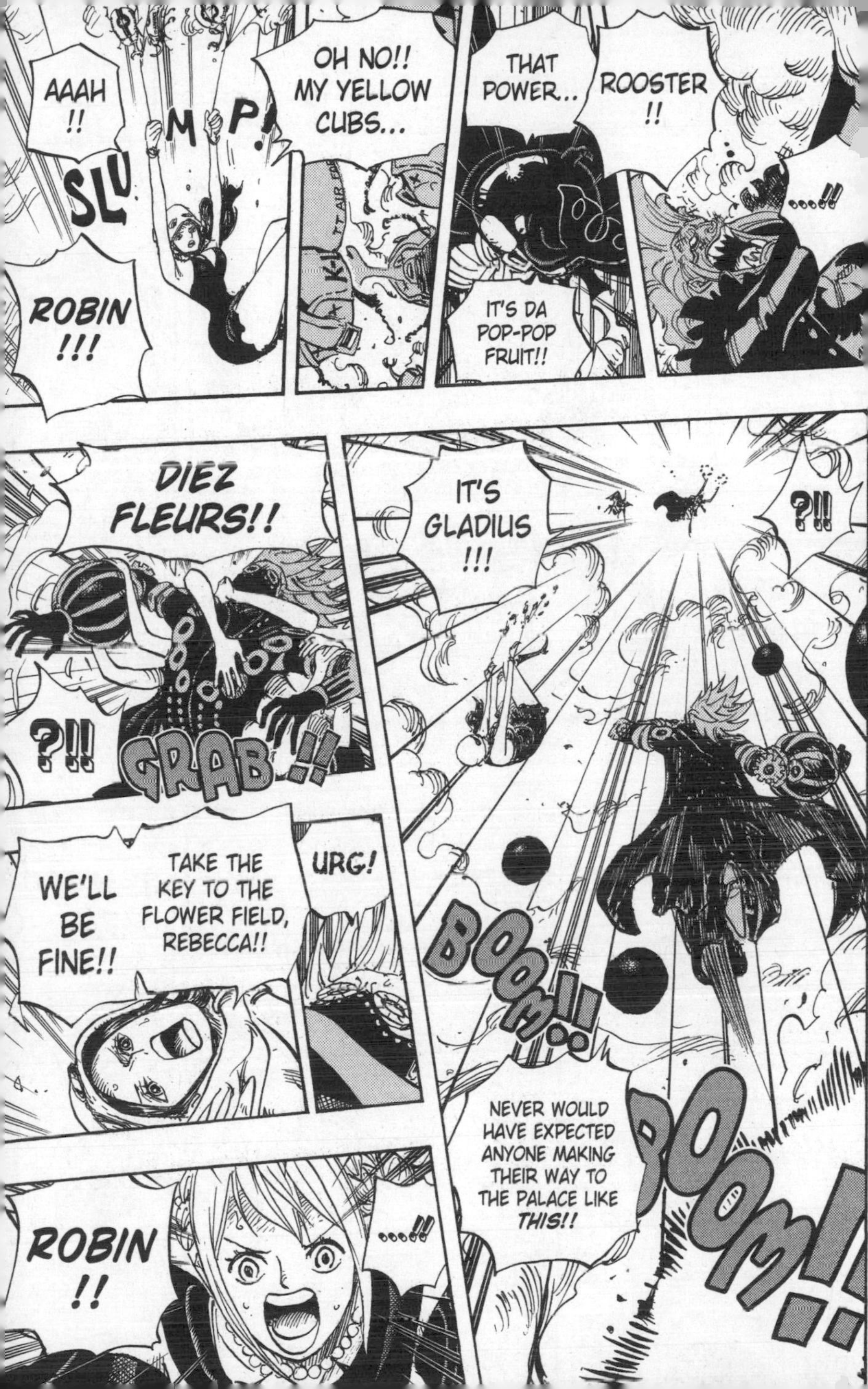
ROOSTER !!
...!!
THAT POWER...
IT'S DA POP-POP FRUIT!!
OH NO!! MY YELLOW CUBS...
AAAH !!
SLUMP!
ROBIN !!!
?!!
IT'S GLADIUS !!!
BOOM!!..
NEVER WOULD HAVE EXPECTED ANYONE MAKING THEIR WAY TO THE PALACE LIKE *THIS!!*
BOOM!!
DIEZ FLEURS!!
?!!
GRAB!!
URG!
TAKE THE KEY TO THE FLOWER FIELD, REBECCA!!
WE'LL BE FINE!!
...!!
ROBIN !!

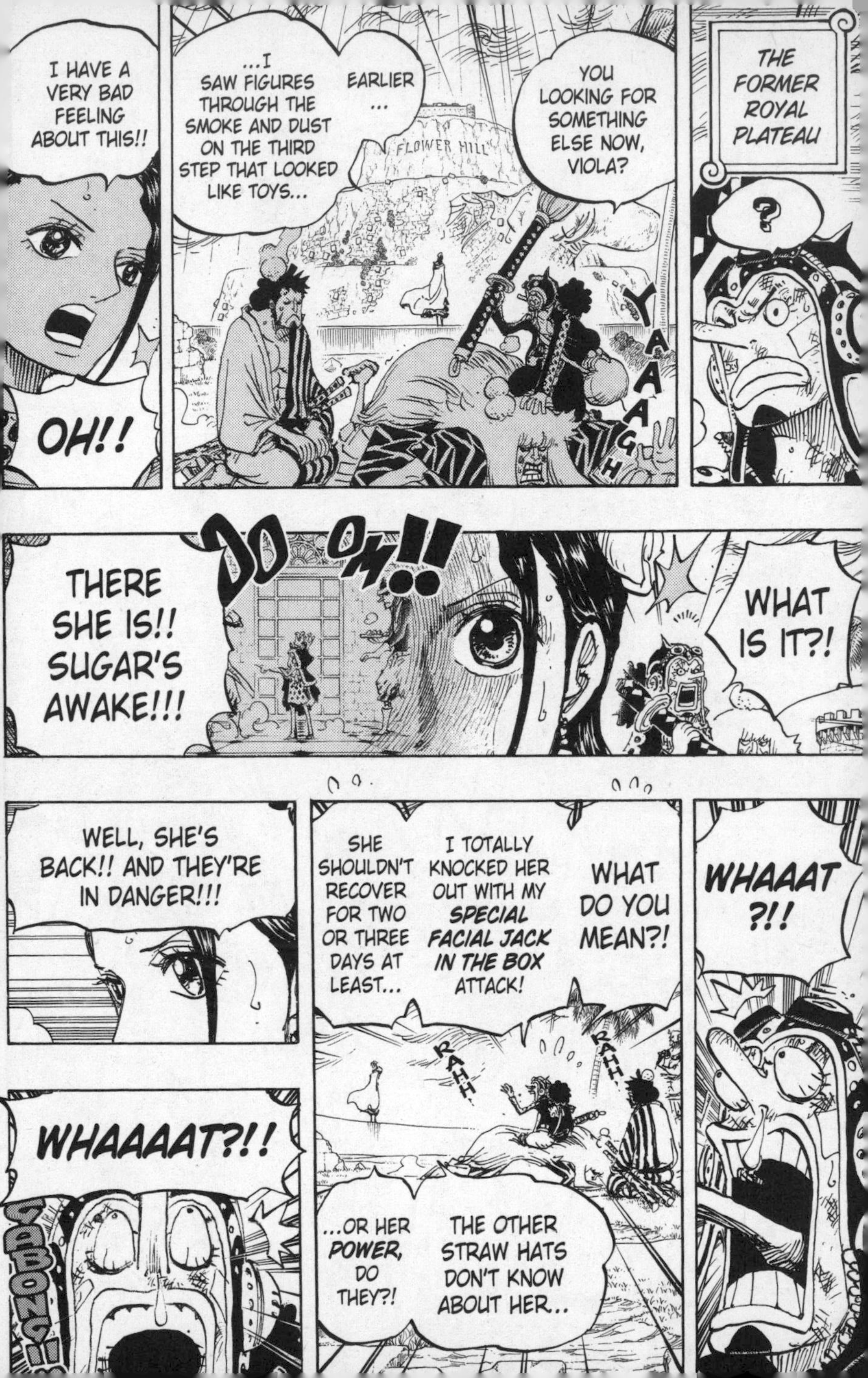

THE FORMER ROYAL PLATEAU
?
YOU LOOKING FOR SOMETHING ELSE NOW, VIOLA?
EARLIER ...
...I SAW FIGURES THROUGH THE SMOKE AND DUST ON THE THIRD STEP THAT LOOKED LIKE TOYS...
FLOWER HILL
YAAAAGH
I HAVE A VERY BAD FEELING ABOUT THIS!!
OH!!
WHAT IS IT?!
DOOM!!
THERE SHE IS!! SUGAR'S AWAKE!!!
WHAAAT ?!!
WHAT DO YOU MEAN?!
I TOTALLY KNOCKED HER OUT WITH MY *SPECIAL FACIAL JACK IN THE BOX* ATTACK!
SHE SHOULDN'T RECOVER FOR TWO OR THREE DAYS AT LEAST...
RAHH
RAHH
THE OTHER STRAW HATS DON'T KNOW ABOUT HER...
...OR HER *POWER,* DO THEY?!
WELL, SHE'S BACK!! AND THEY'RE IN DANGER!!!
WHAAAAT?!!
GABONG!!

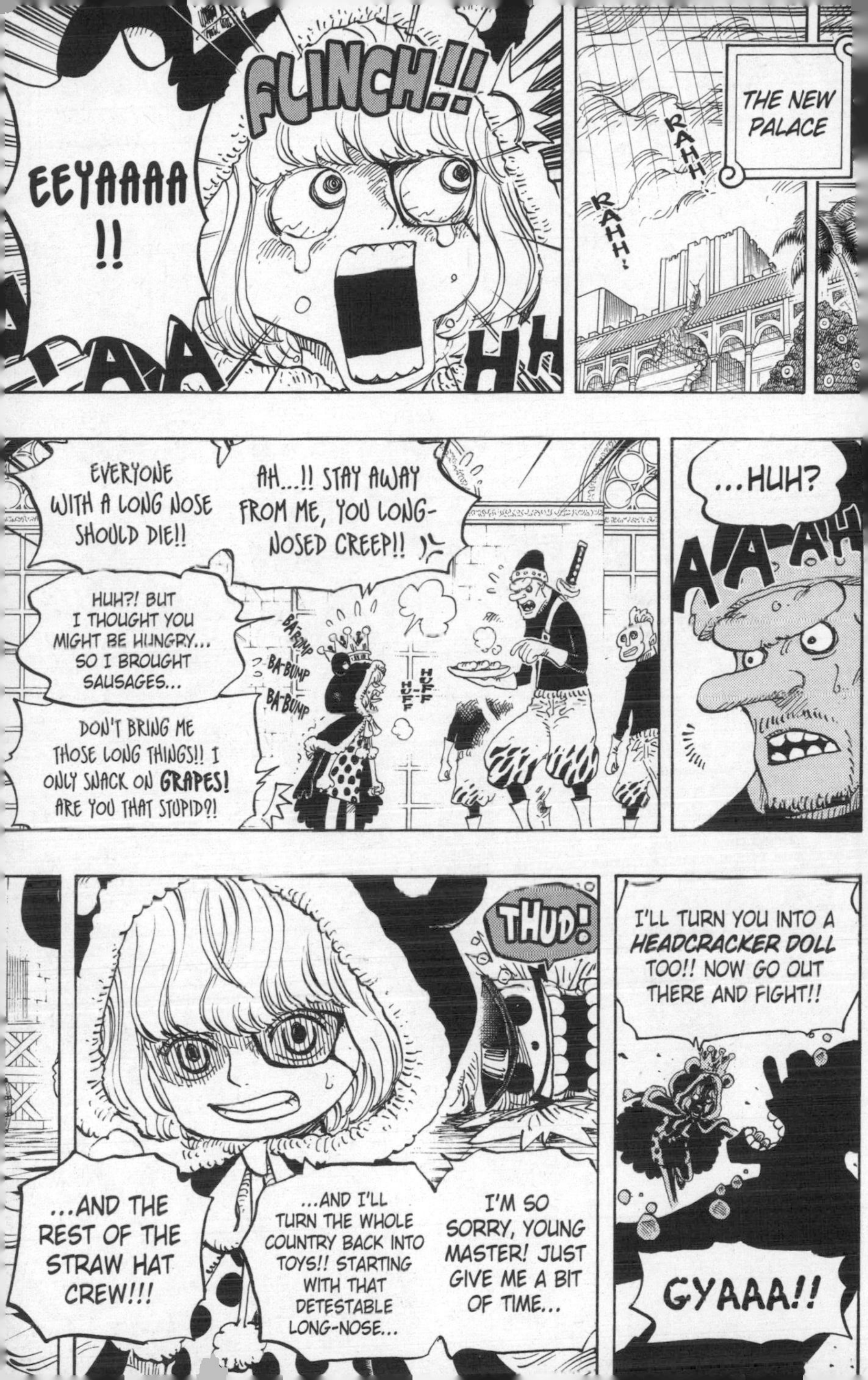
THE NEW PALACE
RAHH
RAHH!
FLINCH!!
EEYAAAA!!
...HUH?
AH...!! STAY AWAY FROM ME, YOU LONG-NOSED CREEP!!
EVERYONE WITH A LONG NOSE SHOULD DIE!!
HUH?! BUT I THOUGHT YOU MIGHT BE HUNGRY... SO I BROUGHT SAUSAGES...
HUFF HUFF
BA-BUMP
BA-BUMP
BA-BUMP
DON'T BRING ME THOSE LONG THINGS!! I ONLY SNACK ON GRAPES! ARE YOU THAT STUPID?!
I'LL TURN YOU INTO A HEADCRACKER DOLL TOO!! NOW GO OUT THERE AND FIGHT!!
GYAAA!!
THUD!
I'M SO SORRY, YOUNG MASTER! JUST GIVE ME A BIT OF TIME...
...AND I'LL TURN THE WHOLE COUNTRY BACK INTO TOYS!! STARTING WITH THAT DETESTABLE LONG-NOSE...
...AND THE REST OF THE STRAW HAT CREW!!!

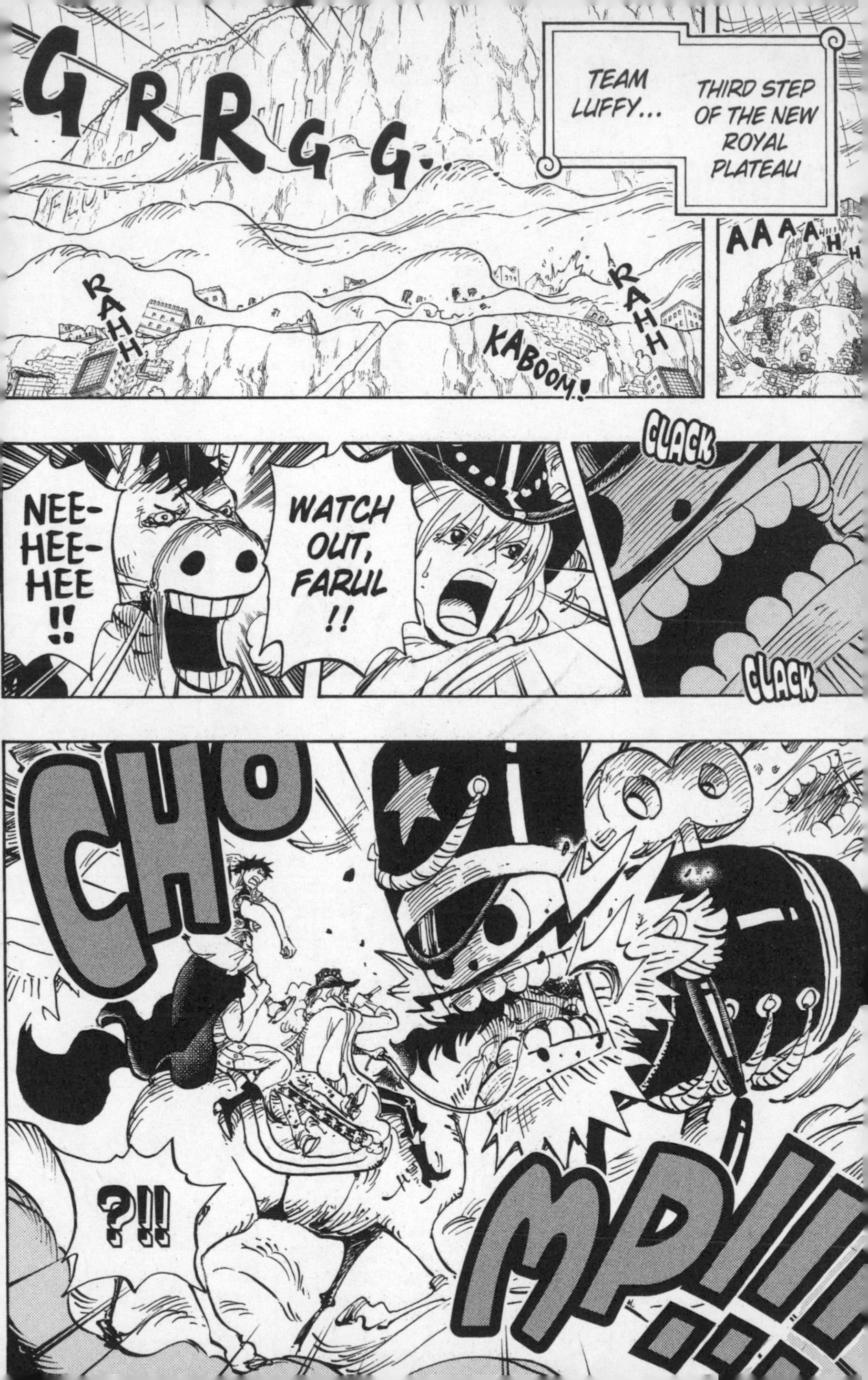
TEAM LUFFY... THIRD STEP OF THE NEW ROYAL PLATEAU
AAAAHHH
GRRRGG...
RAHH
KABOOM!
RAHH
CLACK
CLACK
WATCH OUT, FARUL!!
NEE-HEE-HEE!!
CHOMP!!
?!!

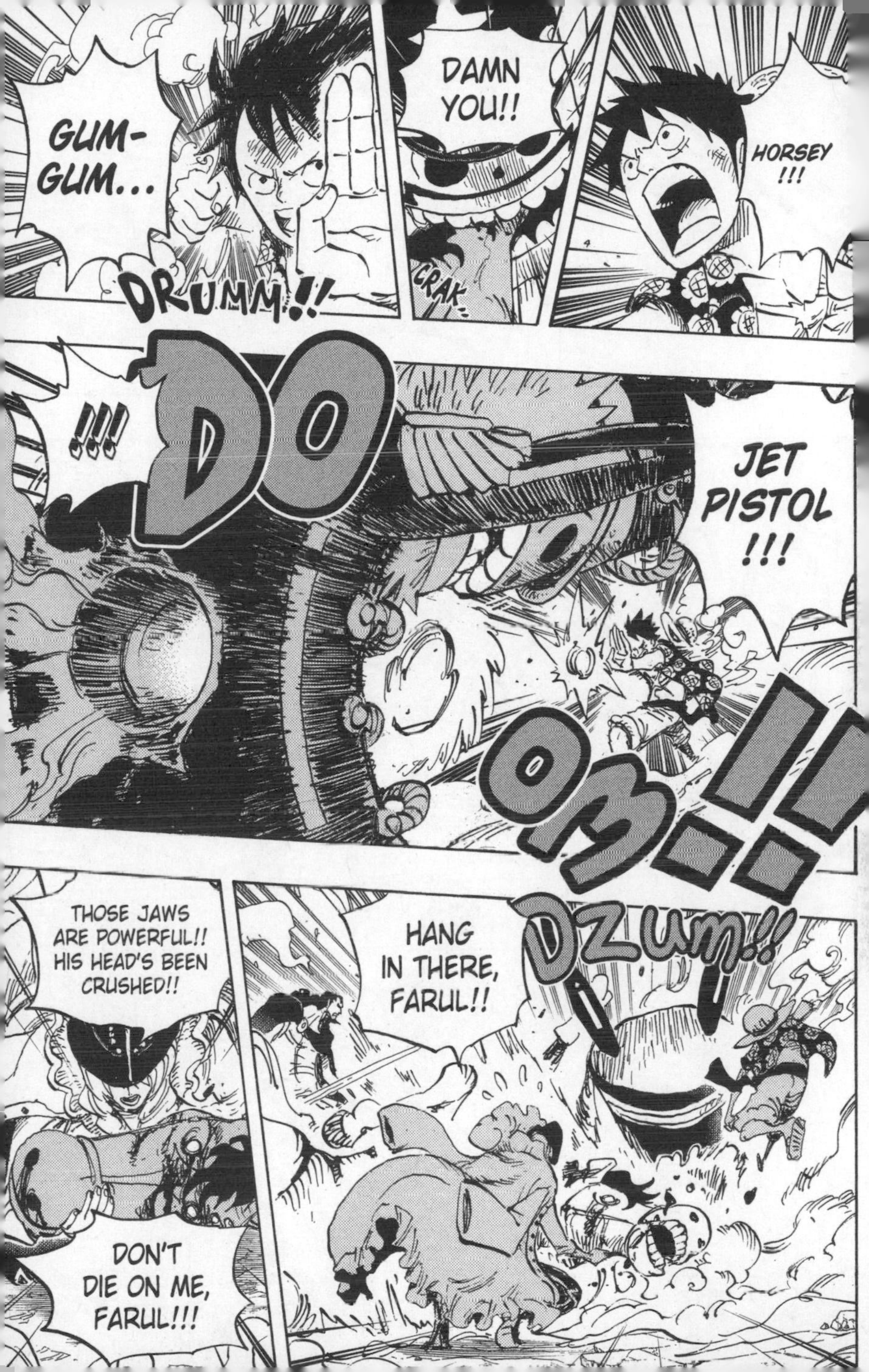
HORSEY !!!
DAMN YOU!!
CRAK
GUM-GUM...
DRUMM!!
JET PISTOL !!!
!!!
DO
OM!!
DZUM!!
HANG IN THERE, FARUL!!
THOSE JAWS ARE POWERFUL!! HIS HEAD'S BEEN CRUSHED!!
DON'T DIE ON ME, FARUL!!!

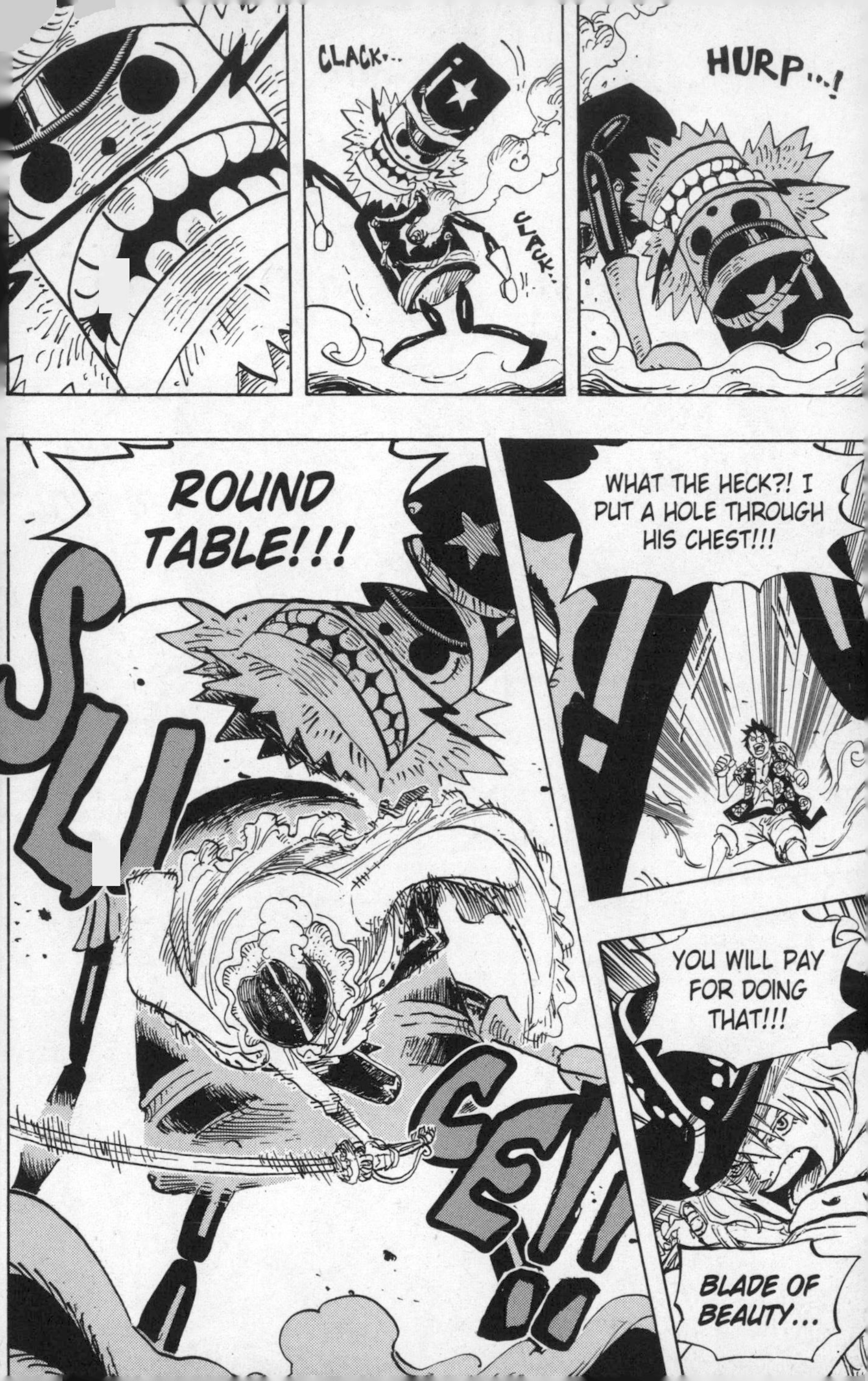
HURP...!
CLACK...
CLACK...
WHAT THE HECK?! I PUT A HOLE THROUGH HIS CHEST!!!
YOU WILL PAY FOR DOING THAT!!!
BLADE OF BEAUTY...
ROUND TABLE!!!

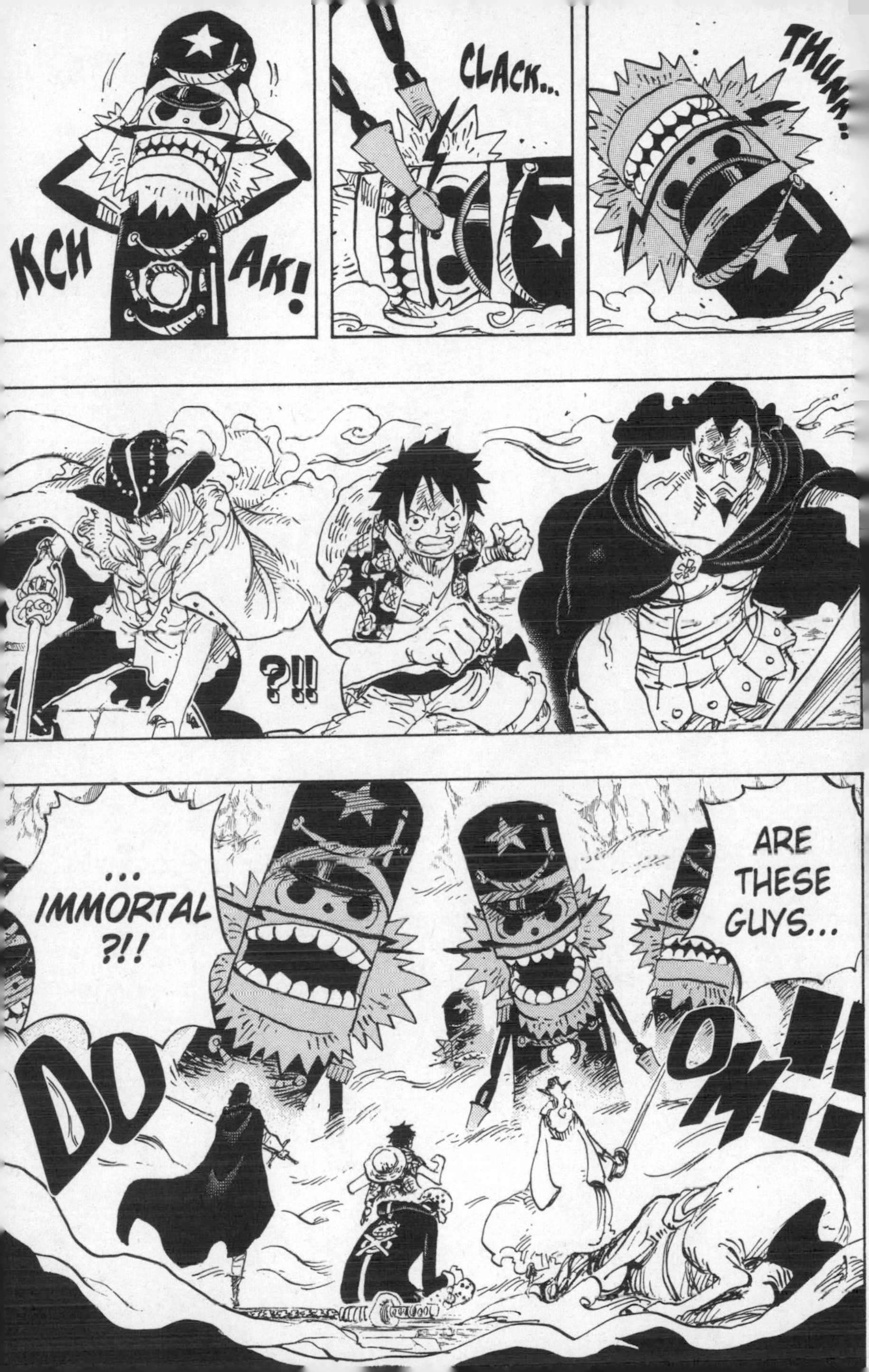
THUNK..
CLACK...
KCHAK!
?!!
ARE THESE GUYS...
... IMMORTAL ?!!
DOOM!!

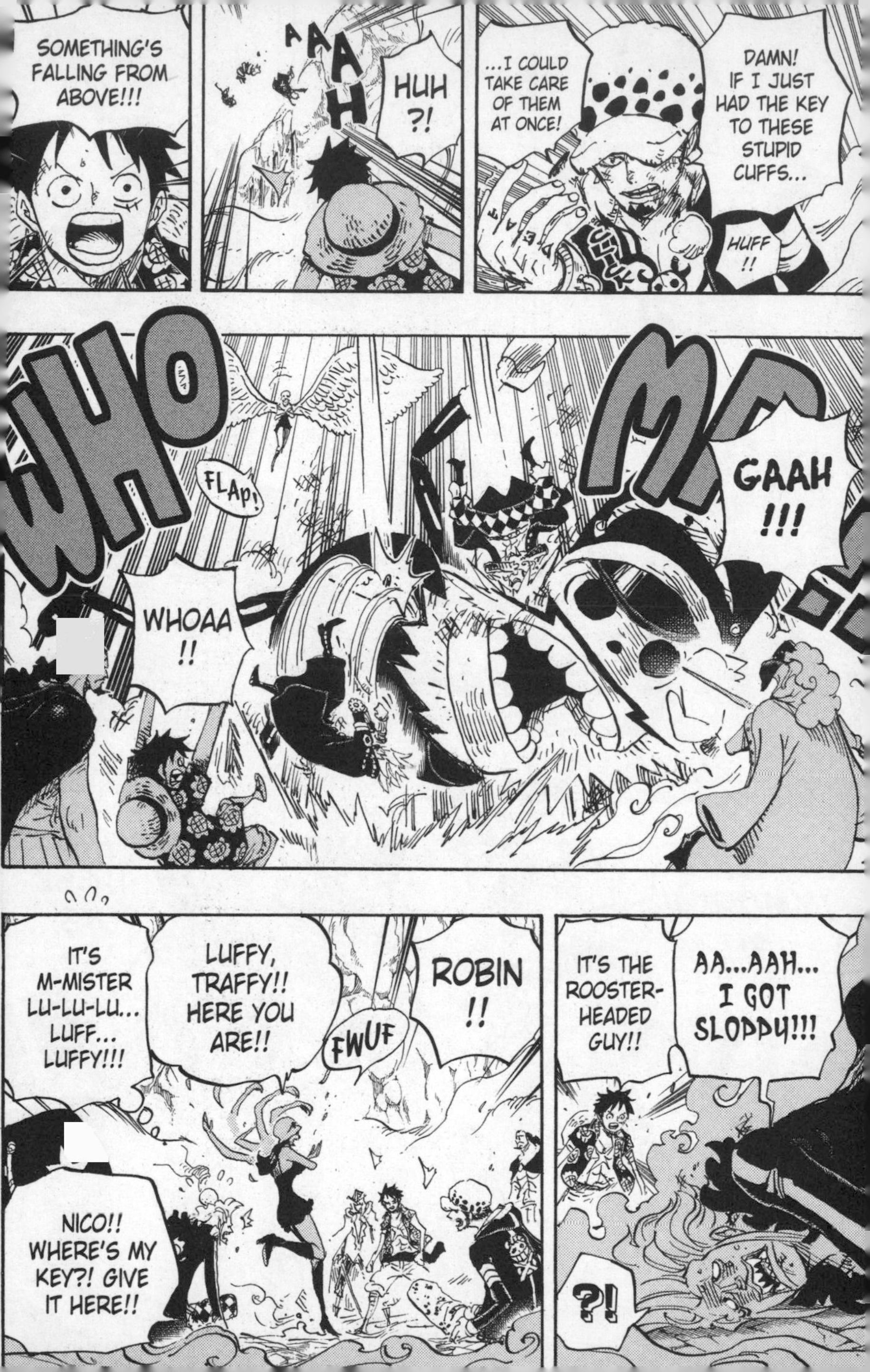
DAMN! IF I JUST HAD THE KEY TO THESE STUPID CUFFS...
...I COULD TAKE CARE OF THEM AT ONCE!
HUFF !!
AAAH
HUH ?!
SOMETHING'S FALLING FROM ABOVE!!!
GAAH !!!
M
WHO
FLAp!
WHOAA !!
AA...AAH... I GOT SLOPPY!!!
IT'S THE ROOSTER-HEADED GUY!!
?!
ROBIN !!
FWUF
LUFFY, TRAFFY!! HERE YOU ARE!!
IT'S M-MISTER LU-LU-LU... LUFF... LUFFY!!!
NICO!! WHERE'S MY KEY?! GIVE IT HERE!!

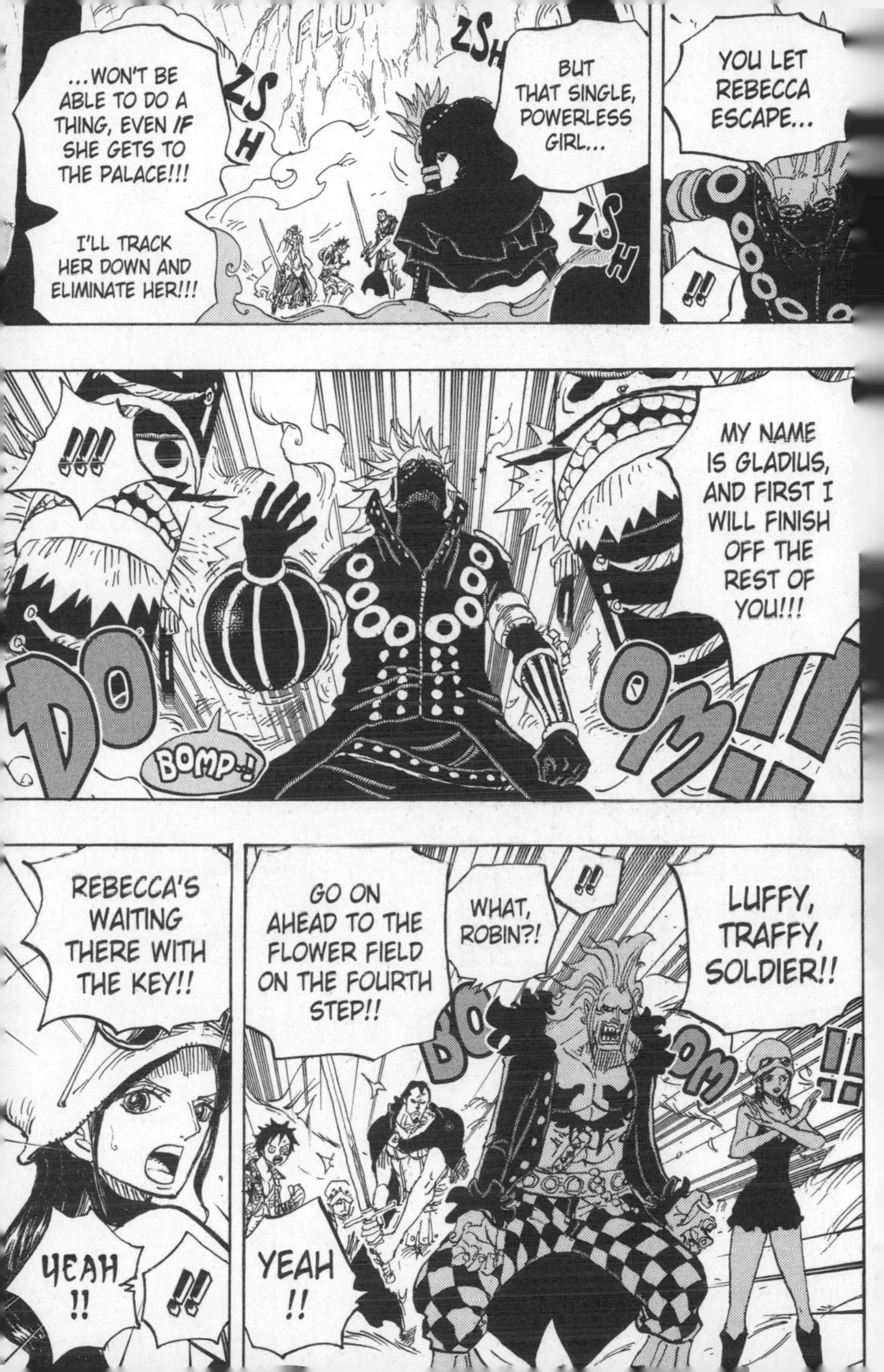
YOU LET REBECCA ESCAPE...
!!
ZSH
BUT THAT SINGLE, POWERLESS GIRL...
ZSH
ZSH
...WON'T BE ABLE TO DO A THING, EVEN IF SHE GETS TO THE PALACE!!!
I'LL TRACK HER DOWN AND ELIMINATE HER!!!
MY NAME IS GLADIUS, AND FIRST I WILL FINISH OFF THE REST OF YOU!!!
!!!
DOOM!!
BOMP-!
LUFFY, TRAFFY, SOLDIER!!
!!
WHAT, ROBIN?!
GO ON AHEAD TO THE FLOWER FIELD ON THE FOURTH STEP!!
BOOM!!
YEAH!!
REBECCA'S WAITING THERE WITH THE KEY!!
!!
YEAH!!

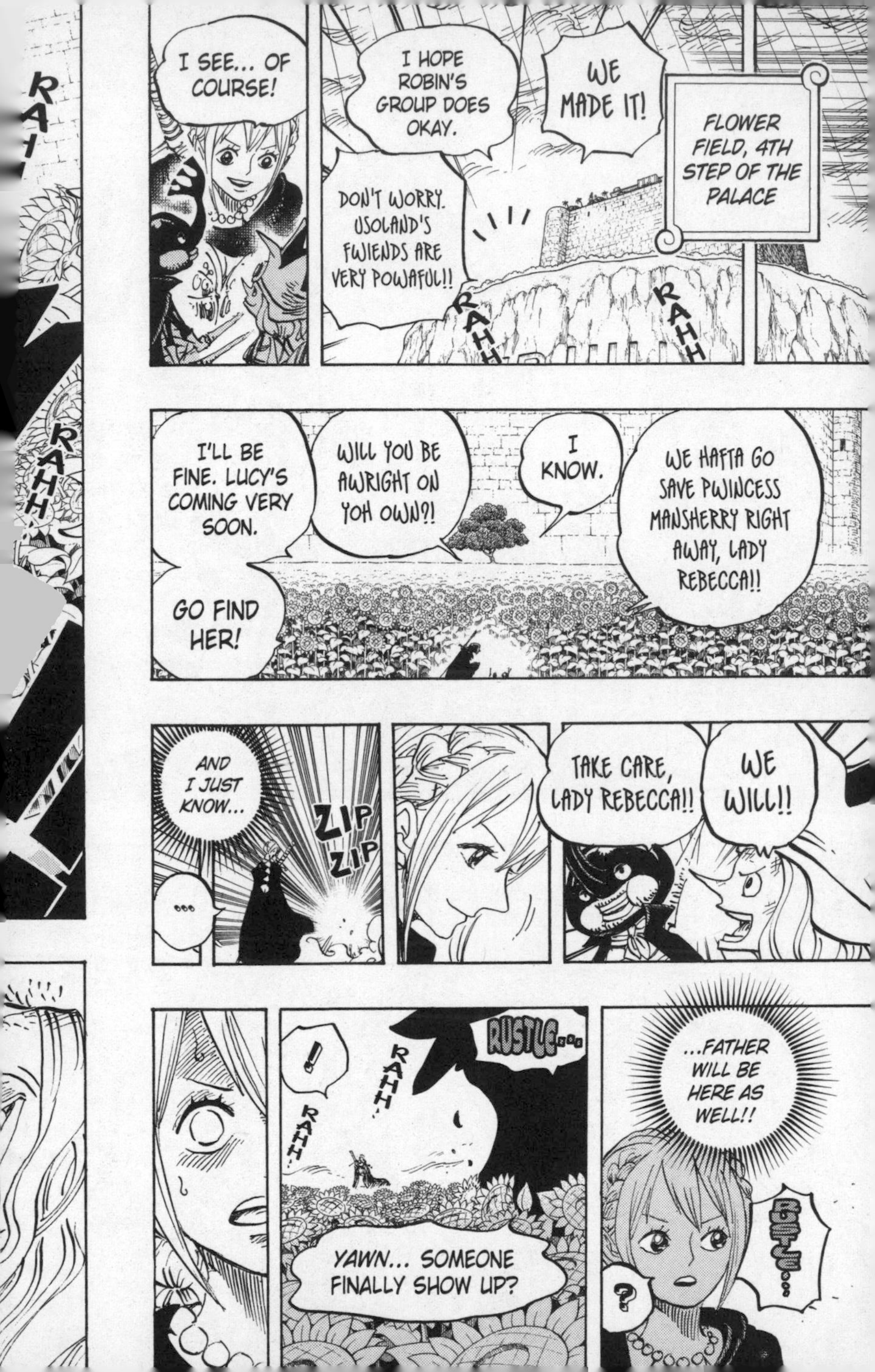
FLOWER FIELD, 4TH STEP OF THE PALACE
WE MADE IT!
RAHH
RAHH
I HOPE ROBIN'S GROUP DOES OKAY.
DON'T WORRY. USOLAND'S FWIENDS ARE VERY POWAFUL!!
I SEE... OF COURSE!
WE HAFTA GO SAVE PWINCESS MANSHERRY RIGHT AWAY, LADY REBECCA!!
I KNOW.
WILL YOU BE AWRIGHT ON YOH OWN?!
I'LL BE FINE. LUCY'S COMING VERY SOON.
GO FIND HER!
WE WILL!!
TAKE CARE, LADY REBECCA!!
ZIP ZIP
AND I JUST KNOW...
...
...FATHER WILL BE HERE AS WELL!!
RUSTLE...
?
RUSTLE...
RAHH
RAHH
!
YAWN... SOMEONE FINALLY SHOW UP?

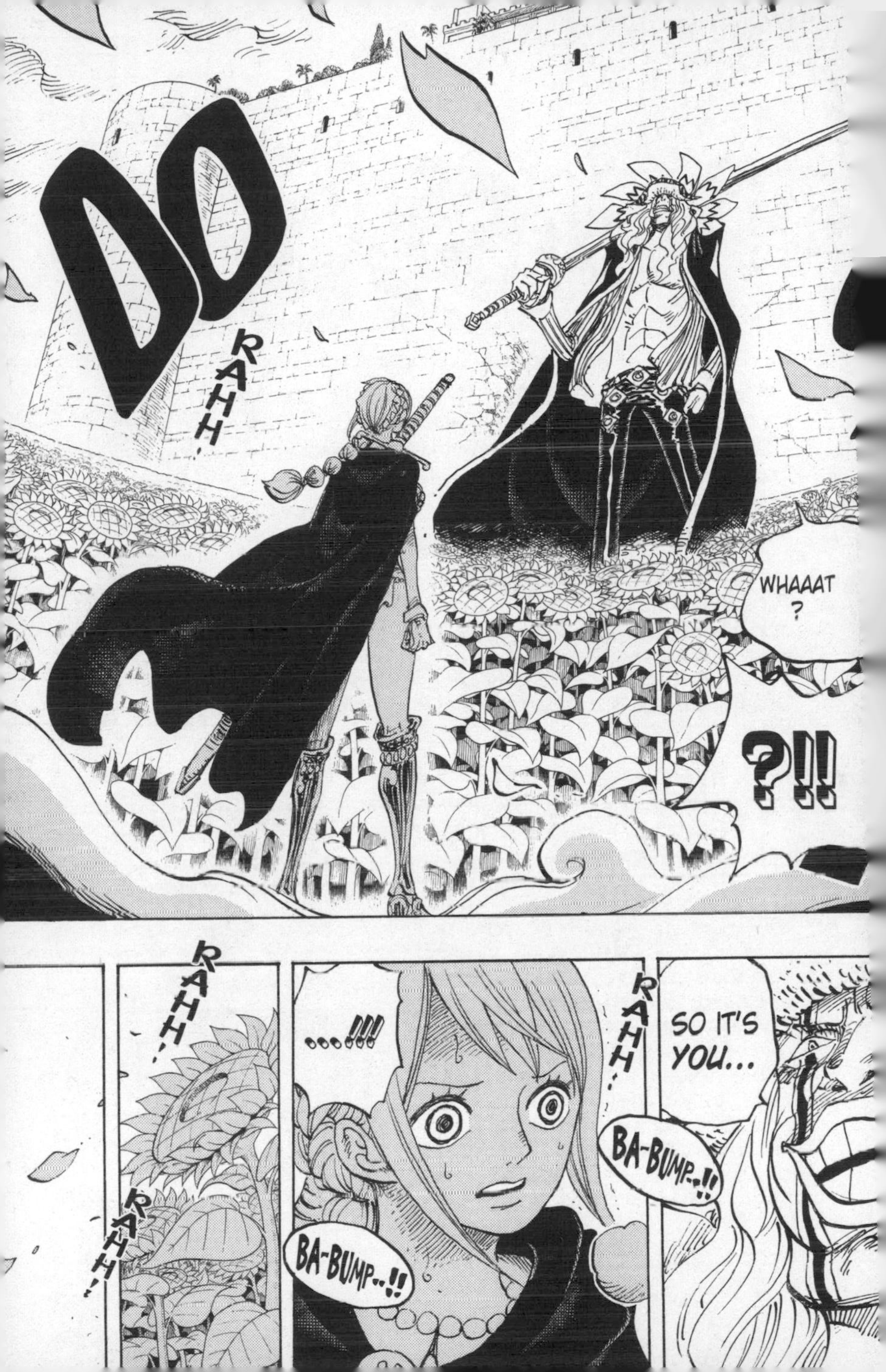
WHAAAT?
?!!
DO
RAHH!
SO IT'S YOU...
RAHH!
BA-BUMP..!!
...!!!
BA-BUMP..!!
RAHH!
RAHH!

(KUPY Family, ? Prefecture)

Q: Mr. Oda, your love of large boobs is so well-documented that it's basically just a disease at this point. But a woman's charms are not limited to her breasts, and so I have long awaited the entrance of a flat-chested character. So…has that day finally arrived?! Yes, let's hear it for Dellinger, age 16, with the most gorgeous legs in the Doflamingo Family! Could this be the first true flat-chested girl in *One Piece?*

--Waremo Wife

A: **Sorry! He's a man!!** I seem to have confused many readers with this one. He was picked up by the family as a baby, and Giolla did most of the work taking care of him. Basically, she raised him like a girl because that was her style.

Q: Hello, Mr. Oda! In Chapter 747, Koala snaps a pic with a little transponder snail. Is that another kind of visual snail? Or does it have a new name, like a "photographic transponder snail"? Tell us!!

--Samurai Ryota

THEY'RE MADE OUT TO LOOK LIKE PIRATE SHIPS...

CLICK!

A: Yes, that's a visual transponder snail. It's the same as the kind on the walls of Impel Down. There are both cam-snails that fulfill the role of a camera, and pro-snails that receive signals and project them onto a wall. As a matter of fact, those are just the juvenile and adult forms of the same snail. A cam-snail can stock still images or videos, while pro-snails can also receive signals and display them.

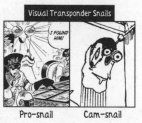

Visual Transponder Snails

I FOUND HIM!

Pro-snail   Cam-snail

Chapter 757:
TRUMP CARD

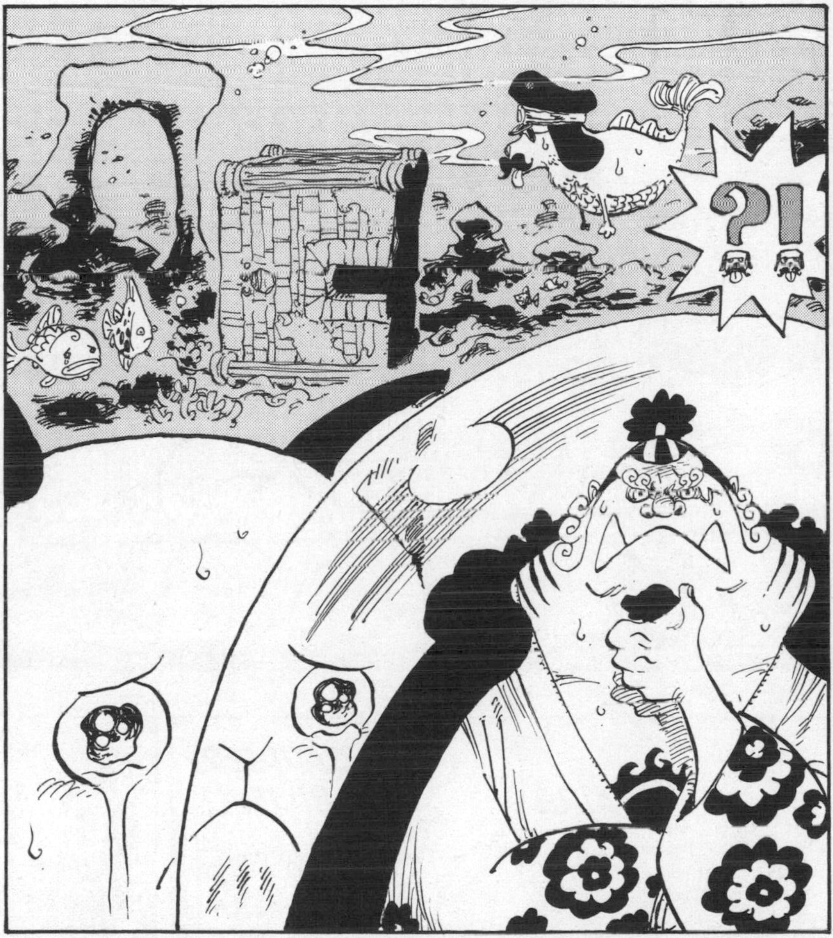
?!

THE SOLITARY JOURNEY OF JIMBEI, FIRST SON OF THE SEA, VOL. 6: "THE OFFICER'S HOUSE IS MIRACULOUSLY FOUND! THE MYSTERY OF THE CRYING SEA-KITTEN DEEPENS"

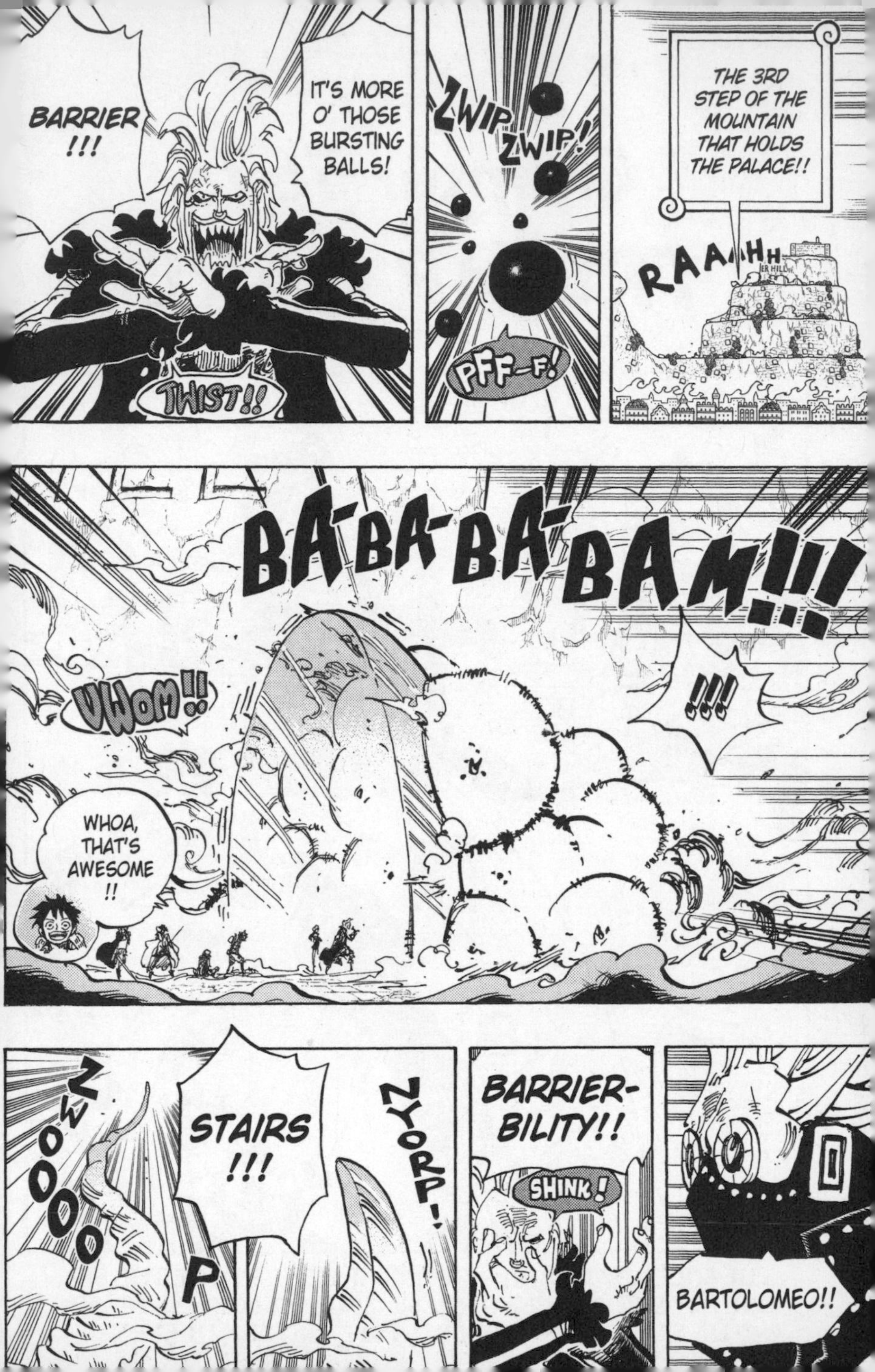
THE 3RD STEP OF THE MOUNTAIN THAT HOLDS THE PALACE!!
RAAAHH
ZWIP ZWIP!
PFF-F!
IT'S MORE O' THOSE BURSTING BALLS!
BARRIER !!!
TWIST!!
BA-BA-BA-BAM!!!
!!!
VWOM!!
WHOA, THAT'S AWESOME !!
BARTOLOMEO!!
BARRIER-BILITY!!
SHINK!
NYORP!
STAIRS !!!
ZWOOOOOP

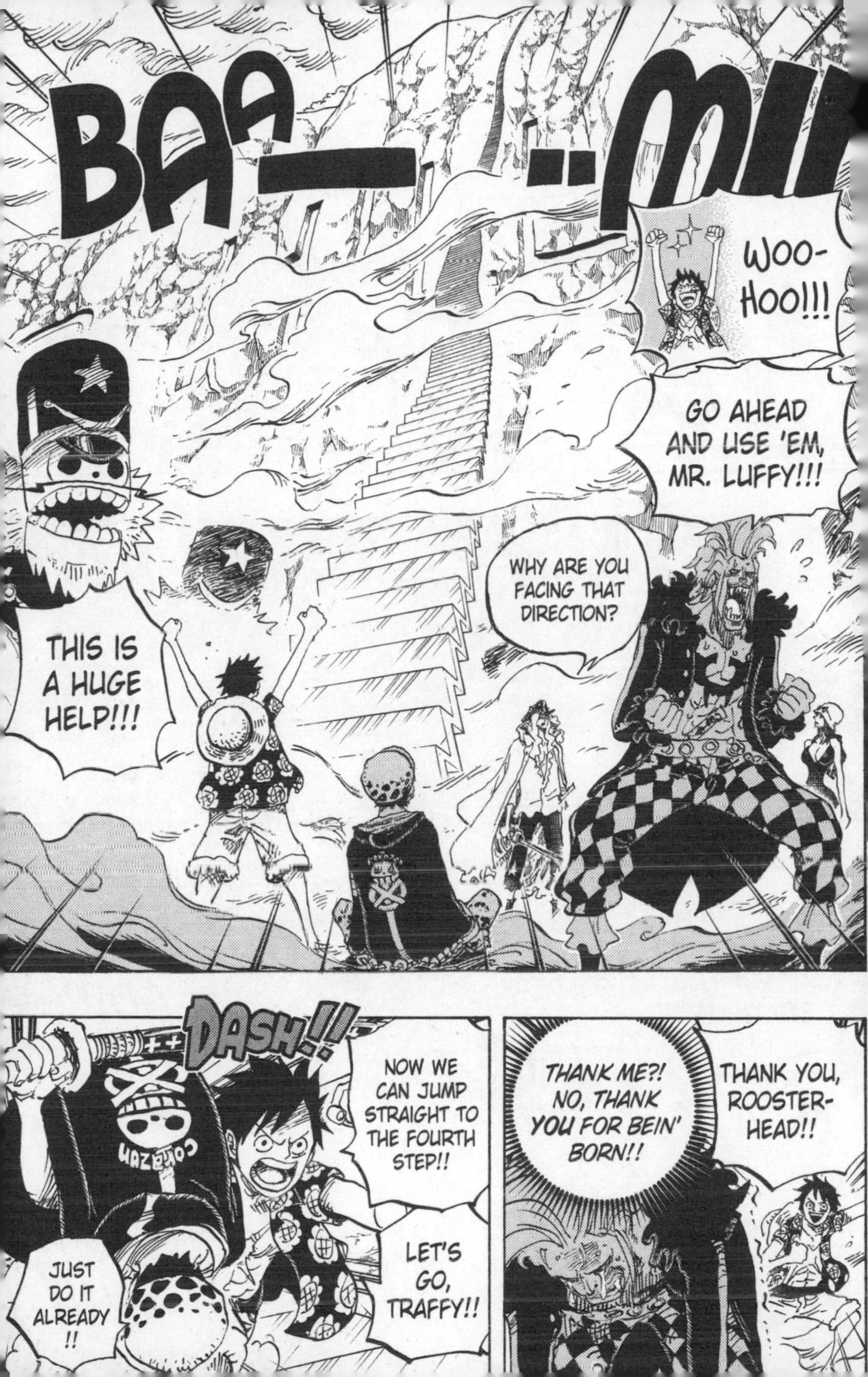
BAA—...M
WOO-HOO!!!
GO AHEAD AND USE 'EM, MR. LUFFY!!!
WHY ARE YOU FACING THAT DIRECTION?
THIS IS A HUGE HELP!!!
THANK YOU, ROOSTER-HEAD!!
THANK ME?! NO, THANK YOU FOR BEIN' BORN!!
DASH!!
NOW WE CAN JUMP STRAIGHT TO THE FOURTH STEP!!
LET'S GO, TRAFFY!!
JUST DO IT ALREADY!!

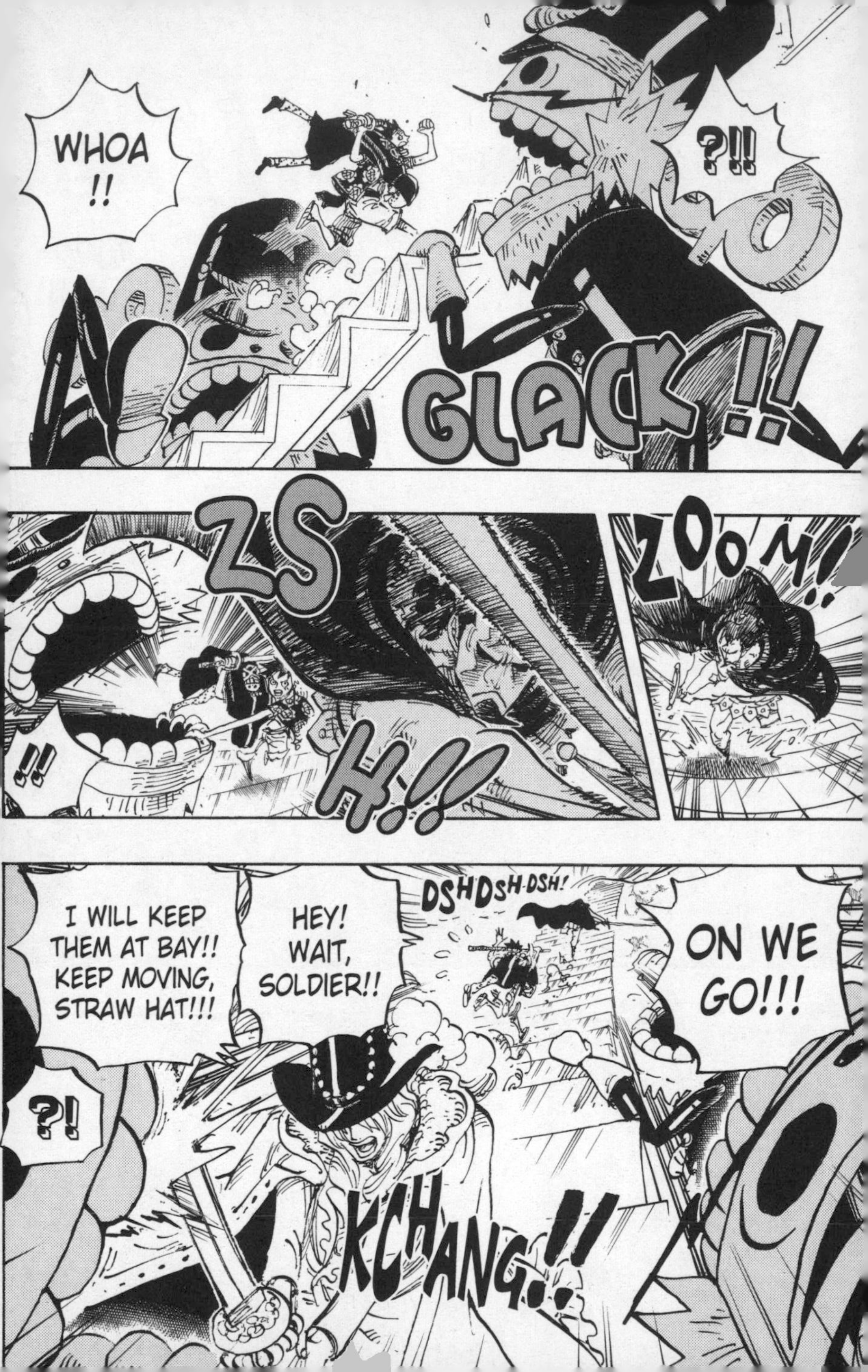
?!!
WHOA !!
GLACK!!
ZOOM!!
ZSH!!
!!
ON WE GO!!!
DSHDSH-DSH!
HEY! WAIT, SOLDIER!!
I WILL KEEP THEM AT BAY!! KEEP MOVING, STRAW HAT!!!
?!
KCHANG!!

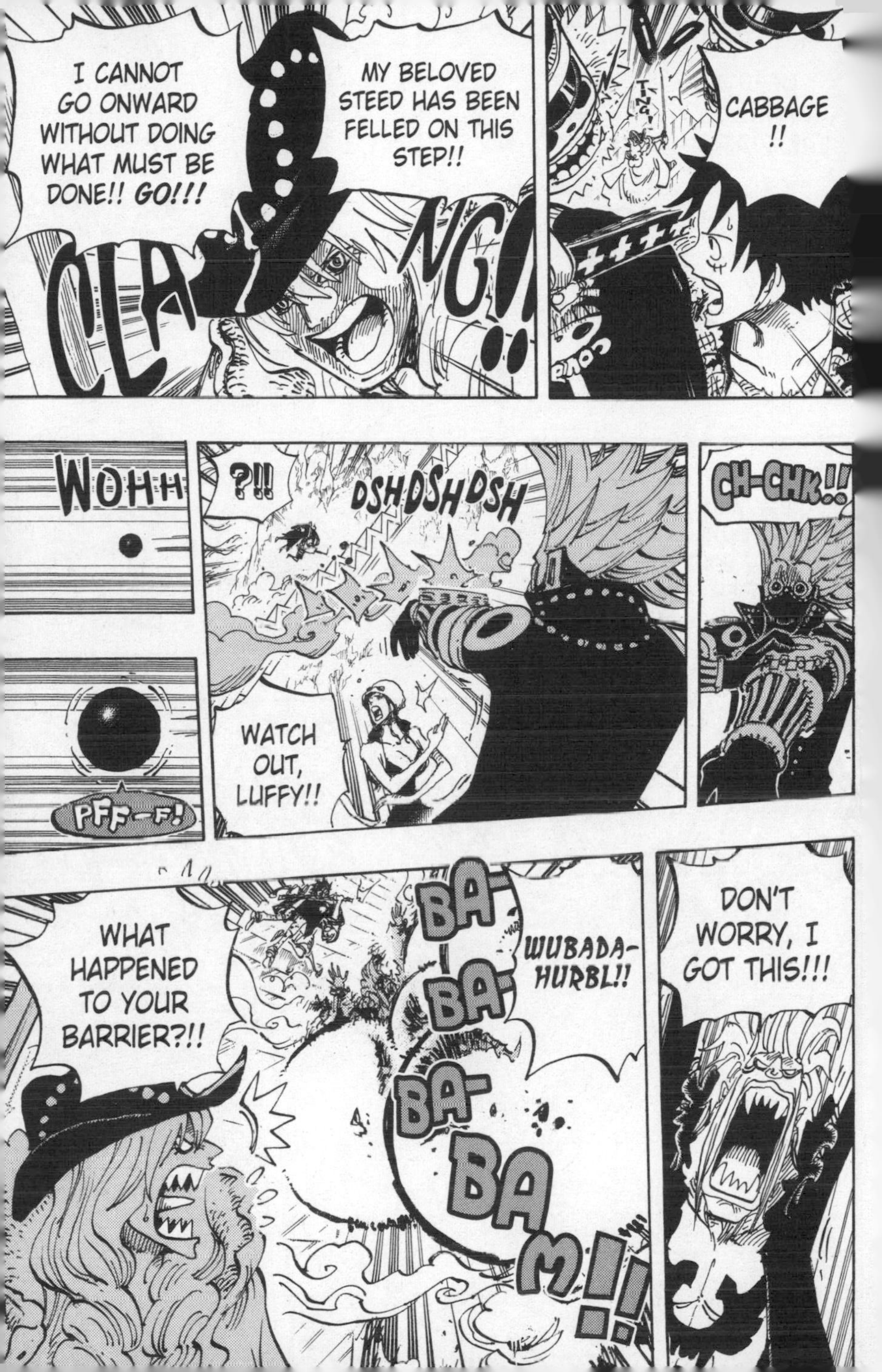
TING!
CABBAGE!!
MY BELOVED STEED HAS BEEN FELLED ON THIS STEP!!
I CANNOT GO ONWARD WITHOUT DOING WHAT MUST BE DONE!! GO!!!
CLANG!!
CH-CHK!!
?!!
DSHDSHDSH
WATCH OUT, LUFFY!!
WOHH
PFF-F!
DON'T WORRY, I GOT THIS!!!
WUBADA-HURBL!!
BA-BA-BA-BA-BAM!!!
WHAT HAPPENED TO YOUR BARRIER?!!

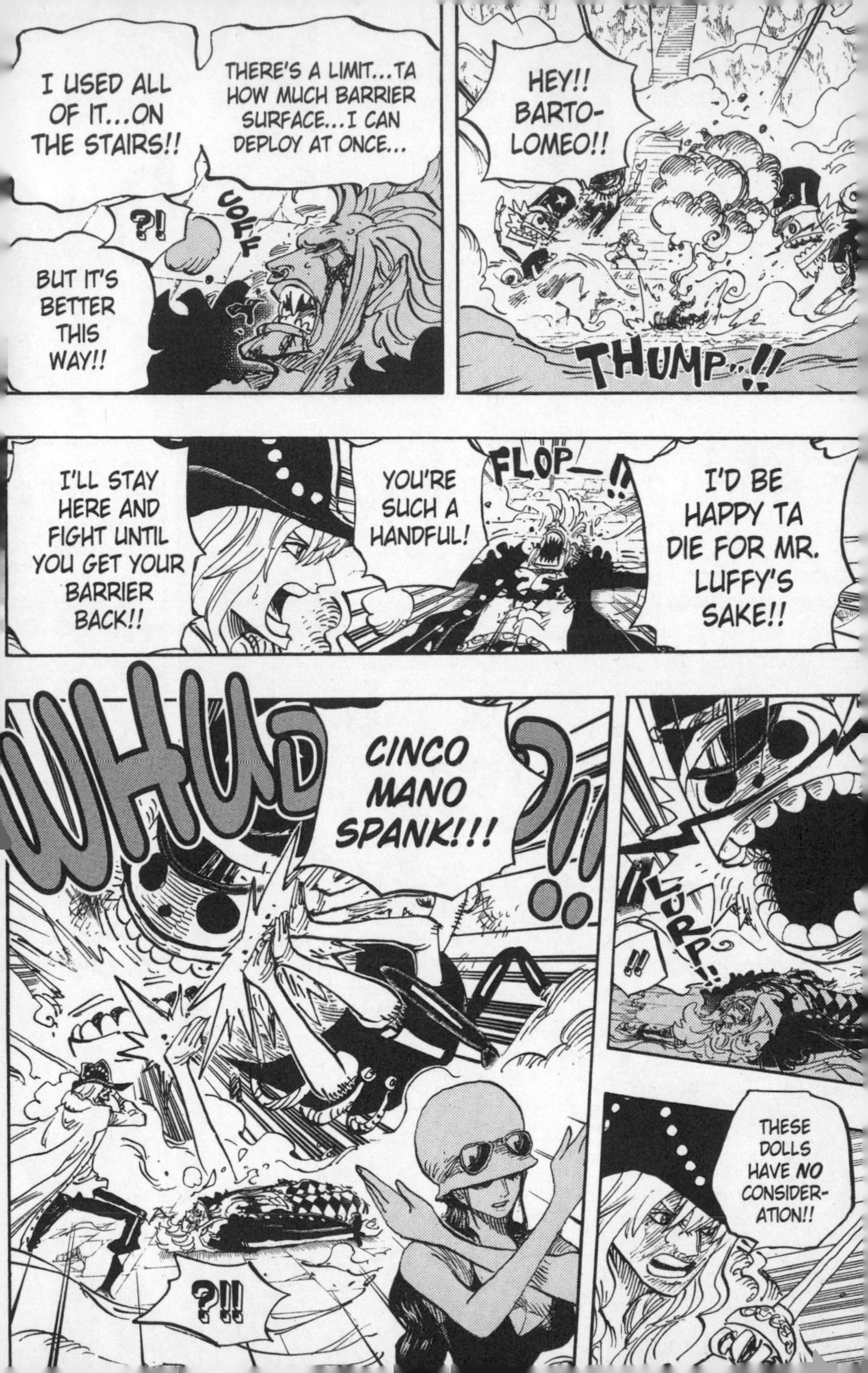
HEY!! BARTO-LOMEO!!
THUMP..!!
THERE'S A LIMIT...TA HOW MUCH BARRIER SURFACE...I CAN DEPLOY AT ONCE...
I USED ALL OF IT...ON THE STAIRS!!
UOFF
?!
BUT IT'S BETTER THIS WAY!!
I'D BE HAPPY TA DIE FOR MR. LUFFY'S SAKE!!
FLOP—!!
YOU'RE SUCH A HANDFUL!
I'LL STAY HERE AND FIGHT UNTIL YOU GET YOUR BARRIER BACK!!
LURP!!
!!
THESE DOLLS HAVE NO CONSIDERATION!!
WHUD
CINCO MANO SPANK!!!
?!!

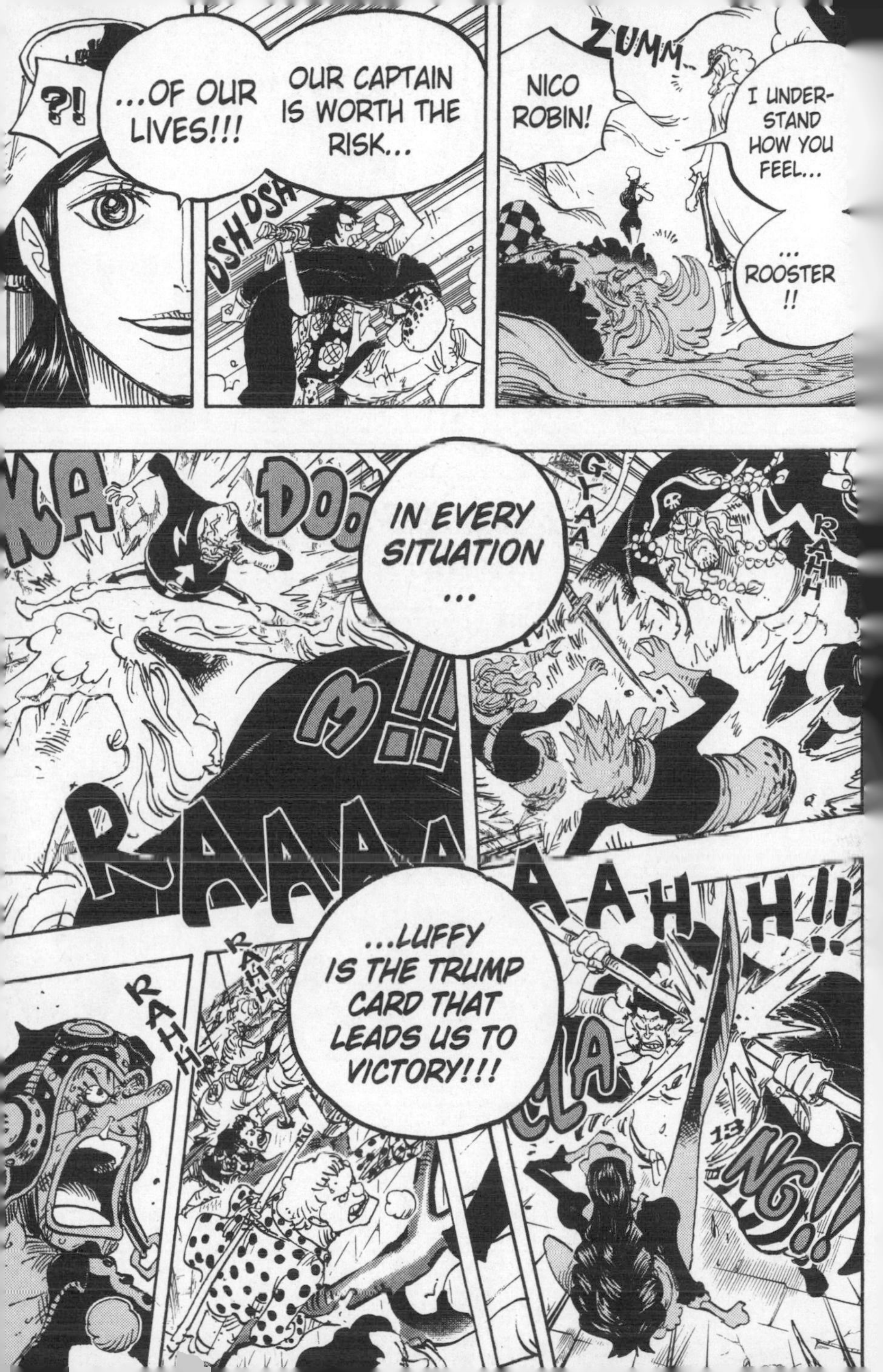
ZUMM
I UNDER-STAND HOW YOU FEEL...
NICO ROBIN!
... ROOSTER !!
OUR CAPTAIN IS WORTH THE RISK...
DSH DSH
...OF OUR LIVES!!!
?!
RAHHH
GYAAA
IN EVERY SITUATION ...
DOOM!!
RAAAAAAAAHH!!
...LUFFY IS THE TRUMP CARD THAT LEADS US TO VICTORY!!!
NG!!
RAHH
RAHH

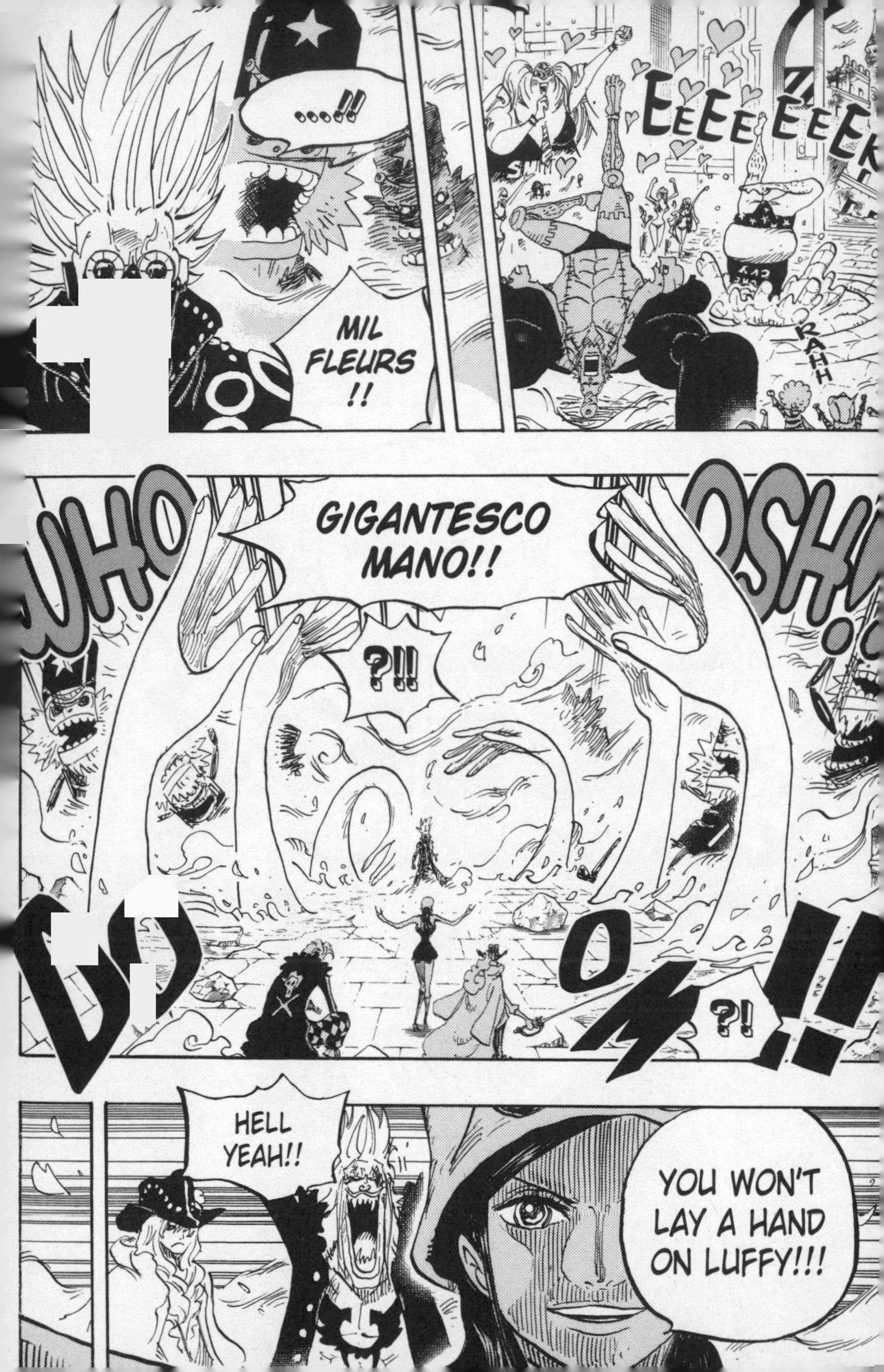
EEEEEEEEK
RAHH
....!!
MIL FLEURS!!
WHO
OSH!!
GIGANTESCO MANO!!
?!!
?!
OM!!
YOU WON'T LAY A HAND ON LUFFY!!!
HELL YEAH!!

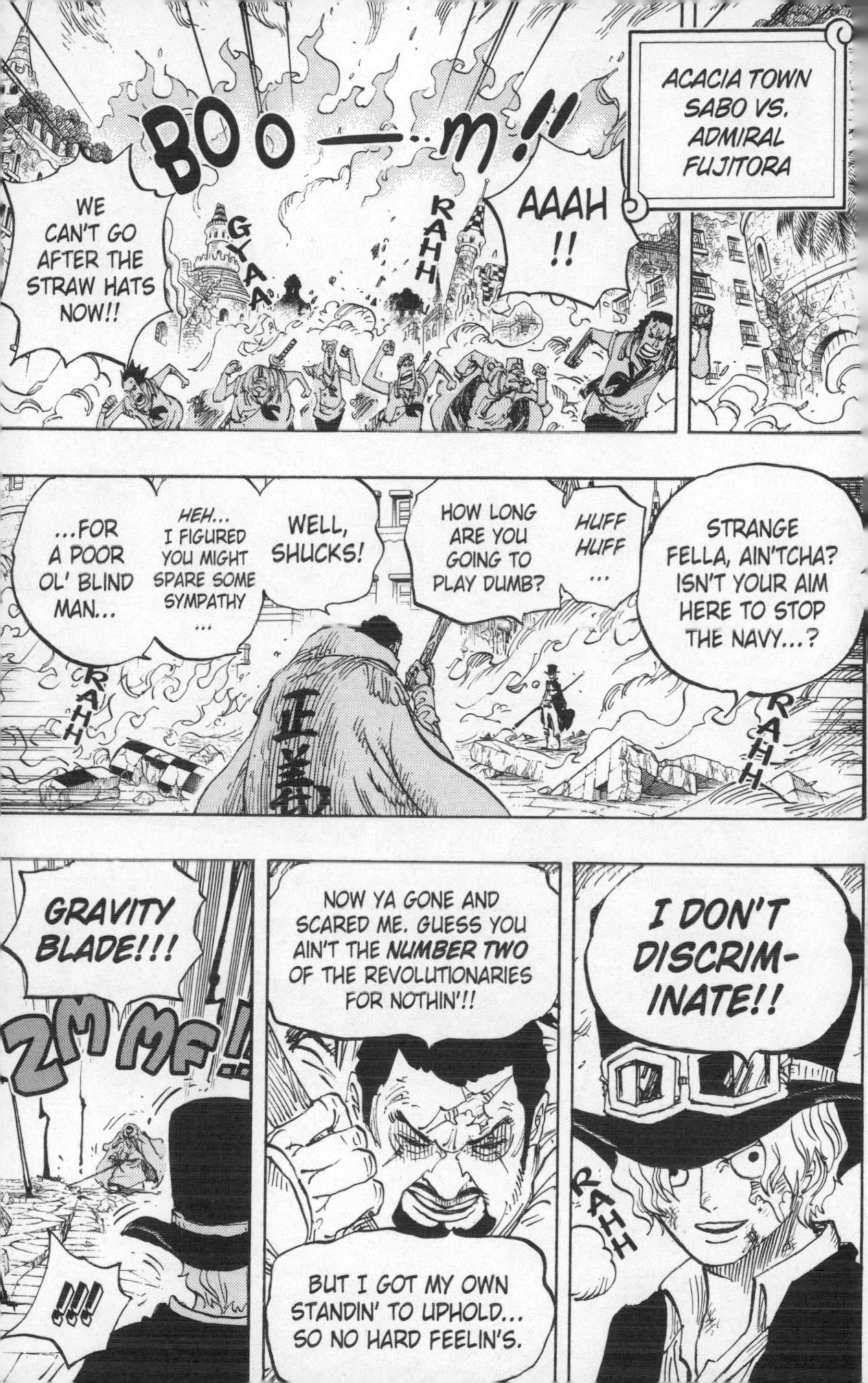
ACACIA TOWN SABO VS. ADMIRAL FUJITORA
BOO—m!!
AAAH!!
RAHH
GYAA
WE CAN'T GO AFTER THE STRAW HATS NOW!!
STRANGE FELLA, AIN'TCHA? ISN'T YOUR AIM HERE TO STOP THE NAVY...?
HUFF HUFF ...
HOW LONG ARE YOU GOING TO PLAY DUMB?
WELL, SHUCKS!
HEH... I FIGURED YOU MIGHT SPARE SOME SYMPATHY ...
...FOR A POOR OL' BLIND MAN...
RAHH
RAHH
I DON'T DISCRIM-INATE!!
RAHH
NOW YA GONE AND SCARED ME. GUESS YOU AIN'T THE NUMBER TWO OF THE REVOLUTIONARIES FOR NOTHIN'!!
BUT I GOT MY OWN STANDIN' TO UPHOLD... SO NO HARD FEELIN'S.
GRAVITY BLADE!!!
ZMMF!!
!!!

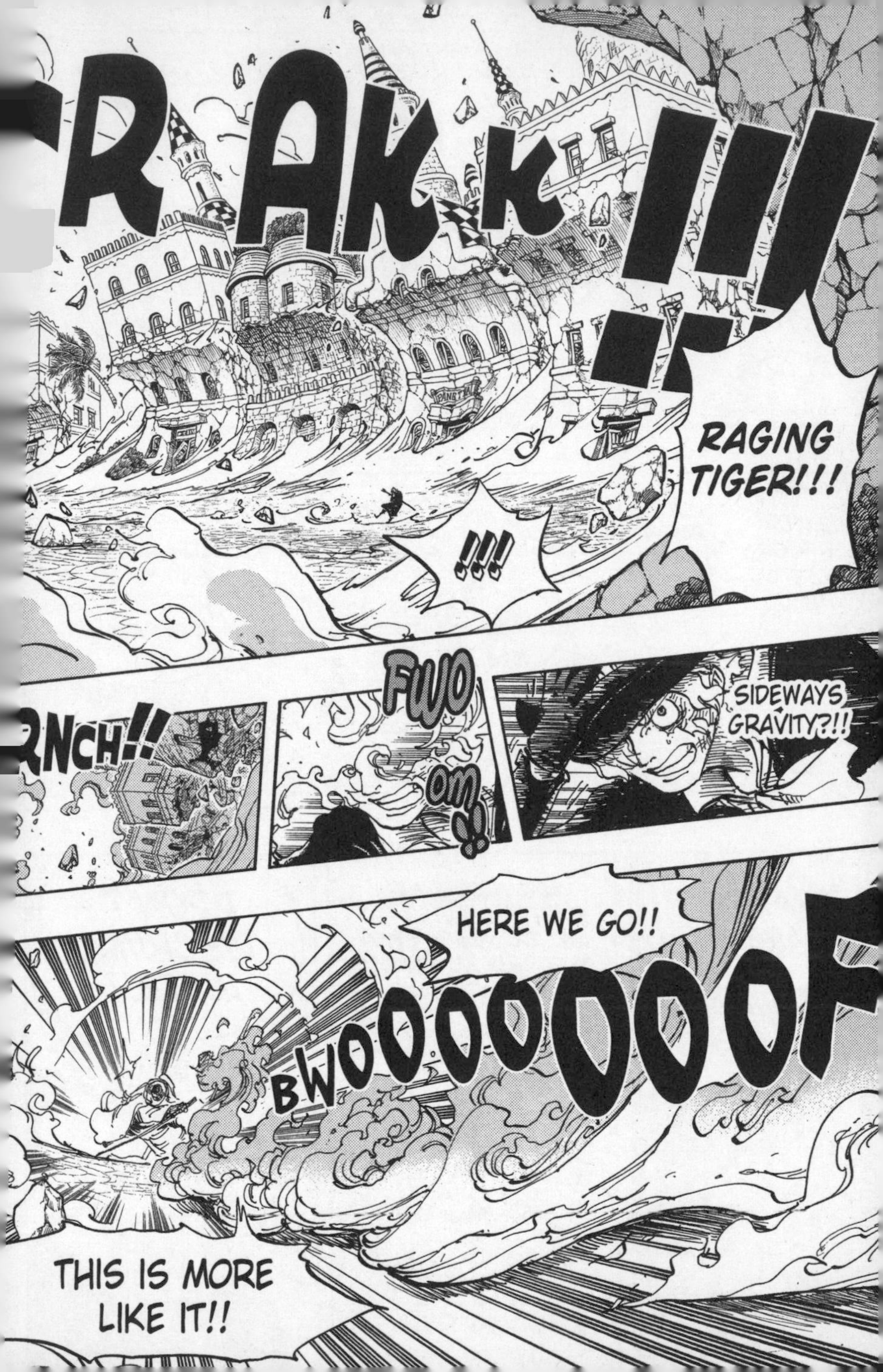
RAKK!!!
RAGING TIGER!!!
!!!
SIDEWAYS GRAVITY?!!
FWO
om!!
RNCH!!
HERE WE GO!!
BWOOOOOOOF
THIS IS MORE LIKE IT!!

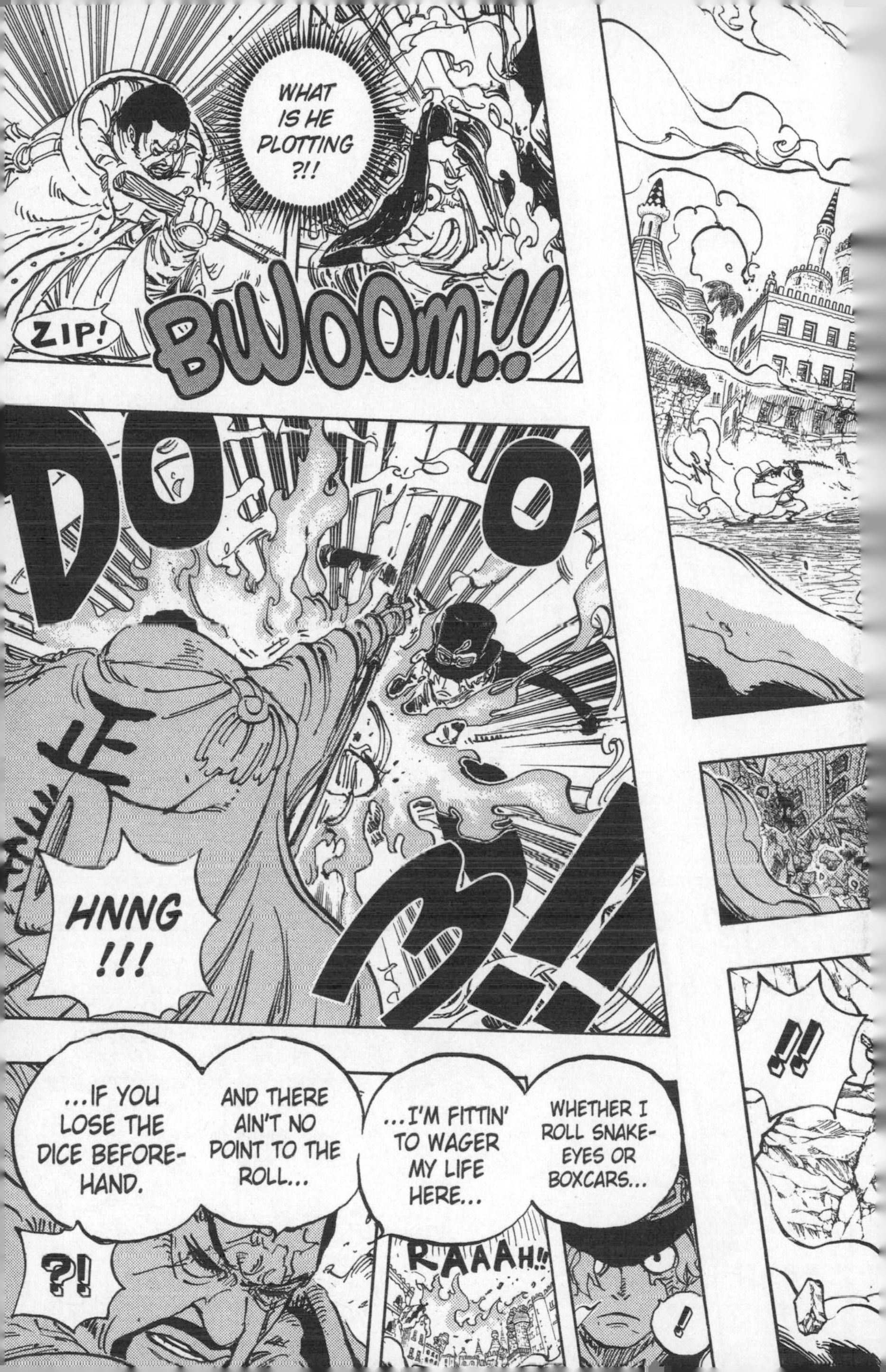
WHAT IS HE PLOTTING ?!!
BWOOM..!!
ZIP!
HNNG !!!
!!
WHETHER I ROLL SNAKE-EYES OR BOXCARS...
...I'M FITTIN' TO WAGER MY LIFE HERE...
!
RAAAH!!
AND THERE AIN'T NO POINT TO THE ROLL...
...IF YOU LOSE THE DICE BEFORE-HAND.
?!

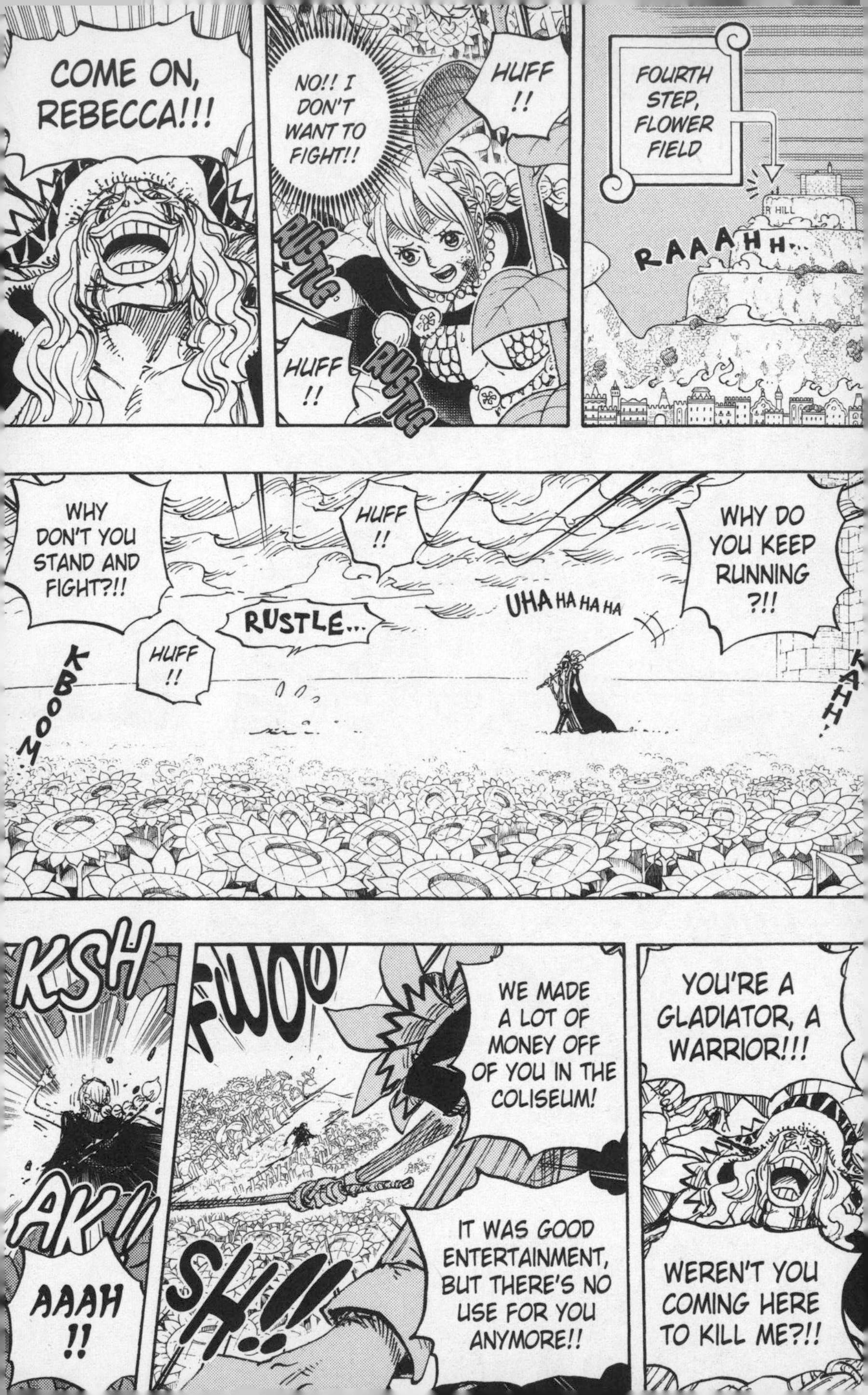
FOURTH STEP, FLOWER FIELD
R HILL
RAAAHH...
HUFF !!
NO!! I DON'T WANT TO FIGHT!!
RUSTLE
RUSTLE
HUFF !!
COME ON, REBECCA!!!
KAHH!
WHY DO YOU KEEP RUNNING ?!!
UHA HA HA HA
HUFF !!
RUSTLE...
WHY DON'T YOU STAND AND FIGHT?!!
HUFF !!
KBOOOM
YOU'RE A GLADIATOR, A WARRIOR!!!
WEREN'T YOU COMING HERE TO KILL ME?!!
FWOO
WE MADE A LOT OF MONEY OFF OF YOU IN THE COLISEUM!
IT WAS GOOD ENTERTAINMENT, BUT THERE'S NO USE FOR YOU ANYMORE!!
SH!!
KSH
AK!!
AAAH !!

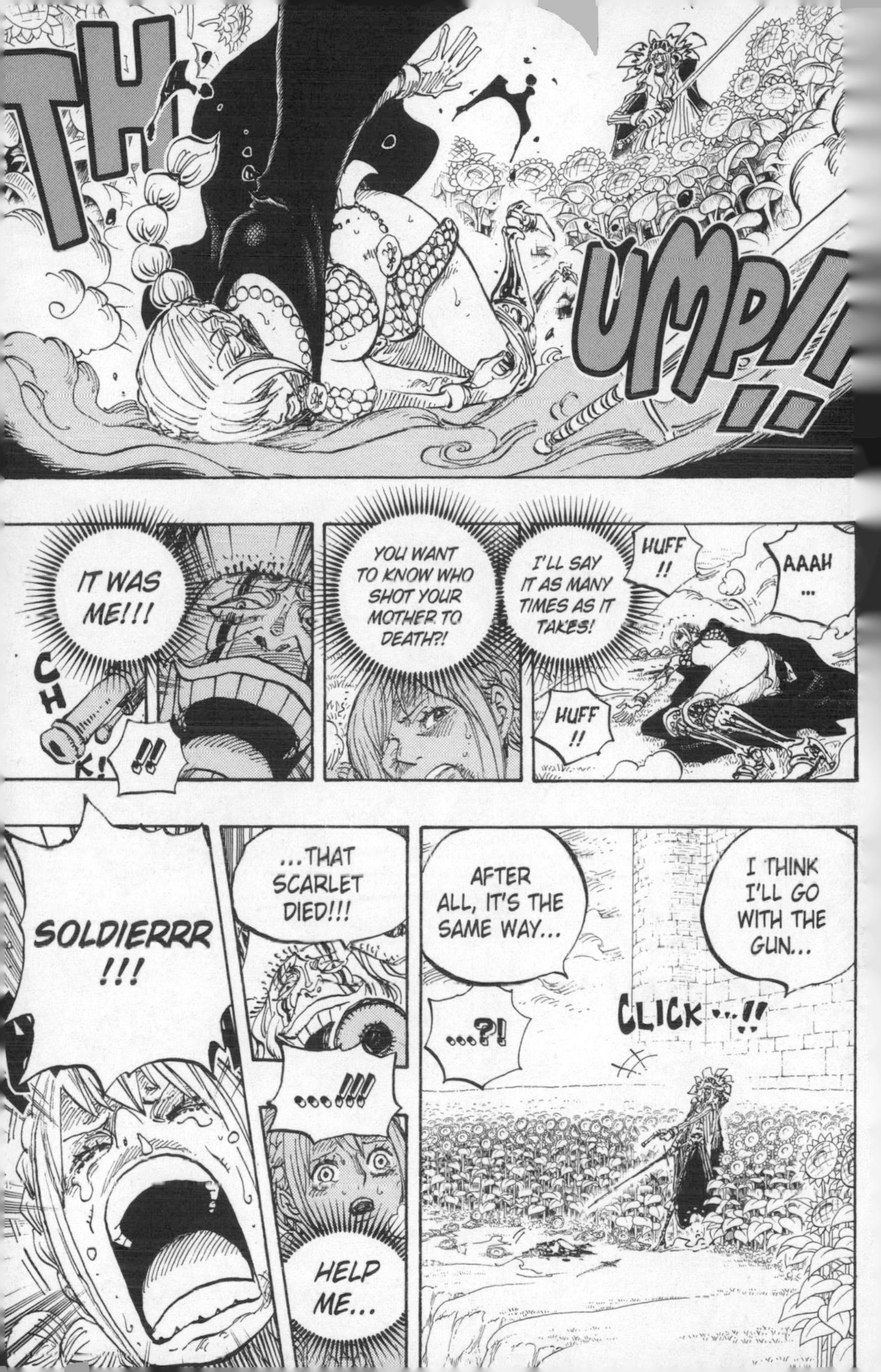
THUMP!!
AAAH ...
HUFF !!
HUFF !!
YOU WANT TO KNOW WHO SHOT YOUR MOTHER TO DEATH?!
I'LL SAY IT AS MANY TIMES AS IT TAKES!
IT WAS ME!!!
CHK!
!!
I THINK I'LL GO WITH THE GUN...
AFTER ALL, IT'S THE SAME WAY...
...?!
CLICK...!!
...THAT SCARLET DIED!!!
...!!!
HELP ME...
SOLDIERRR !!!

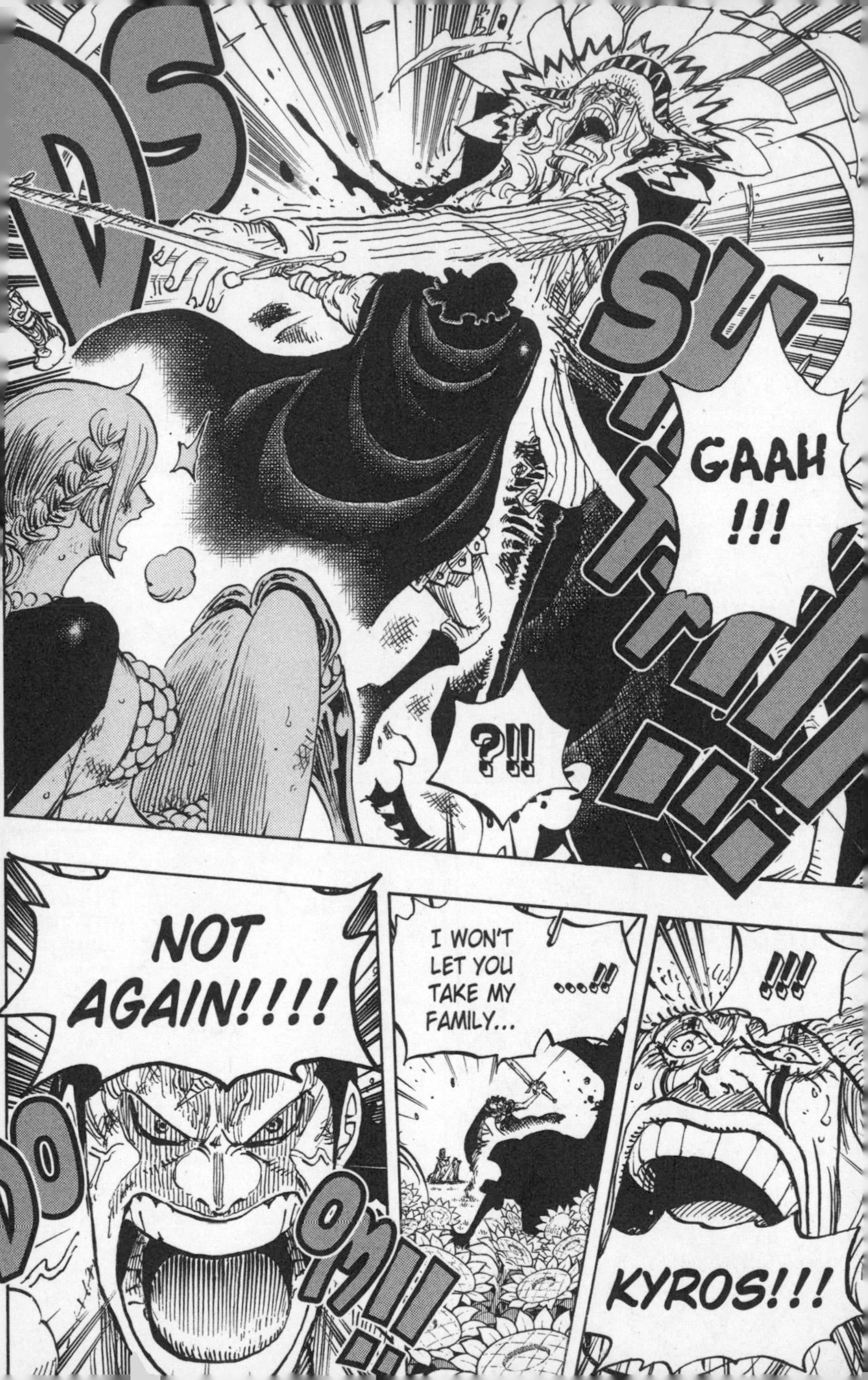
GAAH!!!
?!!
!!!
KYROS!!!
...!!
I WON'T LET YOU TAKE MY FAMILY...
NOT AGAIN!!!!
DOOM!!

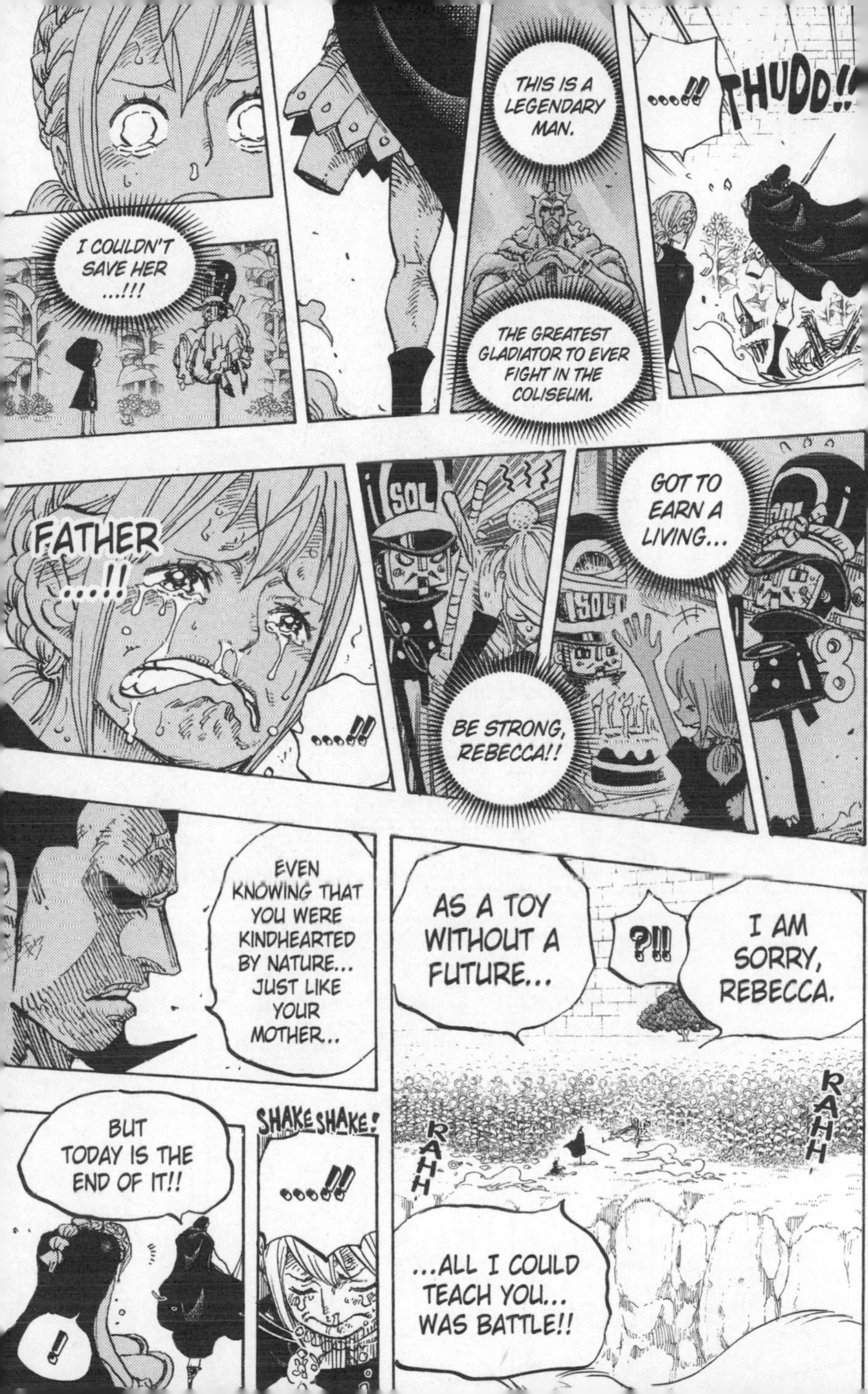

....!!
THUDD!!
THIS IS A LEGENDARY MAN.
THE GREATEST GLADIATOR TO EVER FIGHT IN THE COLISEUM.
I COULDN'T SAVE HER ...!!!
GOT TO EARN A LIVING...
BE STRONG, REBECCA!!
FATHER ...!!
....!!
I AM SORRY, REBECCA.
?!!
AS A TOY WITHOUT A FUTURE...
RAHH
RAHH
...ALL I COULD TEACH YOU... WAS BATTLE!!
EVEN KNOWING THAT YOU WERE KINDHEARTED BY NATURE... JUST LIKE YOUR MOTHER...
SHAKE SHAKE!
....!!
BUT TODAY IS THE END OF IT!!
!

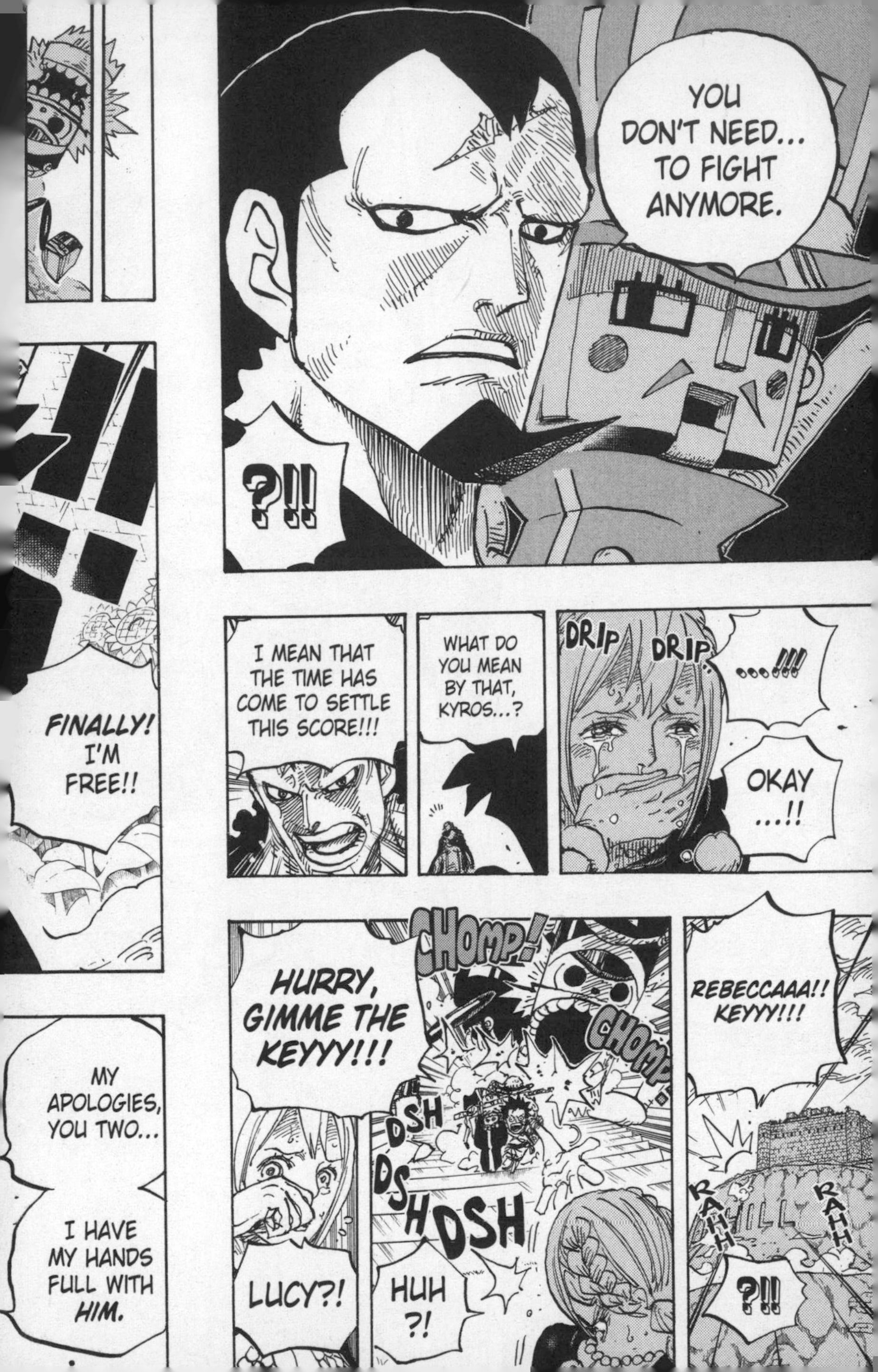
YOU DON'T NEED... TO FIGHT ANYMORE.
?!!
DRIP DRIP
...!!!
OKAY ...!!
WHAT DO YOU MEAN BY THAT, KYROS...?
I MEAN THAT THE TIME HAS COME TO SETTLE THIS SCORE!!!
REBECCAAA!! KEYYY!!!
RAHH RAHH
?!!
CHOMP!
CHOMP
HURRY, GIMME THE KEYYY!!!
DSH DSH DSH DSH
HUH ?!
LUCY?!
FINALLY! I'M FREE!!
MY APOLOGIES, YOU TWO...
I HAVE MY HANDS FULL WITH HIM.

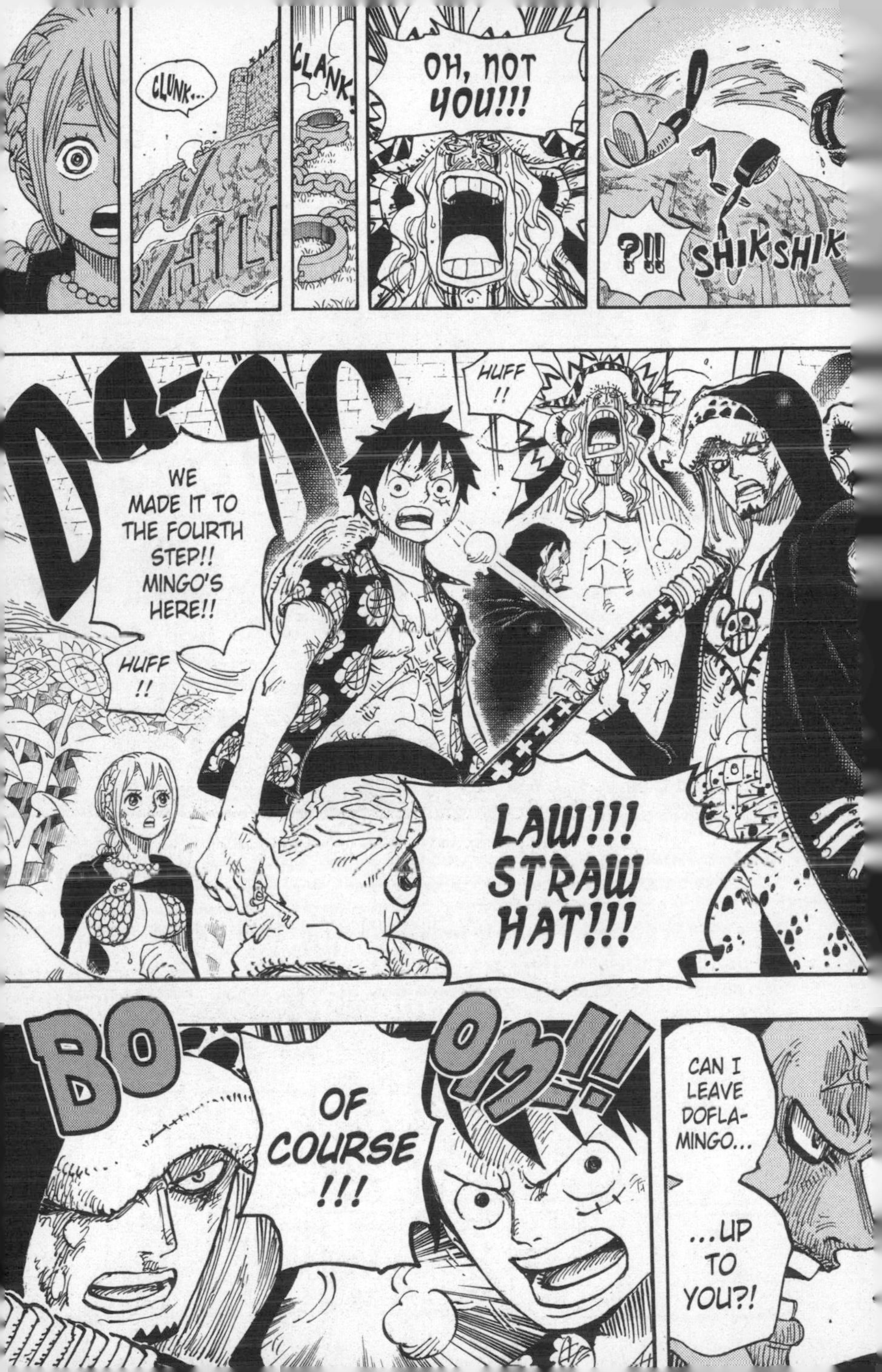
SHIK SHIK
?!!
OH, NOT YOU!!!
CLANK
CLUNK...
HUFF !!
DA-DO
WE MADE IT TO THE FOURTH STEP!! MINGO'S HERE!!
HUFF !!
LAW!!! STRAW HAT!!!
CAN I LEAVE DOFLA-MINGO...
...UP TO YOU?!
BO-OM!!
OF COURSE!!!

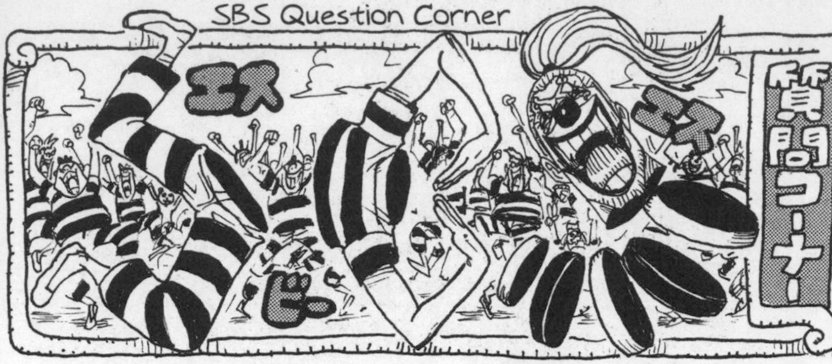
SBS Question Corner
質問コーナー
エス
ビー
エス

(Penae, Aichi)

Q: Odacchi! Question! Are there no women in the Whitebeard Pirates? I'm curious!
--Ringo

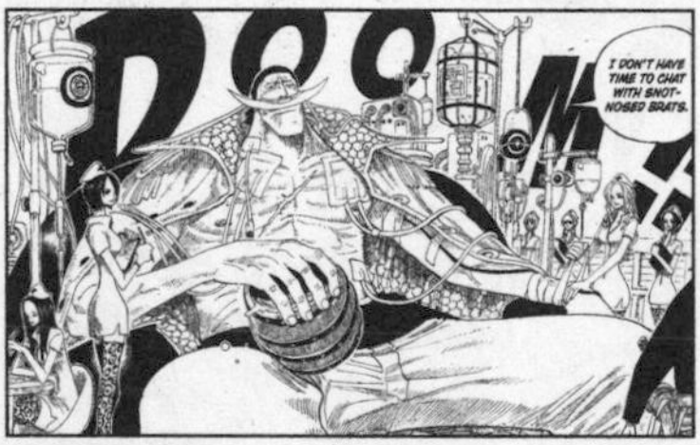
I DON'T HAVE TIME TO CHAT WITH SNOT-NOSED BRATS.

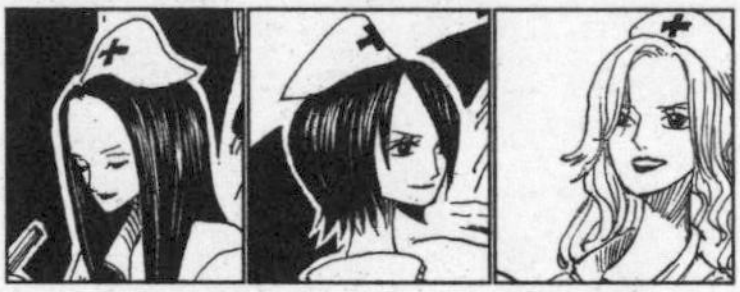

A: Hmm. There were female nurses on his ship during his first appearance in Volume 25. They're actually the medical team of the Whitebeard Pirate Crew. However, Whitebeard never allowed any women on his ship as fighters. That's why there were no women on his ship when they showed up at the Paramount War in Marineford. He was prepared to die in that battle. He ripped off all the medical apparatuses that kept him alive, sent all the tearful nurses off of the ship, and headed off to the final battle with only men at his side!! I didn't draw it, but that was a bit of drama behind his entrance.

Q: Mr. Oda, I've got a problem!! My family can't tell the difference between Zolo and Sanji!! Can you distill it down in a format so iconic, they never get confused again?

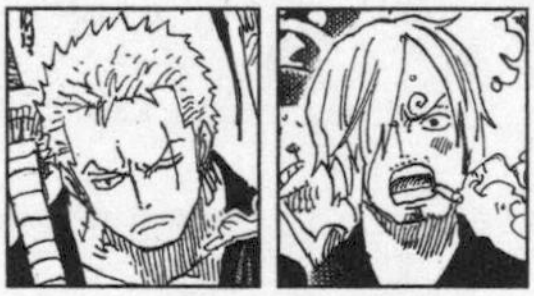

A:

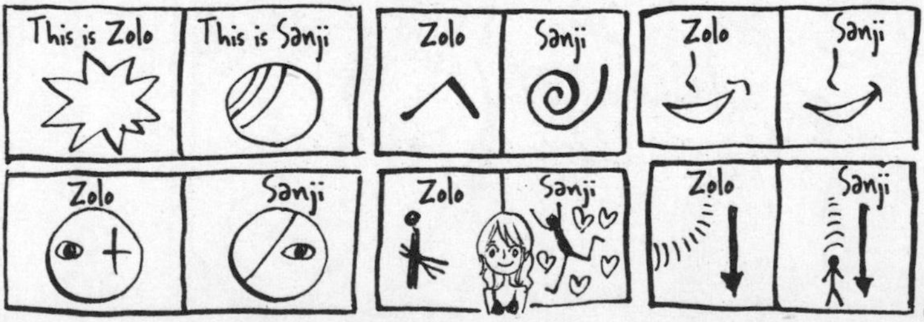
Sanji
Zolo
Sanji
Zolo
This is Sanji
This is Zolo
Sanji
Zolo
Sanji
Zolo
Sanji
Zolo

Chapter 758:
JUST KEEP GOING

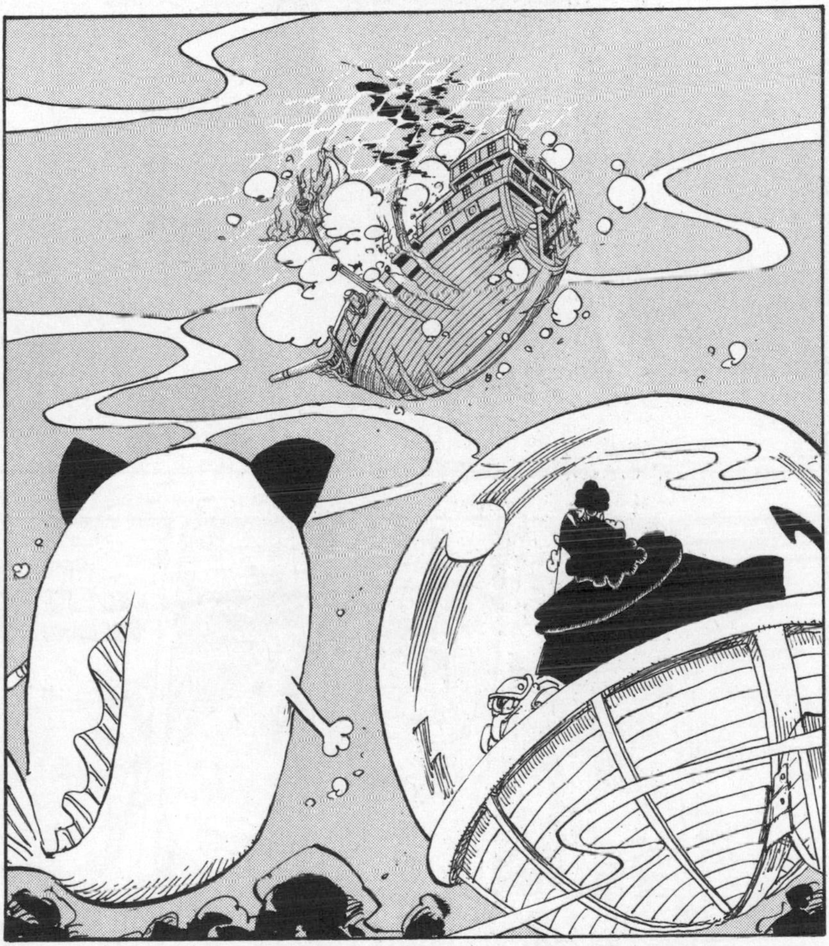

THE SOLITARY JOURNEY OF JIMBEI, FIRST SON OF THE SEA, VOL. 7: "LOOK, A SINKING SHIP!!"

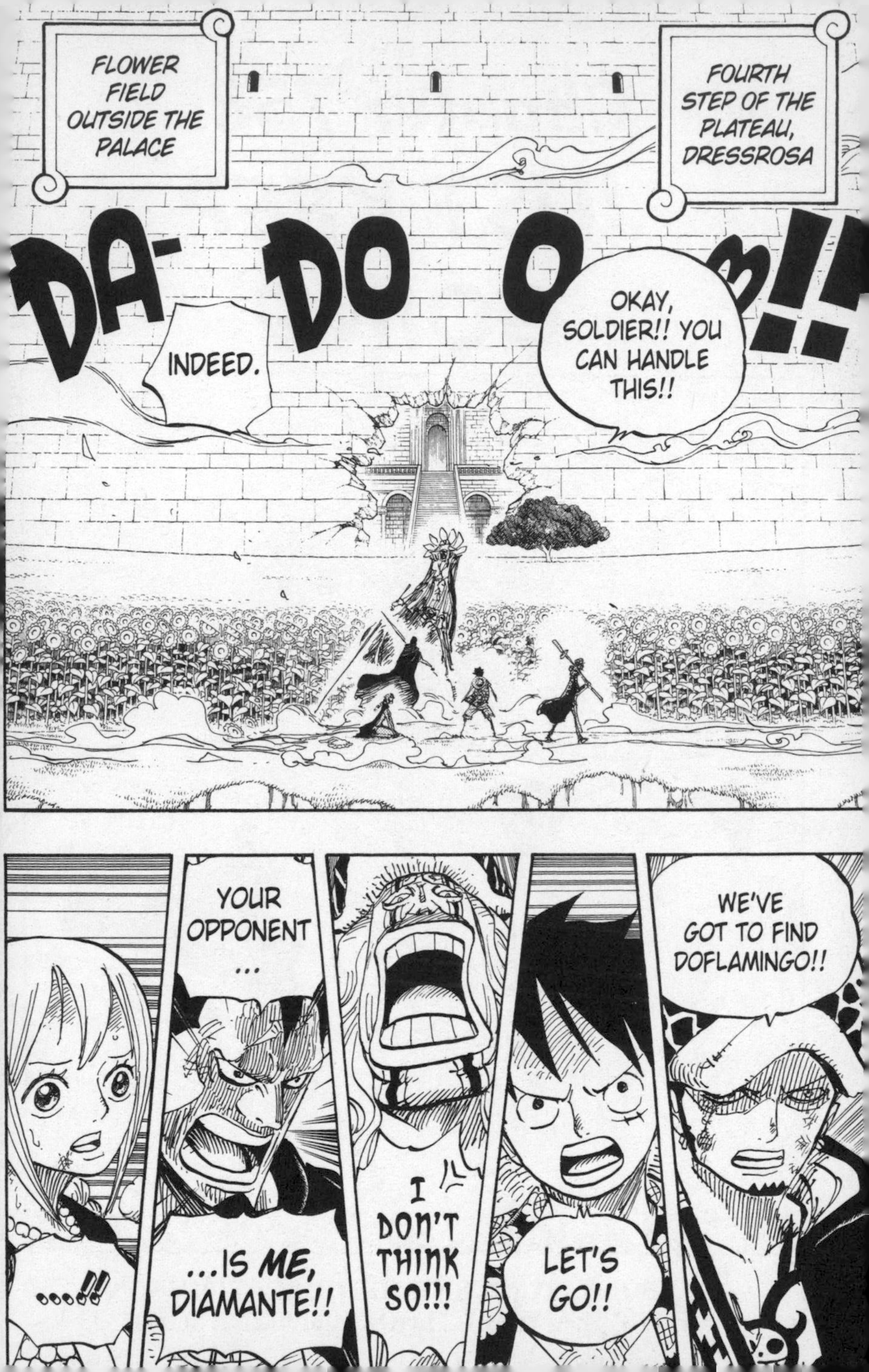
FOURTH STEP OF THE PLATEAU, DRESSROSA
FLOWER FIELD OUTSIDE THE PALACE
DA-DO O M!!
OKAY, SOLDIER!! YOU CAN HANDLE THIS!!
INDEED.
WE'VE GOT TO FIND DOFLAMINGO!!
LET'S GO!!
I DON'T THINK SO!!!
YOUR OPPONENT ...
...IS *ME*, DIAMANTE!!
...!!

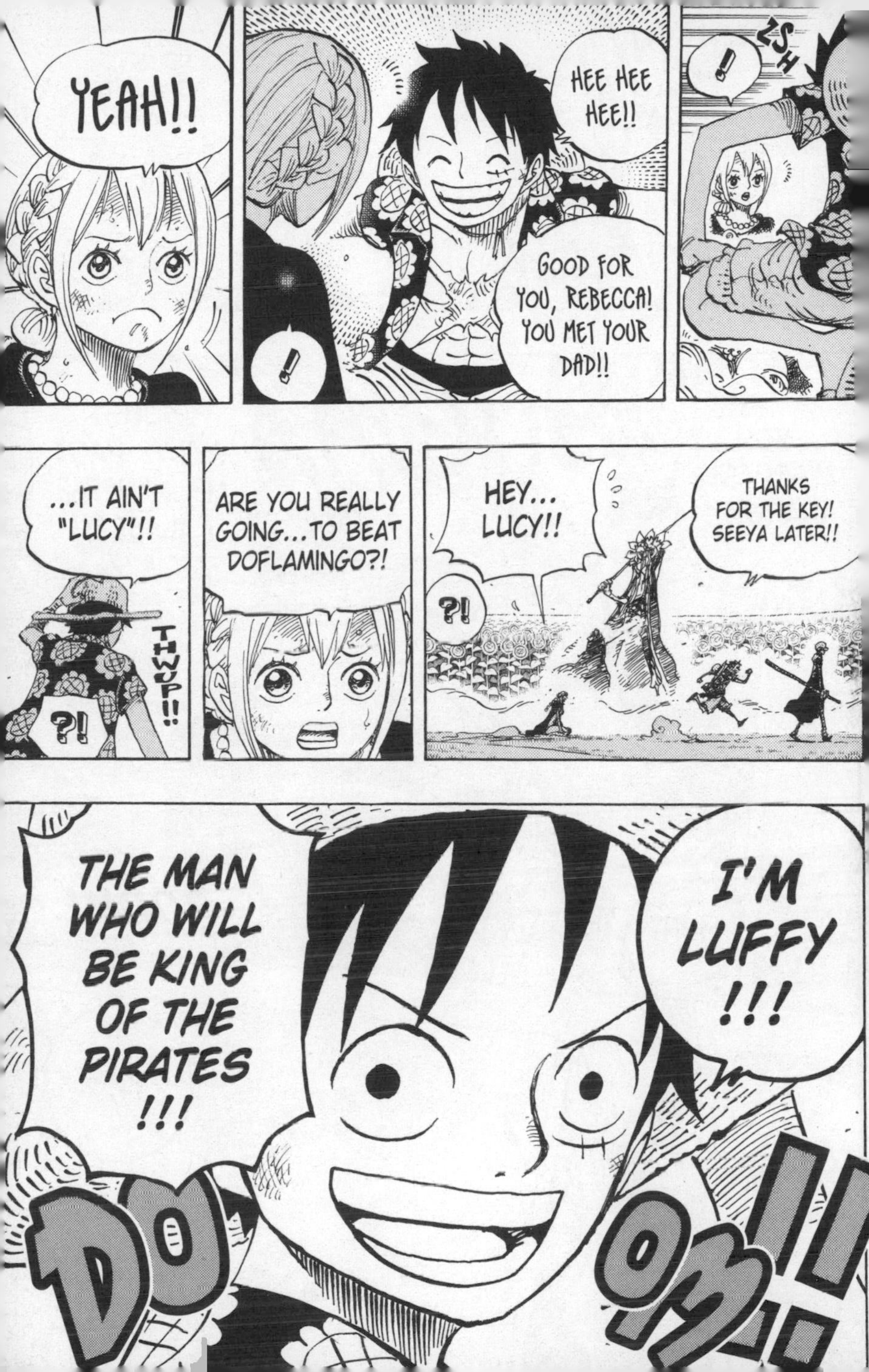
ZSH
!
HEE HEE HEE!!
GOOD FOR YOU, REBECCA! YOU MET YOUR DAD!!
!
YEAH!!
THANKS FOR THE KEY! SEEYA LATER!!
HEY... LUCY!!
?!
ARE YOU REALLY GOING...TO BEAT DOFLAMINGO?!
...IT AIN'T "LUCY"!!
THWUP!!
?!
I'M LUFFY!!!
THE MAN WHO WILL BE KING OF THE PIRATES!!!
DOOM!!

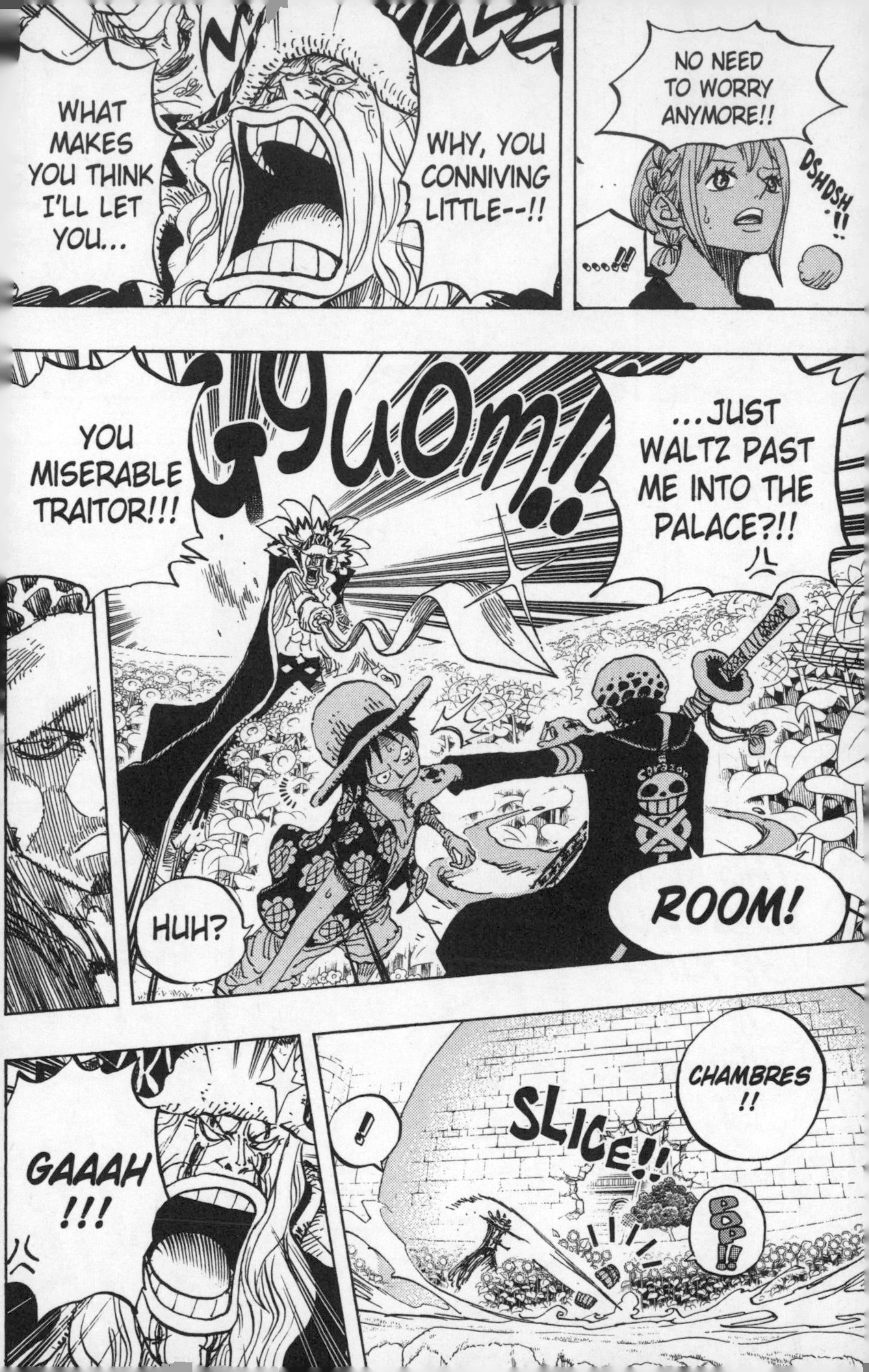
NO NEED TO WORRY ANYMORE!!
DSHDSH!!
...!!
WHY, YOU CONNIVING LITTLE--!!
WHAT MAKES YOU THINK I'LL LET YOU...
...JUST WALTZ PAST ME INTO THE PALACE?!!
GYUON!!
YOU MISERABLE TRAITOR!!!
ROOM!
HUH?
CHAMBRES!!
SLICE!!
!
BOP!
GAAAH!!!

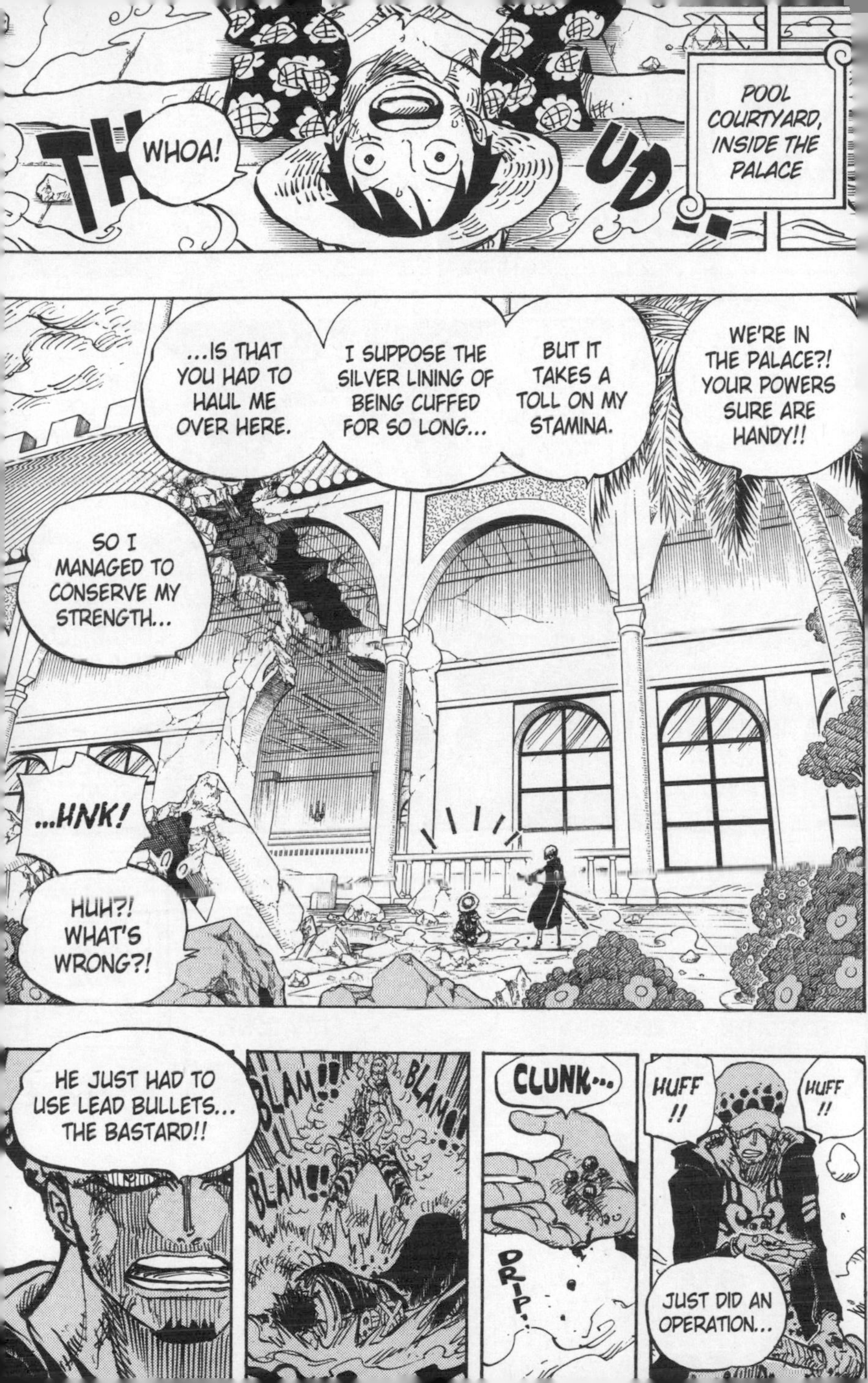
POOL COURTYARD, INSIDE THE PALACE
THUD..
WHOA!
WE'RE IN THE PALACE?! YOUR POWERS SURE ARE HANDY!!
BUT IT TAKES A TOLL ON MY STAMINA.
I SUPPOSE THE SILVER LINING OF BEING CUFFED FOR SO LONG...
...IS THAT YOU HAD TO HAUL ME OVER HERE.
SO I MANAGED TO CONSERVE MY STRENGTH...
...HNK!
HUH?! WHAT'S WRONG?!
HUFF !!
HUFF !!
JUST DID AN OPERATION...
CLUNK...
DRIP..
BLAM!!
BLAM!!
BLAM!!
HE JUST HAD TO USE LEAD BULLETS... THE BASTARD!!

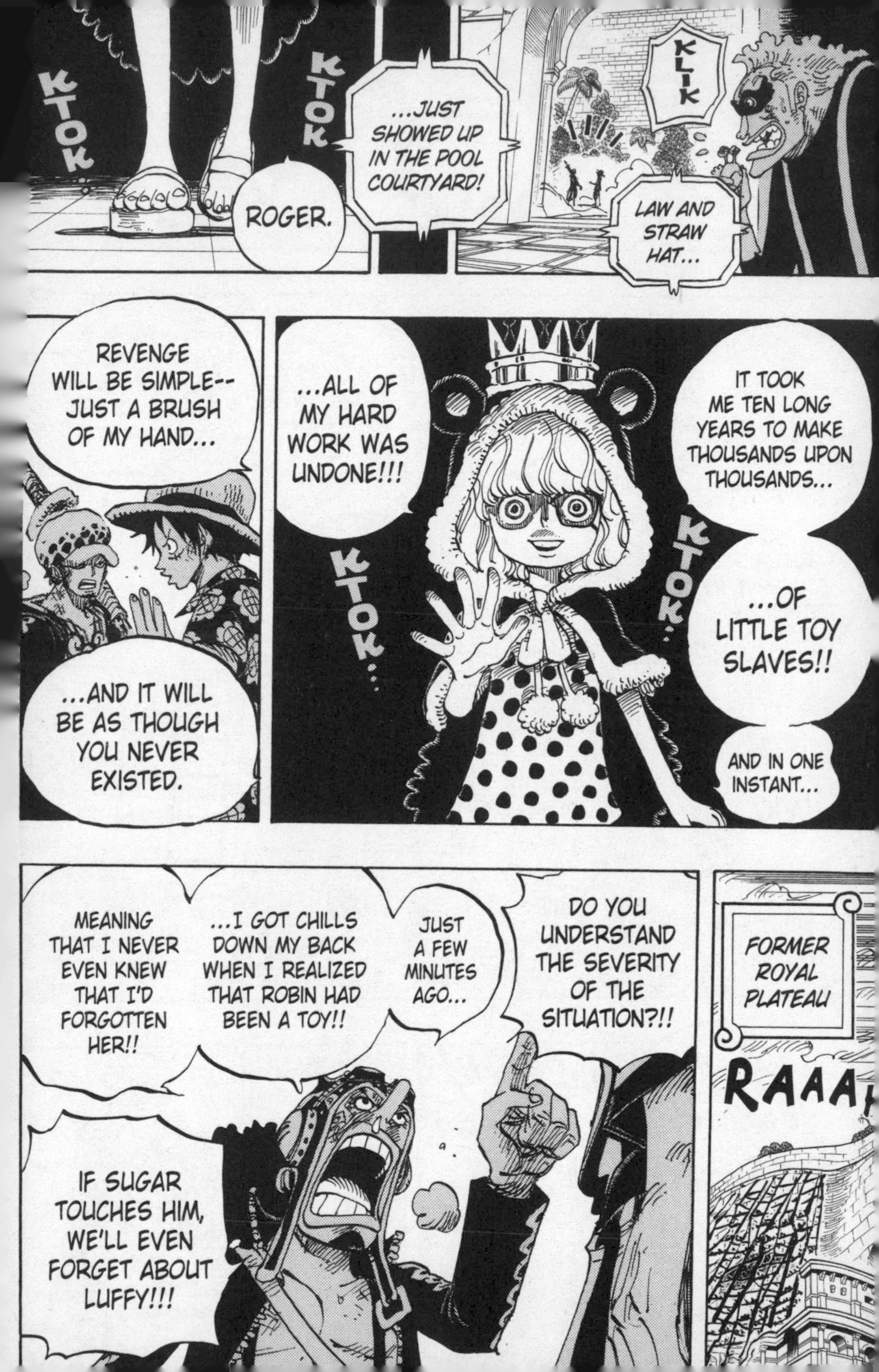
KLIK
LAW AND STRAW HAT...
...JUST SHOWED UP IN THE POOL COURTYARD!
KTOK
KTOK
ROGER.
IT TOOK ME TEN LONG YEARS TO MAKE THOUSANDS UPON THOUSANDS...
...OF LITTLE TOY SLAVES!!
AND IN ONE INSTANT...
KTOK...
...ALL OF MY HARD WORK WAS UNDONE!!!
KTOK...
REVENGE WILL BE SIMPLE-- JUST A BRUSH OF MY HAND...
...AND IT WILL BE AS THOUGH YOU NEVER EXISTED.
FORMER ROYAL PLATEAU
RAAA
DO YOU UNDERSTAND THE SEVERITY OF THE SITUATION?!!
JUST A FEW MINUTES AGO...
...I GOT CHILLS DOWN MY BACK WHEN I REALIZED THAT ROBIN HAD BEEN A TOY!!
MEANING THAT I NEVER EVEN KNEW THAT I'D FORGOTTEN HER!!
IF SUGAR TOUCHES HIM, WE'LL EVEN FORGET ABOUT LUFFY!!!

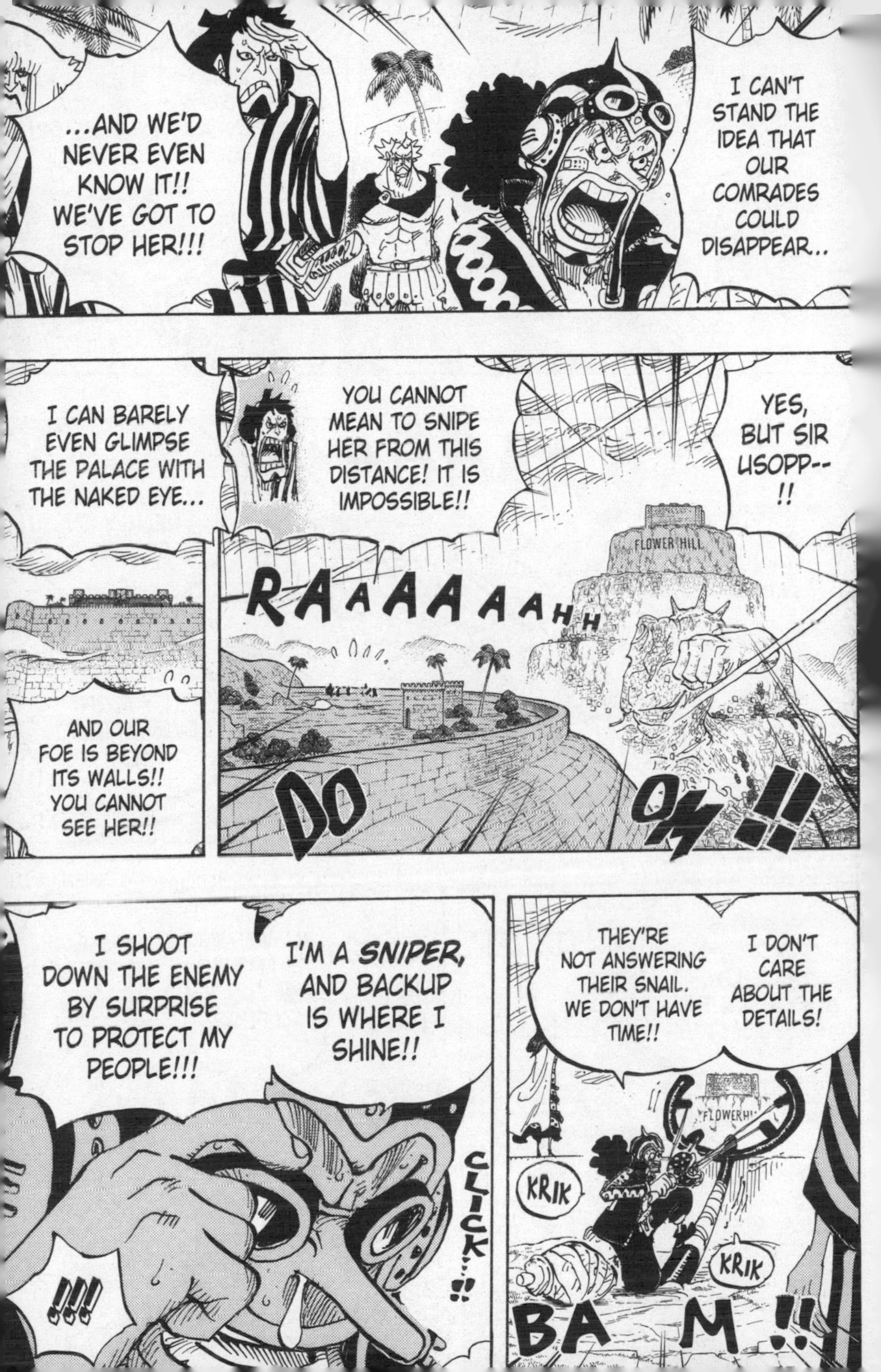
I CAN'T STAND THE IDEA THAT OUR COMRADES COULD DISAPPEAR...
...AND WE'D NEVER EVEN KNOW IT!! WE'VE GOT TO STOP HER!!!
YES, BUT SIR USOPP-- !!
YOU CANNOT MEAN TO SNIPE HER FROM THIS DISTANCE! IT IS IMPOSSIBLE!!
FLOWER HILL
RAAAAAAHH
DO
OM!!
I CAN BARELY EVEN GLIMPSE THE PALACE WITH THE NAKED EYE...
AND OUR FOE IS BEYOND ITS WALLS!! YOU CANNOT SEE HER!!
I DON'T CARE ABOUT THE DETAILS!
THEY'RE NOT ANSWERING THEIR SNAIL. WE DON'T HAVE TIME!!
KRIK
KRIK
BA
M!!
I'M A *SNIPER,* AND BACKUP IS WHERE I SHINE!!
I SHOOT DOWN THE ENEMY BY SURPRISE TO PROTECT MY PEOPLE!!!
CLICK!!
!!!

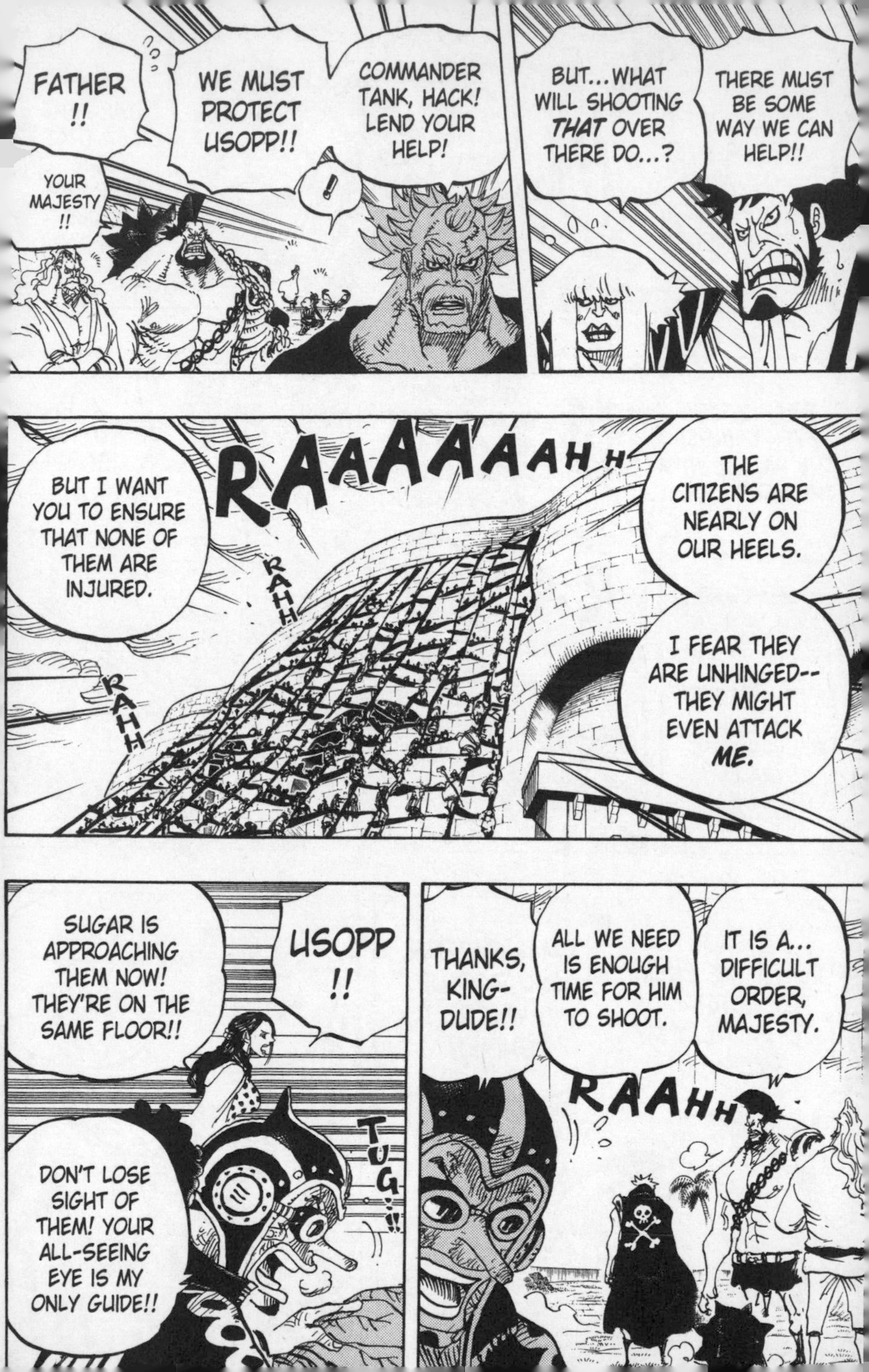
THERE MUST BE SOME WAY WE CAN HELP!!
BUT...WHAT WILL SHOOTING *THAT* OVER THERE DO...?
COMMANDER TANK, HACK! LEND YOUR HELP!
!
WE MUST PROTECT USOPP!!
FATHER !!
YOUR MAJESTY !!
THE CITIZENS ARE NEARLY ON OUR HEELS.
I FEAR THEY ARE UNHINGED-- THEY MIGHT EVEN ATTACK *ME.*
RAAAAAAAHH
BUT I WANT YOU TO ENSURE THAT NONE OF THEM ARE INJURED.
RAHH
RAHH
IT IS A... DIFFICULT ORDER, MAJESTY.
ALL WE NEED IS ENOUGH TIME FOR HIM TO SHOOT.
THANKS, KING-DUDE!!
RAAHH
USOPP !!
SUGAR IS APPROACHING THEM NOW! THEY'RE ON THE SAME FLOOR!!
TUG!!
DON'T LOSE SIGHT OF THEM! YOUR ALL-SEEING EYE IS MY ONLY GUIDE!!

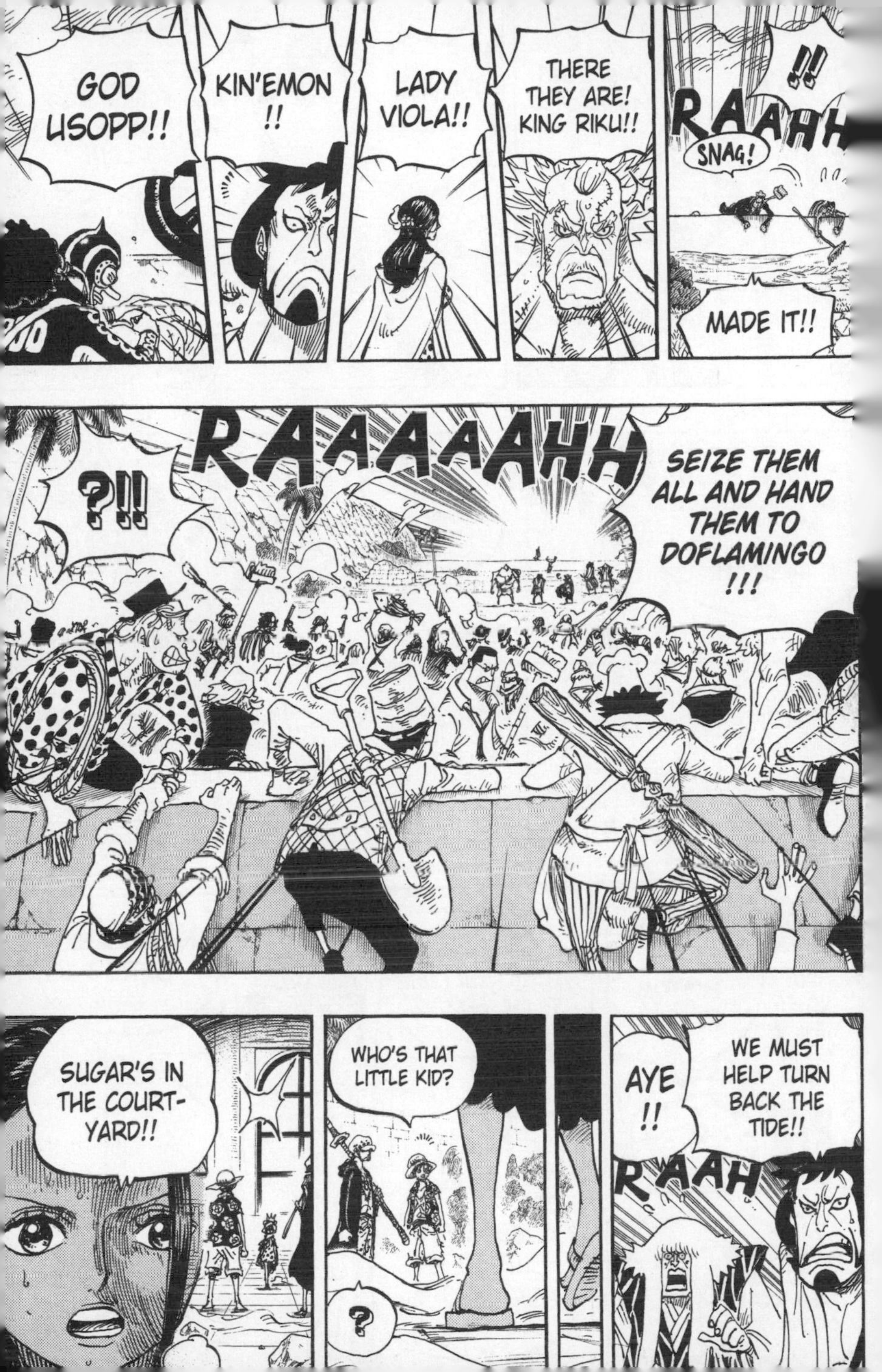
!!
RAAHH
SNAG!
MADE IT!!
THERE THEY ARE! KING RIKU!!
LADY VIOLA!!
KIN'EMON !!
GOD USOPP!!
SEIZE THEM ALL AND HAND THEM TO DOFLAMINGO !!!
RAAAAAHH
?!!
WE MUST HELP TURN BACK THE TIDE!!
AYE !!
RAAH
WHO'S THAT LITTLE KID?
?
SUGAR'S IN THE COURT-YARD!!

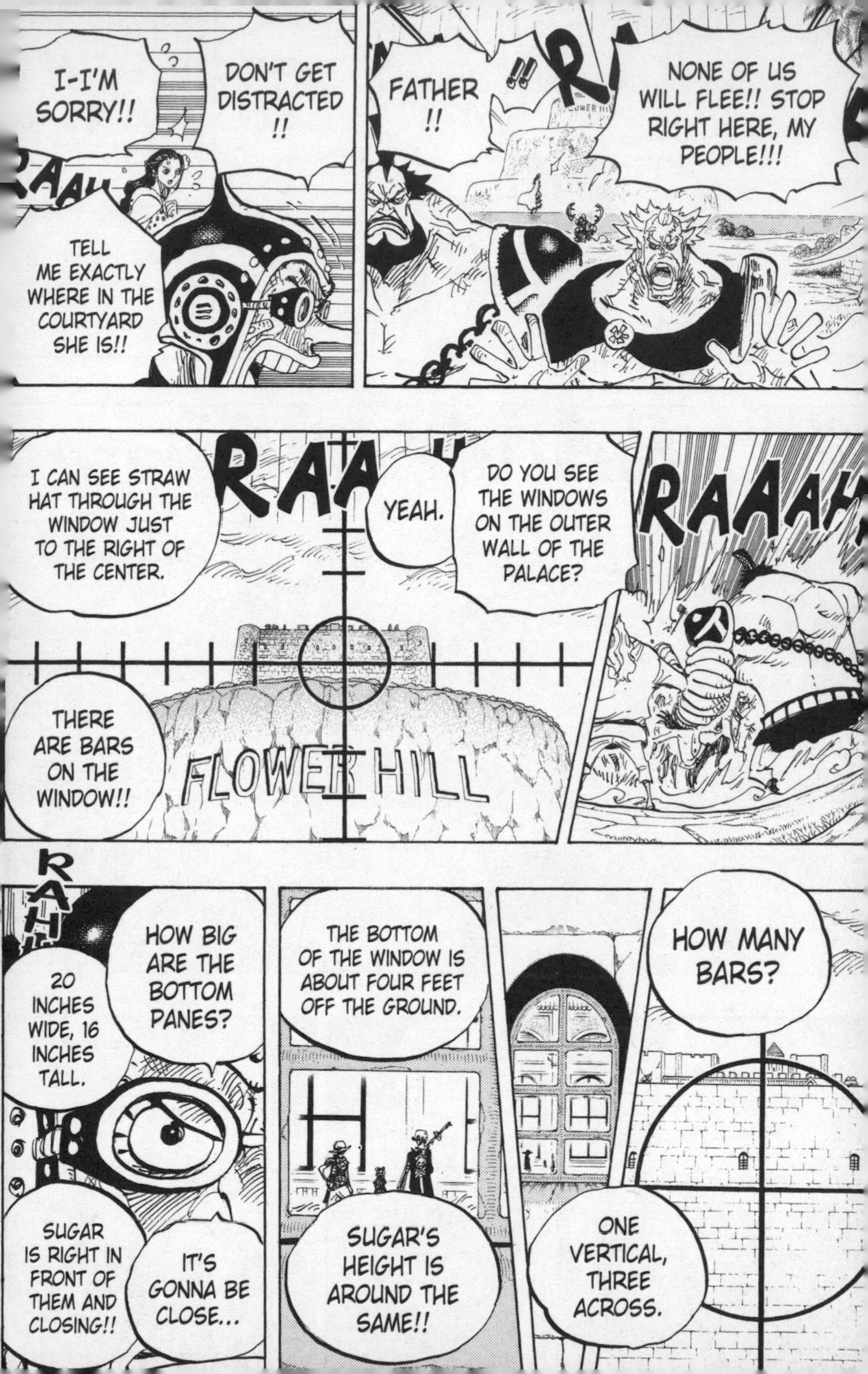
NONE OF US WILL FLEE!! STOP RIGHT HERE, MY PEOPLE!!!
!!
FATHER !!
DON'T GET DISTRACTED !!
I-I'M SORRY!!
TELL ME EXACTLY WHERE IN THE COURTYARD SHE IS!!
RAAAH
DO YOU SEE THE WINDOWS ON THE OUTER WALL OF THE PALACE?
YEAH.
RAA
I CAN SEE STRAW HAT THROUGH THE WINDOW JUST TO THE RIGHT OF THE CENTER.
THERE ARE BARS ON THE WINDOW!!
FLOWER HILL
HOW MANY BARS?
ONE VERTICAL, THREE ACROSS.
THE BOTTOM OF THE WINDOW IS ABOUT FOUR FEET OFF THE GROUND.
SUGAR'S HEIGHT IS AROUND THE SAME!!
RAH
HOW BIG ARE THE BOTTOM PANES?
20 INCHES WIDE, 16 INCHES TALL.
IT'S GONNA BE CLOSE...
SUGAR IS RIGHT IN FRONT OF THEM AND CLOSING!!

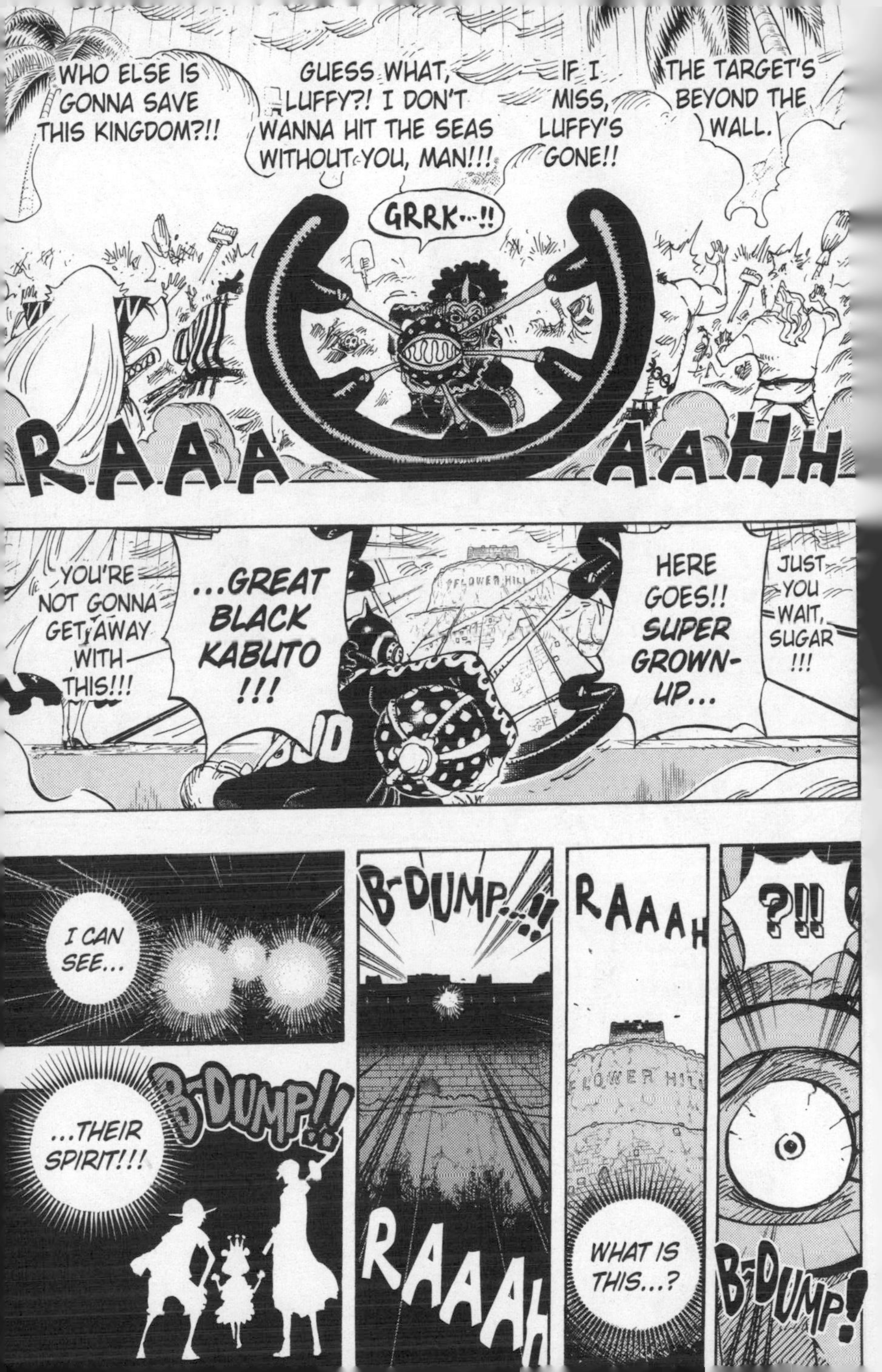
THE TARGET'S BEYOND THE WALL.
IF I MISS, LUFFY'S GONE!!
GUESS WHAT, LUFFY?! I DON'T WANNA HIT THE SEAS WITHOUT YOU, MAN!!!
WHO ELSE IS GONNA SAVE THIS KINGDOM?!!
GRRK...!!
RAAAAAHH
JUST YOU WAIT, SUGAR!!!
HERE GOES!! SUPER GROWN-UP...
...GREAT BLACK KABUTO!!!
YOU'RE NOT GONNA GET AWAY WITH THIS!!!
?!!
B-DUMP!
RAAAH
WHAT IS THIS...?
B-DUMP...!!
RAAAH
I CAN SEE...
B-DUMP!!
...THEIR SPIRIT!!!

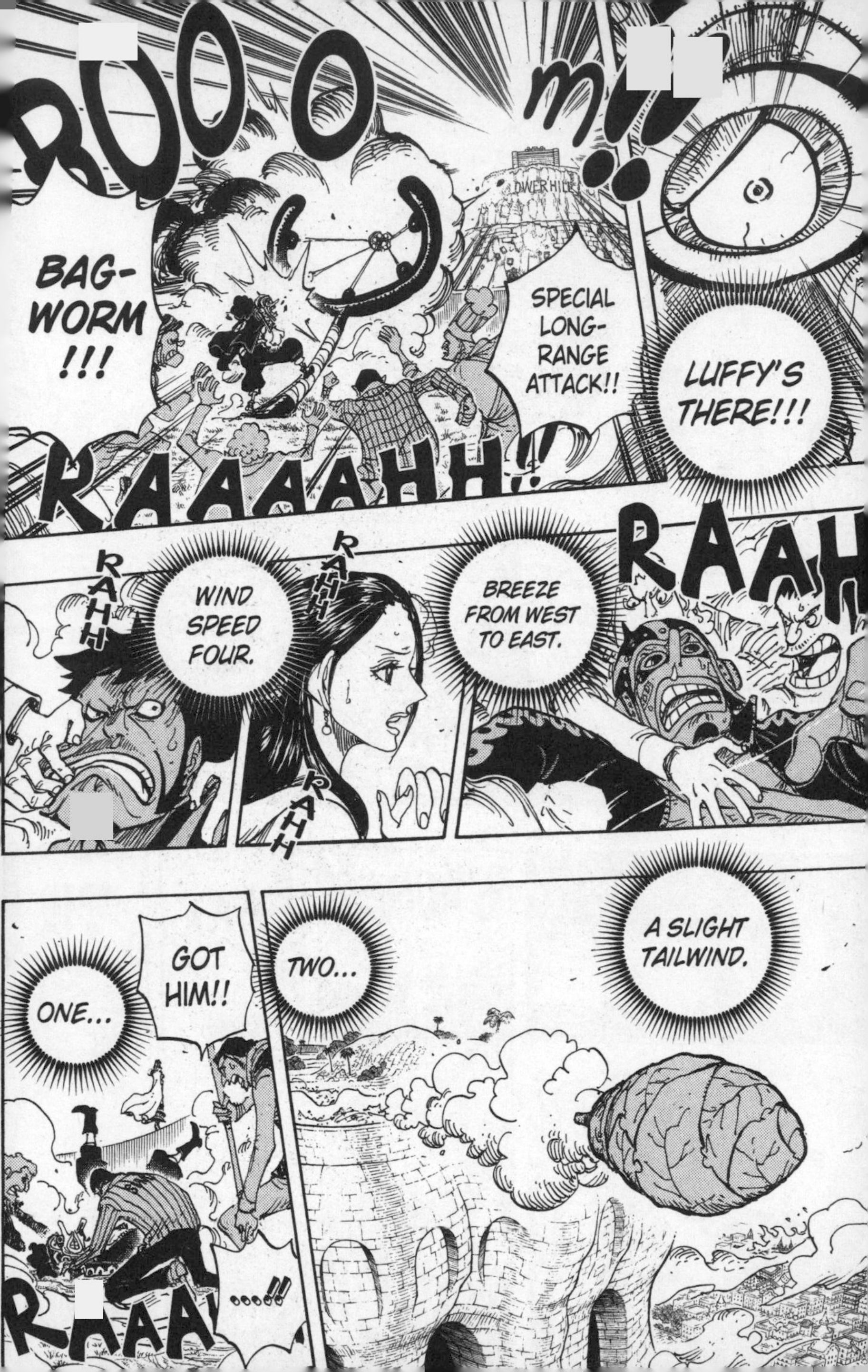
LUFFY'S THERE!!!
SPECIAL LONG-RANGE ATTACK!!
BAG-WORM!!!
RAAAAHH!!
RAAH
BREEZE FROM WEST TO EAST.
RAHH
WIND SPEED FOUR.
RAHH
A SLIGHT TAILWIND.
TWO...
GOT HIM!!
ONE...
....!!
RAAA

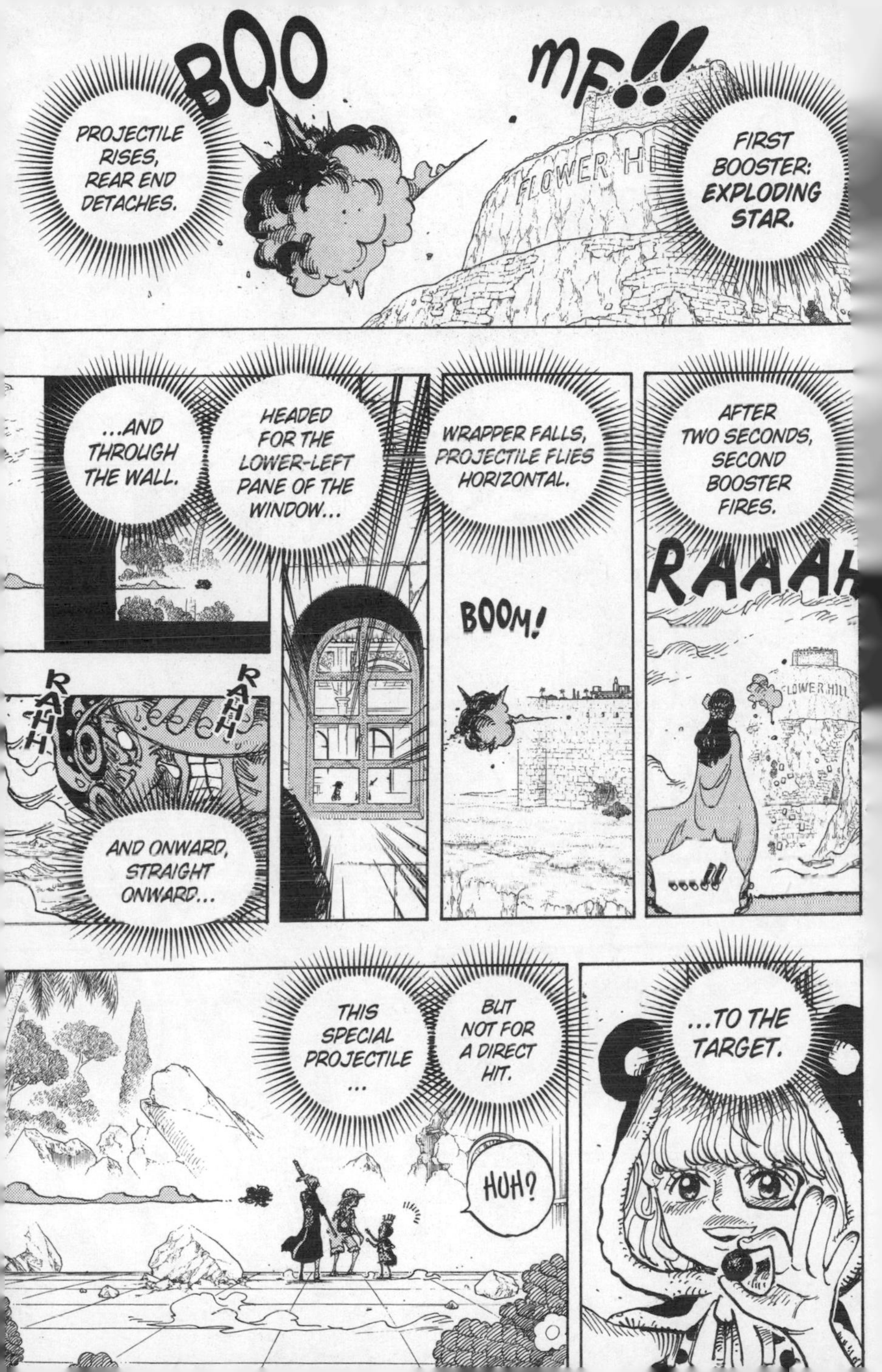
FIRST BOOSTER: EXPLODING STAR.
BOOOMF!!
FLOWER HILL
PROJECTILE RISES, REAR END DETACHES.
AFTER TWO SECONDS, SECOND BOOSTER FIRES.
RAAAH
FLOWER HILL
.....!!
WRAPPER FALLS, PROJECTILE FLIES HORIZONTAL.
BOOM!
HEADED FOR THE LOWER-LEFT PANE OF THE WINDOW...
...AND THROUGH THE WALL.
RAHH
RAHH
AND ONWARD, STRAIGHT ONWARD...
...TO THE TARGET.
BUT NOT FOR A DIRECT HIT.
THIS SPECIAL PROJECTILE ...
HUH?

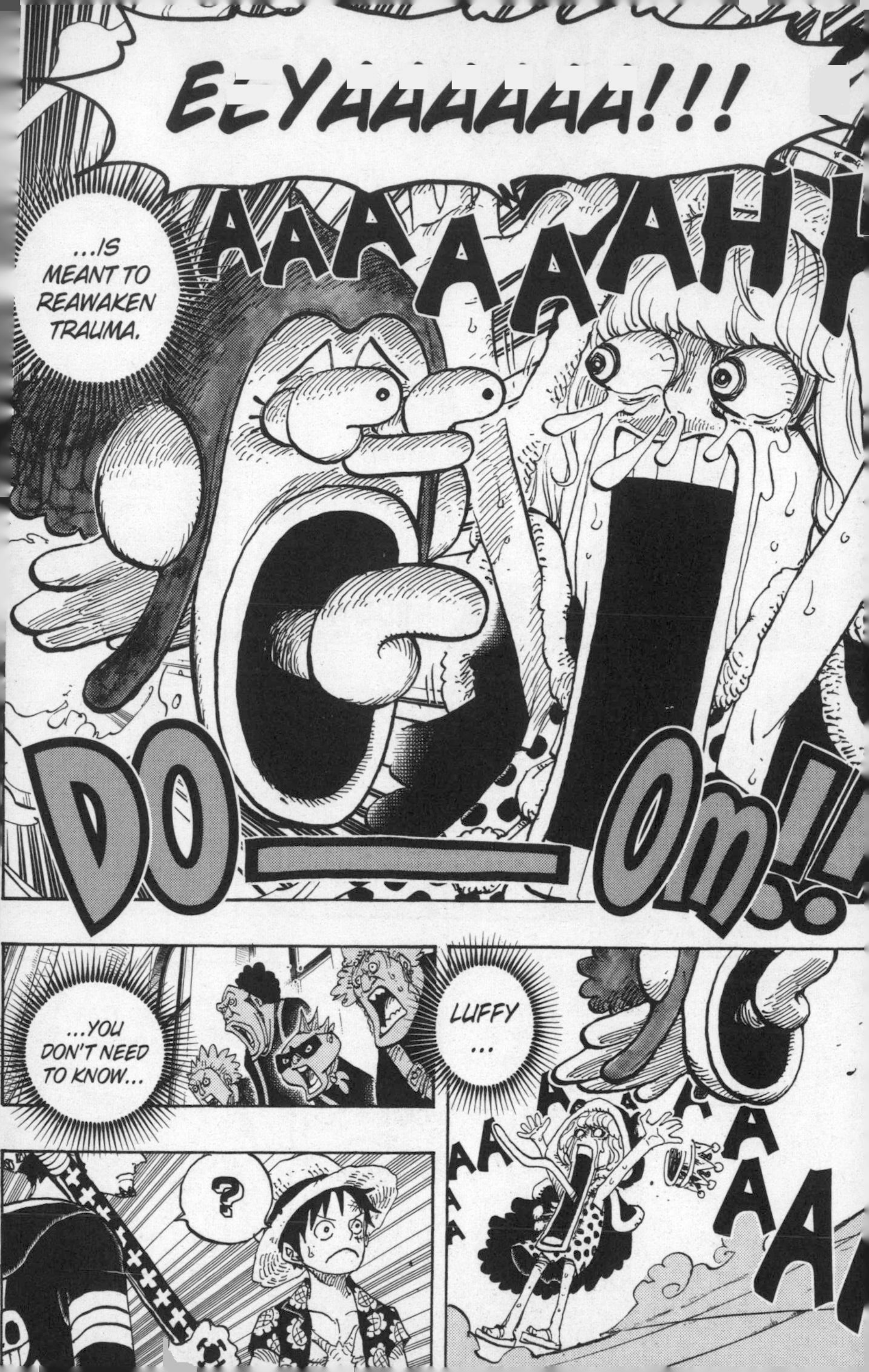
EEYAAAAAAA!!!
AAAAAAAH!!
...IS MEANT TO REAWAKEN TRAUMA.
DO—OM!!
LUFFY ...
AAAAAAAAA
...YOU DON'T NEED TO KNOW...
?

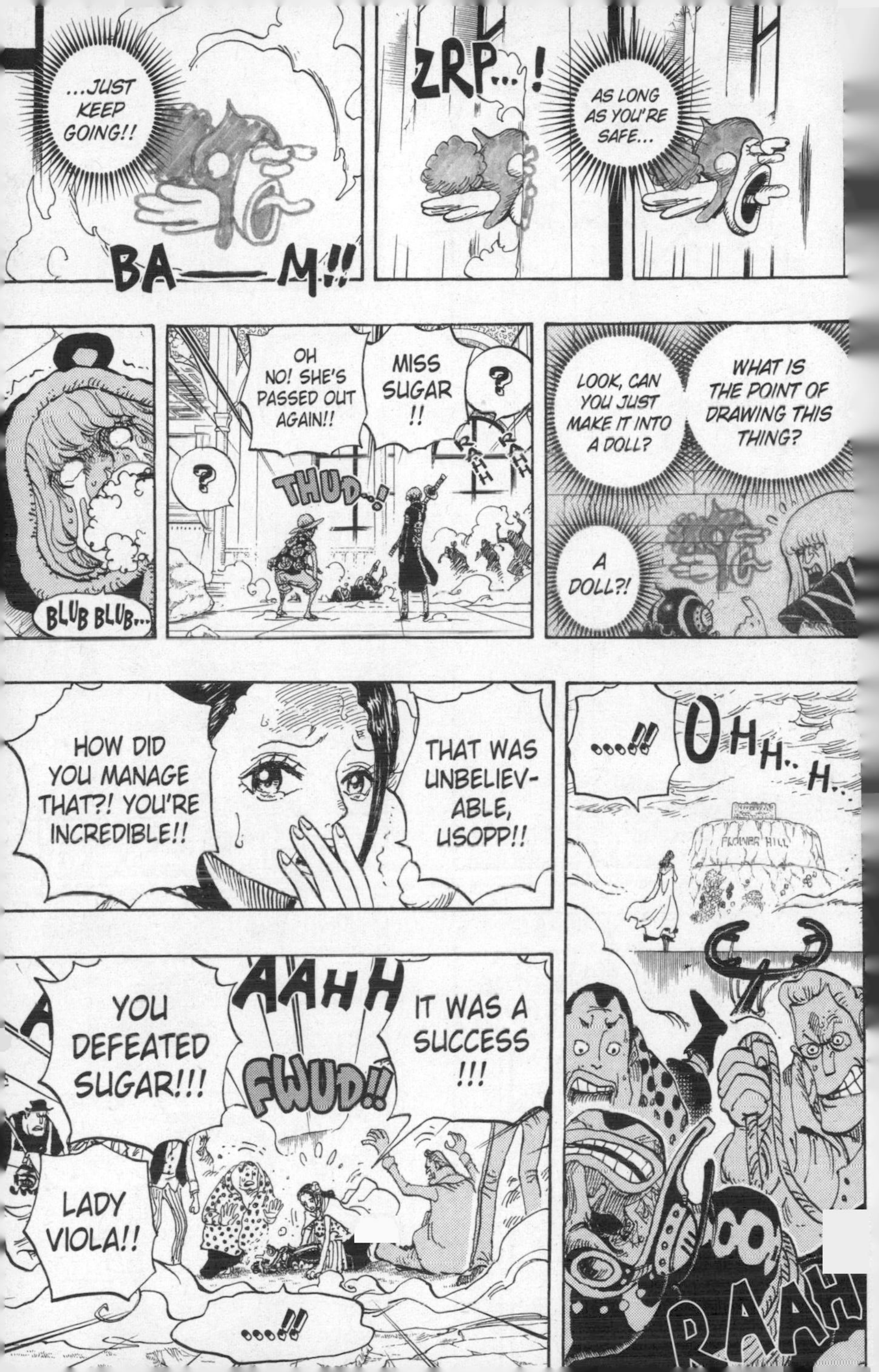
AS LONG AS YOU'RE SAFE...
ZRP...!
...JUST KEEP GOING!!
BA—M!!
WHAT IS THE POINT OF DRAWING THIS THING?
LOOK, CAN YOU JUST MAKE IT INTO A DOLL?
A DOLL?!
?
MISS SUGAR !!
OH NO! SHE'S PASSED OUT AGAIN!!
RAHH RAHH
THUD..!
?
BLUB BLUB...
...!!
OHH..H..
RAAH
THAT WAS UNBELIEV-ABLE, USOPP!!
HOW DID YOU MANAGE THAT?! YOU'RE INCREDIBLE!!
IT WAS A SUCCESS!!!
AAHH
FWUD!!
YOU DEFEATED SUGAR!!!
LADY VIOLA!!
...!!

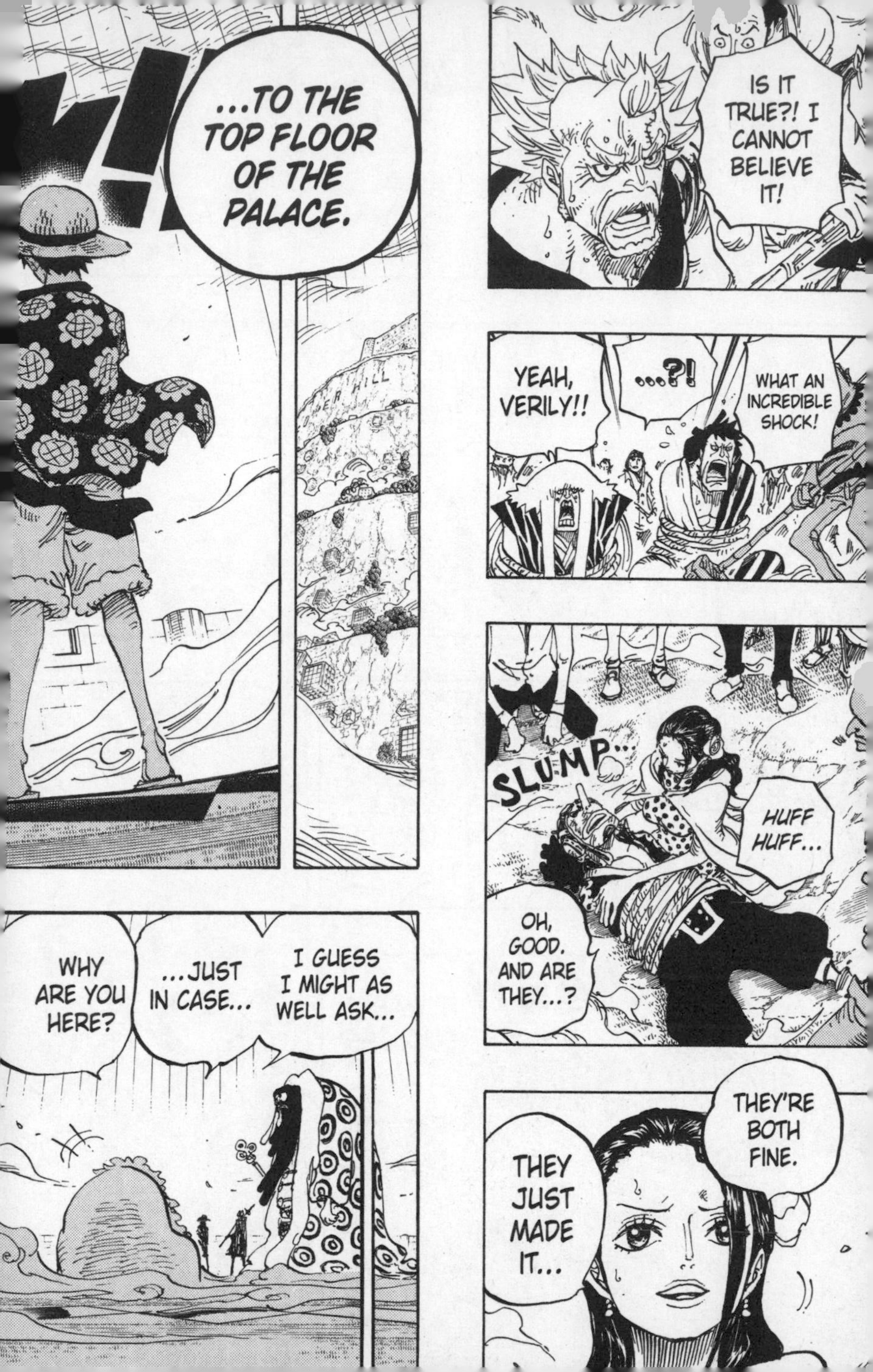
IS IT TRUE?! I CANNOT BELIEVE IT!
WHAT AN INCREDIBLE SHOCK!
...?!
YEAH, VERILY!!
HUFF HUFF...
SLUMP...
OH, GOOD. AND ARE THEY...?
THEY'RE BOTH FINE.
THEY JUST MADE IT...
...TO THE TOP FLOOR OF THE PALACE.
I GUESS I MIGHT AS WELL ASK...
...JUST IN CASE...
WHY ARE YOU HERE?

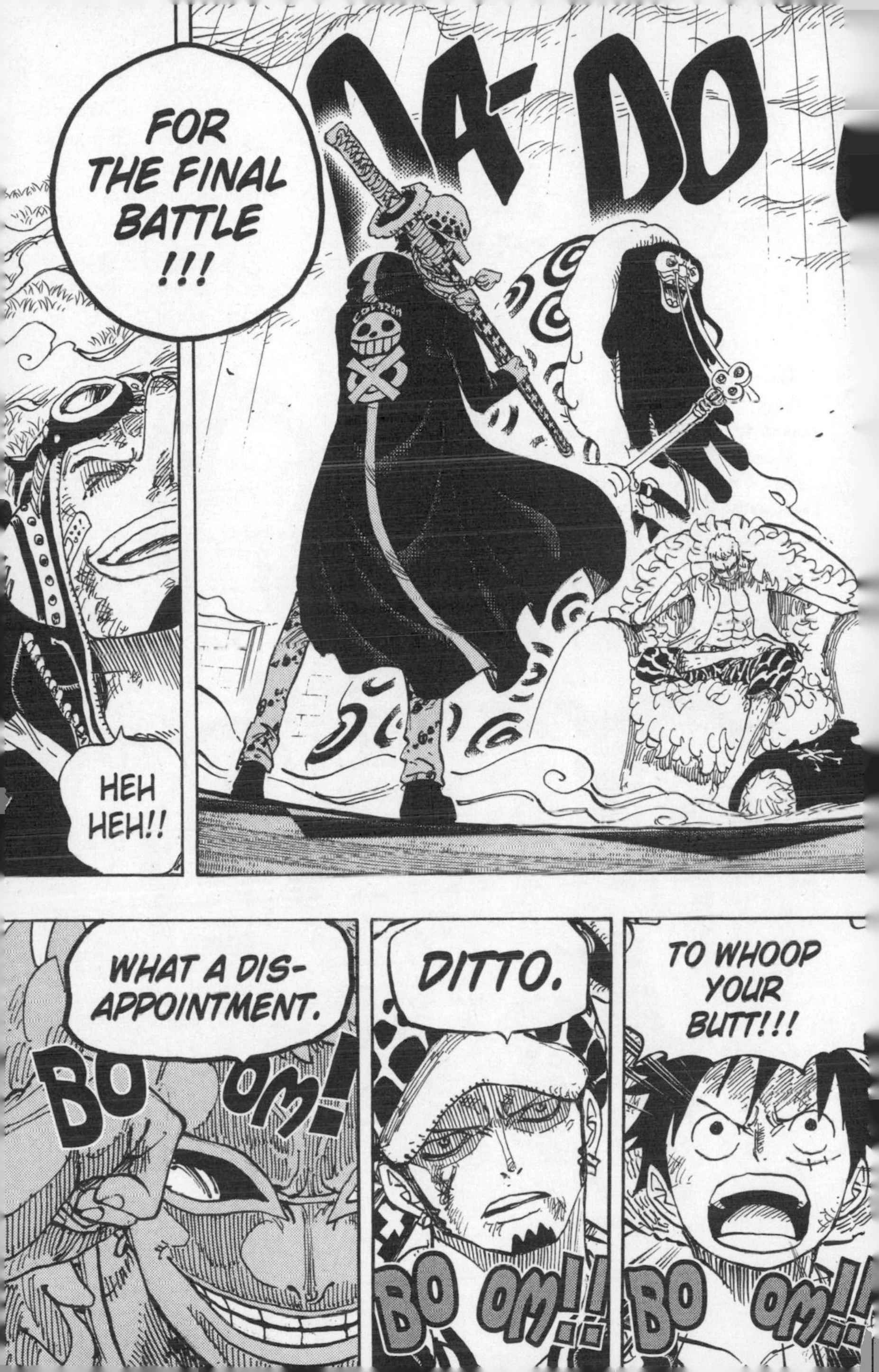
DA-DO
FOR THE FINAL BATTLE!!!
HEH HEH!!
TO WHOOP YOUR BUTT!!!
BOOM!!
DITTO.
BOOM!!
WHAT A DIS-APPOINTMENT.
BOOM!

SBS Question Corner

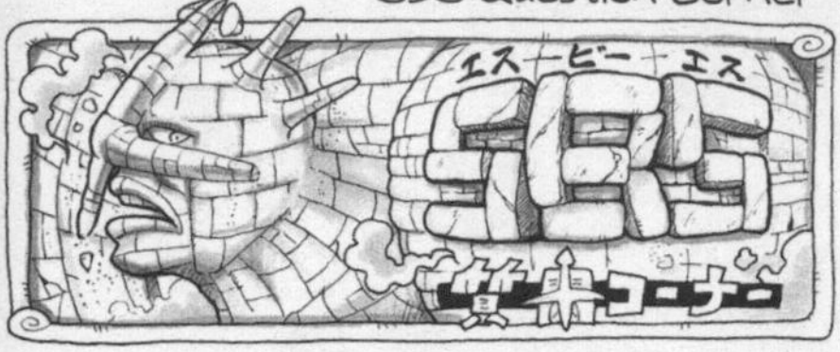
エスービーエス
SBS

(Hippo Iron, Saitama)

Q: What would the various Warlords of the Sea be like if their genders were switched by the power of the Horm-Horm Fruit?

--YMEK

A: Boy, you people really like these things. Don't you find it weird?

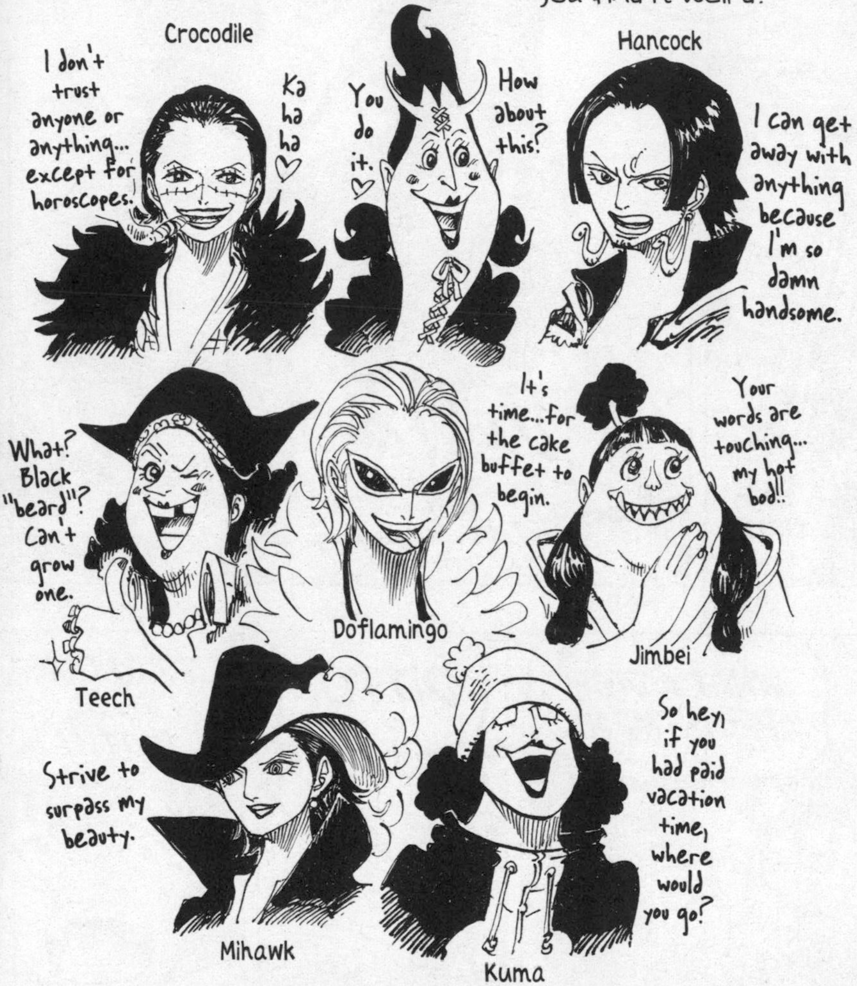
Hancock
I can get away with anything because I'm so damn handsome.
Moria
How about this?
You do it. ♡
Crocodile
Ka ha ha ♡
I don't trust anyone or anything... except for horoscopes.
Jimbei
Your words are touching... my hot bod!!
Doflamingo
It's time...for the cake buffet to begin.
Teech
What? Black "beard"? Can't grow one.
Kuma
So hey, if you had paid vacation time, where would you go?
Mihawk
Strive to surpass my beauty.

Chapter 759:
SECRET PLAN

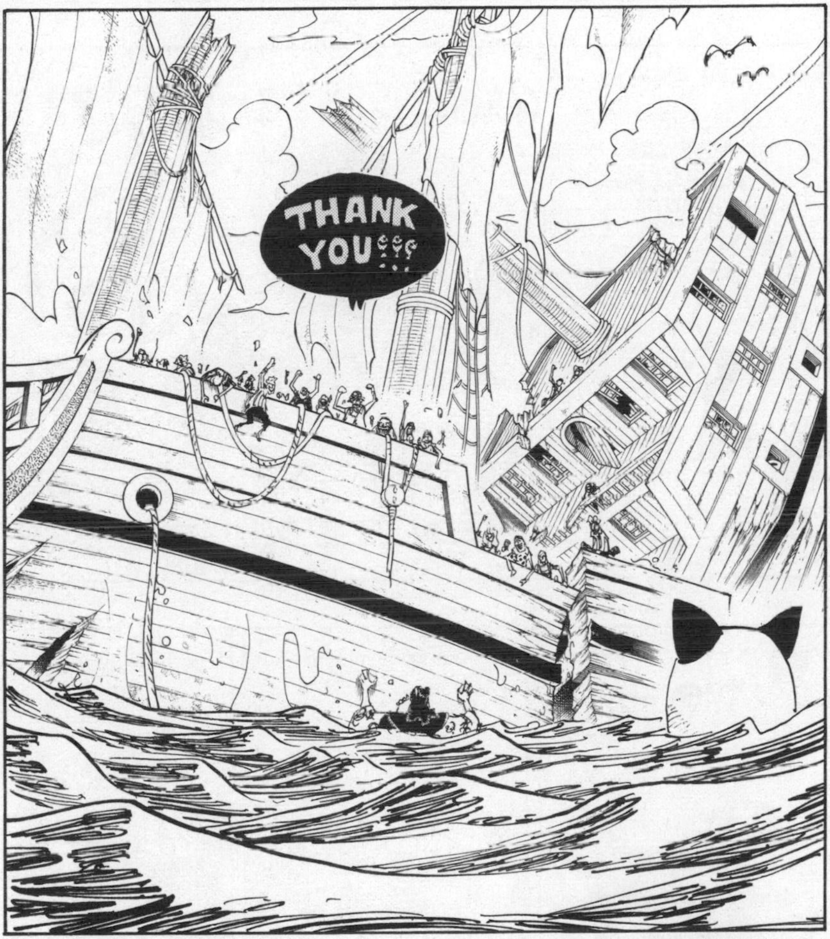
THANK YOU!!!

THE SOLITARY JOURNEY OF JIMBEI, FIRST SON OF THE SEA, VOL. 8: "SAVED THE CAPSIZED SHIP"

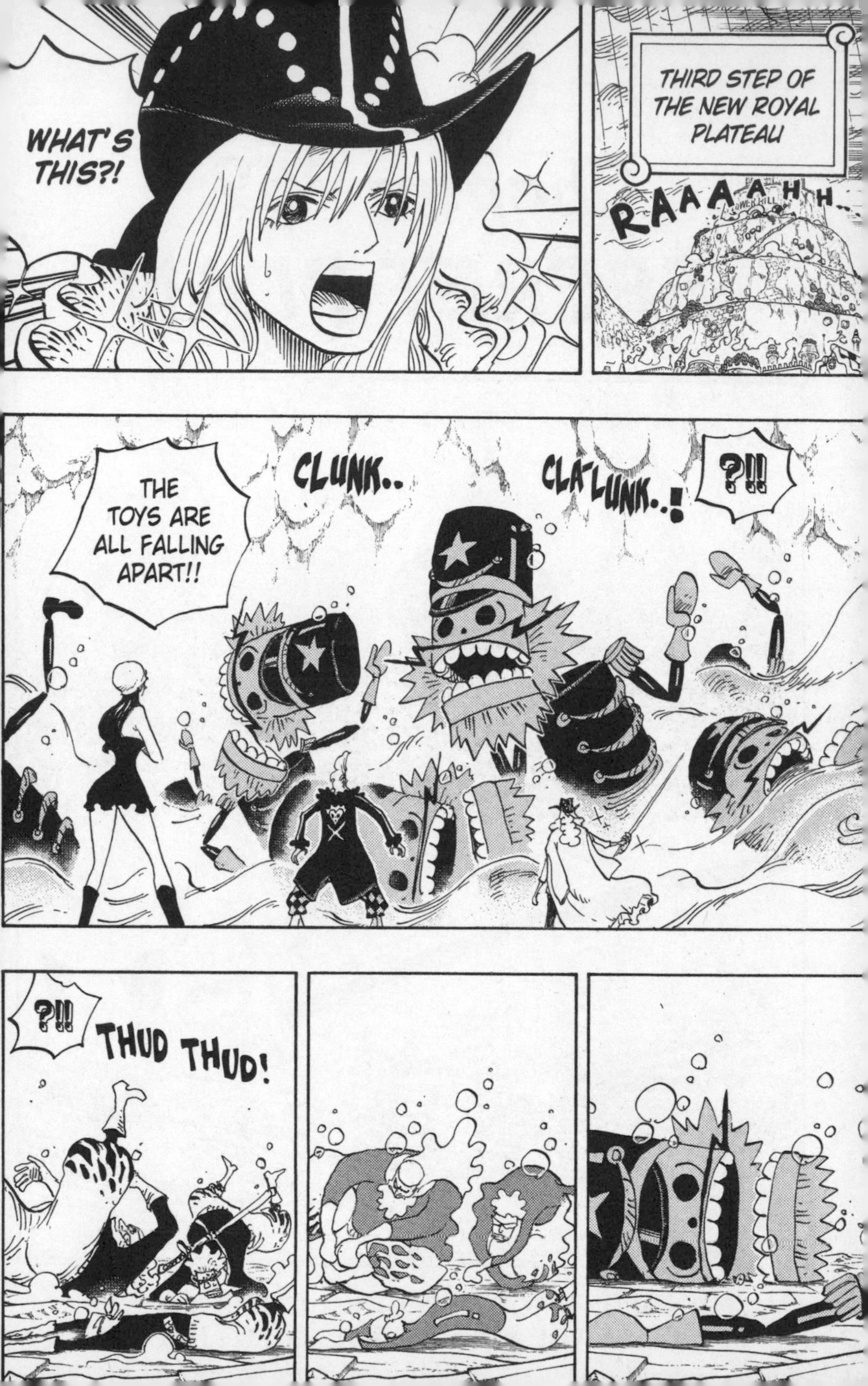
THIRD STEP OF THE NEW ROYAL PLATEAU
RAAAAHH...
WHAT'S THIS?!
?!!
CLA-LUNK..!
CLUNK..
THE TOYS ARE ALL FALLING APART!!
?!!
THUD THUD!

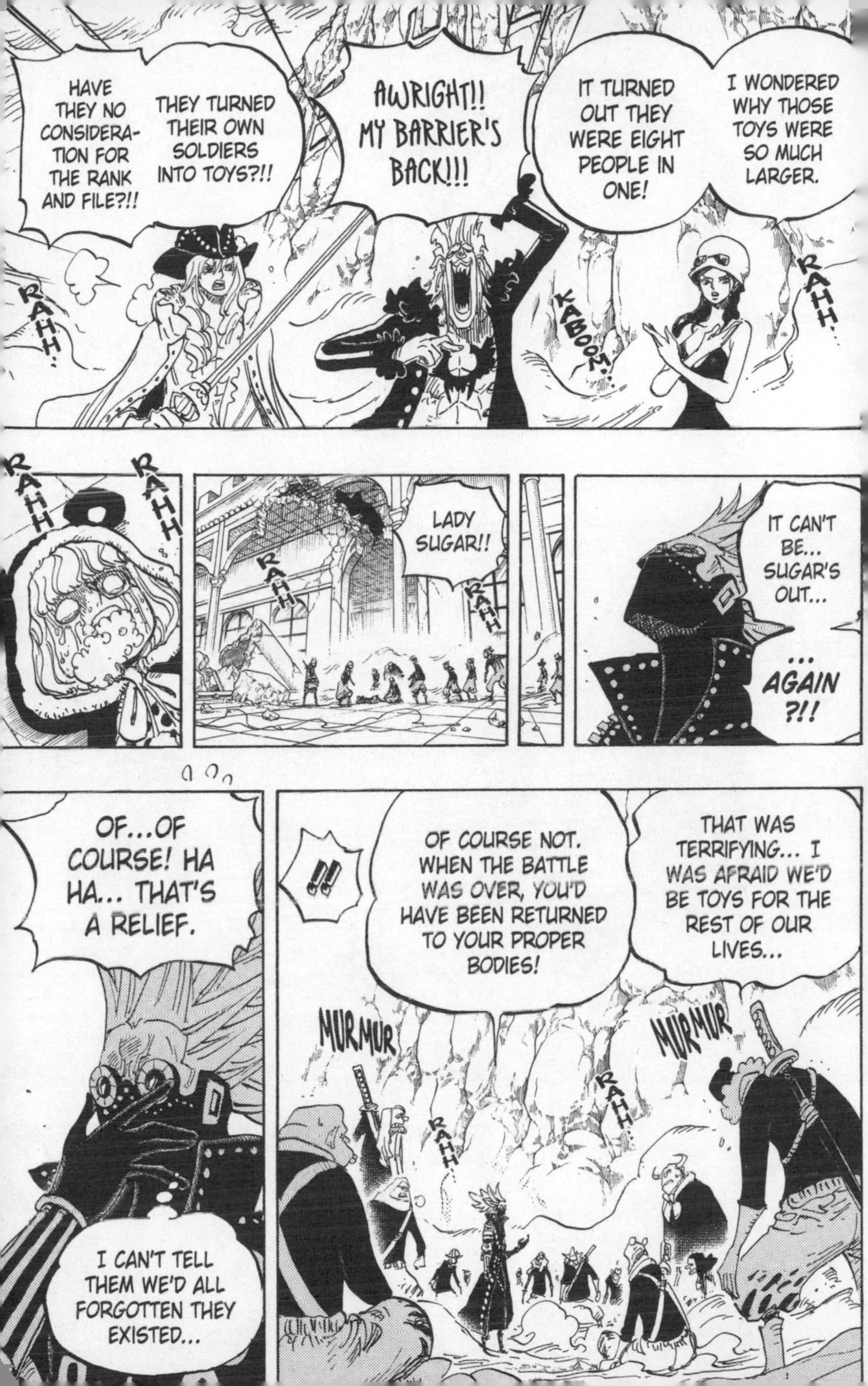
I WONDERED WHY THOSE TOYS WERE SO MUCH LARGER.
IT TURNED OUT THEY WERE EIGHT PEOPLE IN ONE!
RAHH
KABOOM
AWRIGHT!! MY BARRIER'S BACK!!!
THEY TURNED THEIR OWN SOLDIERS INTO TOYS?!!
HAVE THEY NO CONSIDERATION FOR THE RANK AND FILE?!!
RAHH
IT CAN'T BE... SUGAR'S OUT...
...AGAIN?!!
LADY SUGAR!!
RAHH
RAHH
RAHH
RAHH
THAT WAS TERRIFYING... I WAS AFRAID WE'D BE TOYS FOR THE REST OF OUR LIVES...
OF COURSE NOT. WHEN THE BATTLE WAS OVER, YOU'D HAVE BEEN RETURNED TO YOUR PROPER BODIES!
!!
MURMUR
RAHH
RAHH
MURMUR
OF...OF COURSE! HA HA... THAT'S A RELIEF.
I CAN'T TELL THEM WE'D ALL FORGOTTEN THEY EXISTED...

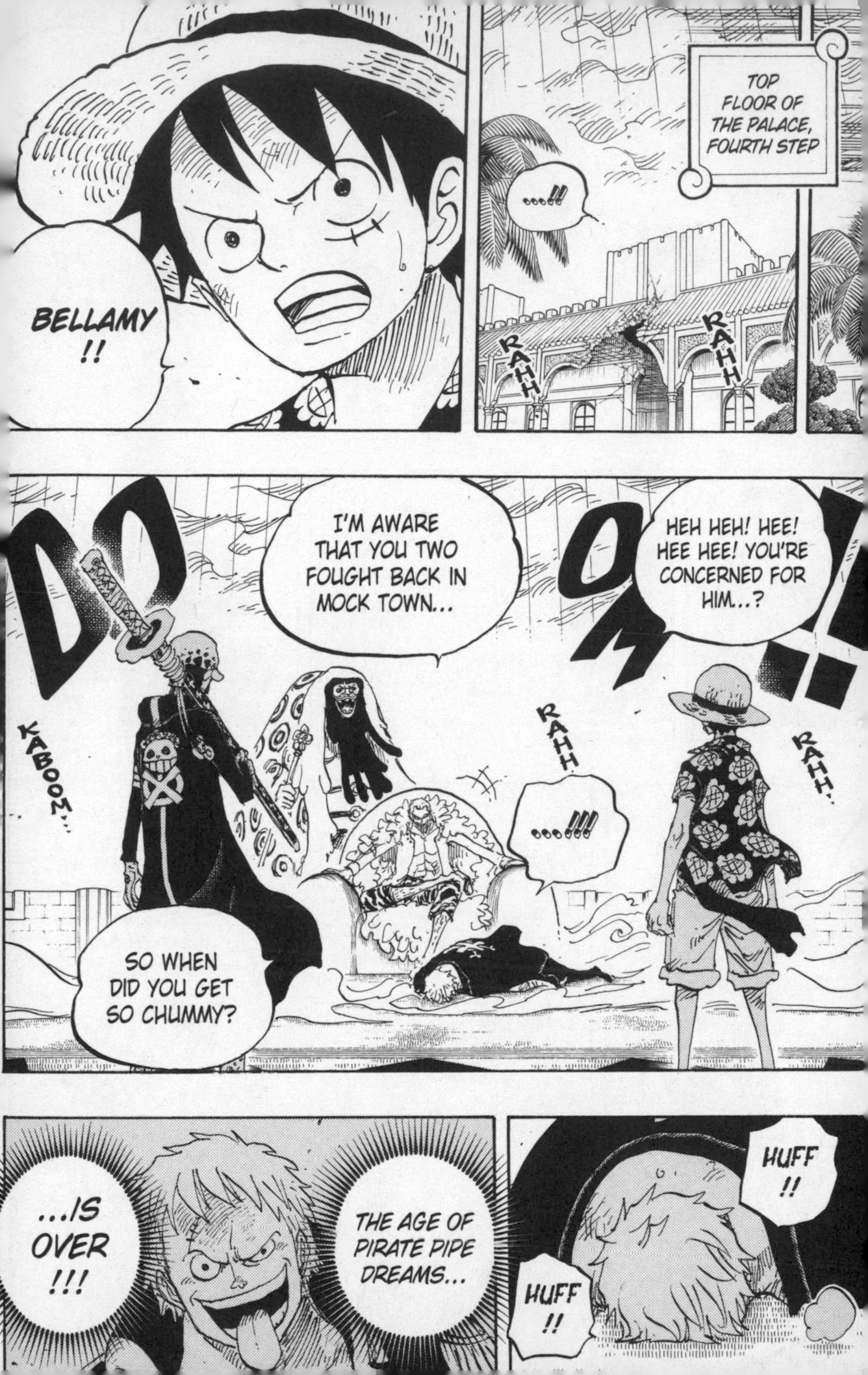
TOP FLOOR OF THE PALACE, FOURTH STEP
....!!
RAHH
RAHH
BELLAMY !!
DOOM!!
HEH HEH! HEE! HEE HEE! YOU'RE CONCERNED FOR HIM...?
RAHH
RAHH
....!!!
I'M AWARE THAT YOU TWO FOUGHT BACK IN MOCK TOWN...
KABOOM...
SO WHEN DID YOU GET SO CHUMMY?
HUFF !!
HUFF !!
THE AGE OF PIRATE PIPE DREAMS...
...IS OVER !!!

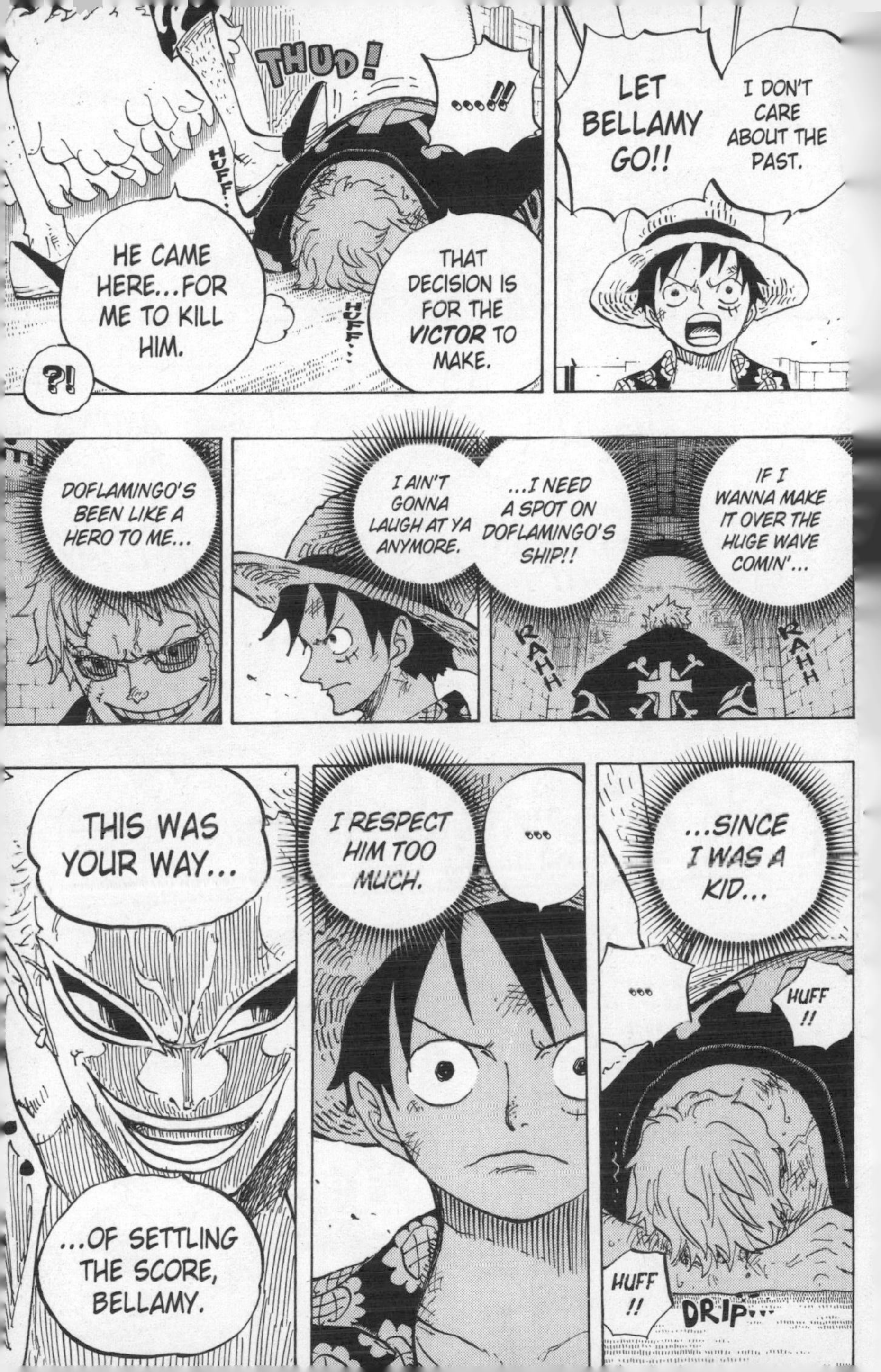
I DON'T CARE ABOUT THE PAST.
LET BELLAMY GO!!
...!!
THUD!
THAT DECISION IS FOR THE VICTOR TO MAKE.
HUFF...
HUFF...
HE CAME HERE...FOR ME TO KILL HIM.
?!
IF I WANNA MAKE IT OVER THE HUGE WAVE COMIN'...
...I NEED A SPOT ON DOFLAMINGO'S SHIP!!
RAHH
RAHH
I AIN'T GONNA LAUGH AT YA ANYMORE.
DOFLAMINGO'S BEEN LIKE A HERO TO ME...
...SINCE I WAS A KID...
...
HUFF !!
HUFF !!
DRIP...
...
I RESPECT HIM TOO MUCH.
THIS WAS YOUR WAY...
...OF SETTLING THE SCORE, BELLAMY.

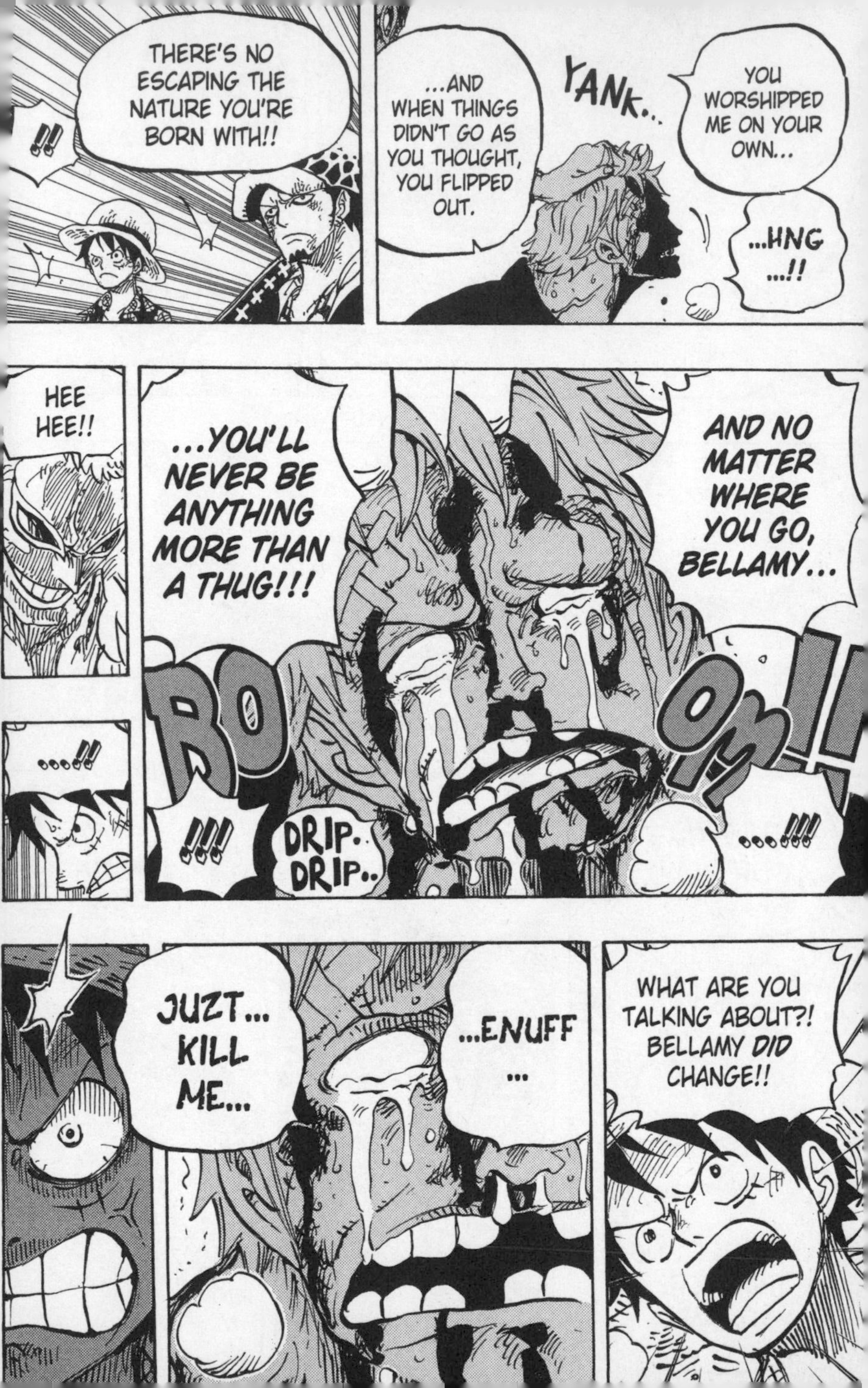
YANK...
YOU WORSHIPPED ME ON YOUR OWN...
...HNG ...!!
...AND WHEN THINGS DIDN'T GO AS YOU THOUGHT, YOU FLIPPED OUT.
THERE'S NO ESCAPING THE NATURE YOU'RE BORN WITH!!
!!
AND NO MATTER WHERE YOU GO, BELLAMY...
...YOU'LL NEVER BE ANYTHING MORE THAN A THUG!!!
RO OM!!
...!!!
DRIP. DRIP..
!!!
HEE HEE!!
...!!
WHAT ARE YOU TALKING ABOUT?! BELLAMY *DID* CHANGE!!
...ENUFF ...
JUZT... KILL ME...

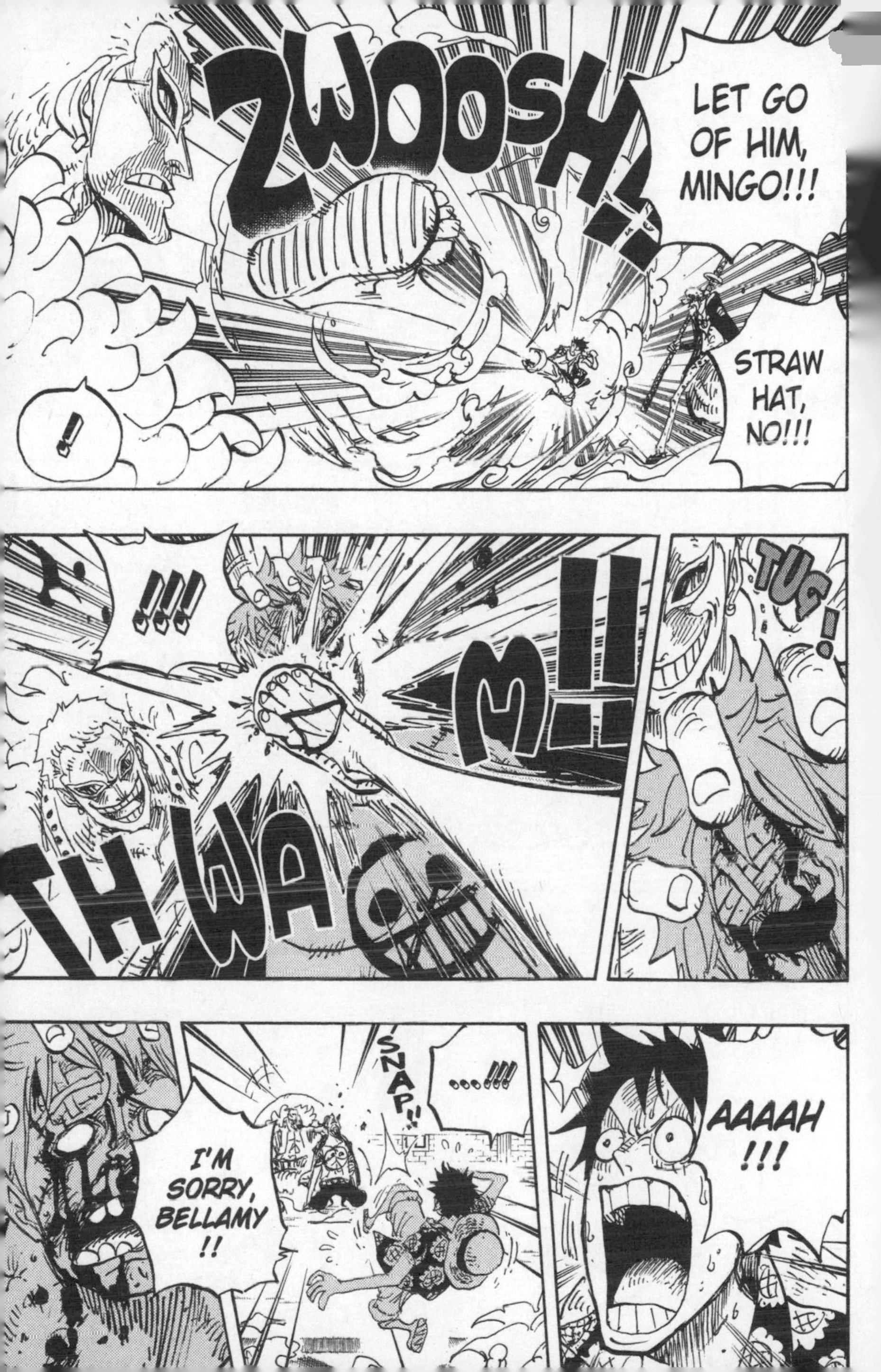
LET GO OF HIM, MINGO!!!
ZWOOSH!!
STRAW HAT, NO!!!
!
TUG!
!!!
THWAM!!
AAAAH!!!
...!!!
SNAP!!
I'M SORRY, BELLAMY!!

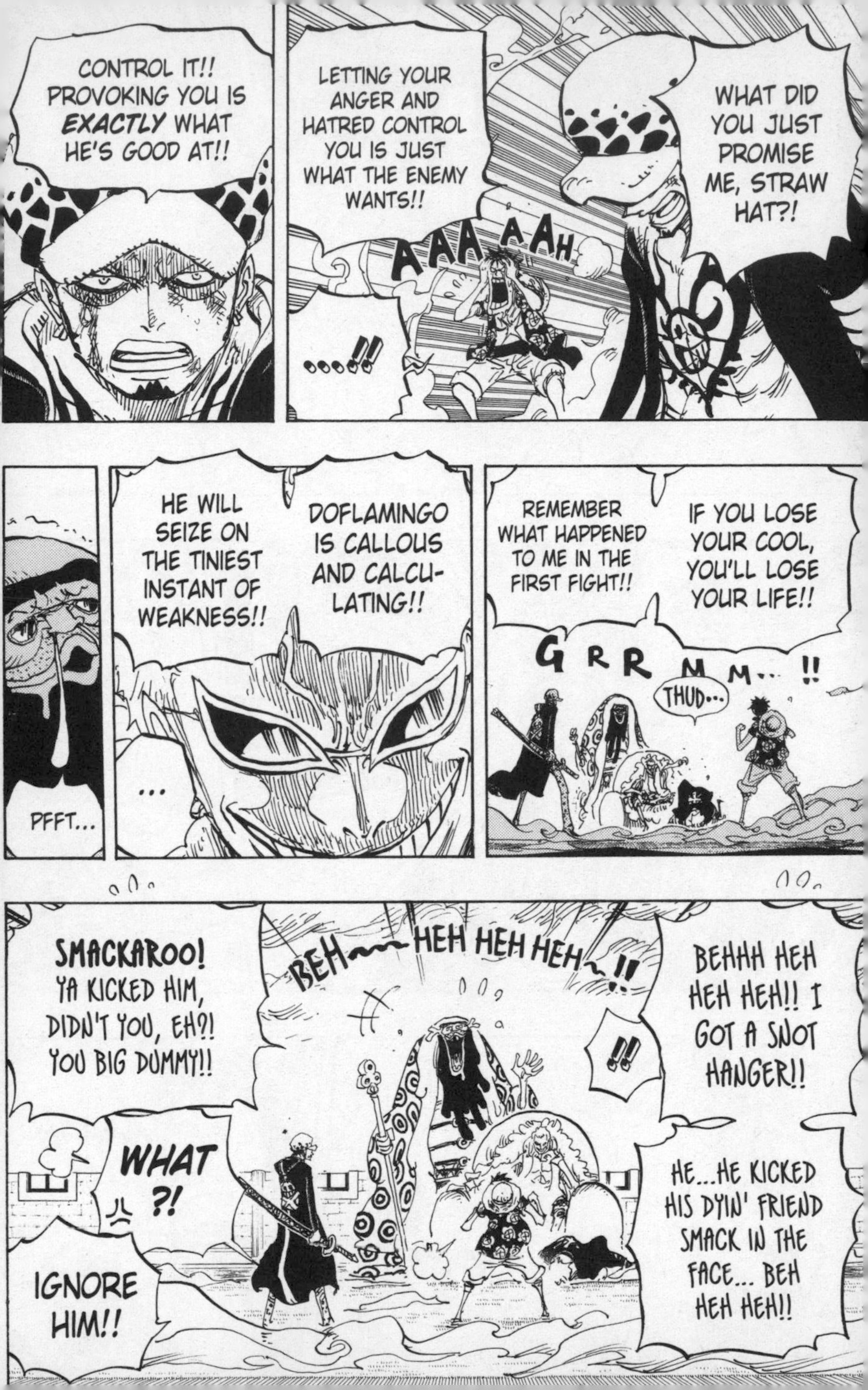
WHAT DID YOU JUST PROMISE ME, STRAW HAT?!
LETTING YOUR ANGER AND HATRED CONTROL YOU IS JUST WHAT THE ENEMY WANTS!!
AAAAAH
....!!
CONTROL IT!! PROVOKING YOU IS *EXACTLY* WHAT HE'S GOOD AT!!
IF YOU LOSE YOUR COOL, YOU'LL LOSE YOUR LIFE!!
REMEMBER WHAT HAPPENED TO ME IN THE FIRST FIGHT!!
GRRMMM...!!
THUD...
DOFLAMINGO IS CALLOUS AND CALCU-LATING!!
HE WILL SEIZE ON THE TINIEST INSTANT OF WEAKNESS!!
...
PFFT...
BEHHH HEH HEH HEH!! I GOT A SNOT HANGER!!
BEH~~HEH HEH HEH~!!
!!
SMACKAROO! YA KICKED HIM, DIDN'T YOU, EH?! YOU BIG DUMMY!!
HE...HE KICKED HIS DYIN' FRIEND SMACK IN THE FACE... BEH HEH HEH!!
WHAT?!
IGNORE HIM!!

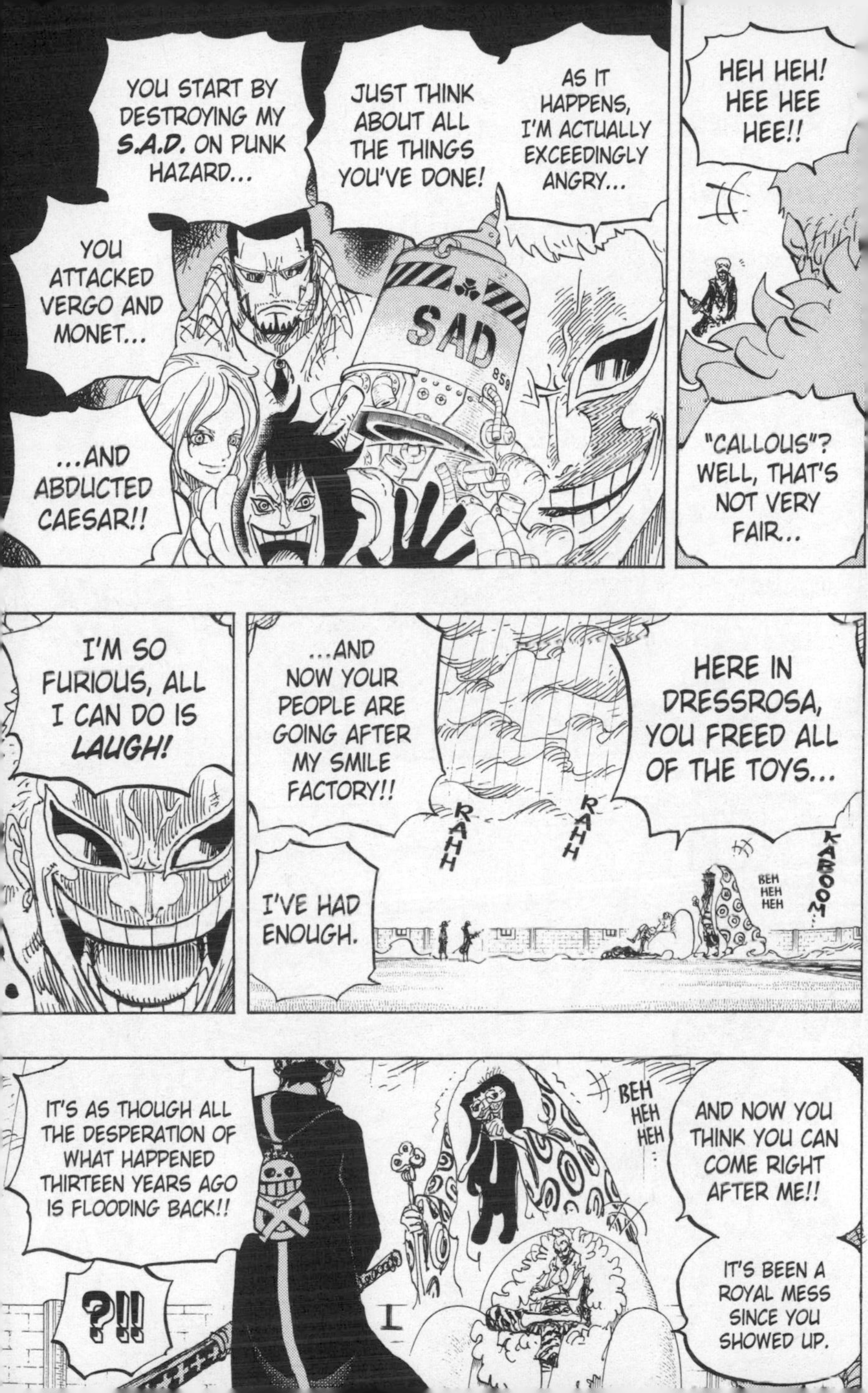
HEH HEH! HEE HEE HEE!!
"CALLOUS"? WELL, THAT'S NOT VERY FAIR...
AS IT HAPPENS, I'M ACTUALLY EXCEEDINGLY ANGRY...
JUST THINK ABOUT ALL THE THINGS YOU'VE DONE!
YOU START BY DESTROYING MY *S.A.D.* ON PUNK HAZARD...
SAD
YOU ATTACKED VERGO AND MONET...
...AND ABDUCTED CAESAR!!
HERE IN DRESSROSA, YOU FREED ALL OF THE TOYS...
KABOOM...
BEH HEH HEH
RAHH
RAHH
...AND NOW YOUR PEOPLE ARE GOING AFTER MY SMILE FACTORY!!
I'VE HAD ENOUGH.
I'M SO FURIOUS, ALL I CAN DO IS *LAUGH!*
AND NOW YOU THINK YOU CAN COME RIGHT AFTER ME!!
IT'S BEEN A ROYAL MESS SINCE YOU SHOWED UP.
BEH HEH HEH
IT'S AS THOUGH ALL THE DESPERATION OF WHAT HAPPENED THIRTEEN YEARS AGO IS FLOODING BACK!!
?!!

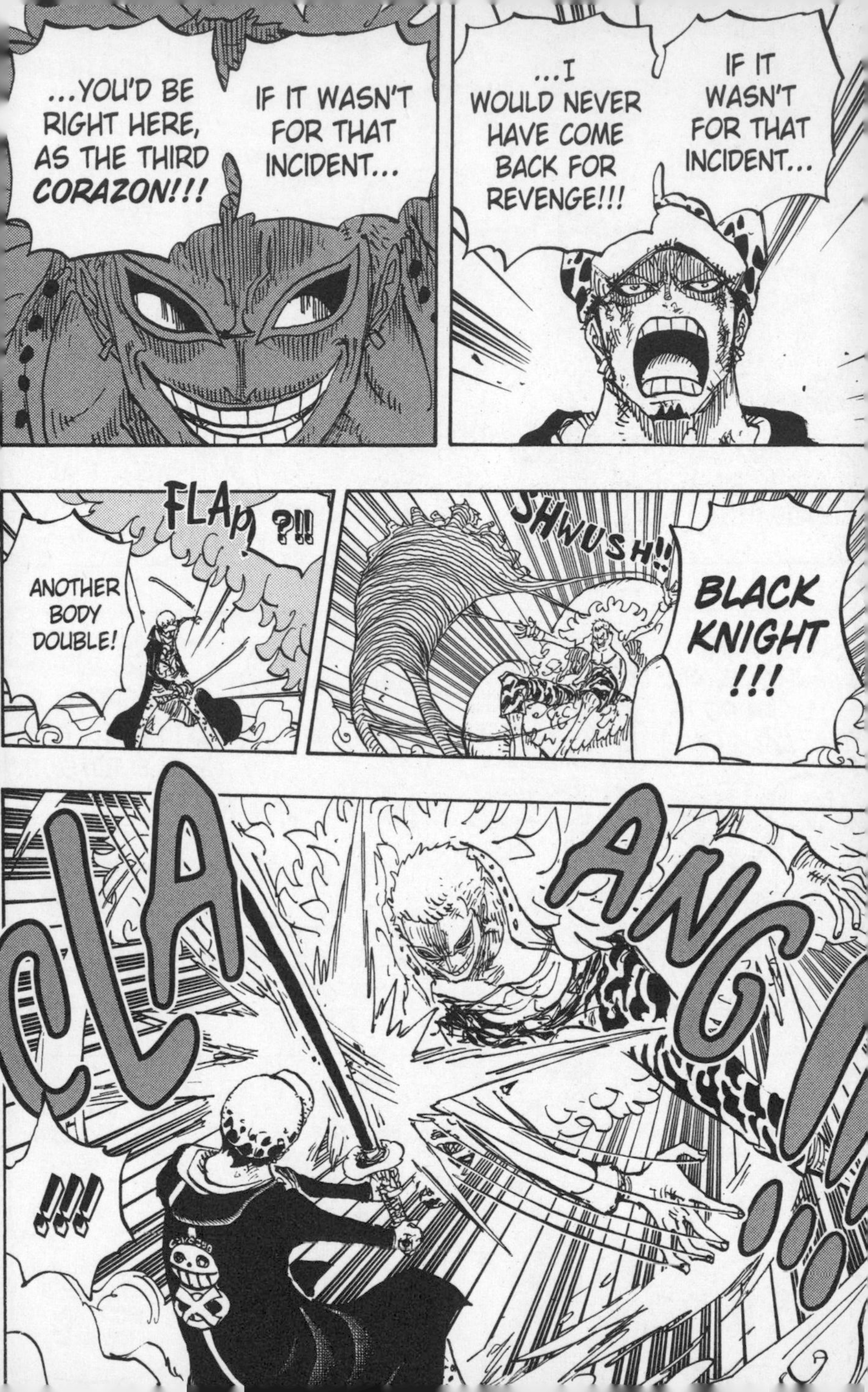

IF IT WASN'T FOR THAT INCIDENT...
...I WOULD NEVER HAVE COME BACK FOR REVENGE!!!
IF IT WASN'T FOR THAT INCIDENT...
...YOU'D BE RIGHT HERE, AS THE THIRD CORAZON!!!
SHWUSH!!
BLACK KNIGHT!!!
FLAP
?!!
ANOTHER BODY DOUBLE!
CLAANG!!
!!!

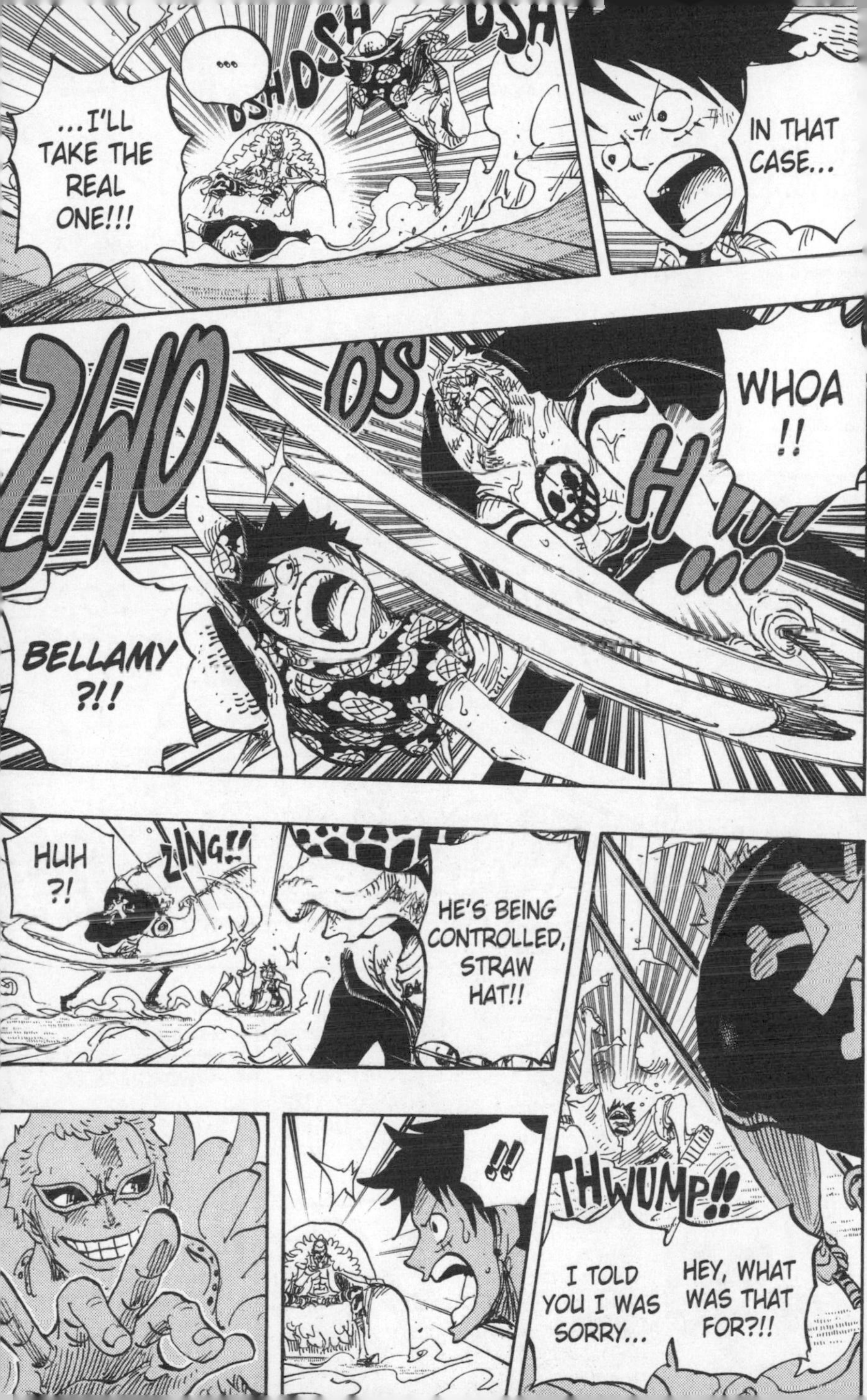
IN THAT CASE...
DSH DSH DSH
...
...I'LL TAKE THE REAL ONE!!!
WHOA!!
ZWOOSH!!!
BELLAMY?!!
THWUMP!!
HEY, WHAT WAS THAT FOR?!!
I TOLD YOU I WAS SORRY...
HE'S BEING CONTROLLED, STRAW HAT!!
ZING!!
HUH?!
!!

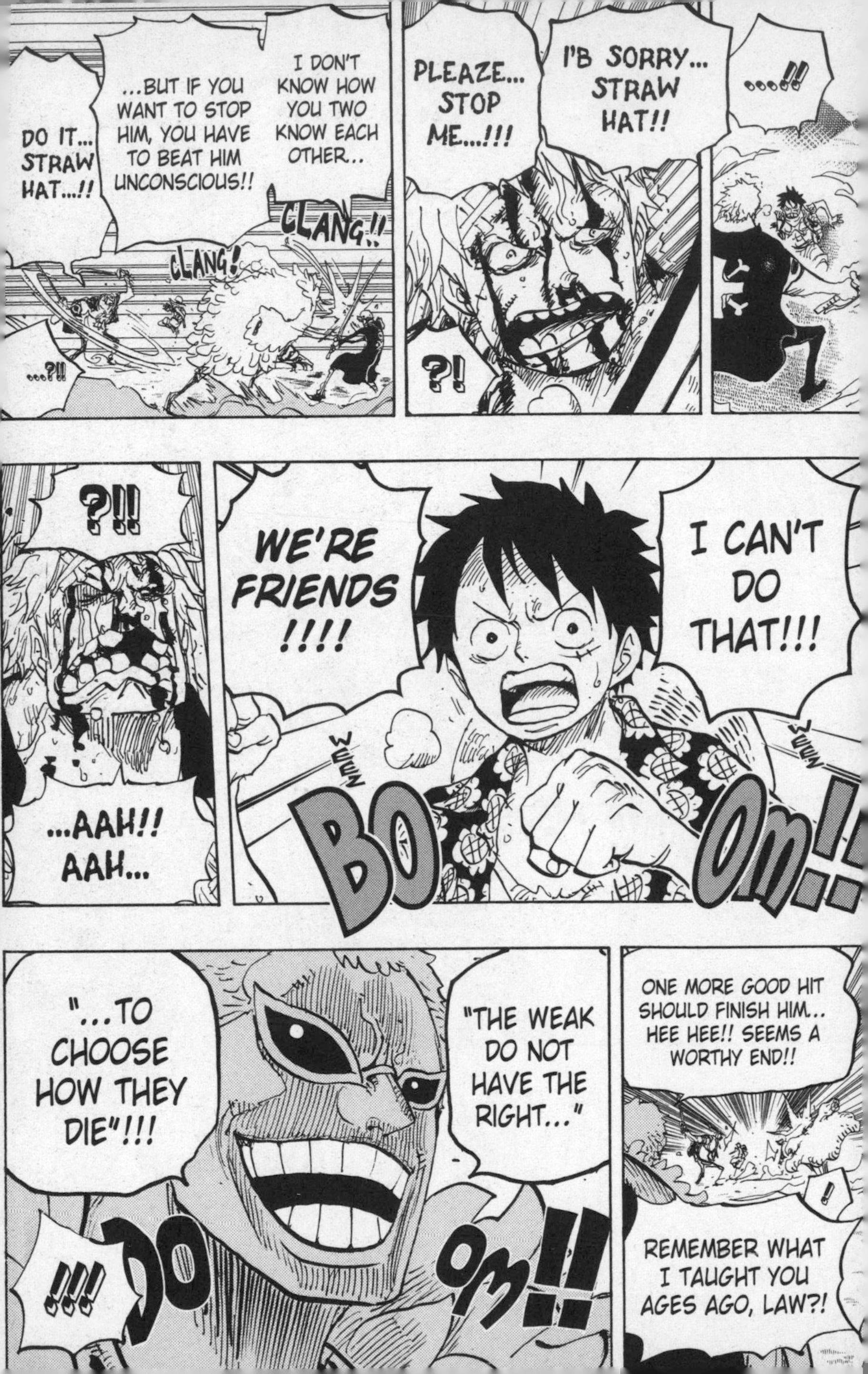
...!!
I'B SORRY... STRAW HAT!!
PLEAZE... STOP ME...!!!
?!
I DON'T KNOW HOW YOU TWO KNOW EACH OTHER...
...BUT IF YOU WANT TO STOP HIM, YOU HAVE TO BEAT HIM UNCONSCIOUS!!
DO IT... STRAW HAT...!!
CLANG!!
CLANG!
...?!!
I CAN'T DO THAT!!!
WE'RE FRIENDS!!!!
WEEN
BOOM!!
WEEN
?!!
...AAH!! AAH...
ONE MORE GOOD HIT SHOULD FINISH HIM.. HEE HEE!! SEEMS A WORTHY END!!
!
REMEMBER WHAT I TAUGHT YOU AGES AGO, LAW?!
"THE WEAK DO NOT HAVE THE RIGHT..."
"...TO CHOOSE HOW THEY DIE"!!!
DOOM!!
!!!

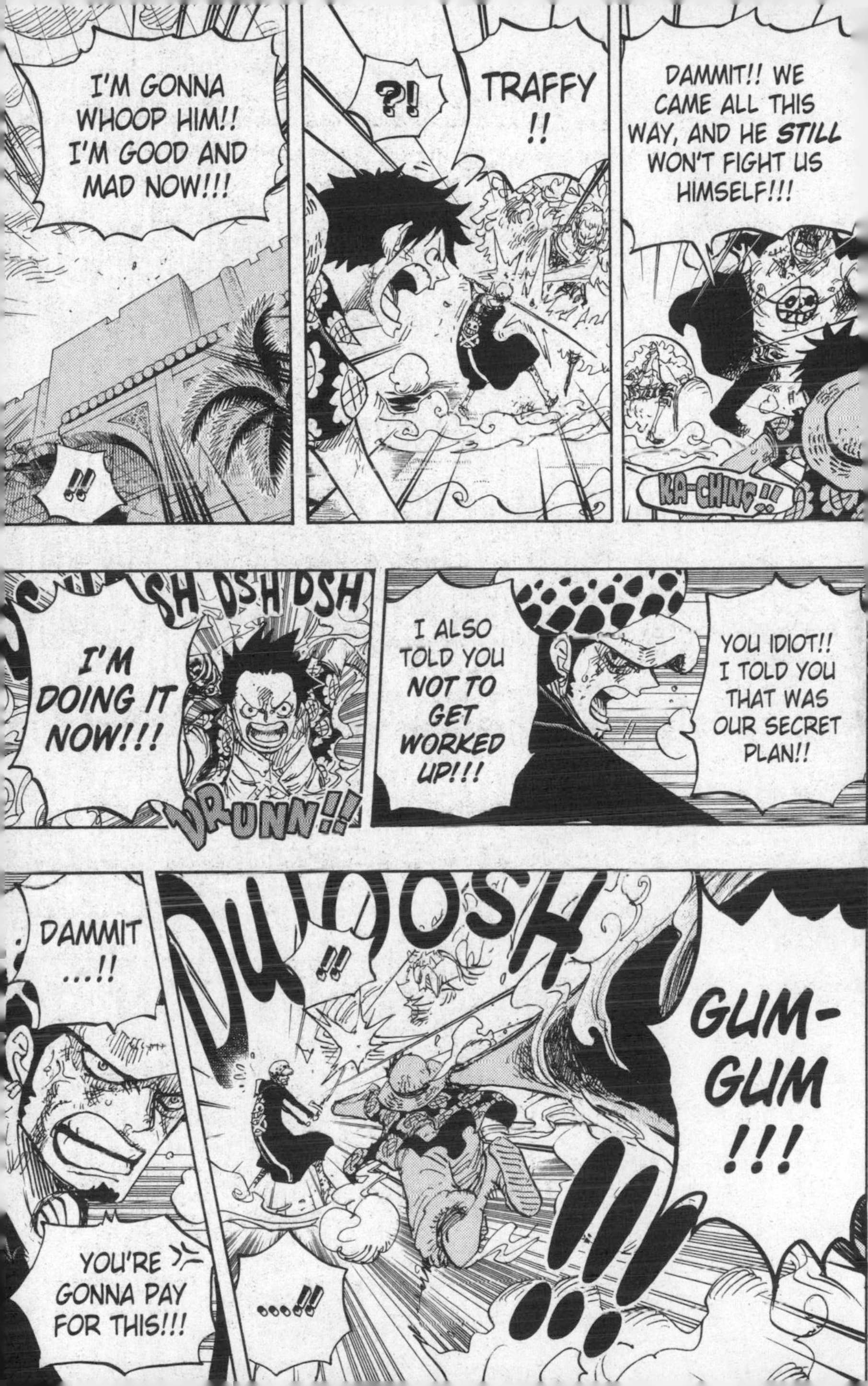
DAMMIT!! WE CAME ALL THIS WAY, AND HE STILL WON'T FIGHT US HIMSELF!!!
KA-CHING!!
TRAFFY!!
?!
I'M GONNA WHOOP HIM!! I'M GOOD AND MAD NOW!!!
!!
YOU IDIOT!! I TOLD YOU THAT WAS OUR SECRET PLAN!!
I ALSO TOLD YOU NOT TO GET WORKED UP!!!
SH DSH DSH
I'M DOING IT NOW!!!
VRUNN!!
DWOOSH
GUM-GUM!!!
!!
....!!
DAMMIT...!!
YOU'RE GONNA PAY FOR THIS!!!

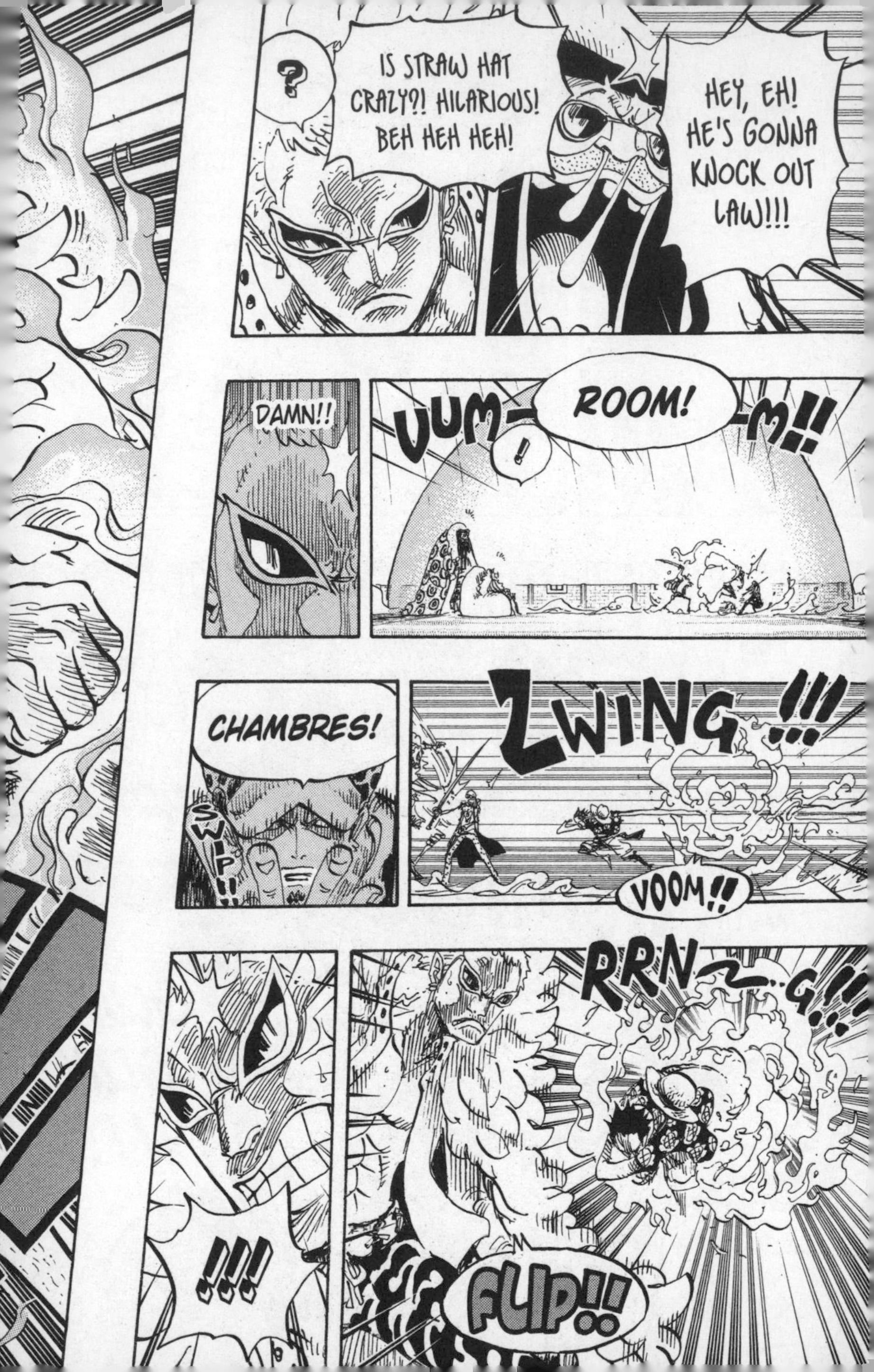
HEY, EH! HE'S GONNA KNOCK OUT LAW!!!
?
IS STRAW HAT CRAZY?! HILARIOUS! BEH HEH HEH!
UUM-
ROOM!
-M!!
!
DAMN!!
ZWING!!!
VOOM!!
CHAMBRES!
SWIP!!
RRN~G!!!
FLIP!!
!!!

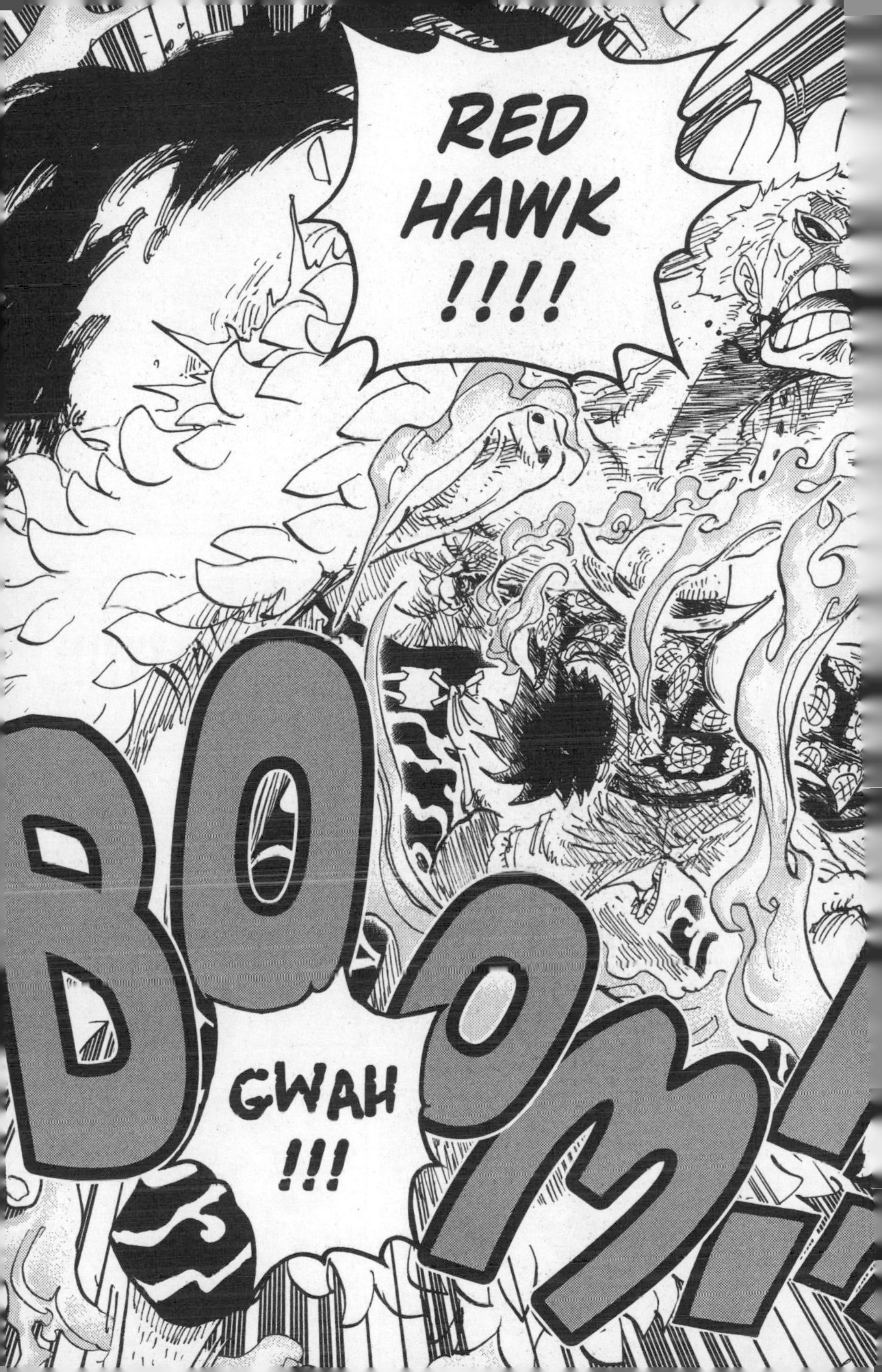
RED HAWK !!!!
BOOSH!!
GWAH !!!

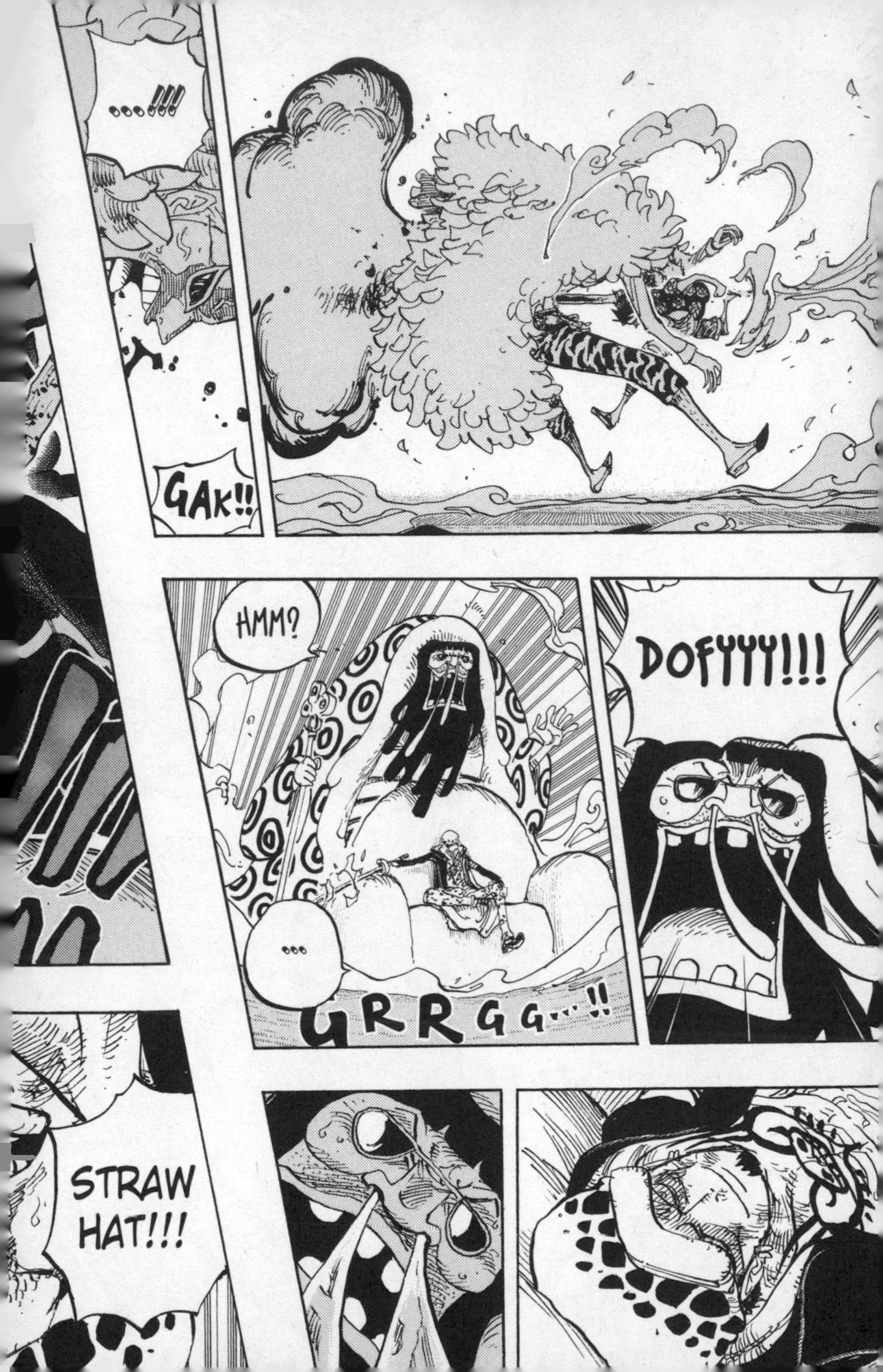
...!!!
GAK!!
DOFYYY!!!
HMM?
...
GRRGG...!!
STRAW HAT!!!

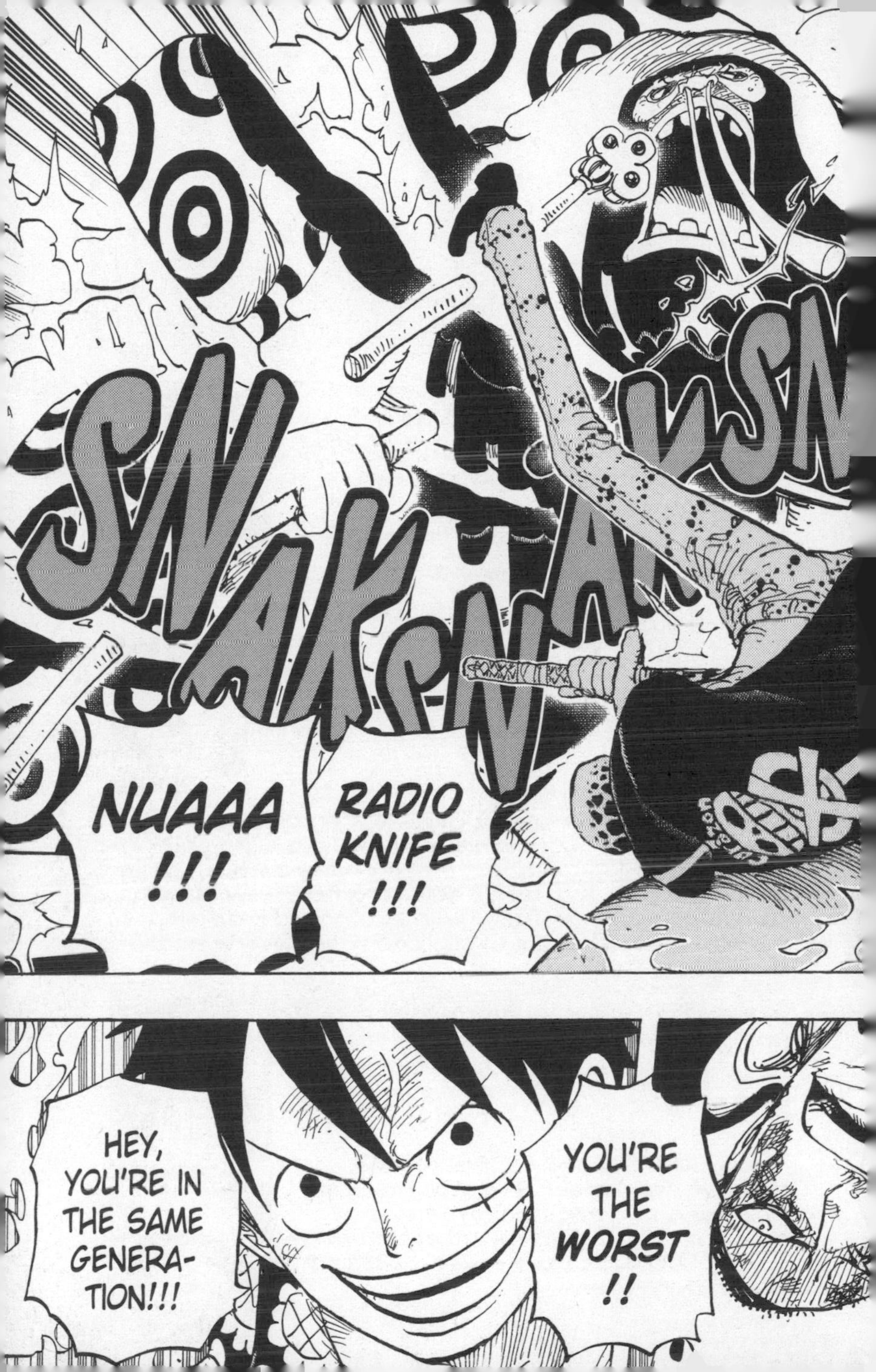
SNAK
RADIO KNIFE!!!
NUAAA!!!
YOU'RE THE WORST!!
HEY, YOU'RE IN THE SAME GENERA-TION!!!

SBS Question Corner

質問コーナー
エス
ビー
エス

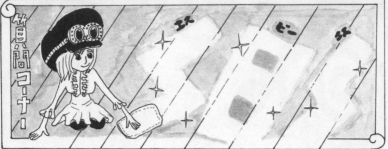

(Moyashicchi, Osaka)

Q: Hello, Odacchi! My question is, this fellow from Chapter 341 in Volume 36 was introduced as Happa in the SBS of Volume 43, but in the data book *One Piece Blue Deep,* it says his name is Mr. Yamao. Explain!

--Bon Voyage

A: Okay. His name is Happa Yamao.

Q: Naaa ha ha ha ha ha ha ha! Howdy! This is UME! If all you do is stare at Nami's chest, you get a blast of orange juice in your eyes! *Squoosh!* Anyway, I noticed that many manga artists have their own Twitter accounts now. Why don't you, Odacchi? Now prepare for a stream of searing citrus juice at your eyes! *Squoosh!*

--UME

A: Yeow! That stings! Knock it off! Is this fresh-squeezed?! Anyway... Twitter. Does everyone really have a Twitter now? Well, I won't. I don't ever put myself directly on the Internet. I haven't before, and I won't now. I only release messages through Shueisha or Toei. The only thing I do is submit scribbled doodles for the official one-piece.com site, because they said so. That's it.

Q: On page 158 of Volume 13, Dorry says that giants live three times as long as humans. How long do the little Tontattas live? It must be long, since Wicka looks like that at age 27.

--OP Girl

(age 159)

(age 27)

A: That's right. Some giants live to 300, some live even longer. The little people all look young, but that's mostly because of their proportions. I've heard they can live to be 150, though. Dey live just a widdle bit longer than humans.

Chapter 760:
THE SAME BET

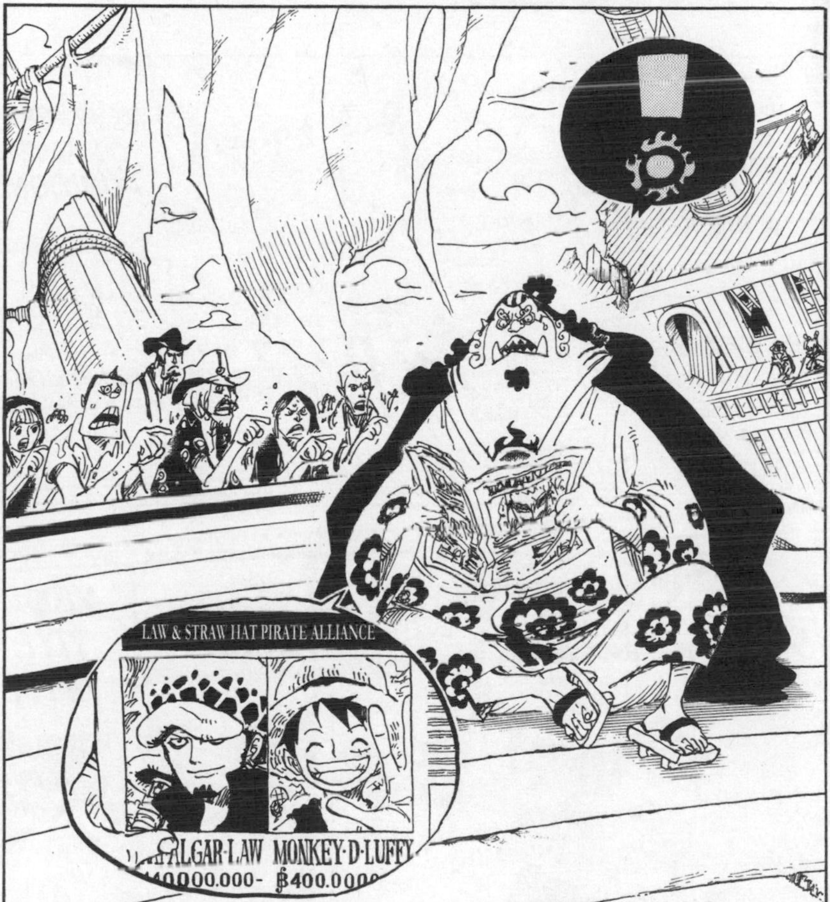
LAW & STRAW HAT PIRATE ALLIANCE
MONKEY·D·LUFFY

THE SOLITARY JOURNEY OF JIMBEI, FIRST SON OF THE SEA, VOL. 9: "THE SAILORS' NEWSPAPER TELLS OF LUFFY'S ALLIANCE"

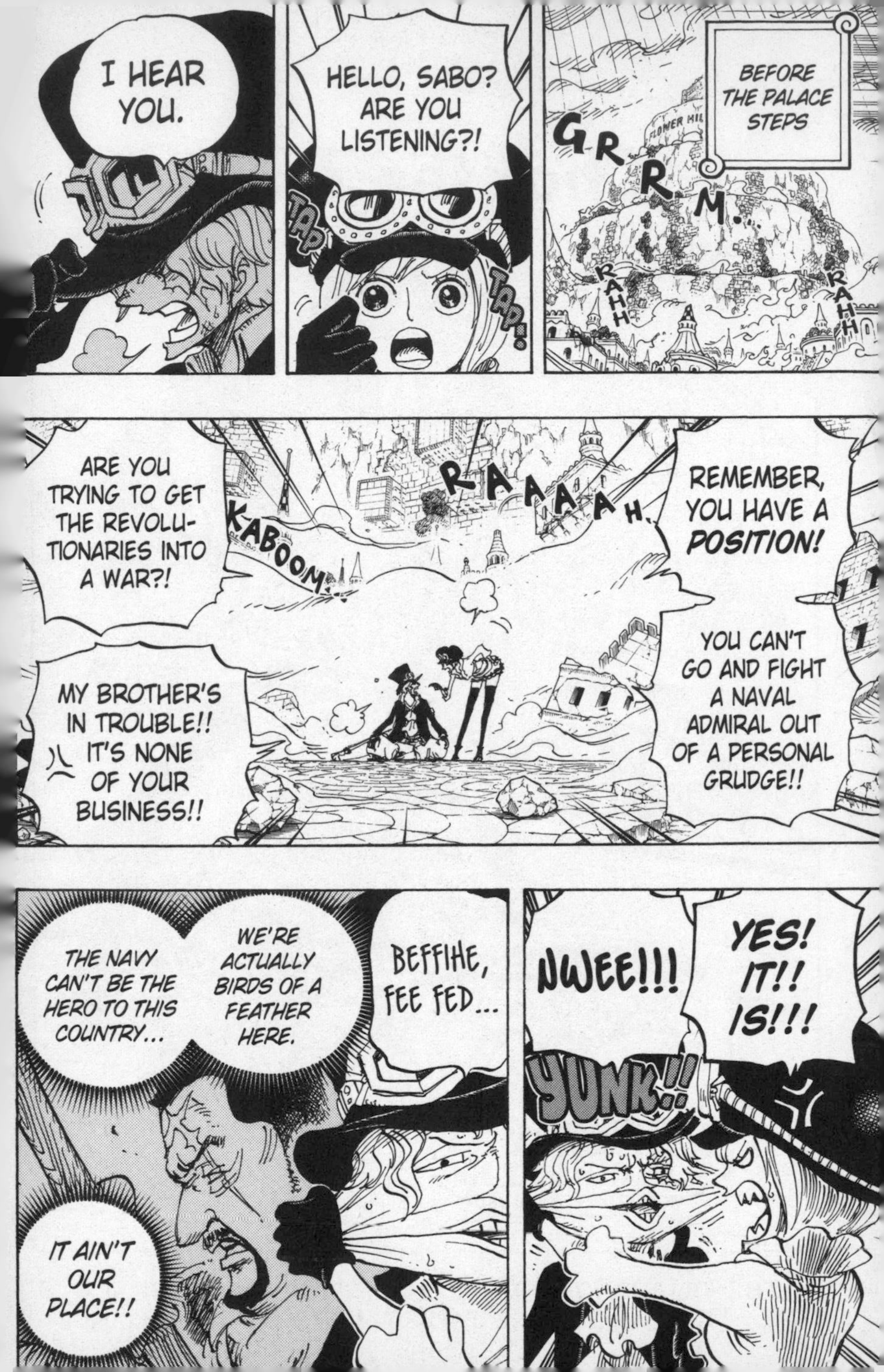
BEFORE THE PALACE STEPS
GRRRM...
RAHH
RAHH
HELLO, SABO? ARE YOU LISTENING?!
TAP
TAP!
I HEAR YOU.
REMEMBER, YOU HAVE A POSITION!
RAAAAAH..
ARE YOU TRYING TO GET THE REVOLUTIONARIES INTO A WAR?!
KABOOM
YOU CAN'T GO AND FIGHT A NAVAL ADMIRAL OUT OF A PERSONAL GRUDGE!!
MY BROTHER'S IN TROUBLE!! IT'S NONE OF YOUR BUSINESS!!
YES! IT!! IS!!!
NWEE!!!
YUNK!!
BEFFIHE, FEE FED...
WE'RE ACTUALLY BIRDS OF A FEATHER HERE.
THE NAVY CAN'T BE THE HERO TO THIS COUNTRY...
IT AIN'T OUR PLACE!!

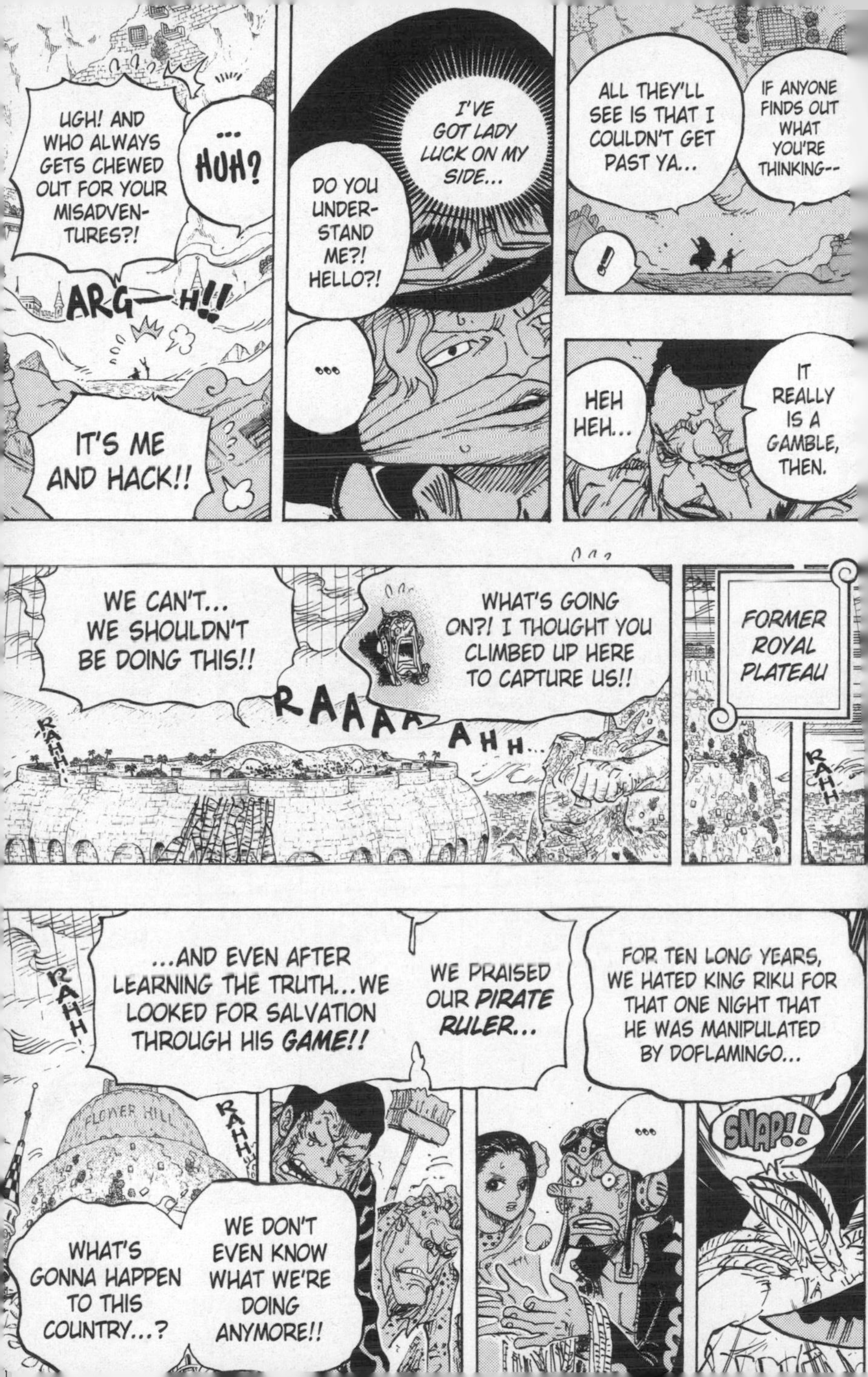
IF ANYONE FINDS OUT WHAT YOU'RE THINKING--
ALL THEY'LL SEE IS THAT I COULDN'T GET PAST YA...
!
IT REALLY IS A GAMBLE, THEN.
HEH HEH...
I'VE GOT LADY LUCK ON MY SIDE...
DO YOU UNDERSTAND ME?! HELLO?!
...
...HUH?
UGH! AND WHO ALWAYS GETS CHEWED OUT FOR YOUR MISADVENTURES?!
ARG—H!!
IT'S ME AND HACK!!
FORMER ROYAL PLATEAU
RAHH
WHAT'S GOING ON?! I THOUGHT YOU CLIMBED UP HERE TO CAPTURE US!!
WE CAN'T... WE SHOULDN'T BE DOING THIS!!
RAAAAAAHH...
RAHH
FOR TEN LONG YEARS, WE HATED KING RIKU FOR THAT ONE NIGHT THAT HE WAS MANIPULATED BY DOFLAMINGO...
WE PRAISED OUR *PIRATE RULER*...
...AND EVEN AFTER LEARNING THE TRUTH...WE LOOKED FOR SALVATION THROUGH HIS *GAME*!!
RAHH
SNAP!!
...
RAHH
WE DON'T EVEN KNOW WHAT WE'RE DOING ANYMORE!!
WHAT'S GONNA HAPPEN TO THIS COUNTRY...?
FLOWER HILL

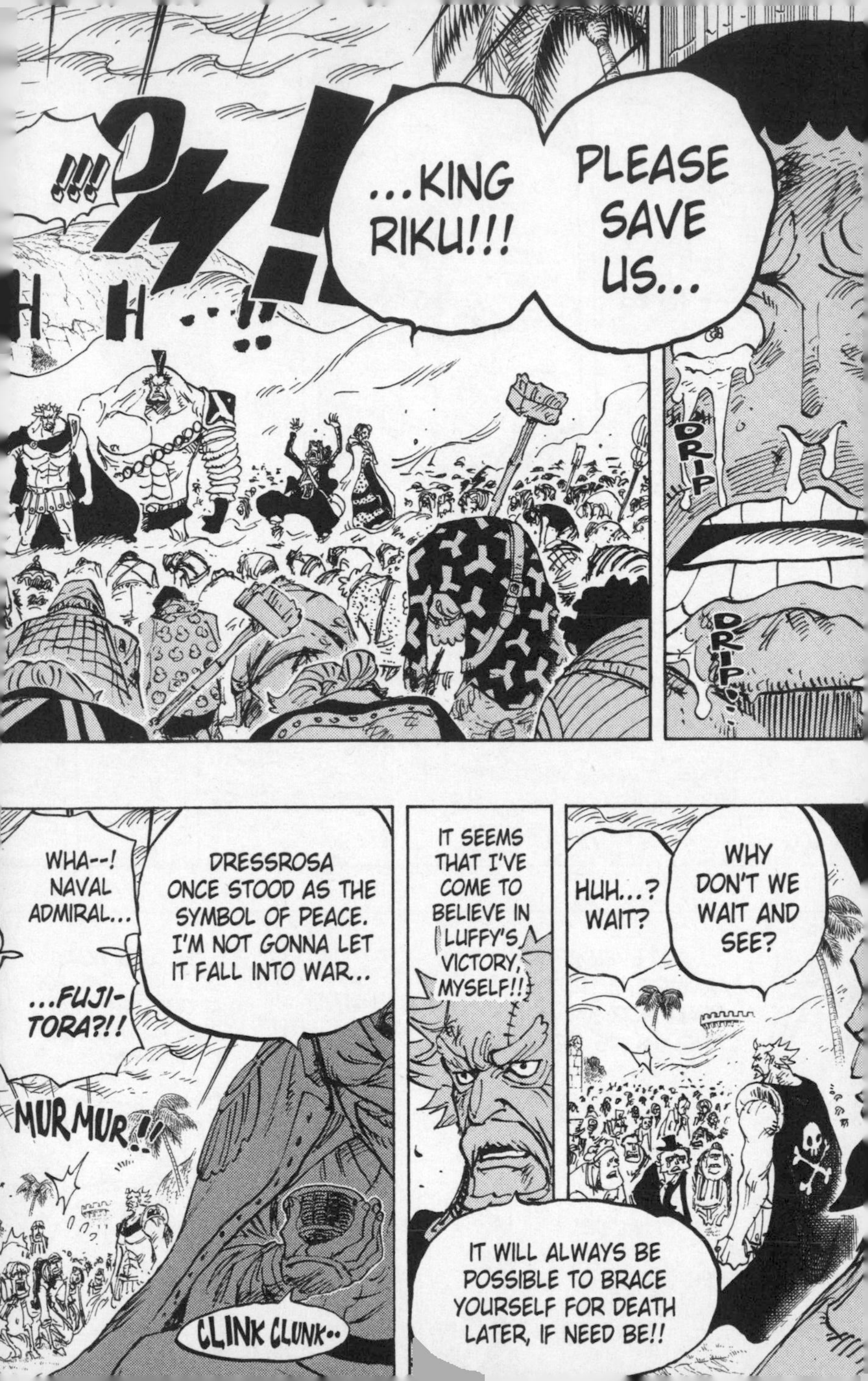
DRIP
DRIP
PLEASE SAVE US...
...KING RIKU!!!
WHY DON'T WE WAIT AND SEE?
HUH...? WAIT?
IT WILL ALWAYS BE POSSIBLE TO BRACE YOURSELF FOR DEATH LATER, IF NEED BE!!
IT SEEMS THAT I'VE COME TO BELIEVE IN LUFFY'S VICTORY, MYSELF!!
DRESSROSA ONCE STOOD AS THE SYMBOL OF PEACE. I'M NOT GONNA LET IT FALL INTO WAR...
WHA--! NAVAL ADMIRAL...
...FUJI-TORA?!!
MUR MUR!!
CLINK CLUNK..

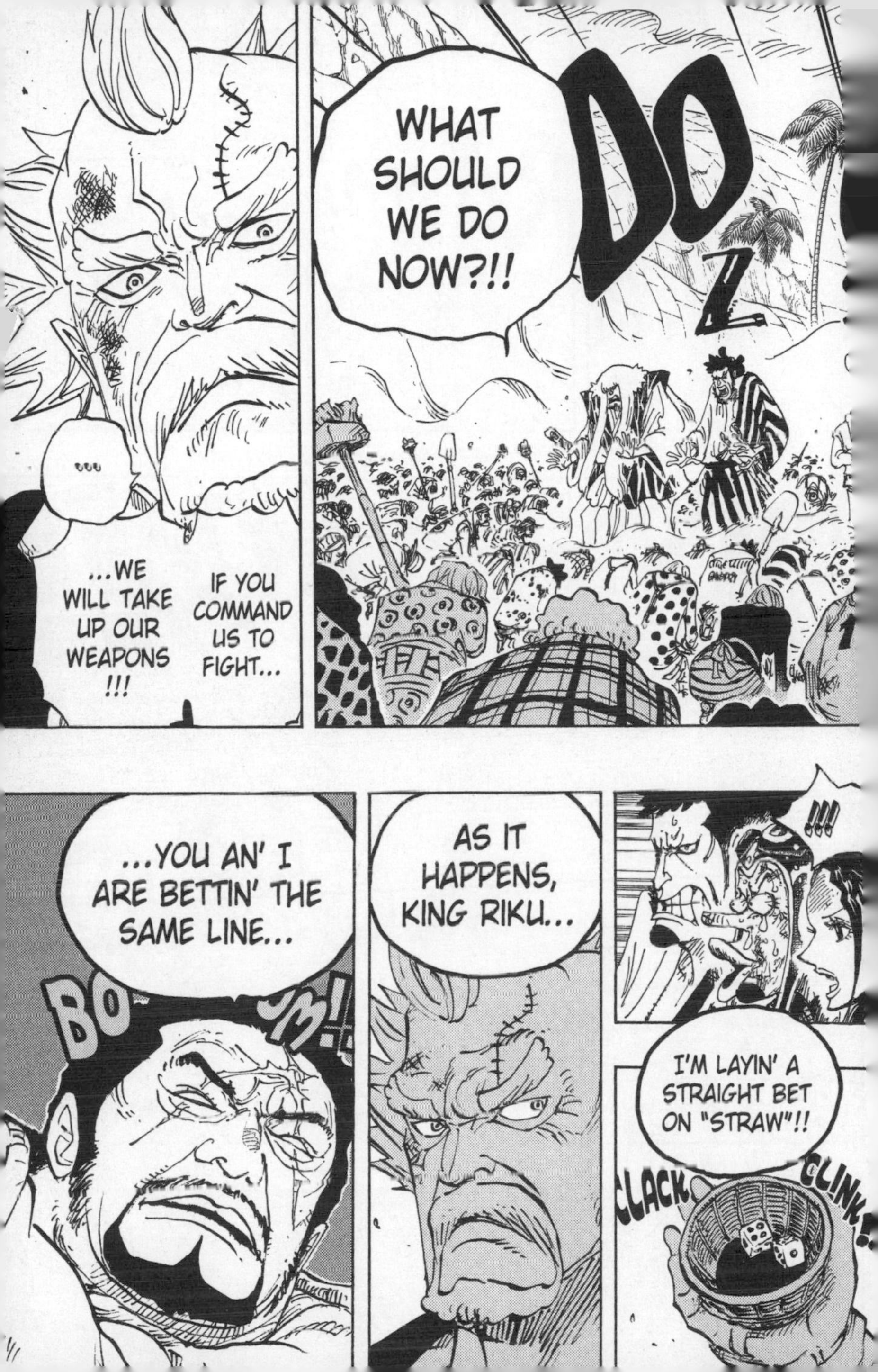
WHAT SHOULD WE DO NOW?!!
DOZ
...
IF YOU COMMAND US TO FIGHT...
...WE WILL TAKE UP OUR WEAPONS !!!
!!!
I'M LAYIN' A STRAIGHT BET ON "STRAW"!!
CLACK
CLINK!!
AS IT HAPPENS, KING RIKU...
...YOU AN' I ARE BETTIN' THE SAME LINE...

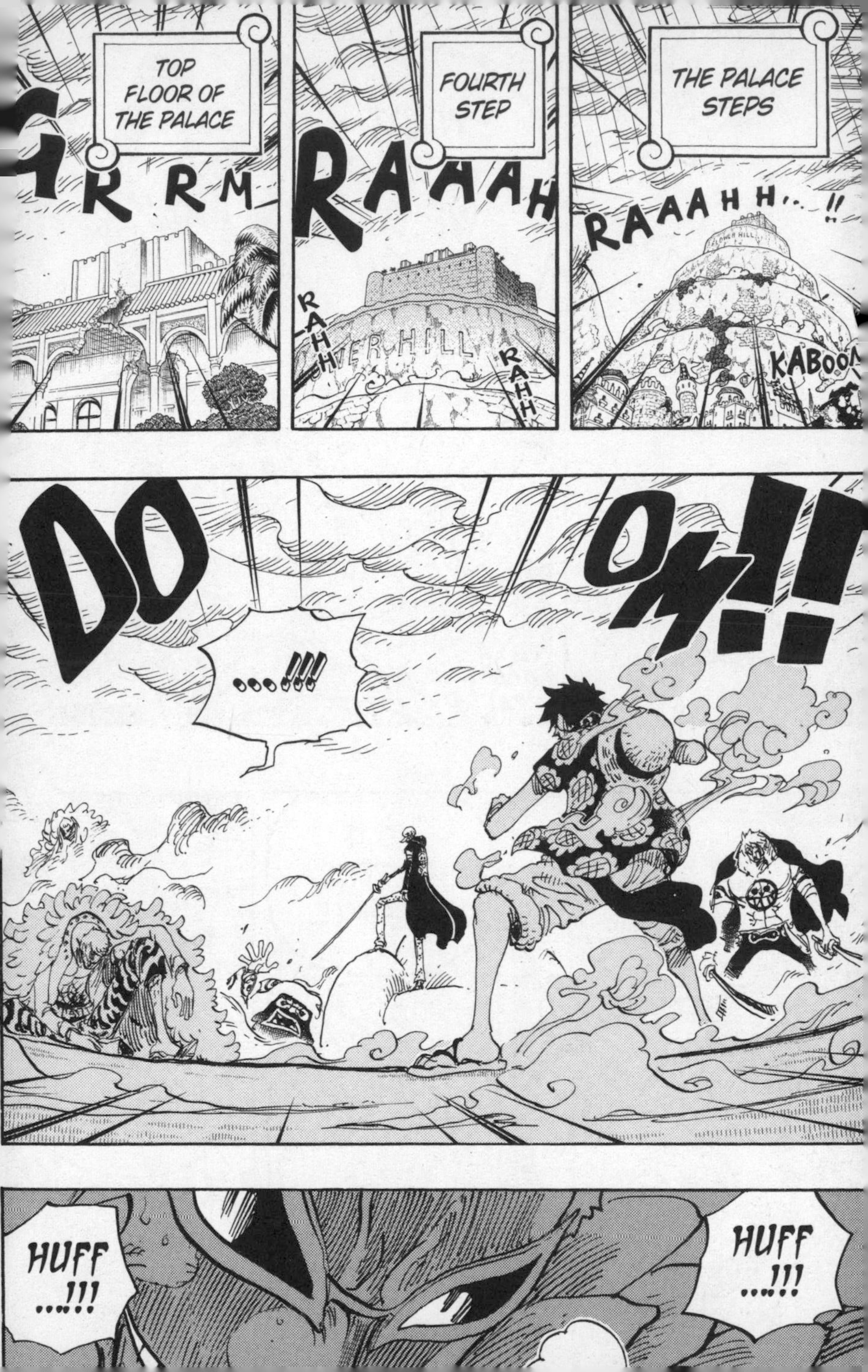
THE PALACE STEPS
RAAAHH...!!
KABOO
FOURTH STEP
RAAAAH
RAHH
RAHH
TOP FLOOR OF THE PALACE
GRRRM
DO
ON!!
...!!!
HUFF ...!!!
HUFF ...!!!

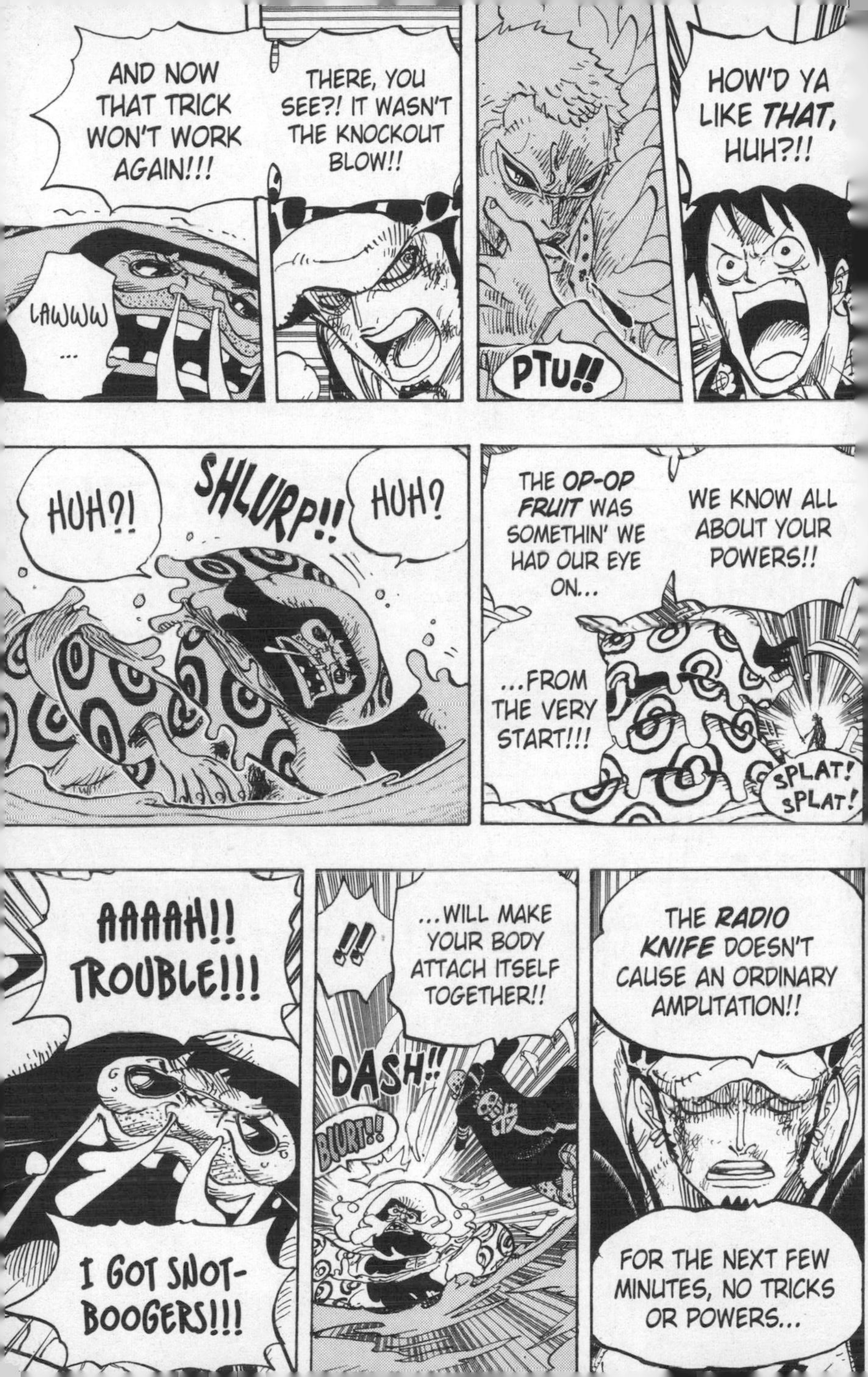
HOW'D YA LIKE THAT, HUH?!!
PTU!!
THERE, YOU SEE?! IT WASN'T THE KNOCKOUT BLOW!!
AND NOW THAT TRICK WON'T WORK AGAIN!!!
LAWWW ...
WE KNOW ALL ABOUT YOUR POWERS!!
THE OP-OP FRUIT WAS SOMETHIN' WE HAD OUR EYE ON...
...FROM THE VERY START!!!
SPLAT! SPLAT!
HUH?
SHLURP!!
HUH?!
THE RADIO KNIFE DOESN'T CAUSE AN ORDINARY AMPUTATION!!
FOR THE NEXT FEW MINUTES, NO TRICKS OR POWERS...
...WILL MAKE YOUR BODY ATTACH ITSELF TOGETHER!!
!!
DASH!!
BLURT!!
AAAAH!! TROUBLE!!!
I GOT SNOT-BOOGERS!!!

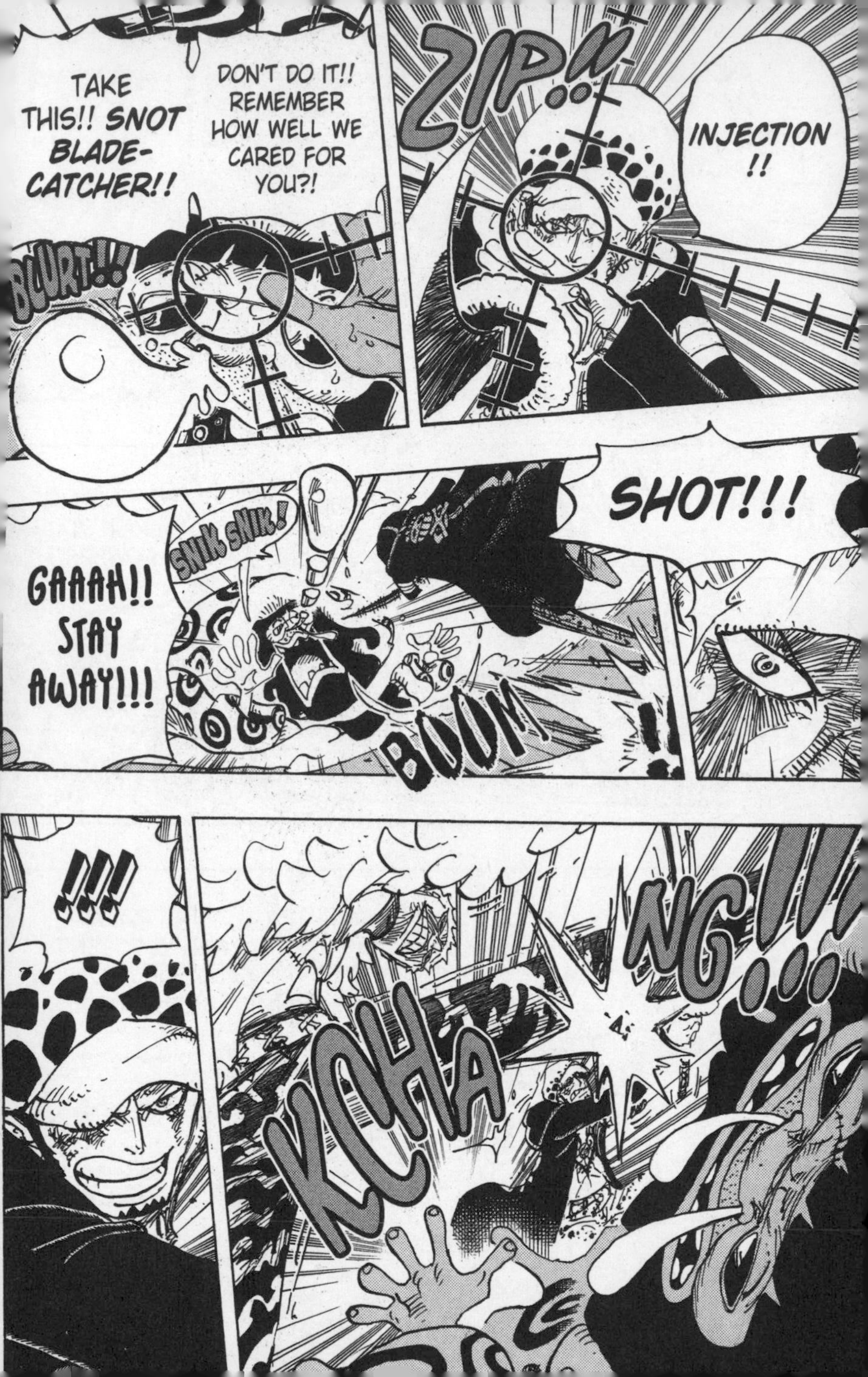
ZIP!!
INJECTION!!
DON'T DO IT!! REMEMBER HOW WELL WE CARED FOR YOU?!
TAKE THIS!! SNOT BLADE-CATCHER!!
BLURT!!!
SHOT!!!
SNIK SNIK!
GAAAH!! STAY AWAY!!!
BOOM!!
NG!!!
KCHA
!!!

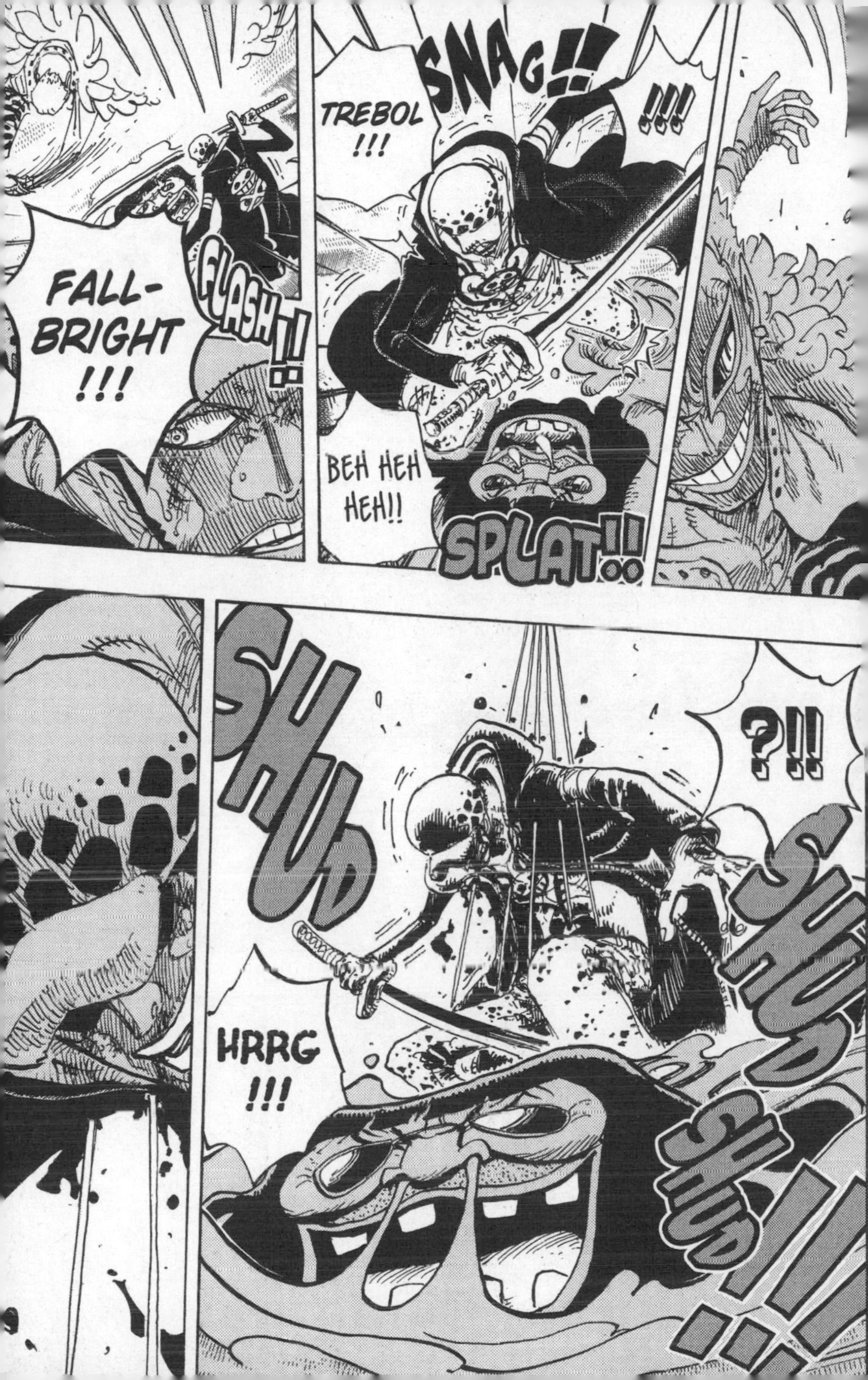
!!!
SNAG!!
TREBOL !!!
BEH HEH HEH!!
SPLAT!!
FALL-BRIGHT !!!
FLASH!!
?!!
SHUD
SHUD
SHUD
SHUD!!
HRRG !!!

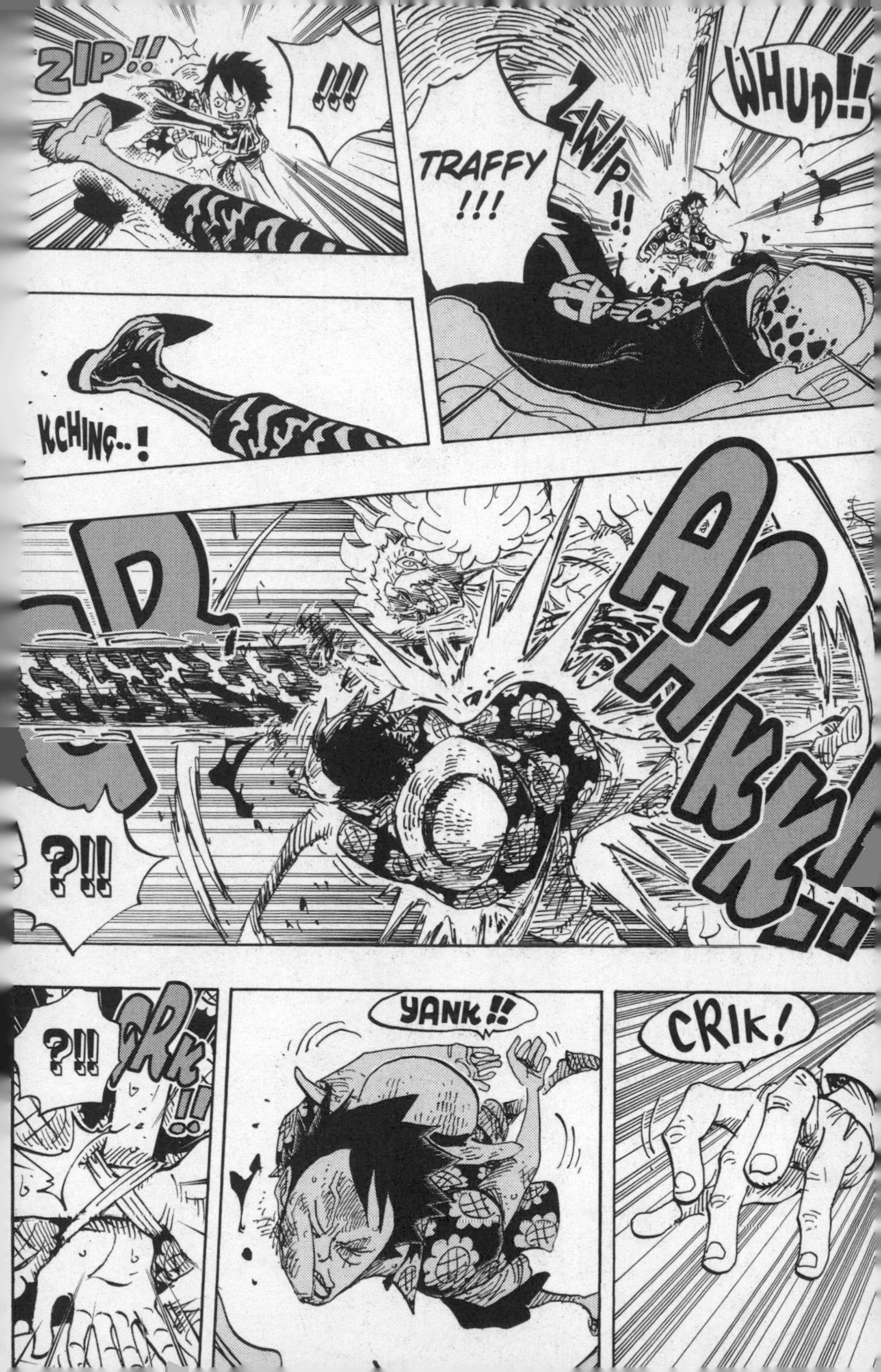
WHUD!!
ZWIP!!
TRAFFY!!!
!!!
ZIP!!
KCHING..!
?!!
CRIK!
YANK!!
?!!

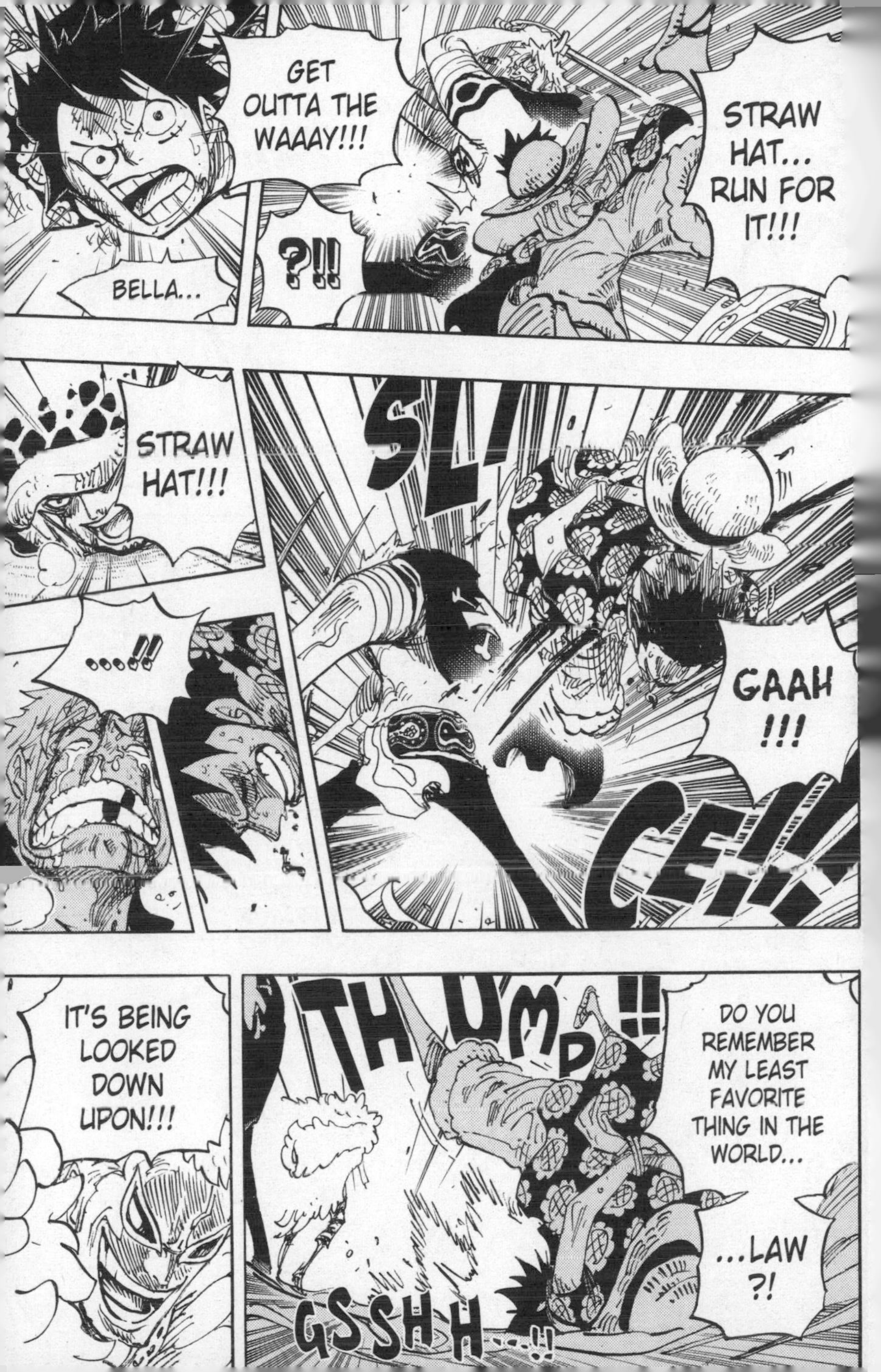
STRAW HAT... RUN FOR IT!!!
?!!
GET OUTTA THE WAAAY!!!
BELLA...
SLI
GAAH!!!
CE
STRAW HAT!!!
....!!
THUMP!!
DO YOU REMEMBER MY LEAST FAVORITE THING IN THE WORLD...
...LAW?!
GSSHH...!!
IT'S BEING LOOKED DOWN UPON!!!

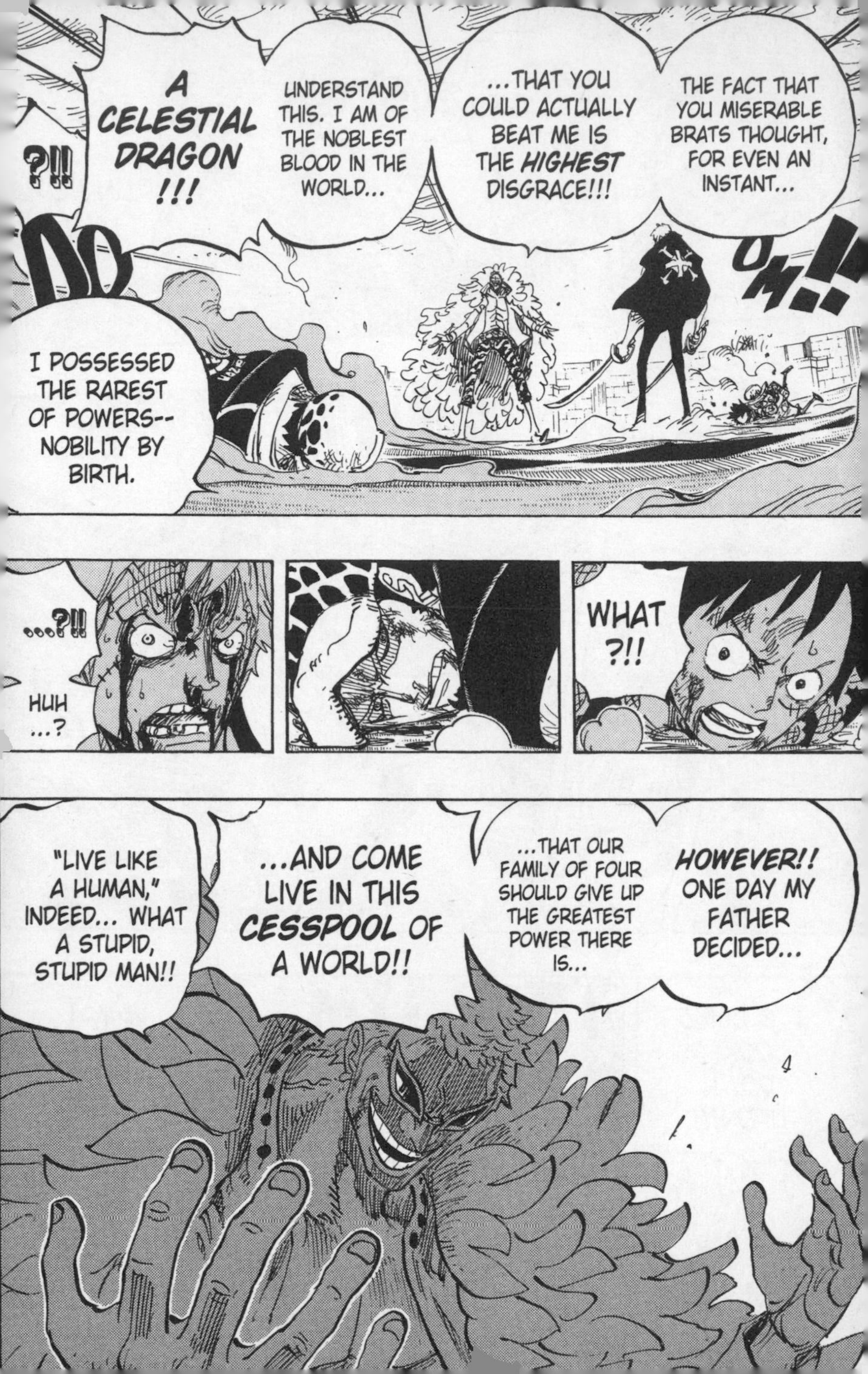
THE FACT THAT YOU MISERABLE BRATS THOUGHT, FOR EVEN AN INSTANT...
...THAT YOU COULD ACTUALLY BEAT ME IS THE HIGHEST DISGRACE!!!
UNDERSTAND THIS. I AM OF THE NOBLEST BLOOD IN THE WORLD...
A CELESTIAL DRAGON!!!
?!!
DOOM!!
I POSSESSED THE RAREST OF POWERS-- NOBILITY BY BIRTH.
WHAT ?!!
...?!!
HUH ...?
HOWEVER!! ONE DAY MY FATHER DECIDED...
...THAT OUR FAMILY OF FOUR SHOULD GIVE UP THE GREATEST POWER THERE IS...
...AND COME LIVE IN THIS CESSPOOL OF A WORLD!!
"LIVE LIKE A HUMAN," INDEED... WHAT A STUPID, STUPID MAN!!

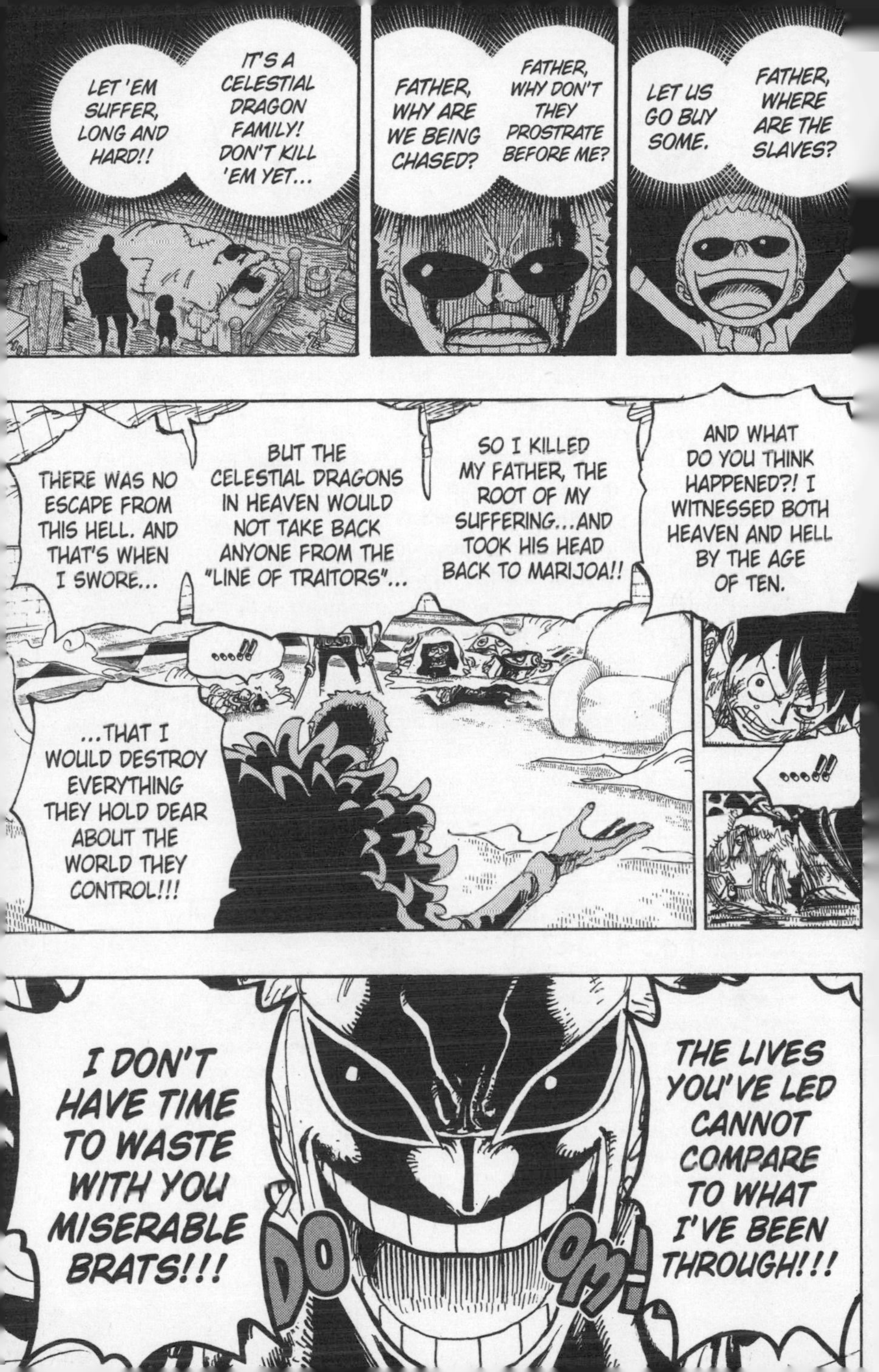
FATHER, WHERE ARE THE SLAVES?
LET US GO BUY SOME.
FATHER, WHY DON'T THEY PROSTRATE BEFORE ME?
FATHER, WHY ARE WE BEING CHASED?
IT'S A CELESTIAL DRAGON FAMILY! DON'T KILL 'EM YET...
LET 'EM SUFFER, LONG AND HARD!!
AND WHAT DO YOU THINK HAPPENED?! I WITNESSED BOTH HEAVEN AND HELL BY THE AGE OF TEN.
....!!
....!!
SO I KILLED MY FATHER, THE ROOT OF MY SUFFERING...AND TOOK HIS HEAD BACK TO MARIJOA!!
BUT THE CELESTIAL DRAGONS IN HEAVEN WOULD NOT TAKE BACK ANYONE FROM THE "LINE OF TRAITORS"...
THERE WAS NO ESCAPE FROM THIS HELL. AND THAT'S WHEN I SWORE...
....!!
...THAT I WOULD DESTROY EVERYTHING THEY HOLD DEAR ABOUT THE WORLD THEY CONTROL!!!
THE LIVES YOU'VE LED CANNOT COMPARE TO WHAT I'VE BEEN THROUGH!!!
DOOM!
I DON'T HAVE TIME TO WASTE WITH YOU MISERABLE BRATS!!!

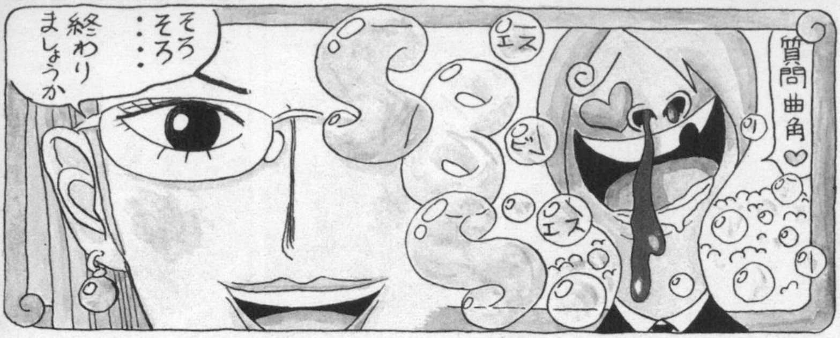
質問曲角♡
エス
ビー
エス
そろそろ……
終わりましょうか

(In My 50s, Oita)

Q: Remember that question in Volume 75 about the reason you used tiger and bull as the animals for the new Naval Admirals?! Well, I've got an idea… We know that the original three of Akainu, Aokiji and Kizaru mean "Red Dog," "Blue Pheasant," and "Yellow Monkey," respectively. And in the fairy tale of Momotaro, the boy born from a peach befriends a dog, pheasant and monkey, who join him on his travels as he seeks to vanquish the army of demonic oni on the island of Onigashima. And how are oni usually depicted? With tigerskin loincloths and bullhorns!
So here's my interpretation: the animals on Momotaro's side stand for law and order, and the oni stand for pirates. Since we know that Fujitora wants to abolish the World Government's Seven Warlords of the Sea system, is it possible that Ryokugyu and Fujitora, the two newest admirals, are both Navy men who bear some kind of rebellious streak against the powers that be? (Assuming that anti-government means pirates.) What do you think? Am I on the right track?

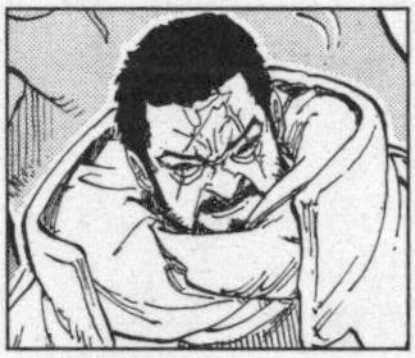

--Rooster Hair Guy

A: **Huh? M-me, panic? (cold sweat) W-why would I do that? That's silly.**
Well, that's a whole lot of complex information you just shared. If anyone wants to read anything into that, they're certainly welcome to do so. I'm not saying if it's right or wrong, that's all! (sweat drop) I'm just saying...this was a letter I received! And now you have seen it for yourselves.
Anyway, **the SBS is now finished!!!**
At the end of the volume, you'll find the results of the latest character popularity poll that we ran in Japan! For some reason we forgot to do a present lottery for those who sent in their votes. It has been six years since the last one, after all...
Thanks to everyone who voted in the poll! Go ahead and see where your favorite placed!

Chapter 761:
THE OP-OP FRUIT

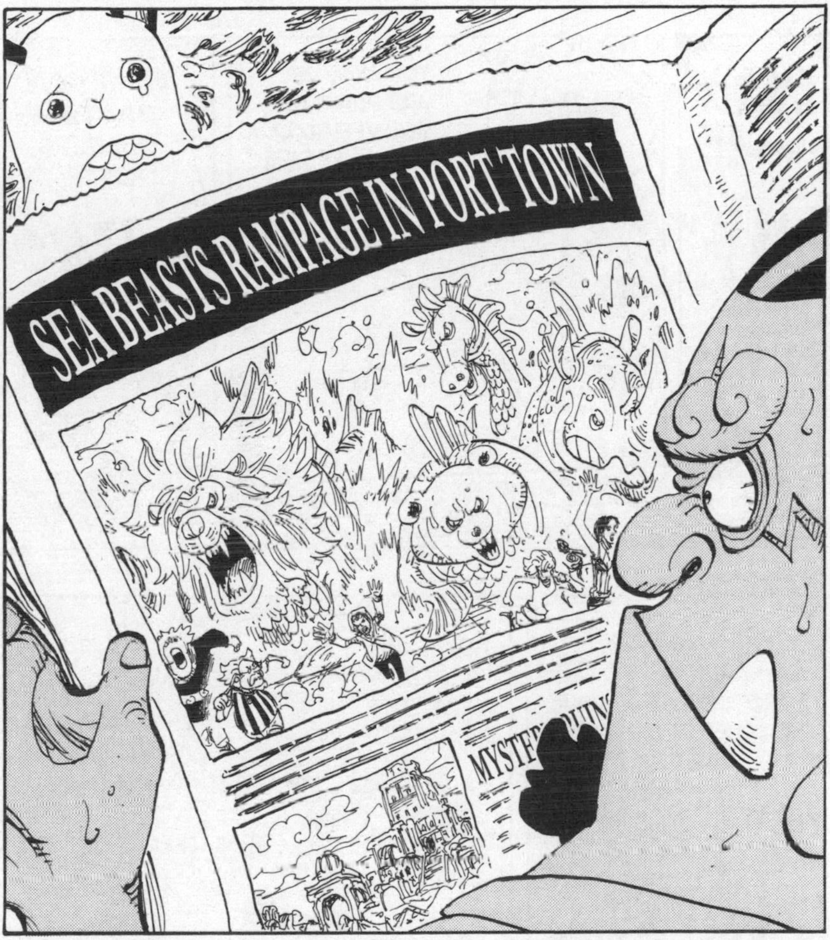
SEA BEASTS RAMPAGE IN PORT TOWN

THE SOLITARY JOURNEY OF JIMBEI, FIRST SON OF THE SEA, VOL. 10: "NOT THAT ARTICLE, THIS ONE! A MOB OF SEA BEASTS"

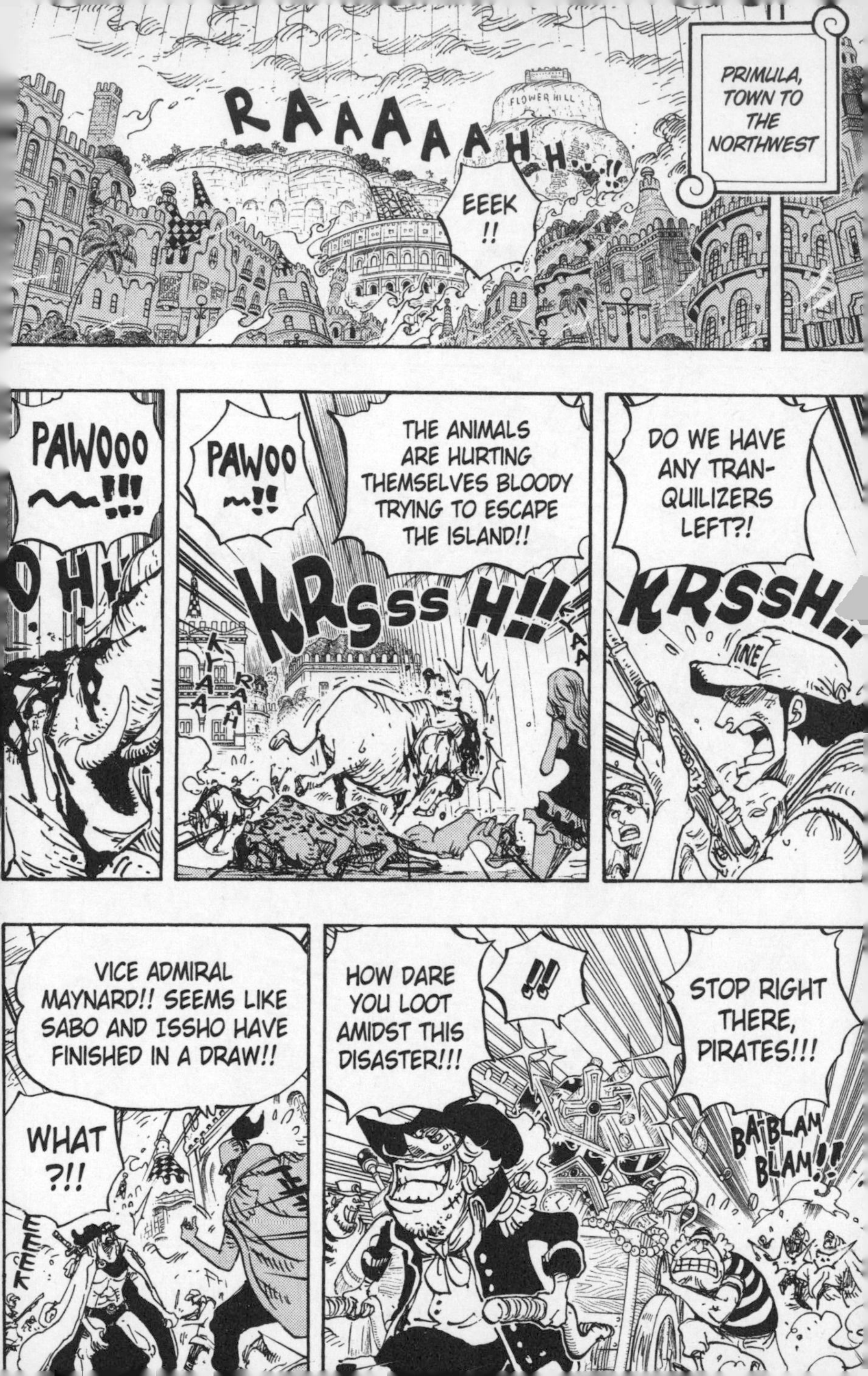
PRIMULA, TOWN TO THE NORTHWEST
FLOWER HILL
EEEK !!
RAAAAAHH...!!
DO WE HAVE ANY TRAN-QUILIZERS LEFT?!
KRSSH..
THE ANIMALS ARE HURTING THEMSELVES BLOODY TRYING TO ESCAPE THE ISLAND!!
PAWOO~!!
KRSSSH!!
KYAA
KYAAA
RAAAH
PAWOOO~!!!
STOP RIGHT THERE, PIRATES!!!
!!
HOW DARE YOU LOOT AMIDST THIS DISASTER!!!
BA BLAM BLAM!!
VICE ADMIRAL MAYNARD!! SEEMS LIKE SABO AND ISSHO HAVE FINISHED IN A DRAW!!
WHAT?!!
EEEEK

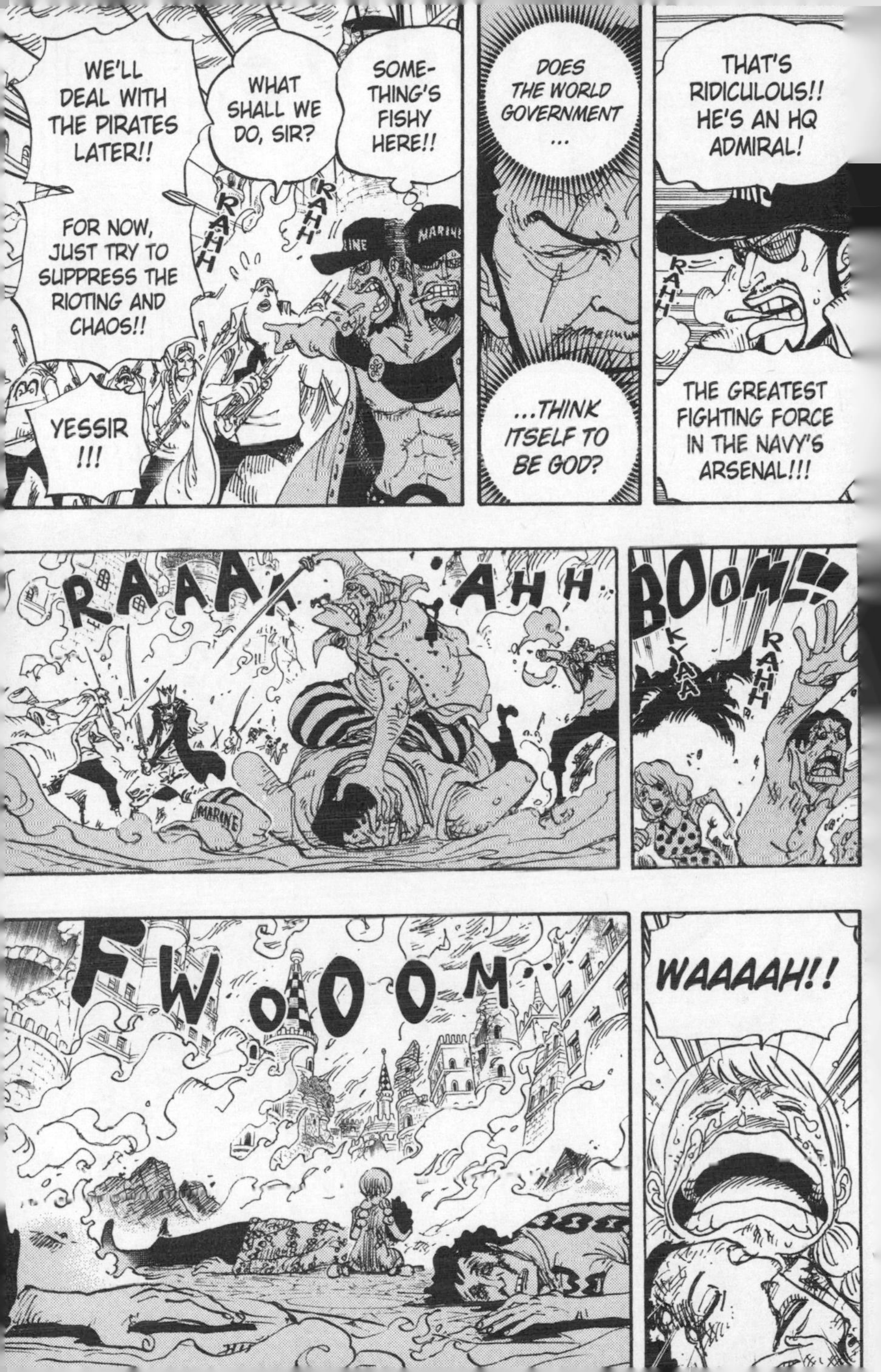
THAT'S RIDICULOUS!! HE'S AN HQ ADMIRAL!
RAHH
THE GREATEST FIGHTING FORCE IN THE NAVY'S ARSENAL!!!
DOES THE WORLD GOVERNMENT ...
...THINK ITSELF TO BE GOD?
SOME-THING'S FISHY HERE!!
WHAT SHALL WE DO, SIR?
RAHH
RAHH
WE'LL DEAL WITH THE PIRATES LATER!!
FOR NOW, JUST TRY TO SUPPRESS THE RIOTING AND CHAOS!!
YESSIR!!!
BOOM!!
KYAA
RAHH
RAAAAAHH
WAAAAH!!
FWOOOM

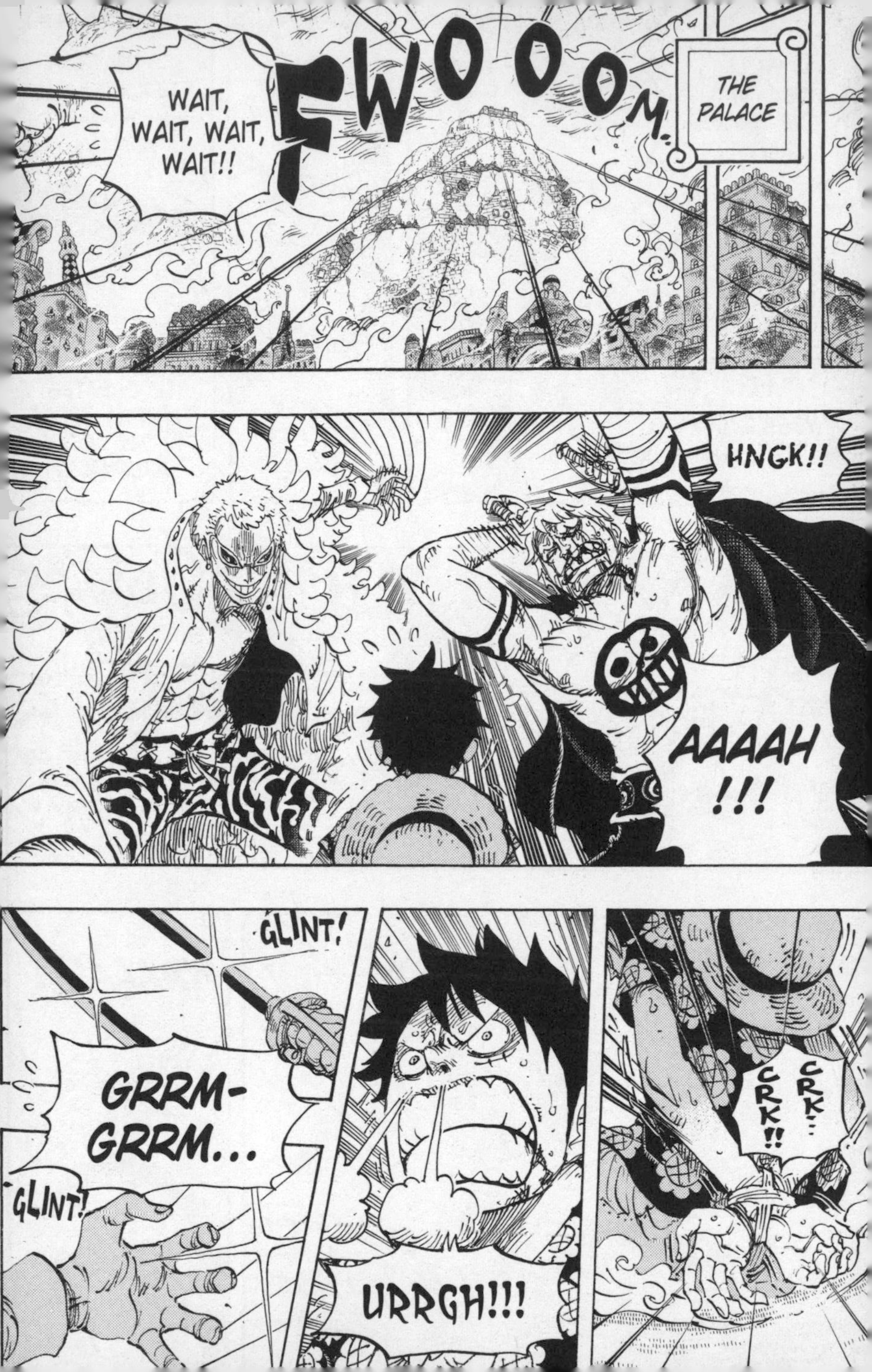
THE PALACE
FWOOOM
WAIT, WAIT, WAIT, WAIT!!
HNGK!!
AAAAH!!!
CRK...
CRK!!
URRGH!!!
GLINT!
GRRM-GRRM...
GLINT!

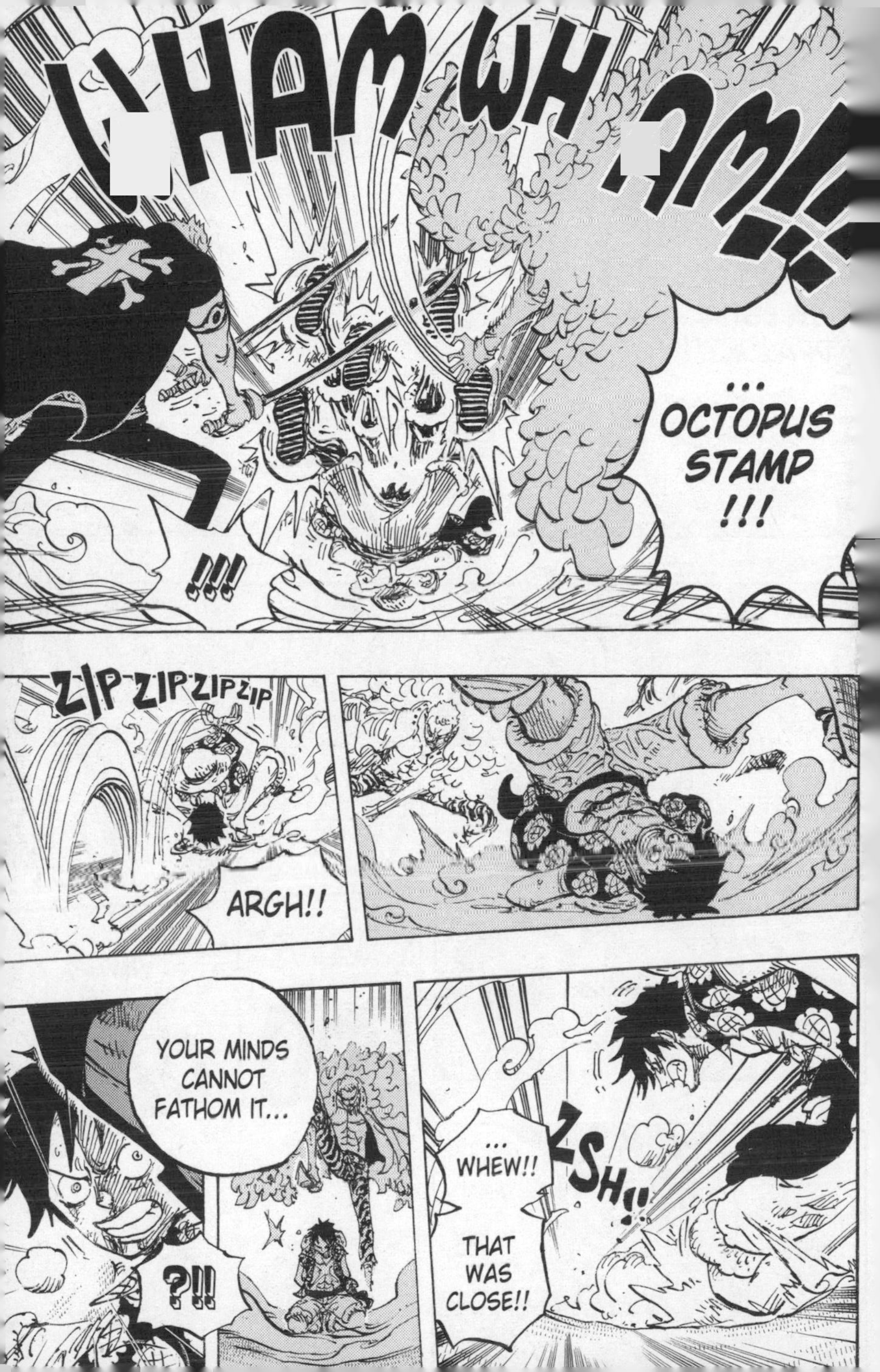
WHAM WHAM!!
... OCTOPUS STAMP !!!
!!!
ZIP ZIP ZIP ZIP
ARGH!!
ZSH!!
... WHEW!!
THAT WAS CLOSE!!
YOUR MINDS CANNOT FATHOM IT...
?!!

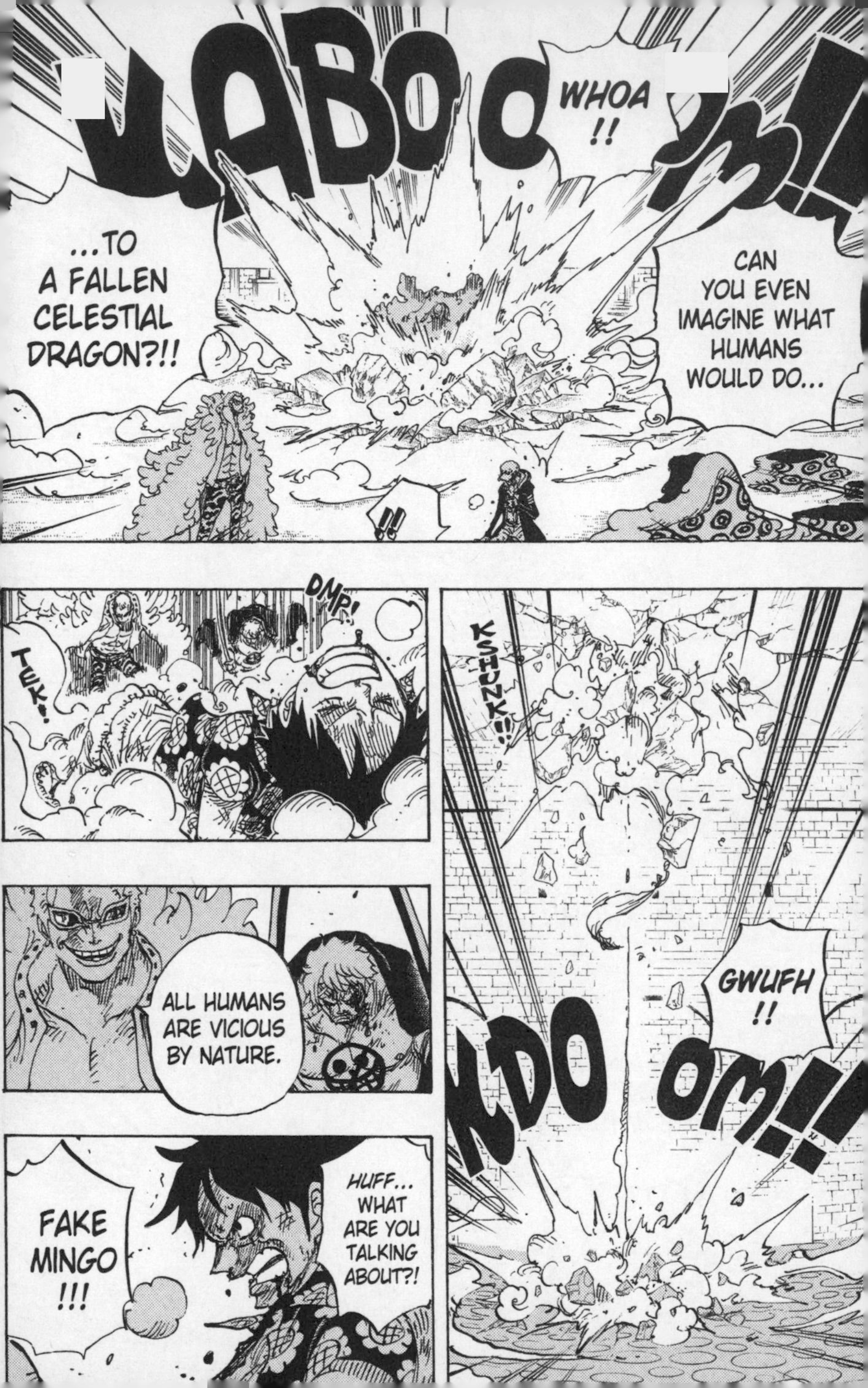

CAN YOU EVEN IMAGINE WHAT HUMANS WOULD DO...
WHOA!!
...TO A FALLEN CELESTIAL DRAGON?!!
KSHUNK!!
GWUFH!!
DMP!
TEK!
ALL HUMANS ARE VICIOUS BY NATURE.
HUFF... WHAT ARE YOU TALKING ABOUT?!
FAKE MINGO!!!

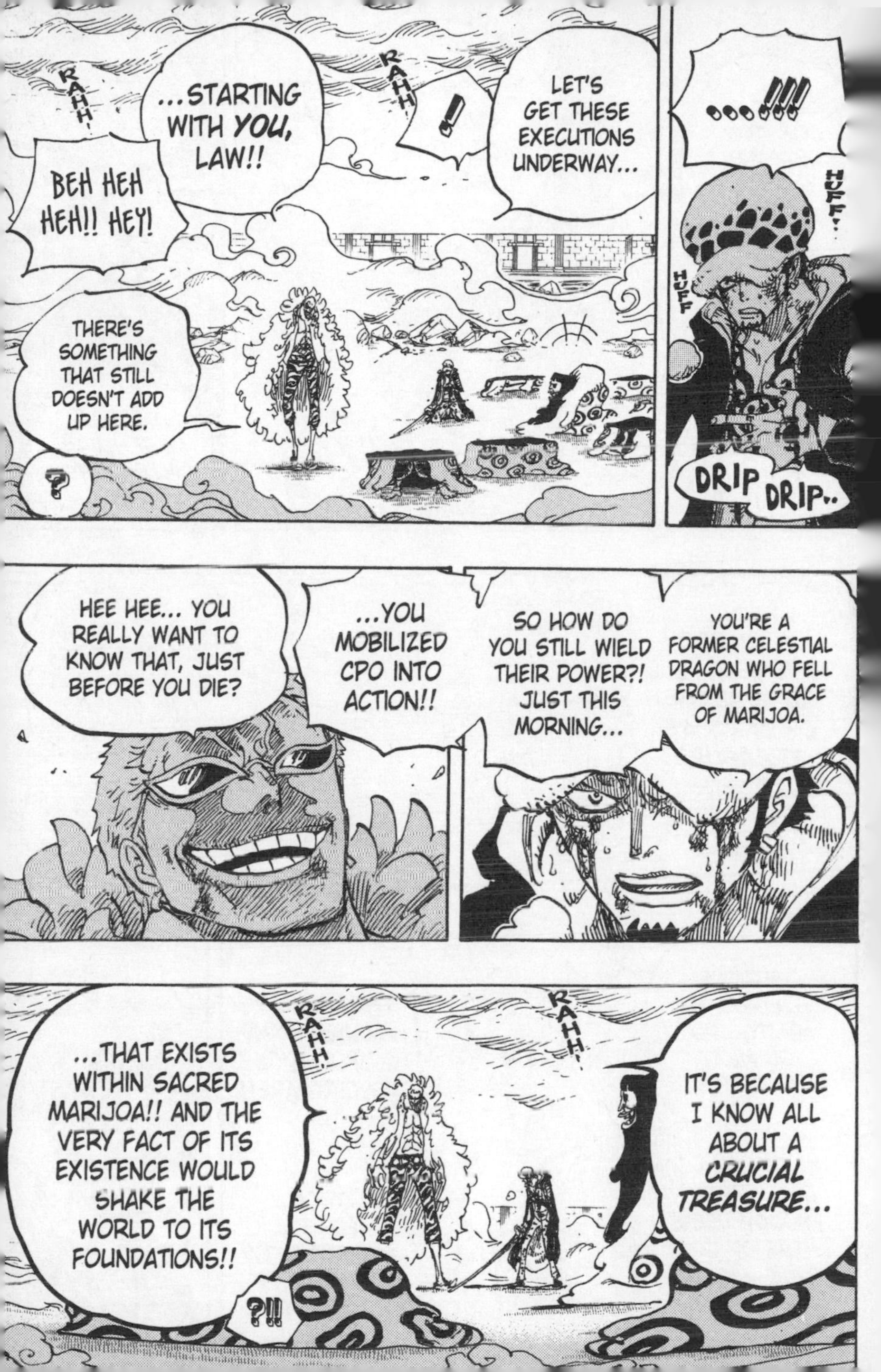
...!!!!
HUFF
HUFF
DRIP DRIP..
LET'S GET THESE EXECUTIONS UNDERWAY...
RAHH
!
...STARTING WITH *YOU*, LAW!!
RAHH
BEH HEH HEH!! HEY!
THERE'S SOMETHING THAT STILL DOESN'T ADD UP HERE.
?
YOU'RE A FORMER CELESTIAL DRAGON WHO FELL FROM THE GRACE OF MARIJOA.
SO HOW DO YOU STILL WIELD THEIR POWER?! JUST THIS MORNING...
...YOU MOBILIZED CPO INTO ACTION!!
HEE HEE... YOU REALLY WANT TO KNOW THAT, JUST BEFORE YOU DIE?
IT'S BECAUSE I KNOW ALL ABOUT A *CRUCIAL TREASURE*...
RAHH
RAHH
...THAT EXISTS WITHIN SACRED MARIJOA!! AND THE VERY FACT OF ITS EXISTENCE WOULD SHAKE THE WORLD TO ITS FOUNDATIONS!!
?!!

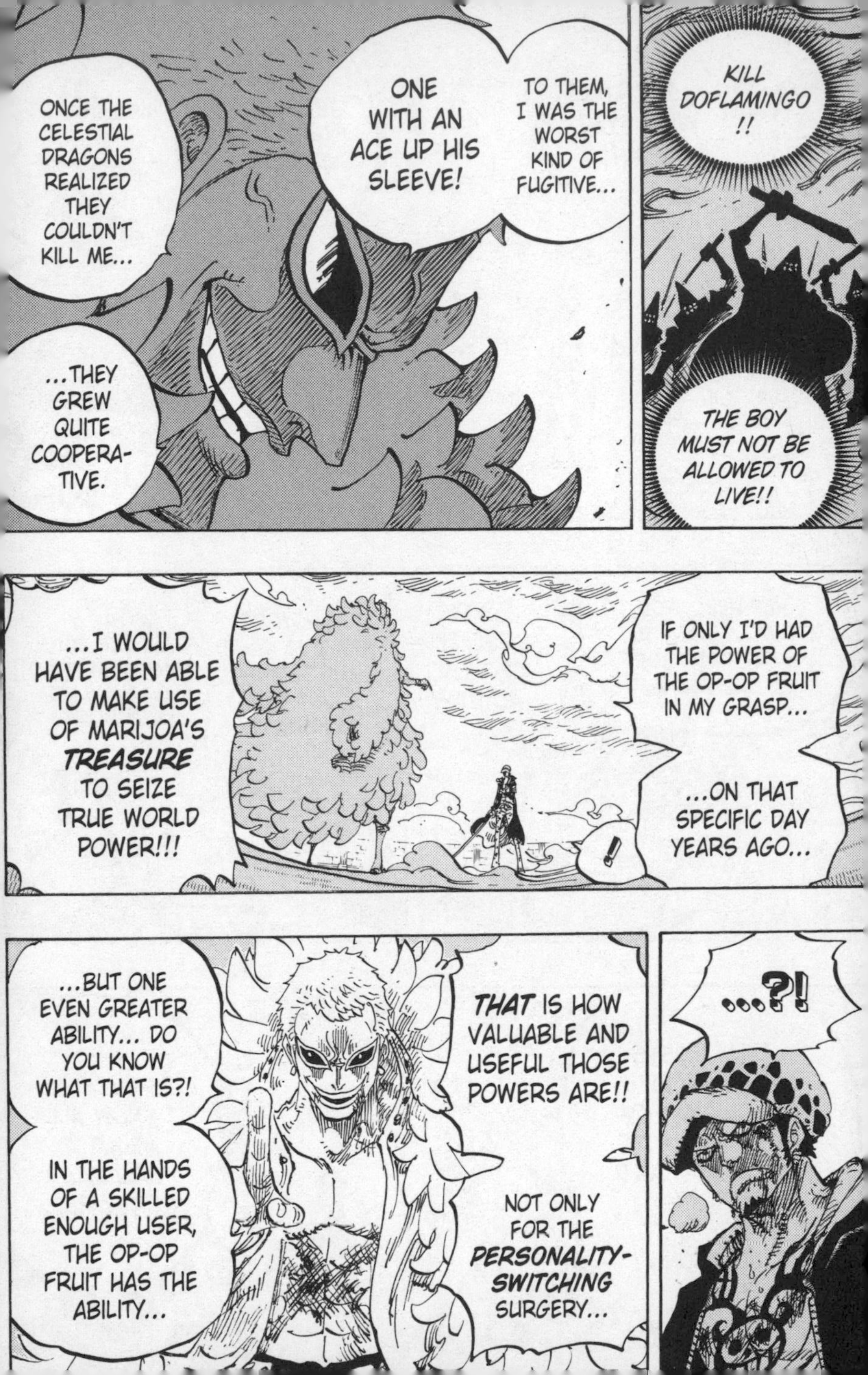
KILL DOFLAMINGO!!
THE BOY MUST NOT BE ALLOWED TO LIVE!!
TO THEM, I WAS THE WORST KIND OF FUGITIVE...
ONE WITH AN ACE UP HIS SLEEVE!
ONCE THE CELESTIAL DRAGONS REALIZED THEY COULDN'T KILL ME...
...THEY GREW QUITE COOPERA-TIVE.
IF ONLY I'D HAD THE POWER OF THE OP-OP FRUIT IN MY GRASP...
...ON THAT SPECIFIC DAY YEARS AGO...
!
...I WOULD HAVE BEEN ABLE TO MAKE USE OF MARIJOA'S ***TREASURE*** TO SEIZE TRUE WORLD POWER!!!
...?!
THAT IS HOW VALUABLE AND USEFUL THOSE POWERS ARE!!
NOT ONLY FOR THE ***PERSONALITY-SWITCHING*** SURGERY...
...BUT ONE EVEN GREATER ABILITY... DO YOU KNOW WHAT THAT IS?!
IN THE HANDS OF A SKILLED ENOUGH USER, THE OP-OP FRUIT HAS THE ABILITY...

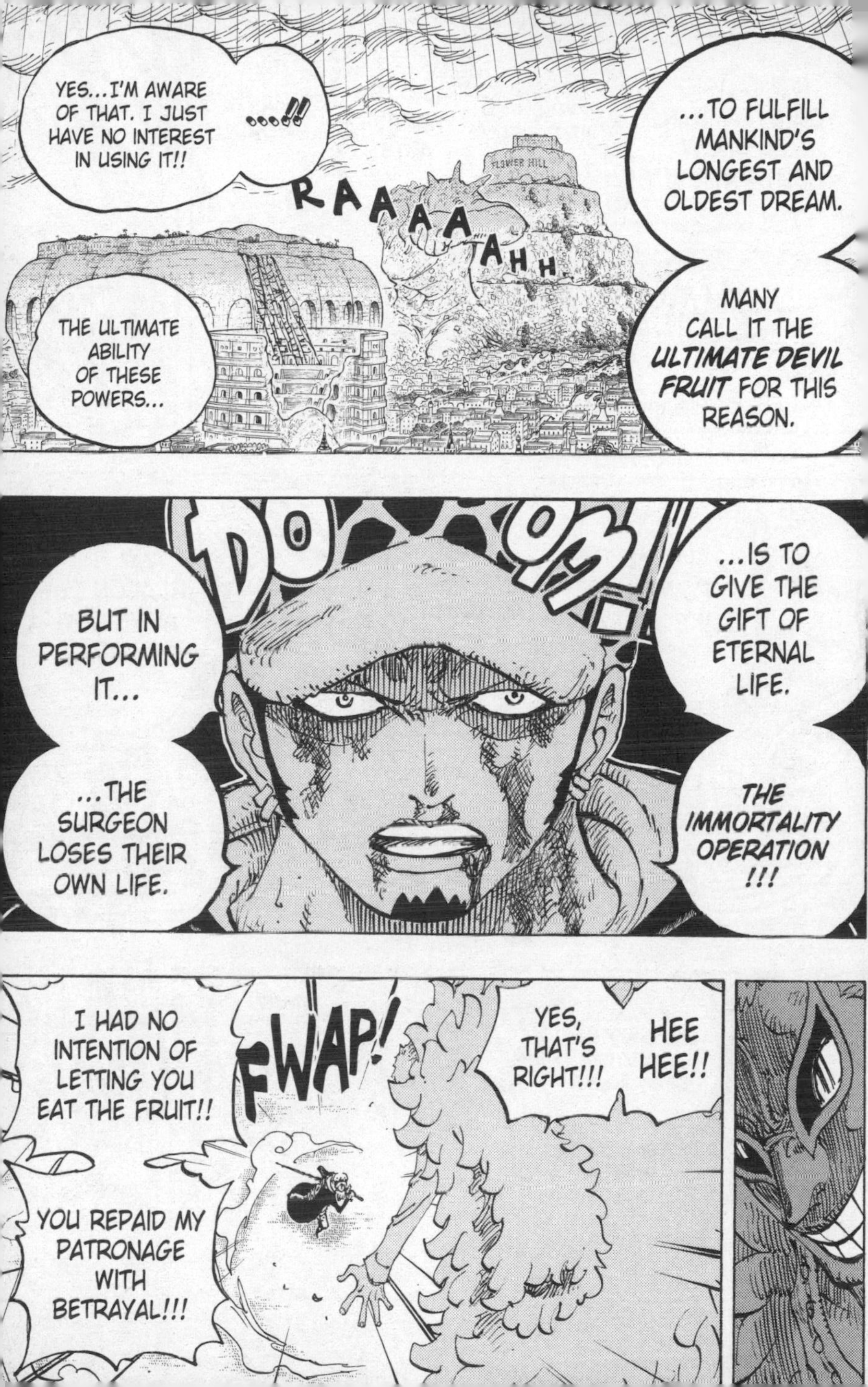
...TO FULFILL MANKIND'S LONGEST AND OLDEST DREAM.
MANY CALL IT THE *ULTIMATE DEVIL FRUIT* FOR THIS REASON.
YES...I'M AWARE OF THAT. I JUST HAVE NO INTEREST IN USING IT!!
....!!
FLOWER HILL
RAAAAAHHH
THE ULTIMATE ABILITY OF THESE POWERS...
...IS TO GIVE THE GIFT OF ETERNAL LIFE.
DOOOM!
THE IMMORTALITY OPERATION !!!
BUT IN PERFORMING IT...
...THE SURGEON LOSES THEIR OWN LIFE.
HEE HEE!!
YES, THAT'S RIGHT!!!
FWAP!
I HAD NO INTENTION OF LETTING YOU EAT THE FRUIT!!
YOU REPAID MY PATRONAGE WITH BETRAYAL!!!

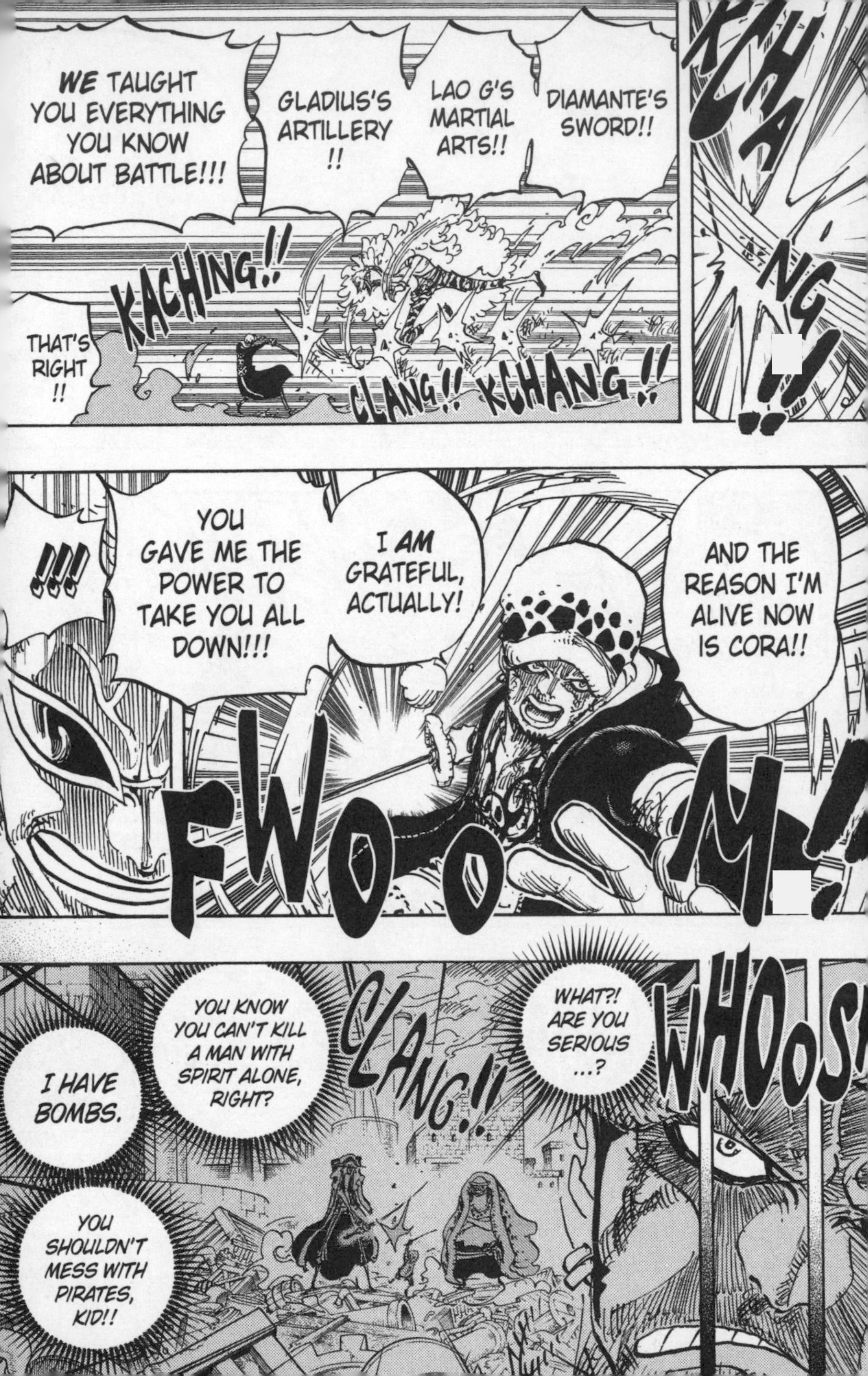
KCHAANG!!
DIAMANTE'S SWORD!!
LAO G'S MARTIAL ARTS!!
GLADIUS'S ARTILLERY !!
WE TAUGHT YOU EVERYTHING YOU KNOW ABOUT BATTLE!!!
KACHING!!
KCHANG!!
CLANG!!
THAT'S RIGHT !!
AND THE REASON I'M ALIVE NOW IS CORA!!
I AM GRATEFUL, ACTUALLY!
YOU GAVE ME THE POWER TO TAKE YOU ALL DOWN!!!
FWOOM!!
!!!
WHOOS
WHAT?! ARE YOU SERIOUS ...?
CLANG!!
YOU KNOW YOU CAN'T KILL A MAN WITH SPIRIT ALONE, RIGHT?
I HAVE BOMBS.
YOU SHOULDN'T MESS WITH PIRATES, KID!!

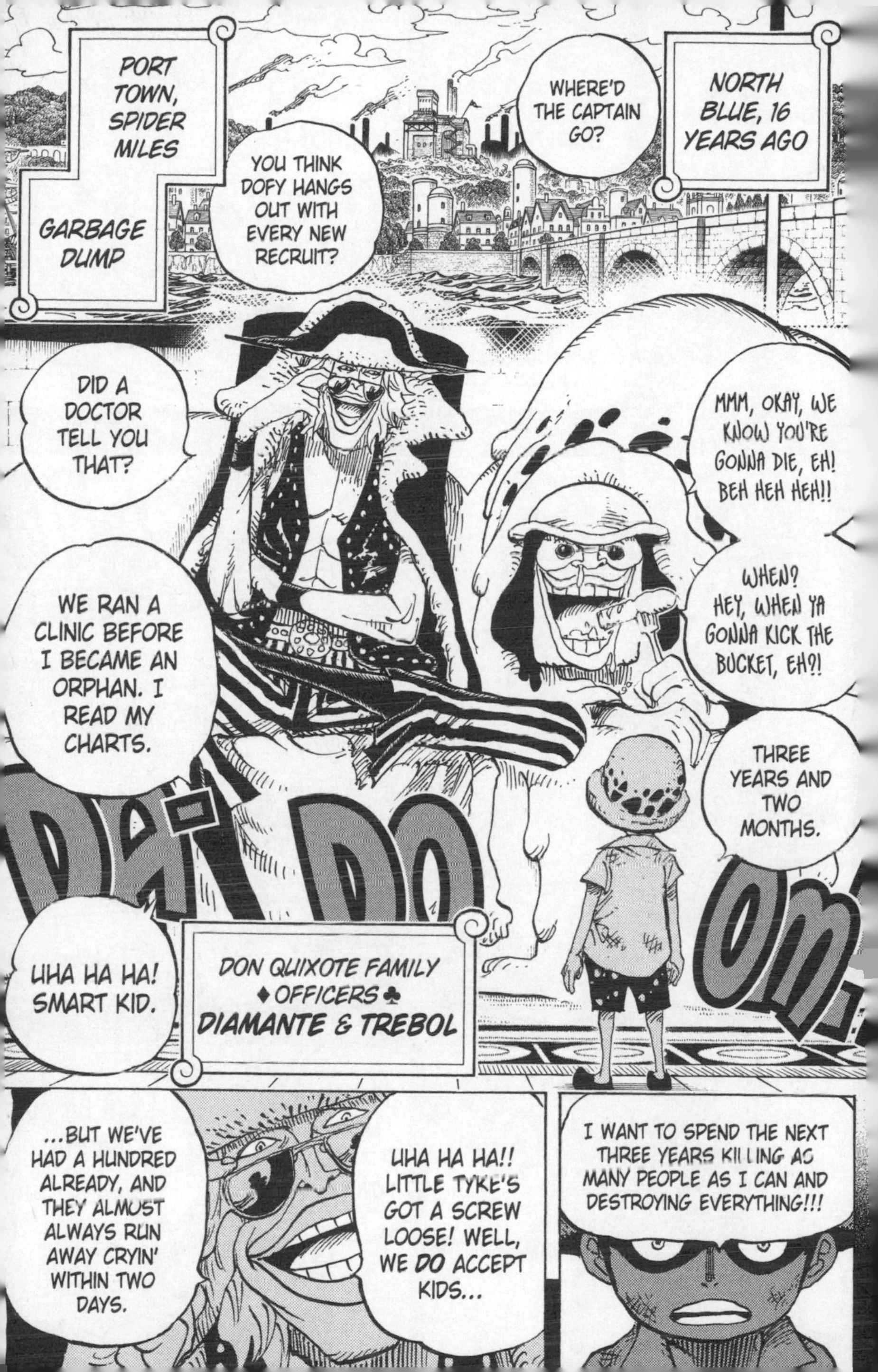
NORTH BLUE, 16 YEARS AGO
WHERE'D THE CAPTAIN GO?
PORT TOWN, SPIDER MILES
YOU THINK DOFY HANGS OUT WITH EVERY NEW RECRUIT?
GARBAGE DUMP
MMM, OKAY, WE KNOW YOU'RE GONNA DIE, EH! BEH HEH HEH!!
WHEN? HEY, WHEN YA GONNA KICK THE BUCKET, EH?!
THREE YEARS AND TWO MONTHS.
DID A DOCTOR TELL YOU THAT?
WE RAN A CLINIC BEFORE I BECAME AN ORPHAN. I READ MY CHARTS.
DA-DOOM
UHA HA HA! SMART KID.
DON QUIXOTE FAMILY ♦OFFICERS♣ DIAMANTE & TREBOL
I WANT TO SPEND THE NEXT THREE YEARS KILLING AS MANY PEOPLE AS I CAN AND DESTROYING EVERYTHING!!!
UHA HA HA!! LITTLE TYKE'S GOT A SCREW LOOSE! WELL, WE *DO* ACCEPT KIDS...
...BUT WE'VE HAD A HUNDRED ALREADY, AND THEY ALMOST ALWAYS RUN AWAY CRYIN' WITHIN TWO DAYS.

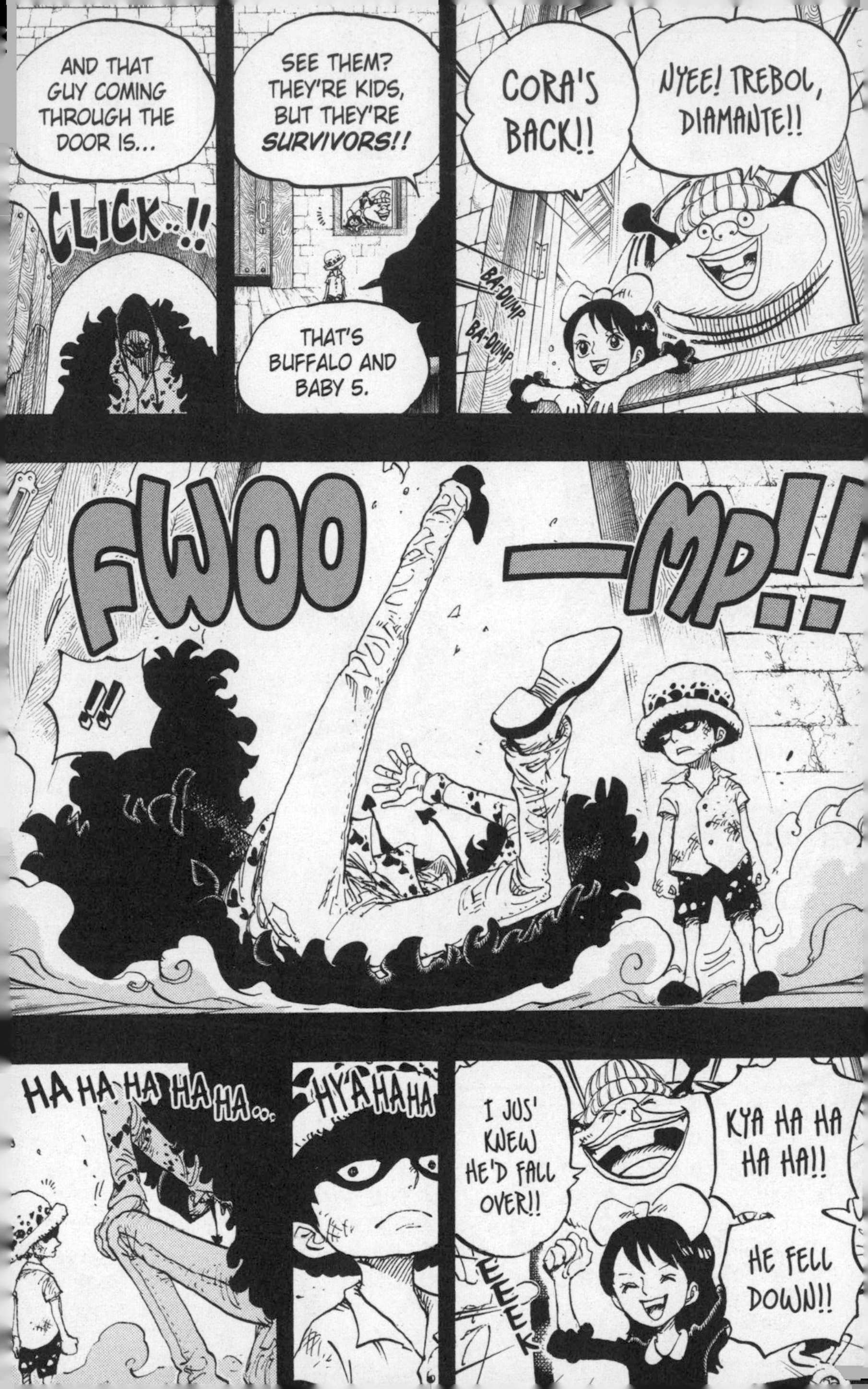
NYEE! TREBOL, DIAMANTE!!
CORA'S BACK!!
BA-DUMP
BA-DUMP
SEE THEM? THEY'RE KIDS, BUT THEY'RE ***SURVIVORS!!***
THAT'S BUFFALO AND BABY 5.
AND THAT GUY COMING THROUGH THE DOOR IS...
CLICK..!!
FWOO—MP!!
!!
KYA HA HA HA HA!!
I JUS' KNEW HE'D FALL OVER!!
HE FELL DOWN!!
EEEEK
HYAHAHAHA
HA HA HA HA HA...

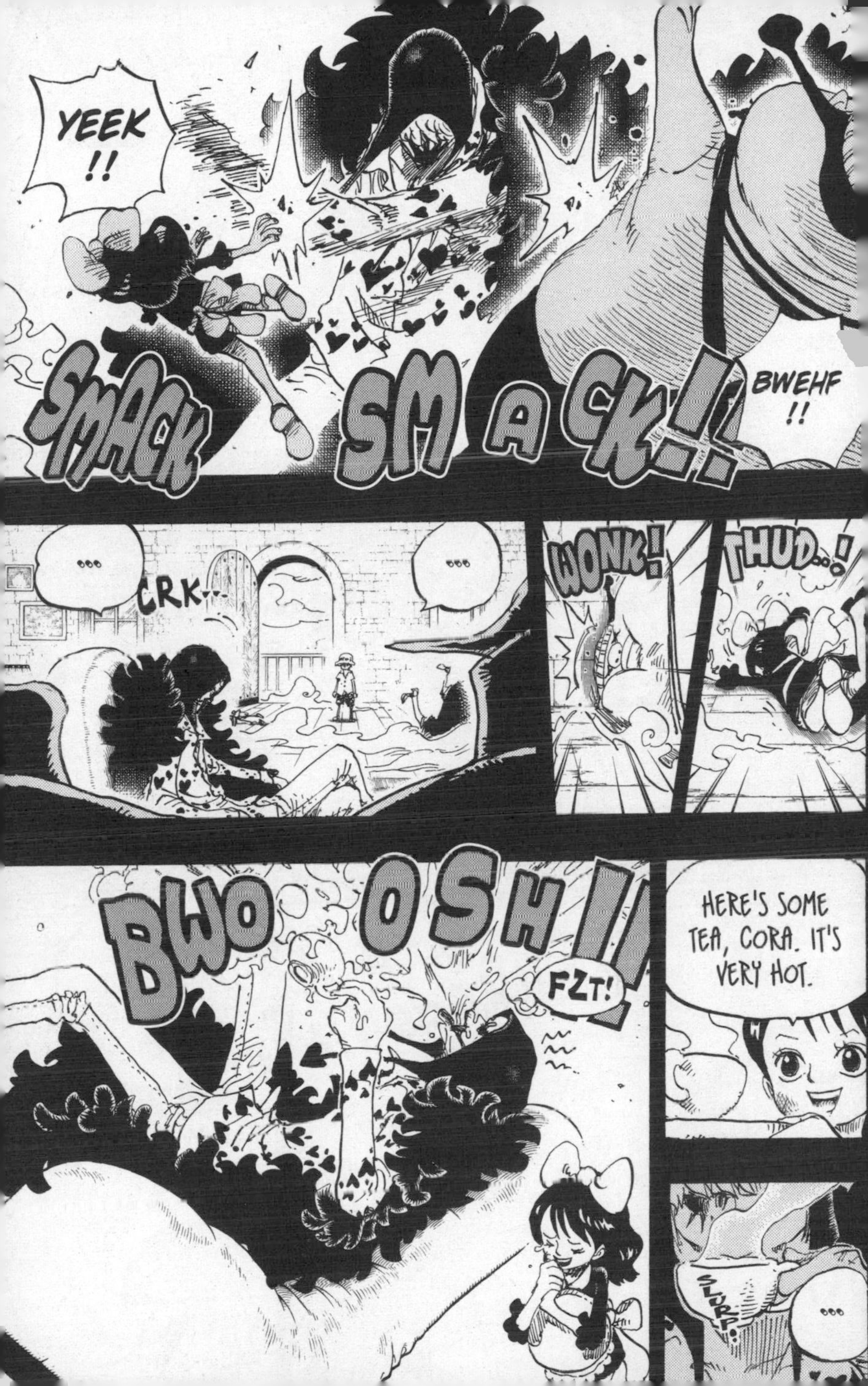
BWEHF!!
YEEK!!
SMACK SMACK!!
THUD...!
WONK!
...
CRK...
...
HERE'S SOME TEA, CORA. IT'S VERY HOT.
SLURP...
...
BWOOSH!!
FZT!

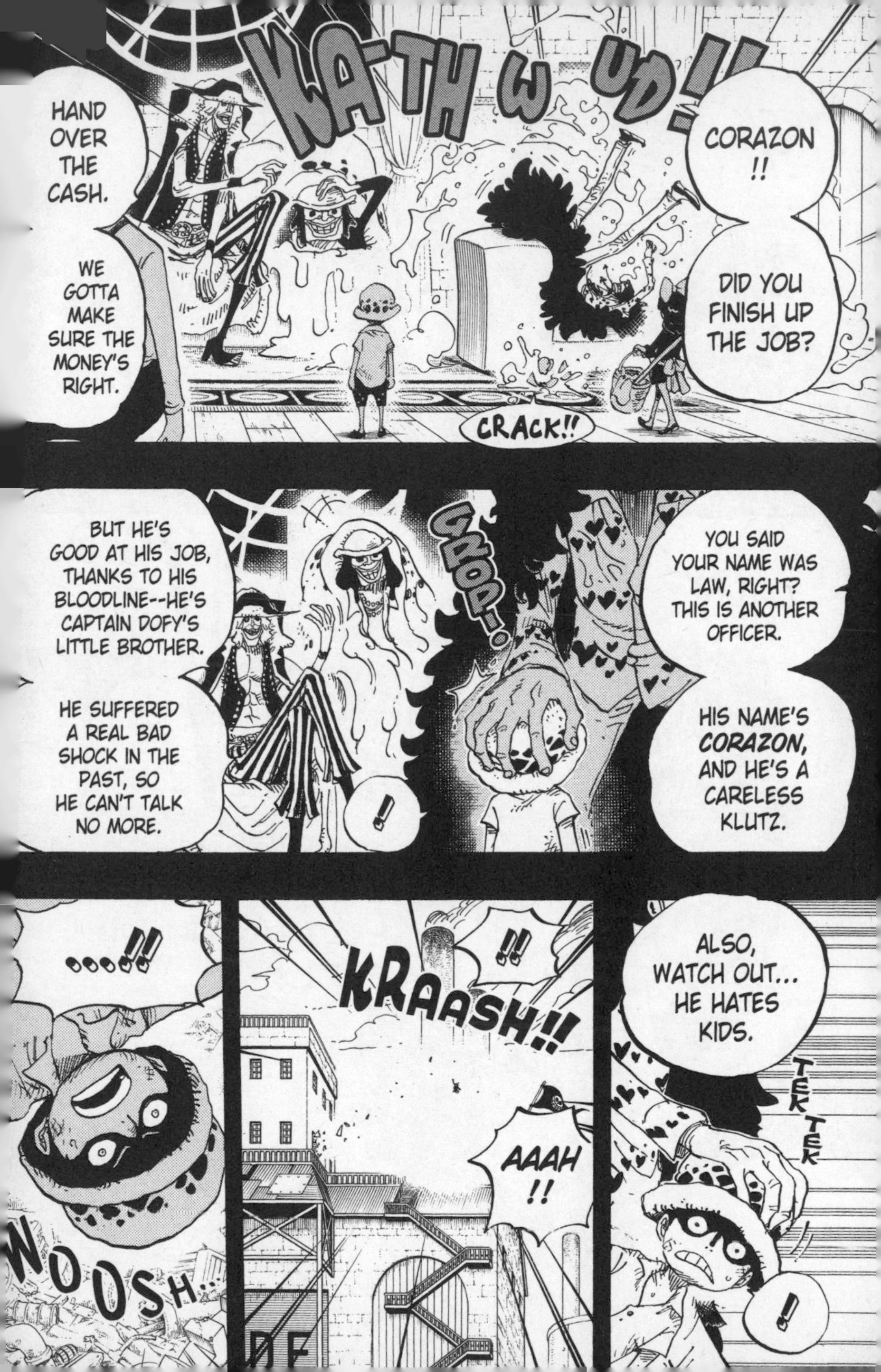

CORAZON !!
DID YOU FINISH UP THE JOB?
KA-THWUD!!
HAND OVER THE CASH.
WE GOTTA MAKE SURE THE MONEY'S RIGHT.
CRACK!!
YOU SAID YOUR NAME WAS LAW, RIGHT? THIS IS ANOTHER OFFICER.
HIS NAME'S *CORAZON,* AND HE'S A CARELESS KLUTZ.
GROP!!
BUT HE'S GOOD AT HIS JOB, THANKS TO HIS BLOODLINE--HE'S CAPTAIN DOFY'S LITTLE BROTHER.
HE SUFFERED A REAL BAD SHOCK IN THE PAST, SO HE CAN'T TALK NO MORE.
!
ALSO, WATCH OUT... HE HATES KIDS.
TEK TEK
!
!!
KRAASH!!
AAAH !!
...!!
WOOSH..

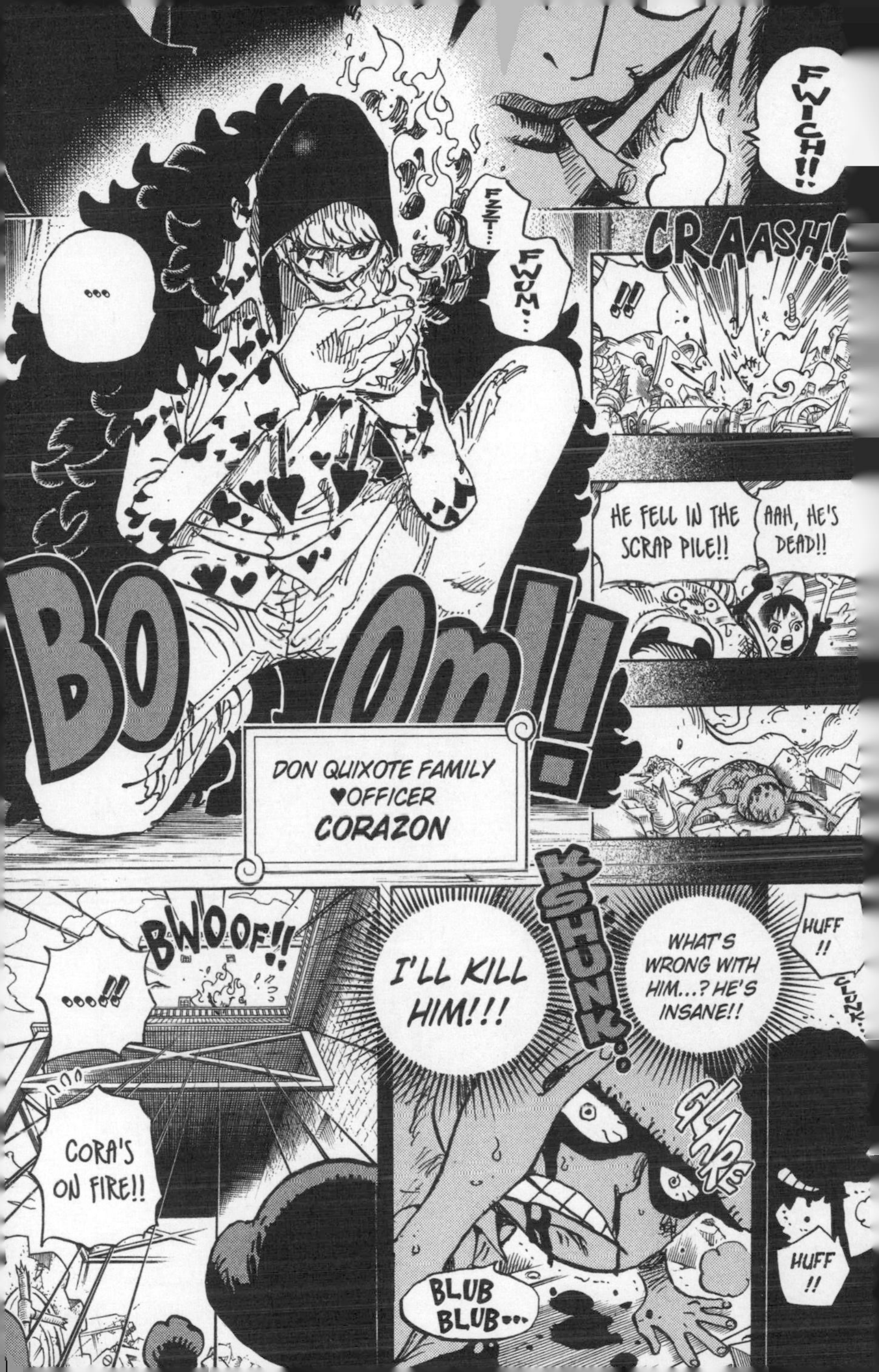
FWICH!!
CRAASH!!
!!
AAH, HE'S DEAD!!
HE FELL IN THE SCRAP PILE!!
FZZT...
FWUM...
...
BOOM!!
DON QUIXOTE FAMILY
♥OFFICER
CORAZON
HUFF!!
WHAT'S WRONG WITH HIM...? HE'S INSANE!!
CLUNK...
KSHUNK
I'LL KILL HIM!!!
GLARE
HUFF!!
BLUB BLUB...
BWOOF!!
...!!
CORA'S ON FIRE!!

KSHUNK!!
GWUFH !!
KDO OM!!

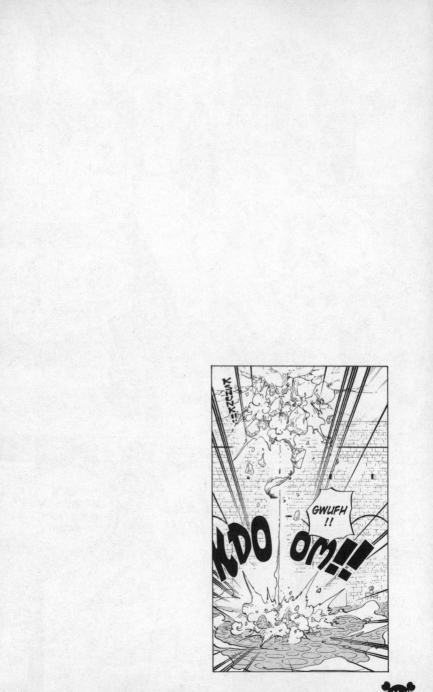

Chapter 762:

THE WHITE TOWN

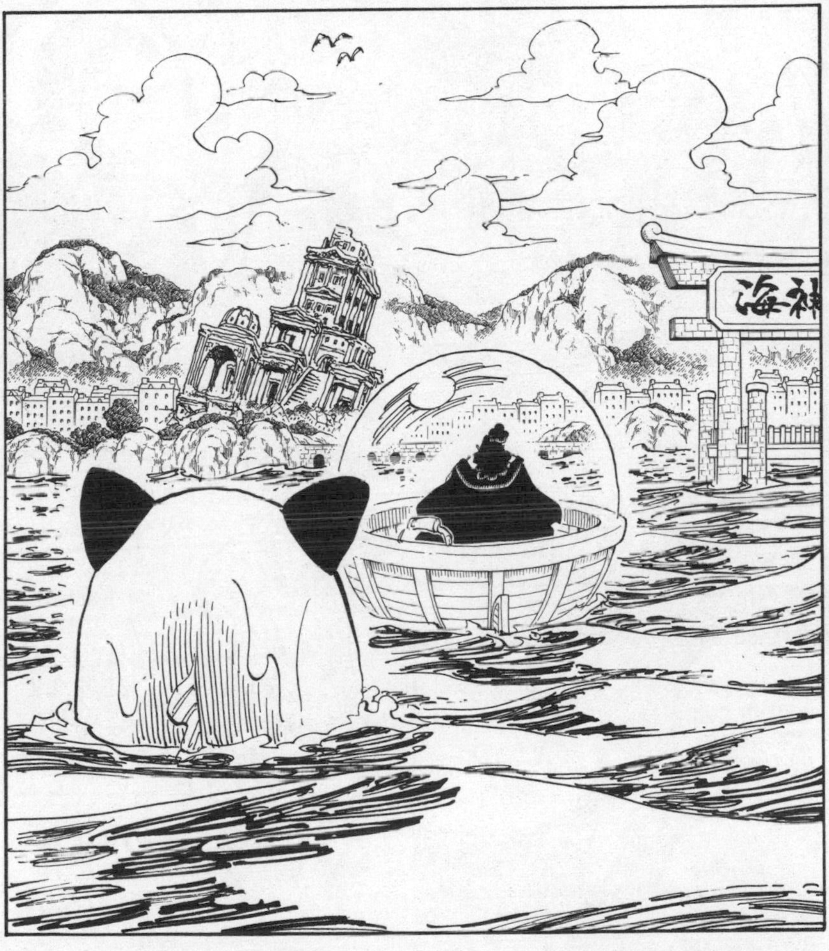
海神
*SEA GOD

THE SOLITARY JOURNEY OF JIMBEI, FIRST SON OF THE SEA, VOL. 11: "LET'S VISIT THE PORT TOWN"

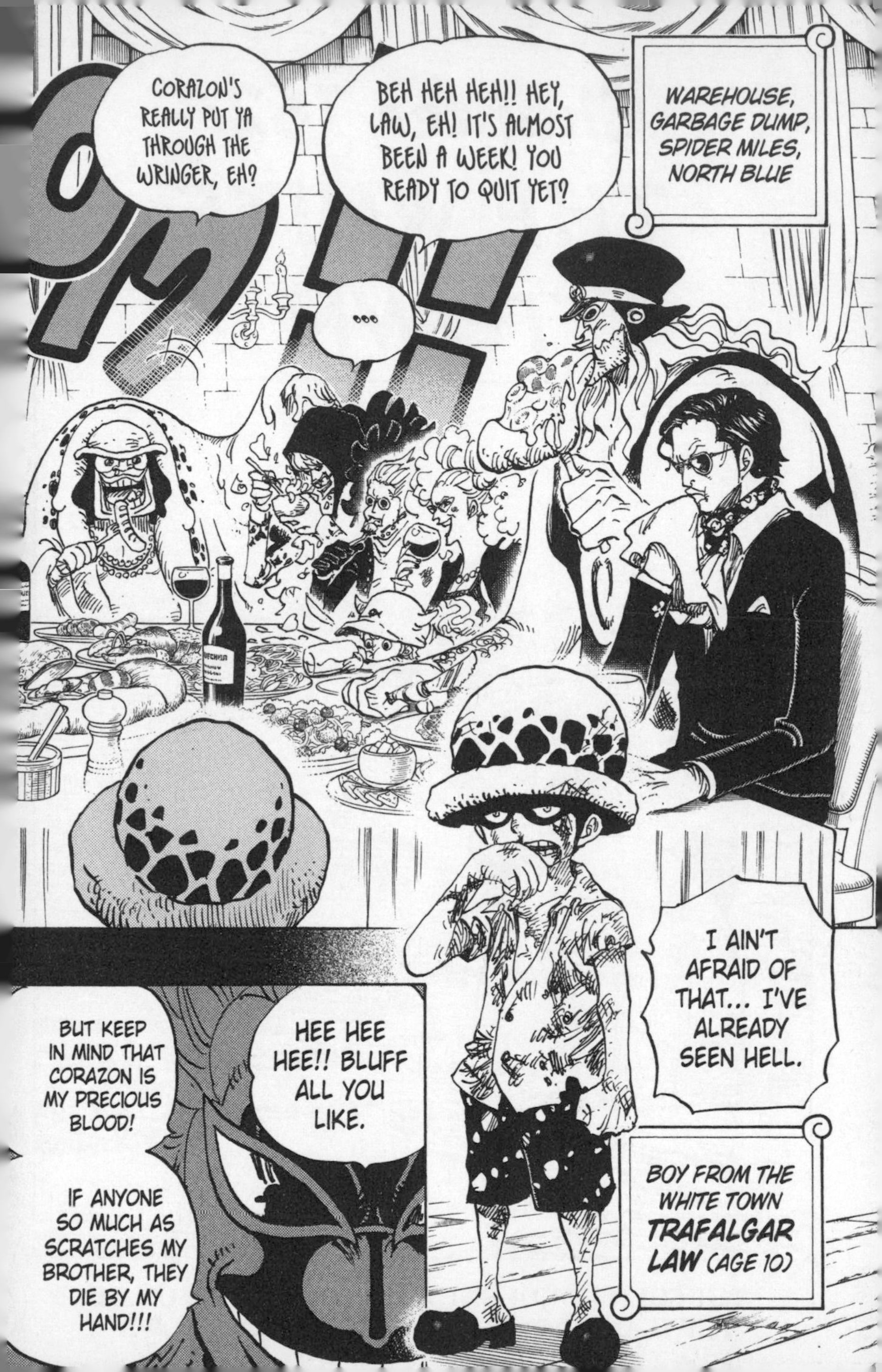
WAREHOUSE, GARBAGE DUMP, SPIDER MILES, NORTH BLUE
BEH HEH HEH!! HEY, LAW, EH! IT'S ALMOST BEEN A WEEK! YOU READY TO QUIT YET?
CORAZON'S REALLY PUT YA THROUGH THE WRINGER, EH?
...
I AIN'T AFRAID OF THAT... I'VE ALREADY SEEN HELL.
BOY FROM THE WHITE TOWN **TRAFALGAR LAW** (AGE 10)
HEE HEE HEE!! BLUFF ALL YOU LIKE.
BUT KEEP IN MIND THAT CORAZON IS MY PRECIOUS BLOOD!
IF ANYONE SO MUCH AS SCRATCHES MY BROTHER, THEY DIE BY MY HAND!!!

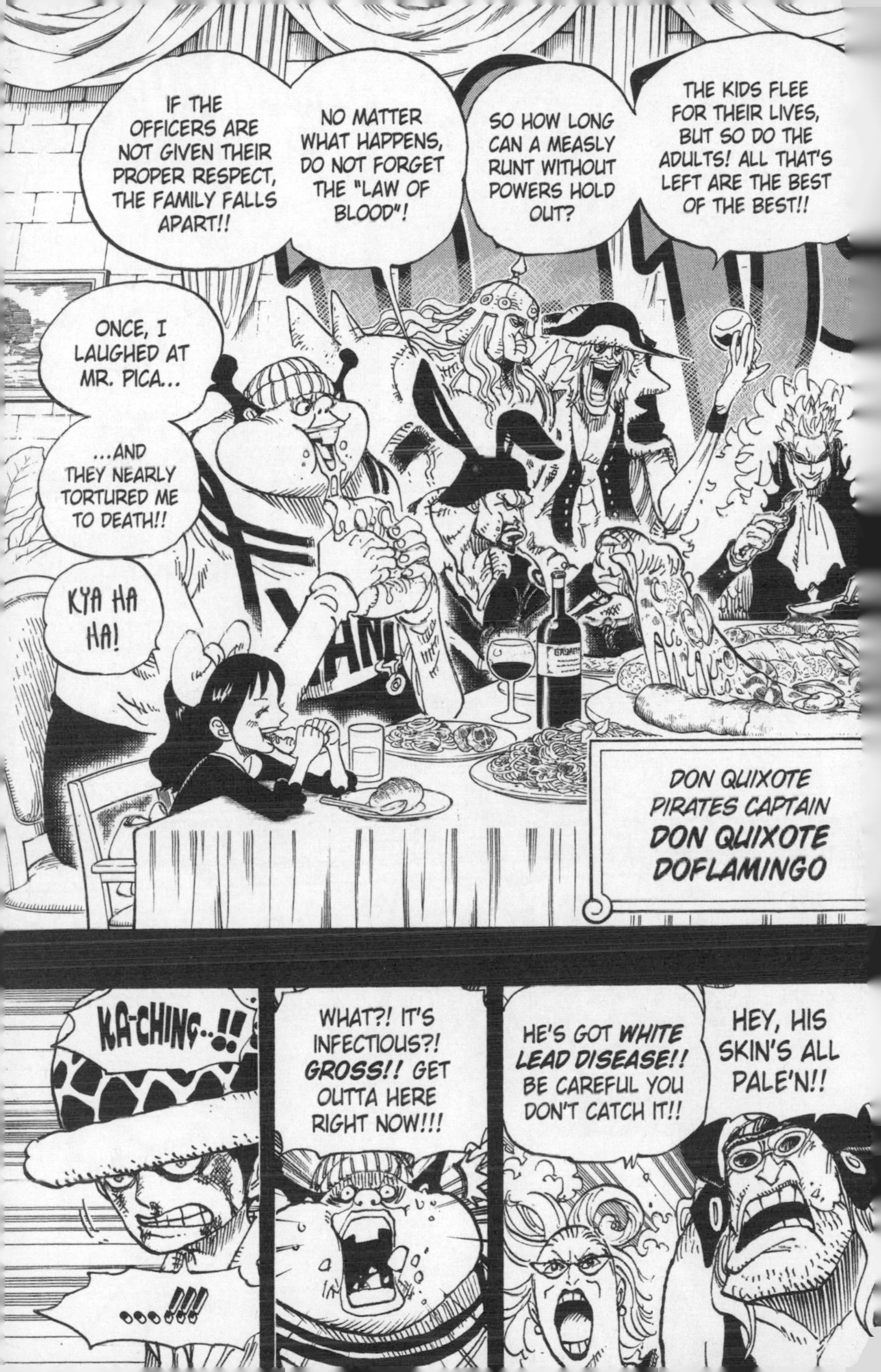
THE KIDS FLEE FOR THEIR LIVES, BUT SO DO THE ADULTS! ALL THAT'S LEFT ARE THE BEST OF THE BEST!!
SO HOW LONG CAN A MEASLY RUNT WITHOUT POWERS HOLD OUT?
NO MATTER WHAT HAPPENS, DO NOT FORGET THE "LAW OF BLOOD"!
IF THE OFFICERS ARE NOT GIVEN THEIR PROPER RESPECT, THE FAMILY FALLS APART!!
ONCE, I LAUGHED AT MR. PICA...
...AND THEY NEARLY TORTURED ME TO DEATH!!
KYA HA HA!
DON QUIXOTE PIRATES CAPTAIN
DON QUIXOTE DOFLAMINGO
HEY, HIS SKIN'S ALL PALE'N!!
HE'S GOT WHITE LEAD DISEASE!! BE CAREFUL YOU DON'T CATCH IT!!
WHAT?! IT'S INFECTIOUS?! GROSS!! GET OUTTA HERE RIGHT NOW!!!
KA-CHING..!!
....!!!

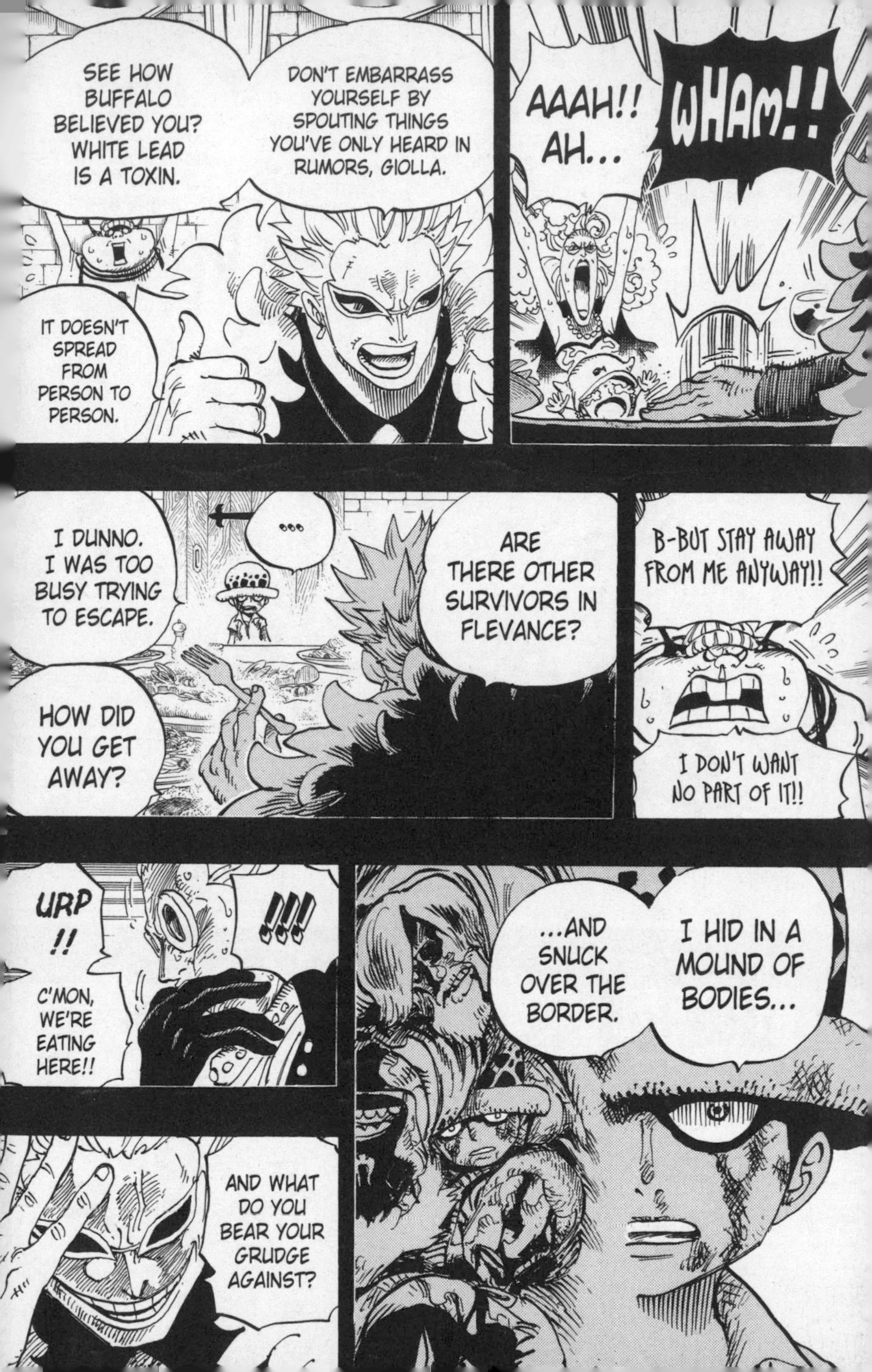
AAAH!! AH...
WHAM!!
DON'T EMBARRASS YOURSELF BY SPOUTING THINGS YOU'VE ONLY HEARD IN RUMORS, GIOLLA.
SEE HOW BUFFALO BELIEVED YOU? WHITE LEAD IS A TOXIN.
IT DOESN'T SPREAD FROM PERSON TO PERSON.
B-BUT STAY AWAY FROM ME ANYWAY!!
I DON'T WANT NO PART OF IT!!
ARE THERE OTHER SURVIVORS IN FLEVANCE?
...
I DUNNO. I WAS TOO BUSY TRYING TO ESCAPE.
HOW DID YOU GET AWAY?
I HID IN A MOUND OF BODIES...
...AND SNUCK OVER THE BORDER.
!!!
URP !!
C'MON, WE'RE EATING HERE!!
AND WHAT DO YOU BEAR YOUR GRUDGE AGAINST?

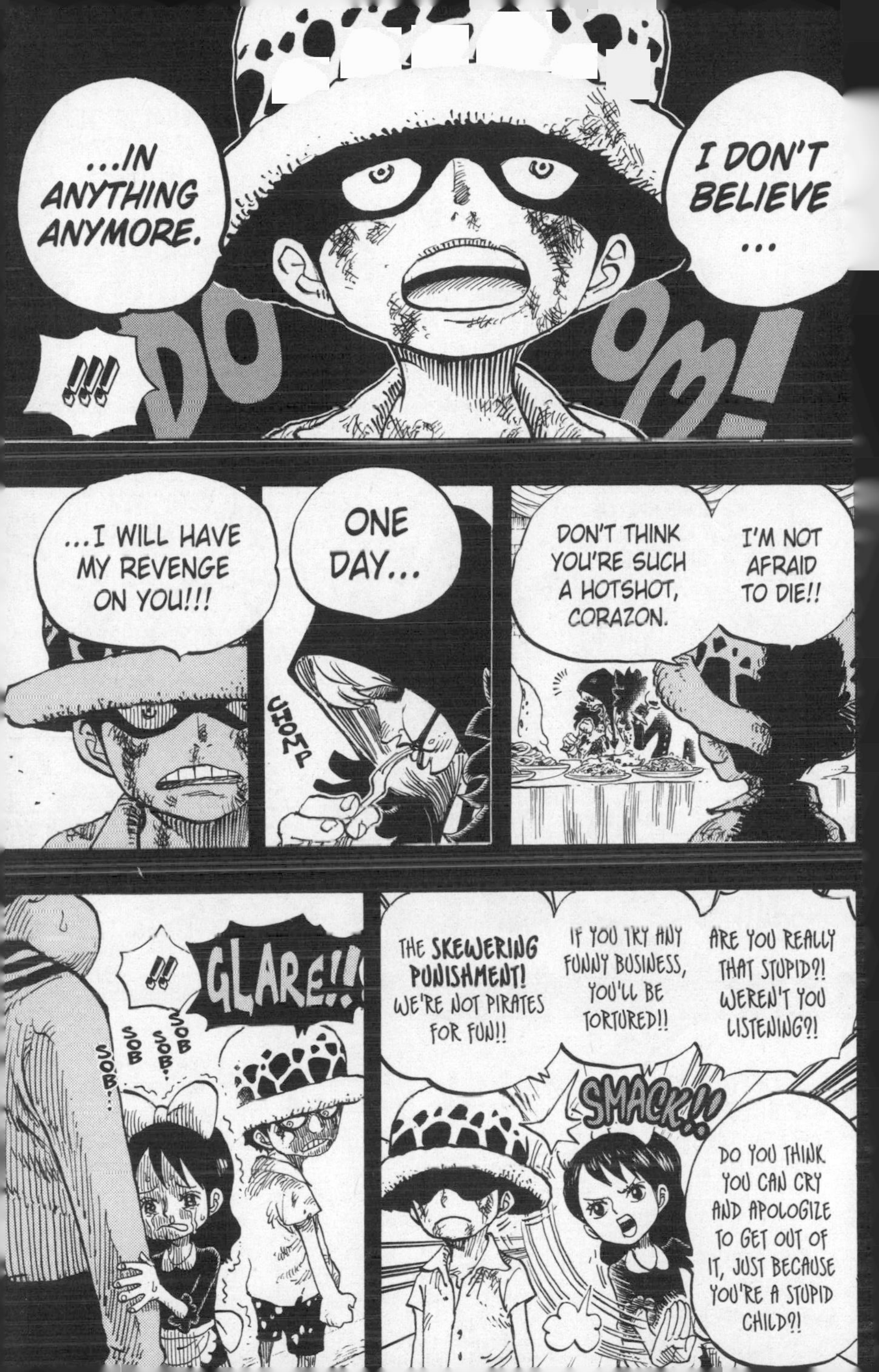
I DON'T BELIEVE ...
...IN ANYTHING ANYMORE.
!!!
DOOM!
I'M NOT AFRAID TO DIE!!
DON'T THINK YOU'RE SUCH A HOTSHOT, CORAZON.
ONE DAY...
CHOMP
...I WILL HAVE MY REVENGE ON YOU!!!
ARE YOU REALLY THAT STUPID?! WEREN'T YOU LISTENING?!
IF YOU TRY ANY FUNNY BUSINESS, YOU'LL BE TORTURED!!
THE SKEWERING PUNISHMENT! WE'RE NOT PIRATES FOR FUN!!
SMACK!!
DO YOU THINK YOU CAN CRY AND APOLOGIZE TO GET OUT OF IT, JUST BECAUSE YOU'RE A STUPID CHILD?!
GLARE!!
!!
SOB SOB...
SOB SOB...

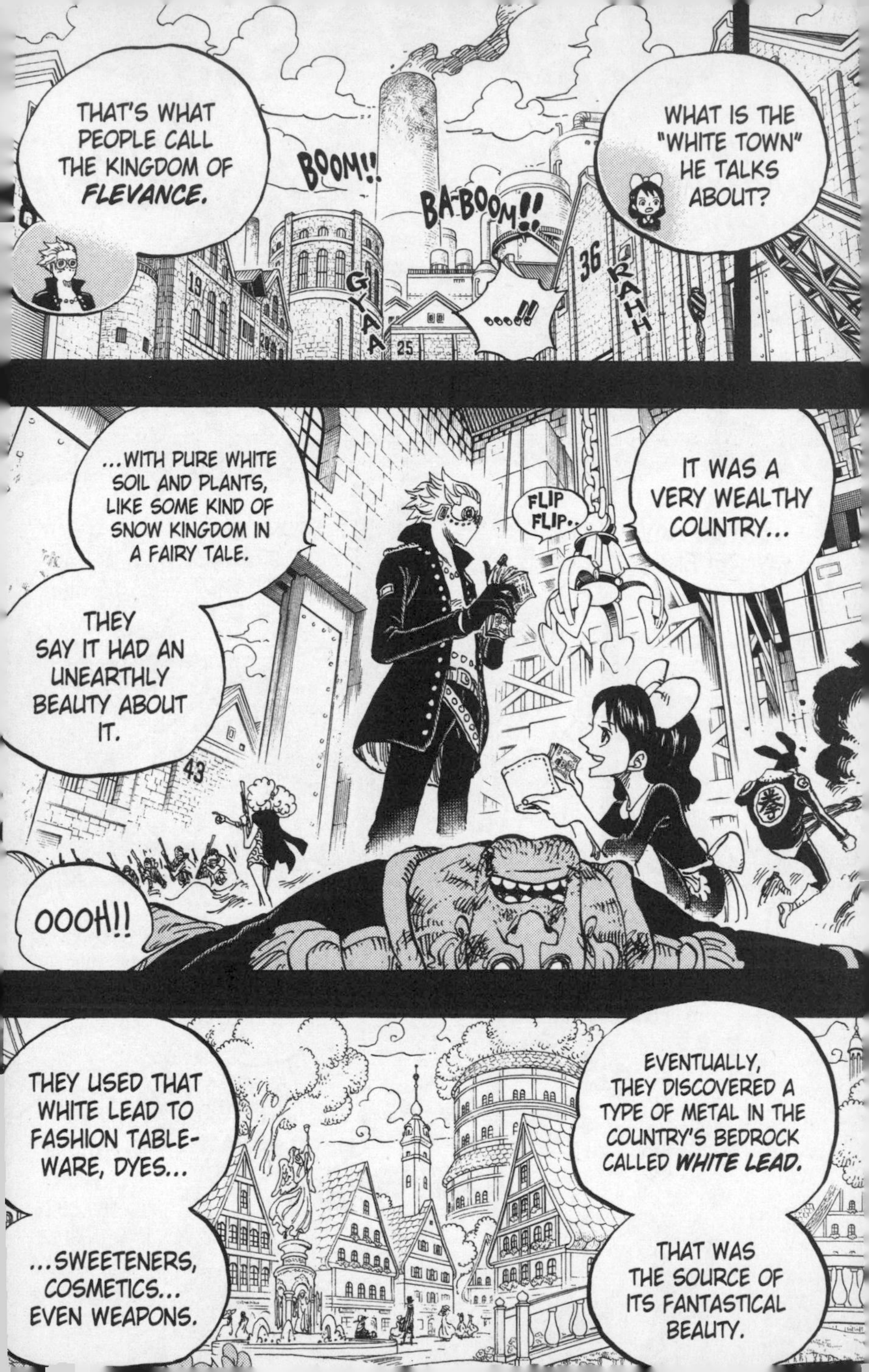
WHAT IS THE "WHITE TOWN" HE TALKS ABOUT?
THAT'S WHAT PEOPLE CALL THE KINGDOM OF *FLEVANCE.*
BA-BOOM!!
BOOM!!
RAHH
....!!
GYAA
IT WAS A VERY WEALTHY COUNTRY...
FLIP FLIP..
...WITH PURE WHITE SOIL AND PLANTS, LIKE SOME KIND OF SNOW KINGDOM IN A FAIRY TALE.
THEY SAY IT HAD AN UNEARTHLY BEAUTY ABOUT IT.
OOOH!!
EVENTUALLY, THEY DISCOVERED A TYPE OF METAL IN THE COUNTRY'S BEDROCK CALLED ***WHITE LEAD.***
THAT WAS THE SOURCE OF ITS FANTASTICAL BEAUTY.
THEY USED THAT WHITE LEAD TO FASHION TABLE-WARE, DYES...
...SWEETENERS, COSMETICS... EVEN WEAPONS.

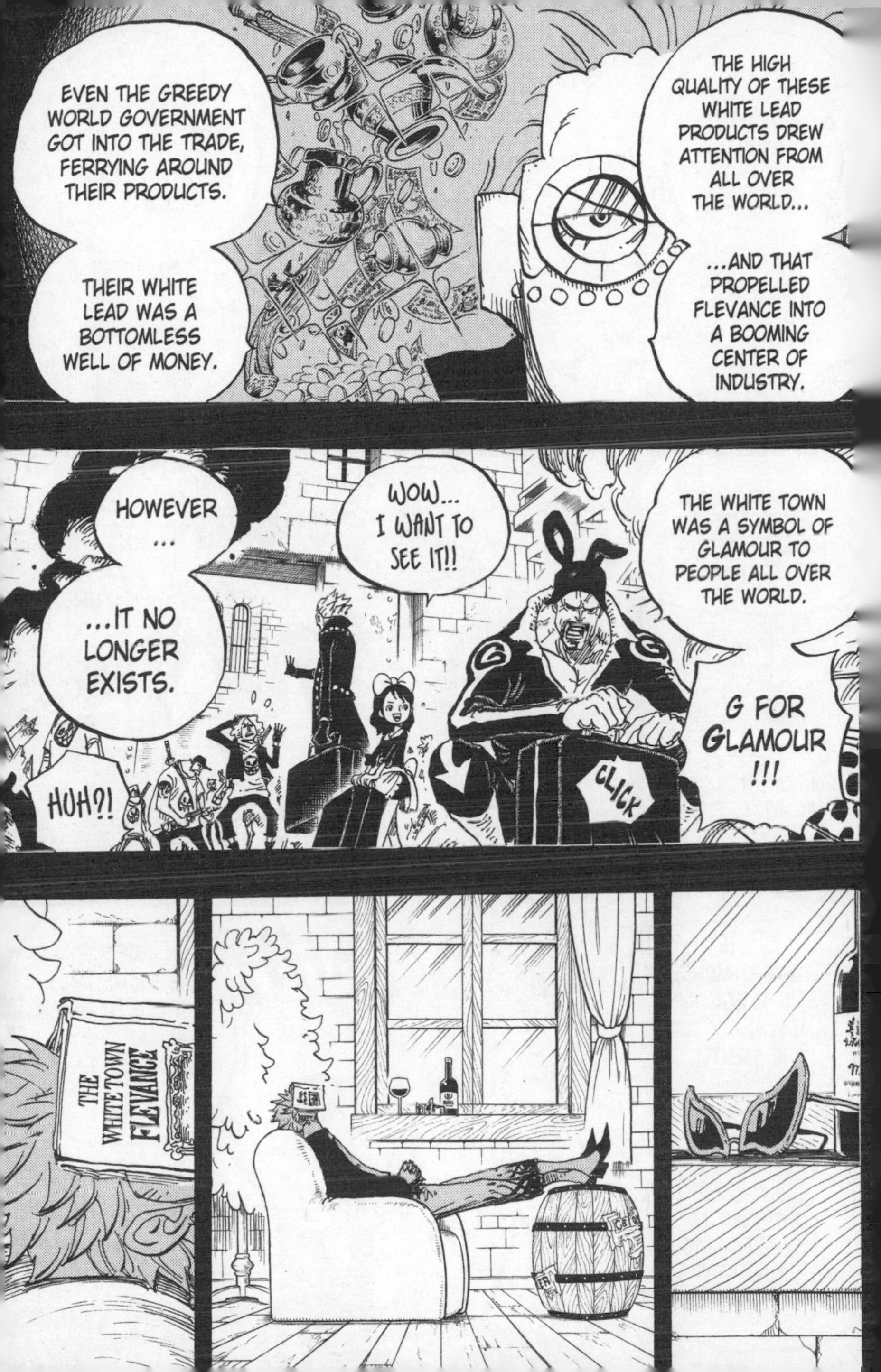
THE HIGH QUALITY OF THESE WHITE LEAD PRODUCTS DREW ATTENTION FROM ALL OVER THE WORLD...
...AND THAT PROPELLED FLEVANCE INTO A BOOMING CENTER OF INDUSTRY.
EVEN THE GREEDY WORLD GOVERNMENT GOT INTO THE TRADE, FERRYING AROUND THEIR PRODUCTS.
THEIR WHITE LEAD WAS A BOTTOMLESS WELL OF MONEY.
THE WHITE TOWN WAS A SYMBOL OF GLAMOUR TO PEOPLE ALL OVER THE WORLD.
G FOR GLAMOUR!!!
CLICK
WOW... I WANT TO SEE IT!!
HOWEVER...
...IT NO LONGER EXISTS.
HUH?!
THE WHITE TOWN FLEVANCE

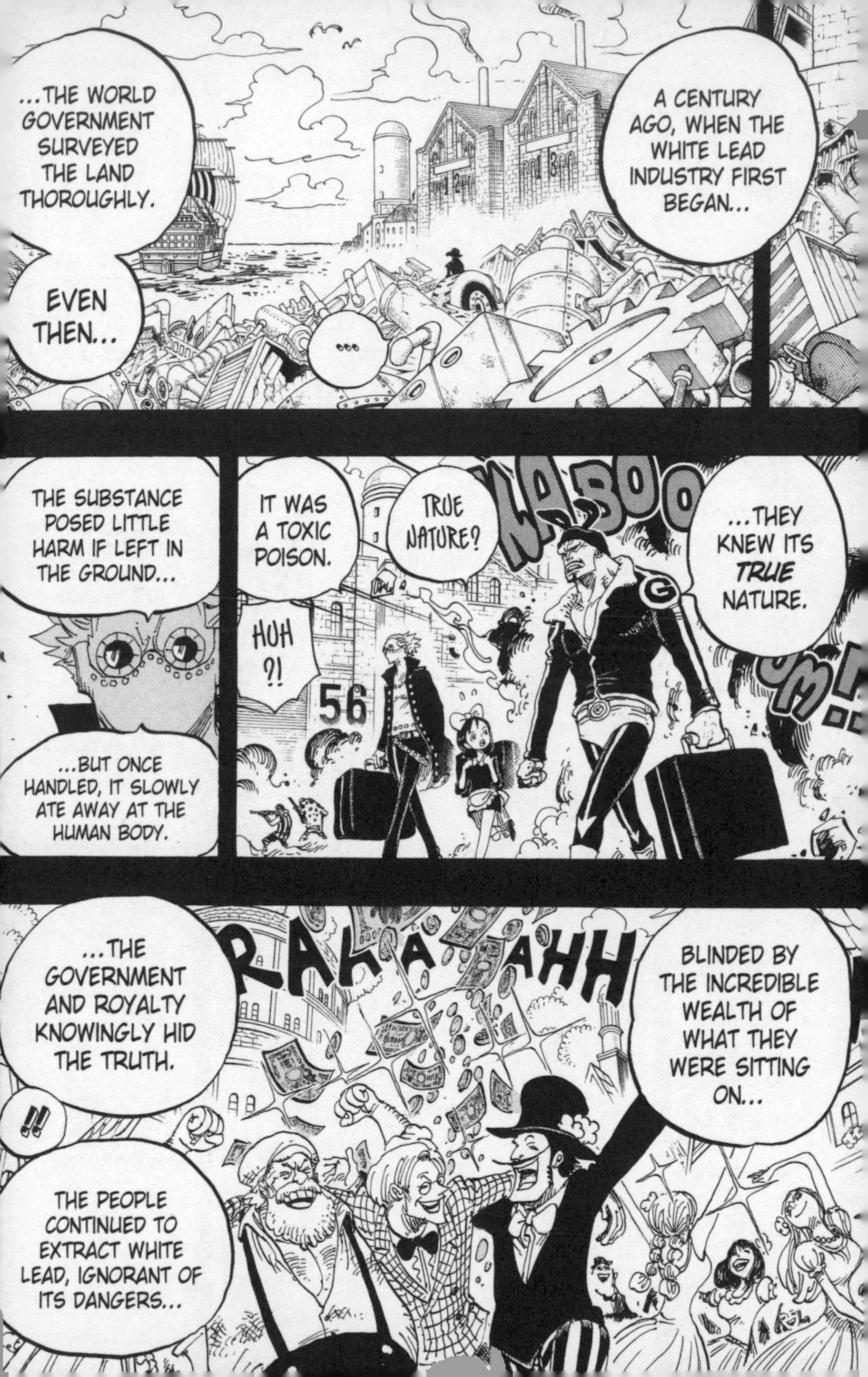
A CENTURY AGO, WHEN THE WHITE LEAD INDUSTRY FIRST BEGAN...
...THE WORLD GOVERNMENT SURVEYED THE LAND THOROUGHLY.
EVEN THEN...
...
...THEY KNEW ITS TRUE NATURE.
TRUE NATURE?
IT WAS A TOXIC POISON.
HUH ?!
56
THE SUBSTANCE POSED LITTLE HARM IF LEFT IN THE GROUND...
...BUT ONCE HANDLED, IT SLOWLY ATE AWAY AT THE HUMAN BODY.
BLINDED BY THE INCREDIBLE WEALTH OF WHAT THEY WERE SITTING ON...
...THE GOVERNMENT AND ROYALTY KNOWINGLY HID THE TRUTH.
!!
THE PEOPLE CONTINUED TO EXTRACT WHITE LEAD, IGNORANT OF ITS DANGERS...

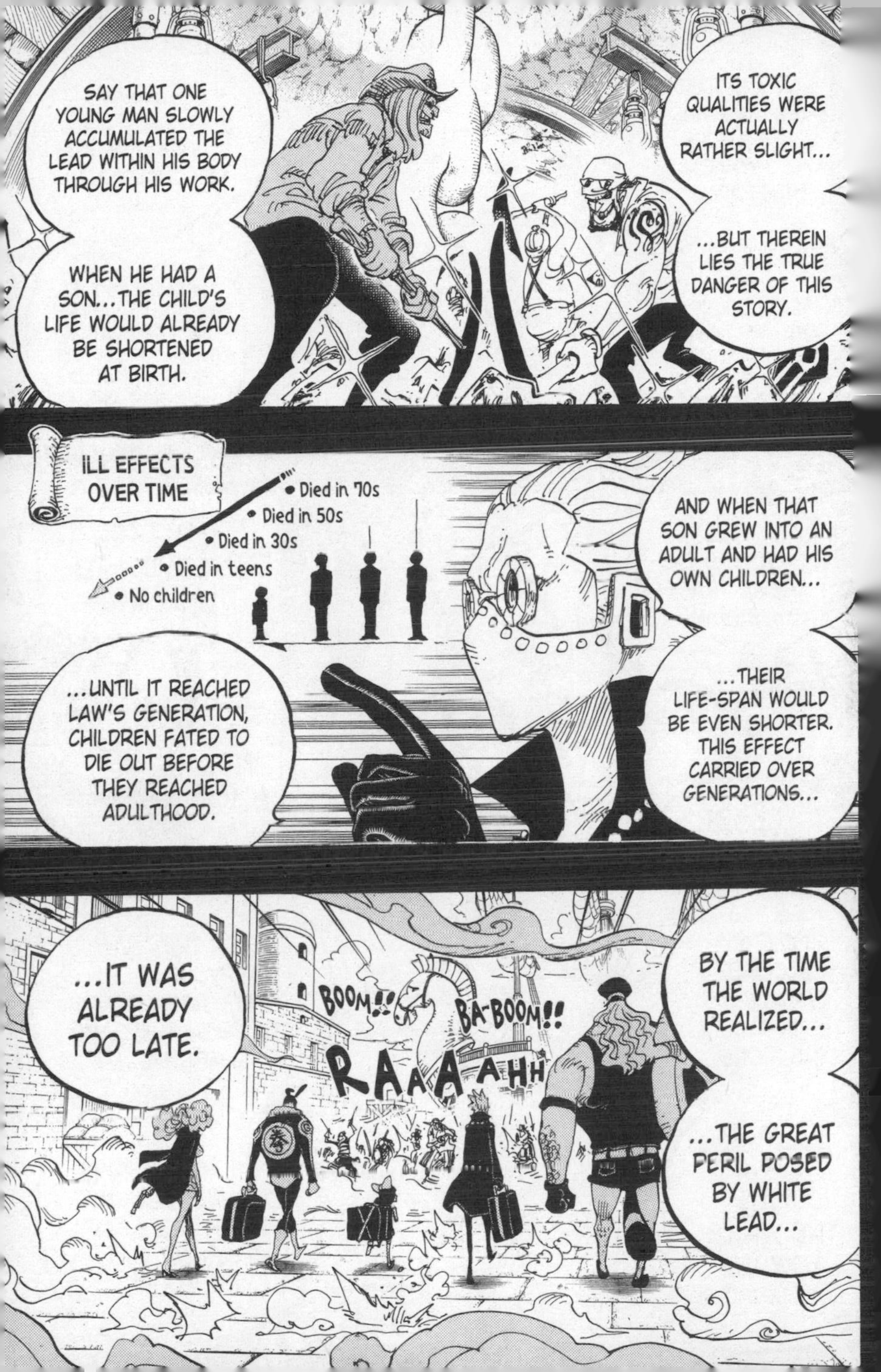
ITS TOXIC QUALITIES WERE ACTUALLY RATHER SLIGHT...
...BUT THEREIN LIES THE TRUE DANGER OF THIS STORY.
SAY THAT ONE YOUNG MAN SLOWLY ACCUMULATED THE LEAD WITHIN HIS BODY THROUGH HIS WORK.
WHEN HE HAD A SON...THE CHILD'S LIFE WOULD ALREADY BE SHORTENED AT BIRTH.
AND WHEN THAT SON GREW INTO AN ADULT AND HAD HIS OWN CHILDREN...
...THEIR LIFE-SPAN WOULD BE EVEN SHORTER. THIS EFFECT CARRIED OVER GENERATIONS...
ILL EFFECTS OVER TIME
Died in 70s
Died in 50s
Died in 30s
Died in teens
No children
...UNTIL IT REACHED LAW'S GENERATION, CHILDREN FATED TO DIE OUT BEFORE THEY REACHED ADULTHOOD.
BY THE TIME THE WORLD REALIZED...
...THE GREAT PERIL POSED BY WHITE LEAD...
...IT WAS ALREADY TOO LATE.
BA-BOOM!!
BOOM!!
RAAAAHH

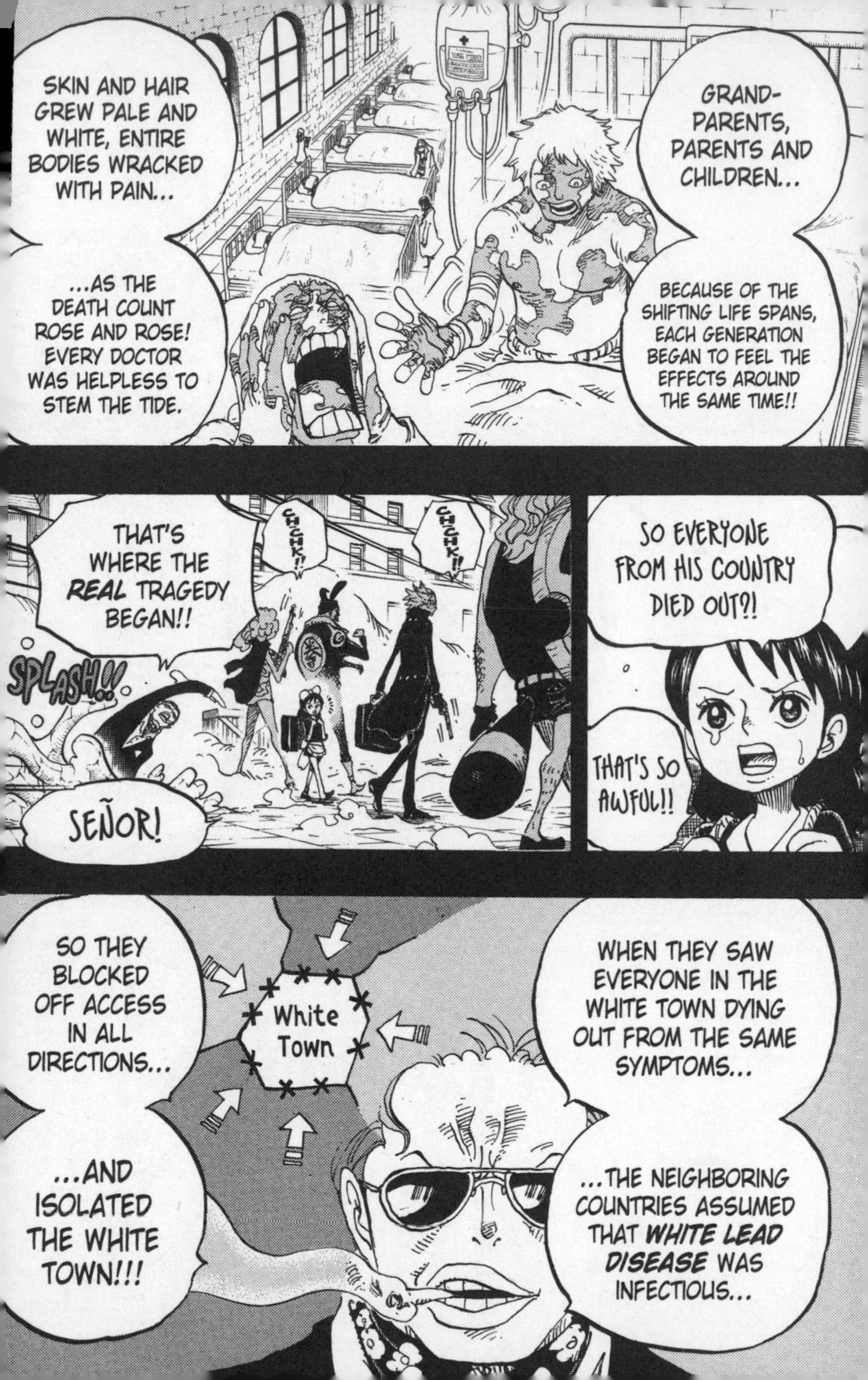
GRAND-PARENTS, PARENTS AND CHILDREN...
BECAUSE OF THE SHIFTING LIFE SPANS, EACH GENERATION BEGAN TO FEEL THE EFFECTS AROUND THE SAME TIME!!
SKIN AND HAIR GREW PALE AND WHITE, ENTIRE BODIES WRACKED WITH PAIN...
...AS THE DEATH COUNT ROSE AND ROSE! EVERY DOCTOR WAS HELPLESS TO STEM THE TIDE.
SO EVERYONE FROM HIS COUNTRY DIED OUT?!
THAT'S SO AWFUL!!
CHCHK!!
CHCHK!!
THAT'S WHERE THE ***REAL*** TRAGEDY BEGAN!!
SPLASH!!
SEÑOR!
WHEN THEY SAW EVERYONE IN THE WHITE TOWN DYING OUT FROM THE SAME SYMPTOMS...
...THE NEIGHBORING COUNTRIES ASSUMED THAT ***WHITE LEAD DISEASE*** WAS INFECTIOUS...
White Town
SO THEY BLOCKED OFF ACCESS IN ALL DIRECTIONS...
...AND ISOLATED THE WHITE TOWN!!!

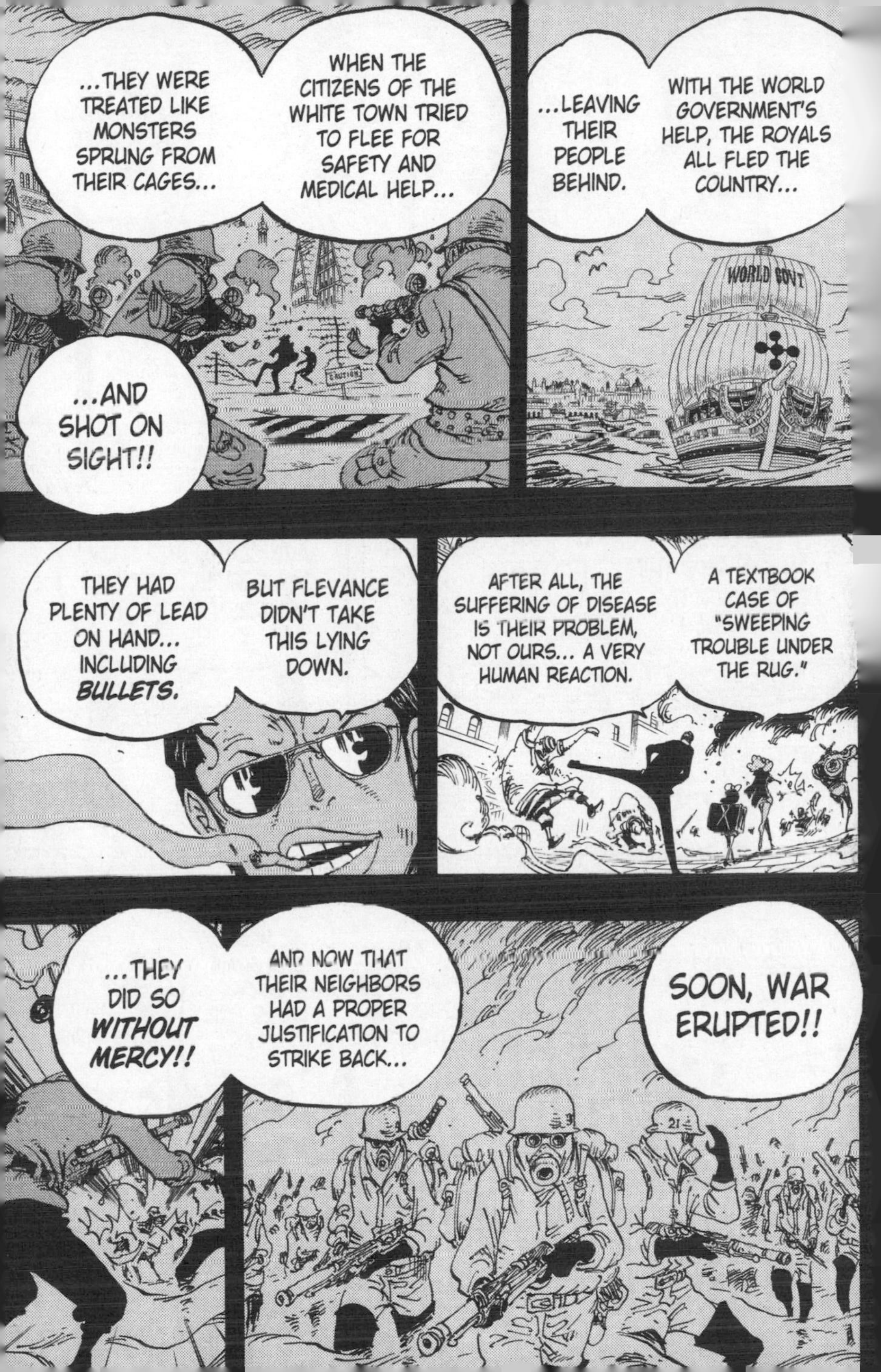
WITH THE WORLD GOVERNMENT'S HELP, THE ROYALS ALL FLED THE COUNTRY...
...LEAVING THEIR PEOPLE BEHIND.
WORLD GOVT
WHEN THE CITIZENS OF THE WHITE TOWN TRIED TO FLEE FOR SAFETY AND MEDICAL HELP...
...THEY WERE TREATED LIKE MONSTERS SPRUNG FROM THEIR CAGES...
...AND SHOT ON SIGHT!!
A TEXTBOOK CASE OF "SWEEPING TROUBLE UNDER THE RUG."
AFTER ALL, THE SUFFERING OF DISEASE IS THEIR PROBLEM, NOT OURS... A VERY HUMAN REACTION.
BUT FLEVANCE DIDN'T TAKE THIS LYING DOWN.
THEY HAD PLENTY OF LEAD ON HAND... INCLUDING *BULLETS.*
SOON, WAR ERUPTED!!
AND NOW THAT THEIR NEIGHBORS HAD A PROPER JUSTIFICATION TO STRIKE BACK...
...THEY DID SO *WITHOUT MERCY!!*

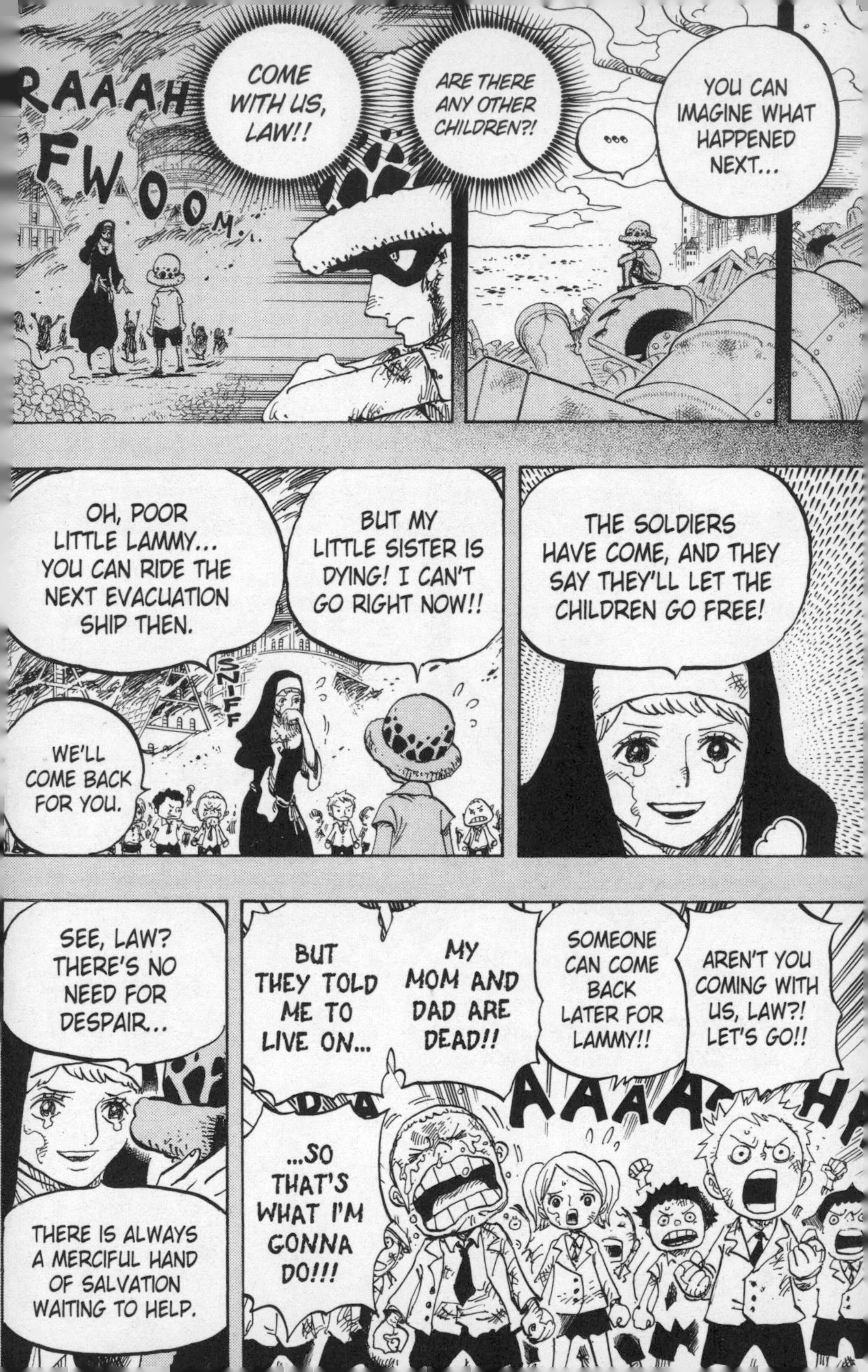
YOU CAN IMAGINE WHAT HAPPENED NEXT...
...
ARE THERE ANY OTHER CHILDREN?!
COME WITH US, LAW!!
RAAAH
FWOOM.
THE SOLDIERS HAVE COME, AND THEY SAY THEY'LL LET THE CHILDREN GO FREE!
BUT MY LITTLE SISTER IS DYING! I CAN'T GO RIGHT NOW!!
OH, POOR LITTLE LAMMY... YOU CAN RIDE THE NEXT EVACUATION SHIP THEN.
SNIFF
WE'LL COME BACK FOR YOU.
AREN'T YOU COMING WITH US, LAW?! LET'S GO!!
SOMEONE CAN COME BACK LATER FOR LAMMY!!
MY MOM AND DAD ARE DEAD!!
BUT THEY TOLD ME TO LIVE ON...
...SO THAT'S WHAT I'M GONNA DO!!!
SEE, LAW? THERE'S NO NEED FOR DESPAIR...
THERE IS ALWAYS A MERCIFUL HAND OF SALVATION WAITING TO HELP.

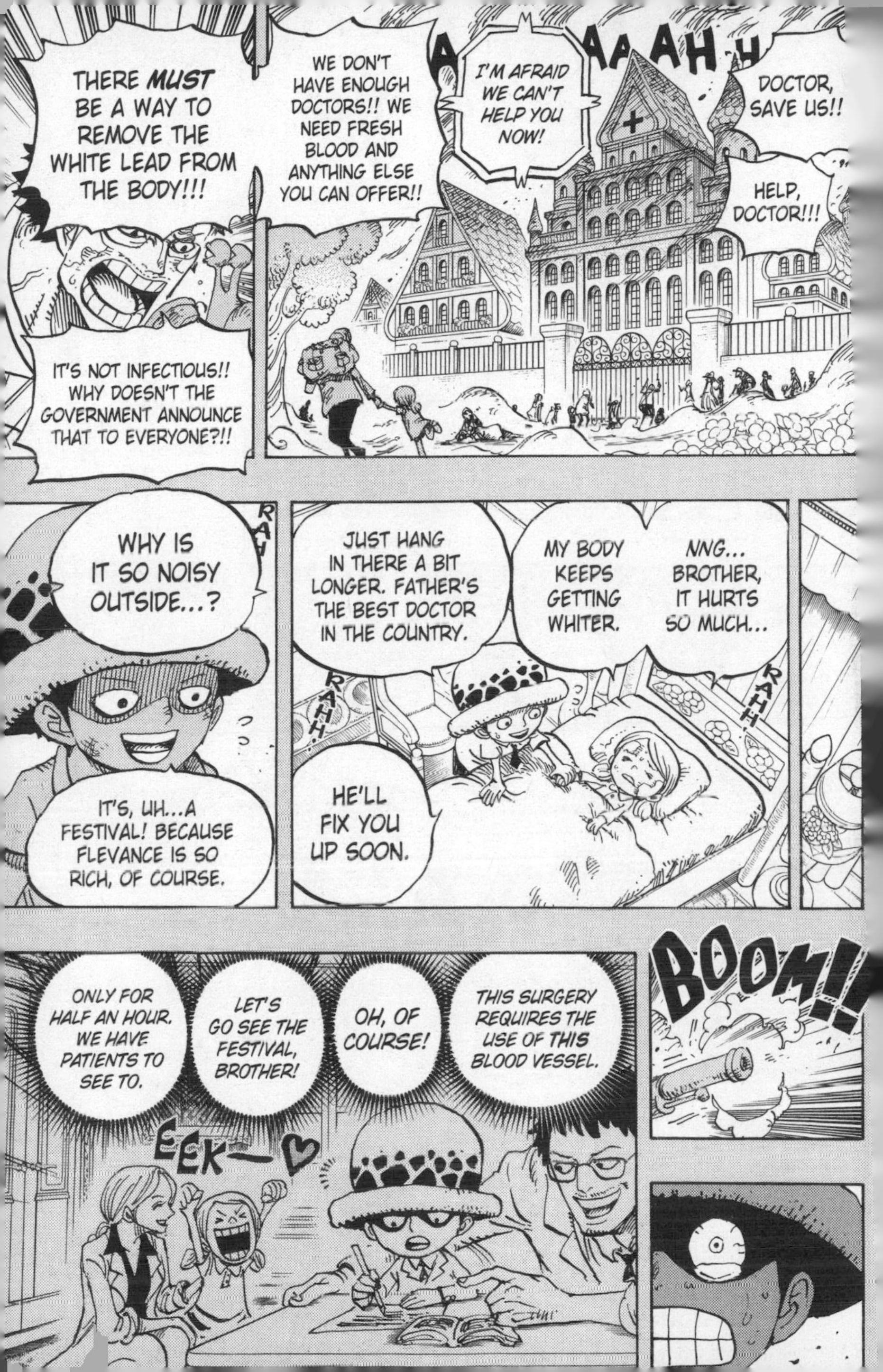
AAAAH
DOCTOR, SAVE US!!
I'M AFRAID WE CAN'T HELP YOU NOW!
WE DON'T HAVE ENOUGH DOCTORS!! WE NEED FRESH BLOOD AND ANYTHING ELSE YOU CAN OFFER!!
HELP, DOCTOR!!!
THERE MUST BE A WAY TO REMOVE THE WHITE LEAD FROM THE BODY!!!
IT'S NOT INFECTIOUS!! WHY DOESN'T THE GOVERNMENT ANNOUNCE THAT TO EVERYONE?!!
NNG... BROTHER, IT HURTS SO MUCH...
MY BODY KEEPS GETTING WHITER.
RAHH
JUST HANG IN THERE A BIT LONGER. FATHER'S THE BEST DOCTOR IN THE COUNTRY.
RAHH
HE'LL FIX YOU UP SOON.
RAH
WHY IS IT SO NOISY OUTSIDE...?
IT'S, UH...A FESTIVAL! BECAUSE FLEVANCE IS SO RICH, OF COURSE.
BOOM!!
THIS SURGERY REQUIRES THE USE OF THIS BLOOD VESSEL.
OH, OF COURSE!
LET'S GO SEE THE FESTIVAL, BROTHER!
ONLY FOR HALF AN HOUR. WE HAVE PATIENTS TO SEE TO.
EEK—♥

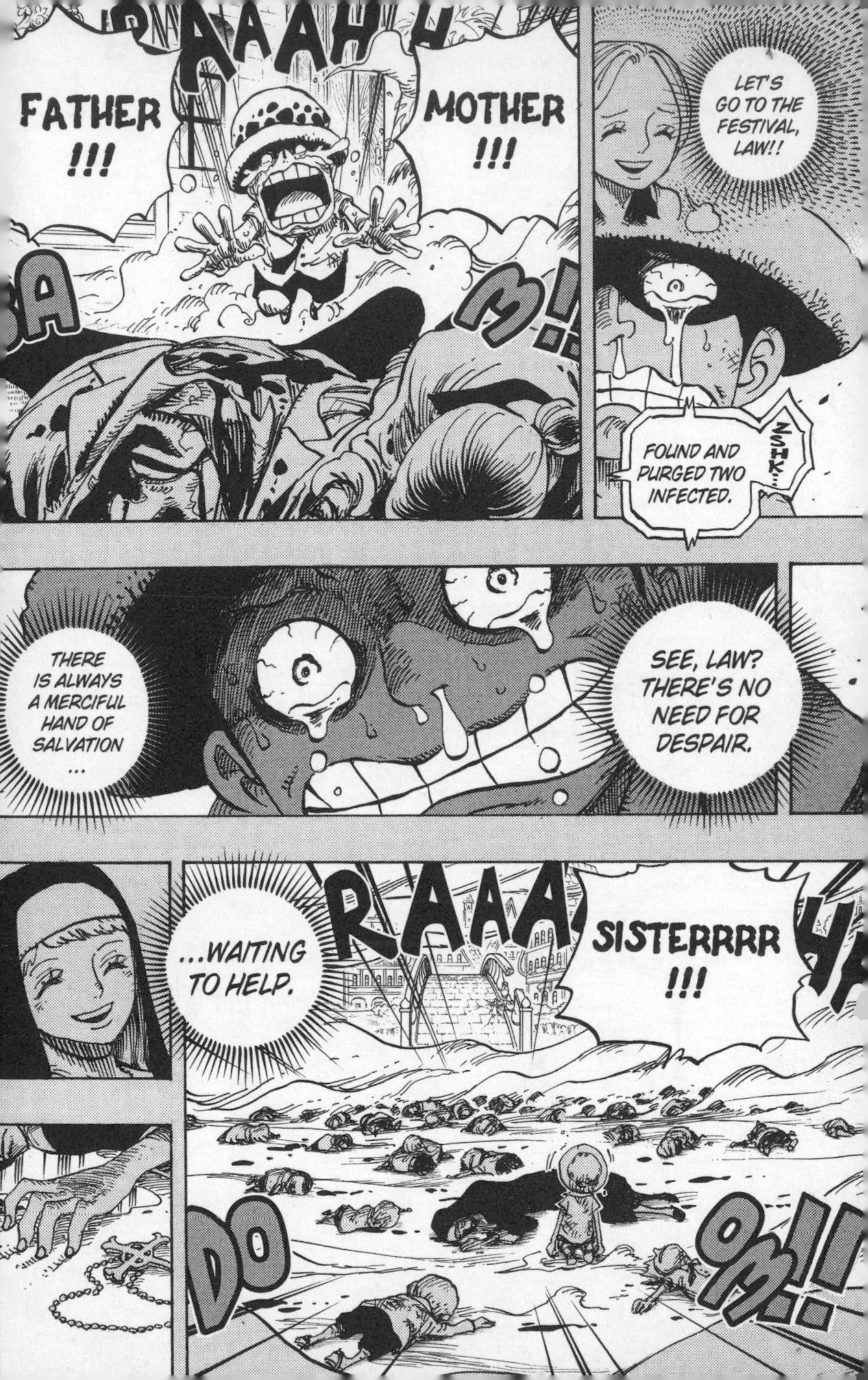
LET'S GO TO THE FESTIVAL, LAW!!
ZSHK...
FOUND AND PURGED TWO INFECTED.
RAAAHH
MOTHER !!!
FATHER !!!
M!!
BA
SEE, LAW? THERE'S NO NEED FOR DESPAIR.
THERE IS ALWAYS A MERCIFUL HAND OF SALVATION ...
SISTERRRR !!!
RAAA
OM!!
DO
...WAITING TO HELP.

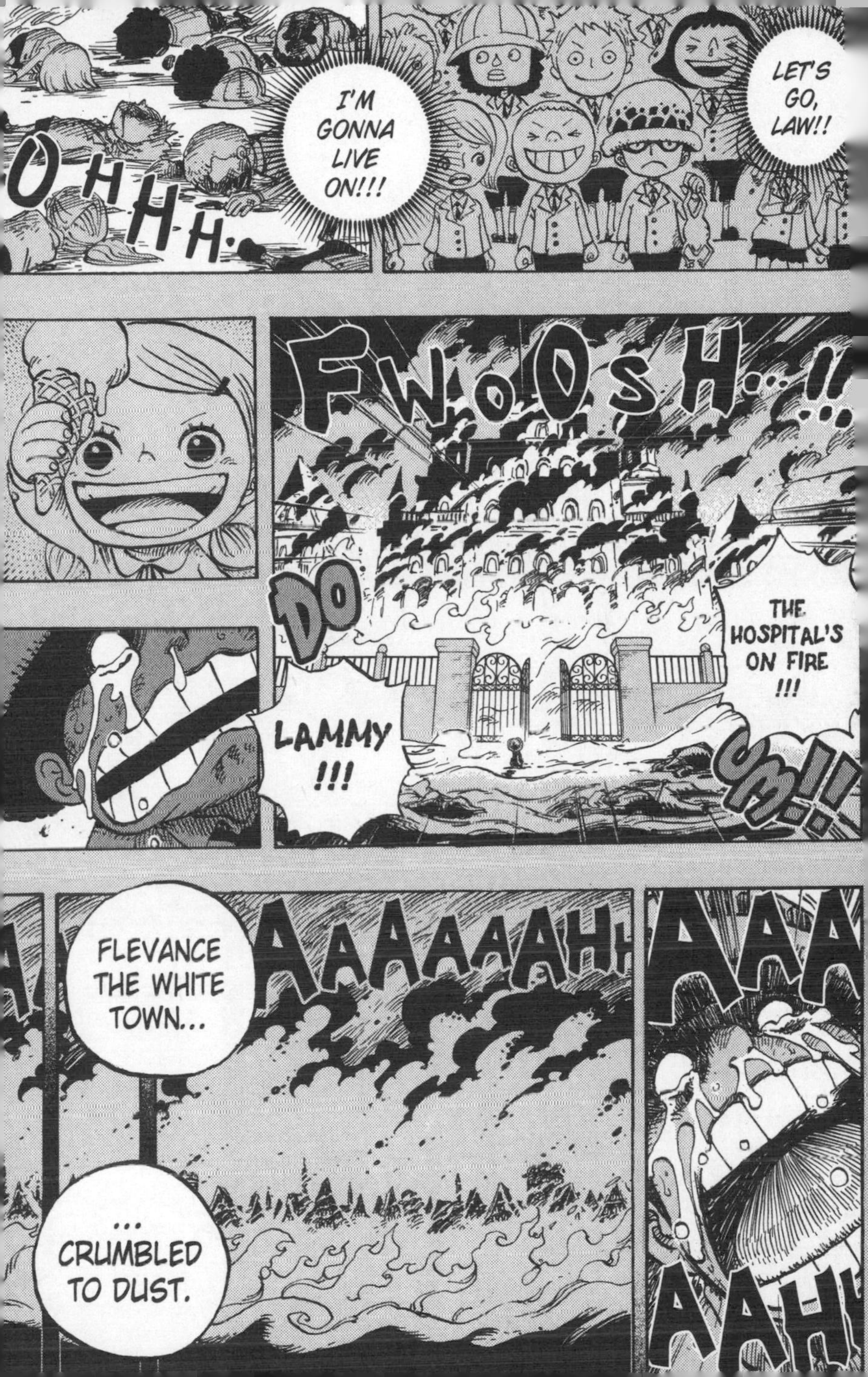
LET'S GO, LAW!!
I'M GONNA LIVE ON!!!
OHHHH.
FWOOSH...!!
THE HOSPITAL'S ON FIRE!!!
DOOM!!
LAMMY!!!
AAAAH
AAAAAAAH
FLEVANCE THE WHITE TOWN...
...CRUMBLED TO DUST.

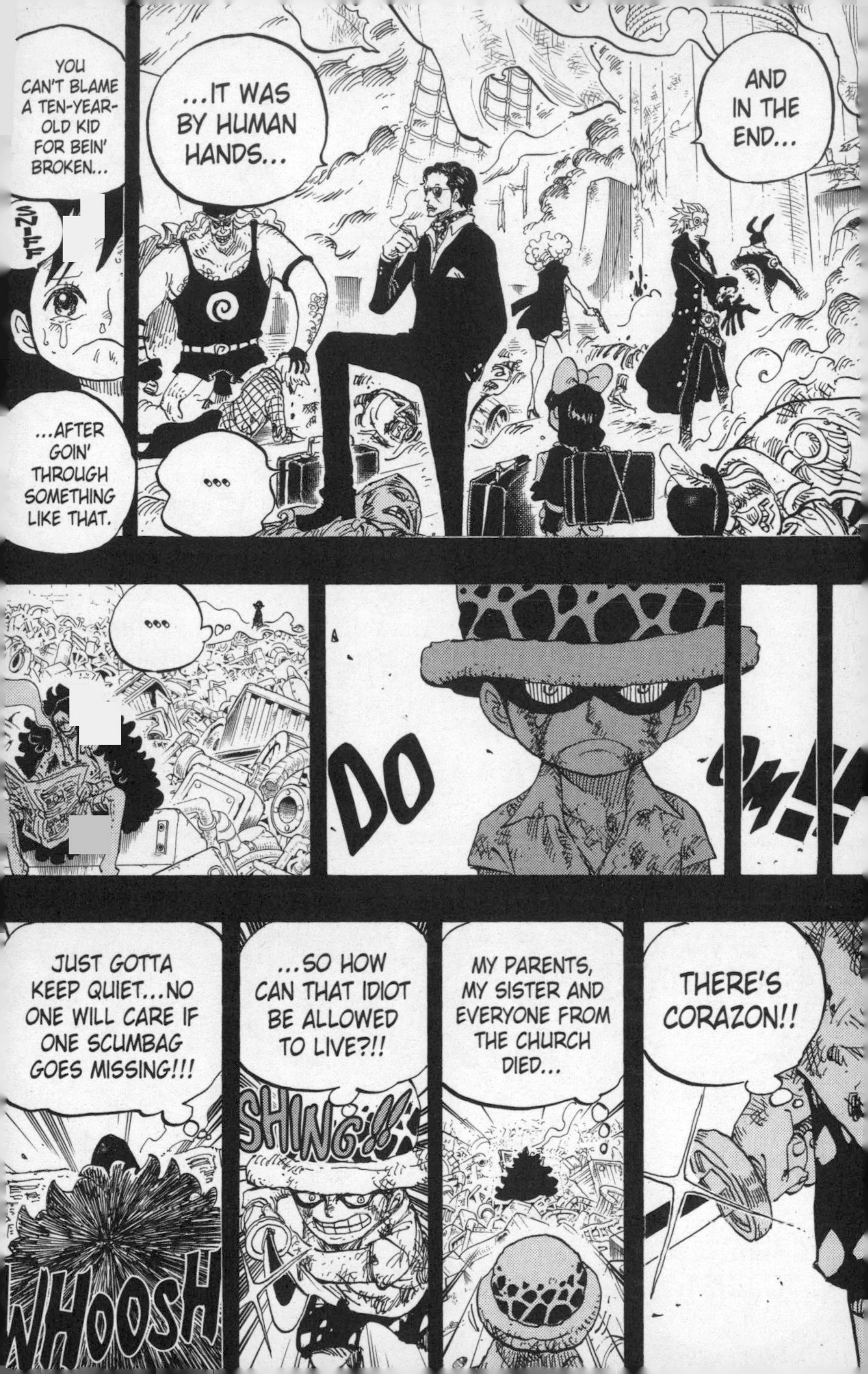
AND IN THE END...
...IT WAS BY HUMAN HANDS...
...
YOU CAN'T BLAME A TEN-YEAR-OLD KID FOR BEIN' BROKEN...
SNIFF
...AFTER GOIN' THROUGH SOMETHING LIKE THAT.
DO
...
THERE'S CORAZON!!
MY PARENTS, MY SISTER AND EVERYONE FROM THE CHURCH DIED...
...SO HOW CAN THAT IDIOT BE ALLOWED TO LIVE?!!
SHING!!
JUST GOTTA KEEP QUIET...NO ONE WILL CARE IF ONE SCUMBAG GOES MISSING!!!
WHOOSH

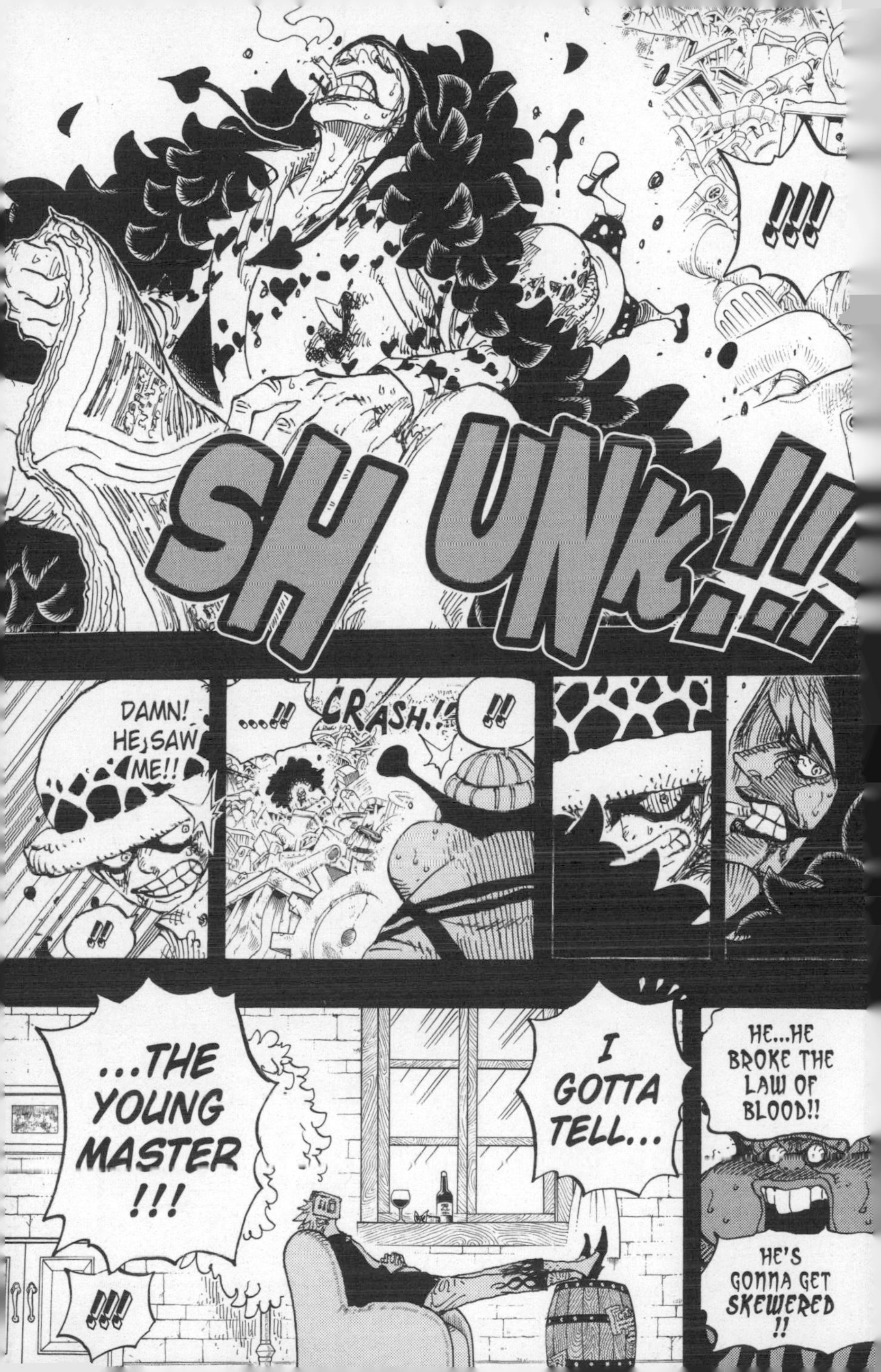
!!!
SHUNK!!!
!!
CRASH!?
...!!
DAMN! HE SAW ME!!
!!
HE...HE BROKE THE LAW OF BLOOD!!
HE'S GONNA GET SKEWERED!!
I GOTTA TELL...
...THE YOUNG MASTER!!!
!!!

Chapter 763:
DECLARATION OF HUMANITY

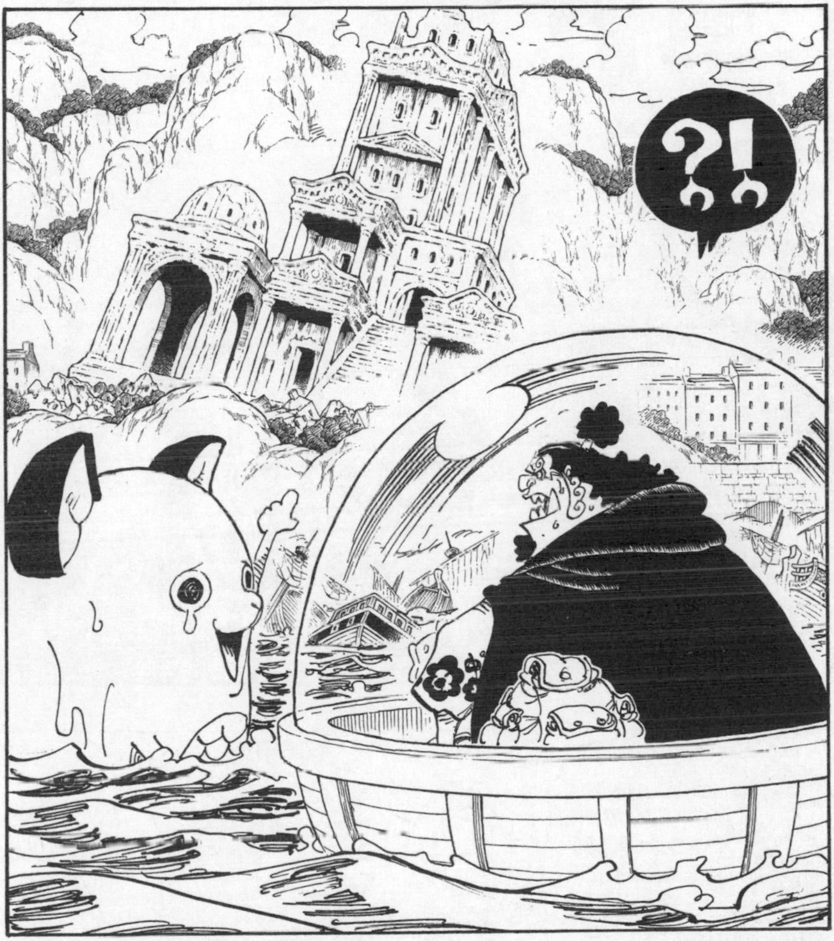
?!

THE SOLITARY JOURNEY OF JIMBEI, FIRST SON OF THE SEA, VOL. 12: "THE RUINS ATOP THE PORT ARE THE SEA-KITTEN'S TOWN"

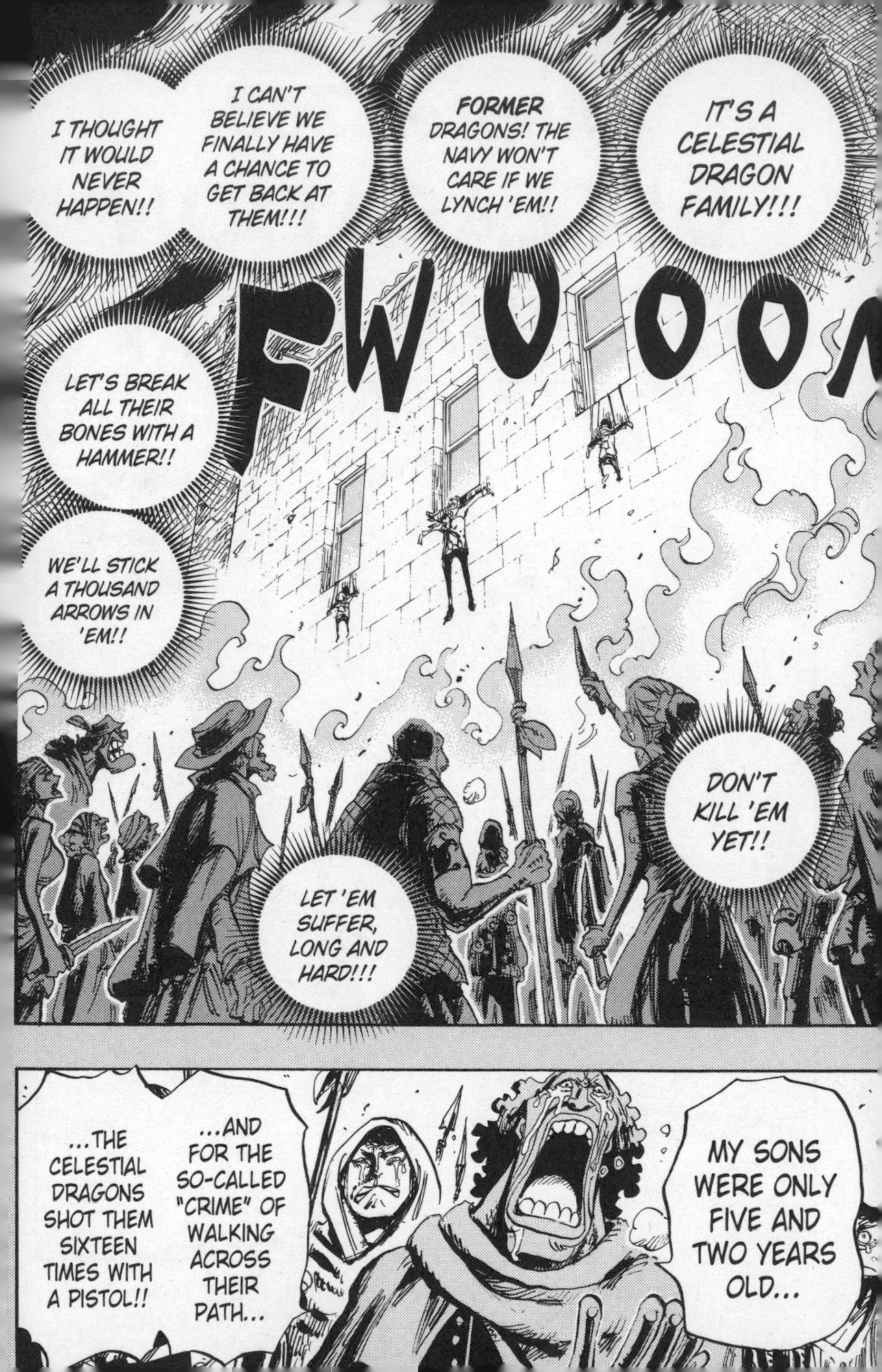
IT'S A CELESTIAL DRAGON FAMILY!!!
FORMER DRAGONS! THE NAVY WON'T CARE IF WE LYNCH 'EM!!
I CAN'T BELIEVE WE FINALLY HAVE A CHANCE TO GET BACK AT THEM!!!
I THOUGHT IT WOULD NEVER HAPPEN!!
FWOOO
LET'S BREAK ALL THEIR BONES WITH A HAMMER!!
WE'LL STICK A THOUSAND ARROWS IN 'EM!!
DON'T KILL 'EM YET!!
LET 'EM SUFFER, LONG AND HARD!!!
MY SONS WERE ONLY FIVE AND TWO YEARS OLD...
...AND FOR THE SO-CALLED "CRIME" OF WALKING ACROSS THEIR PATH...
...THE CELESTIAL DRAGONS SHOT THEM SIXTEEN TIMES WITH A PISTOL!!

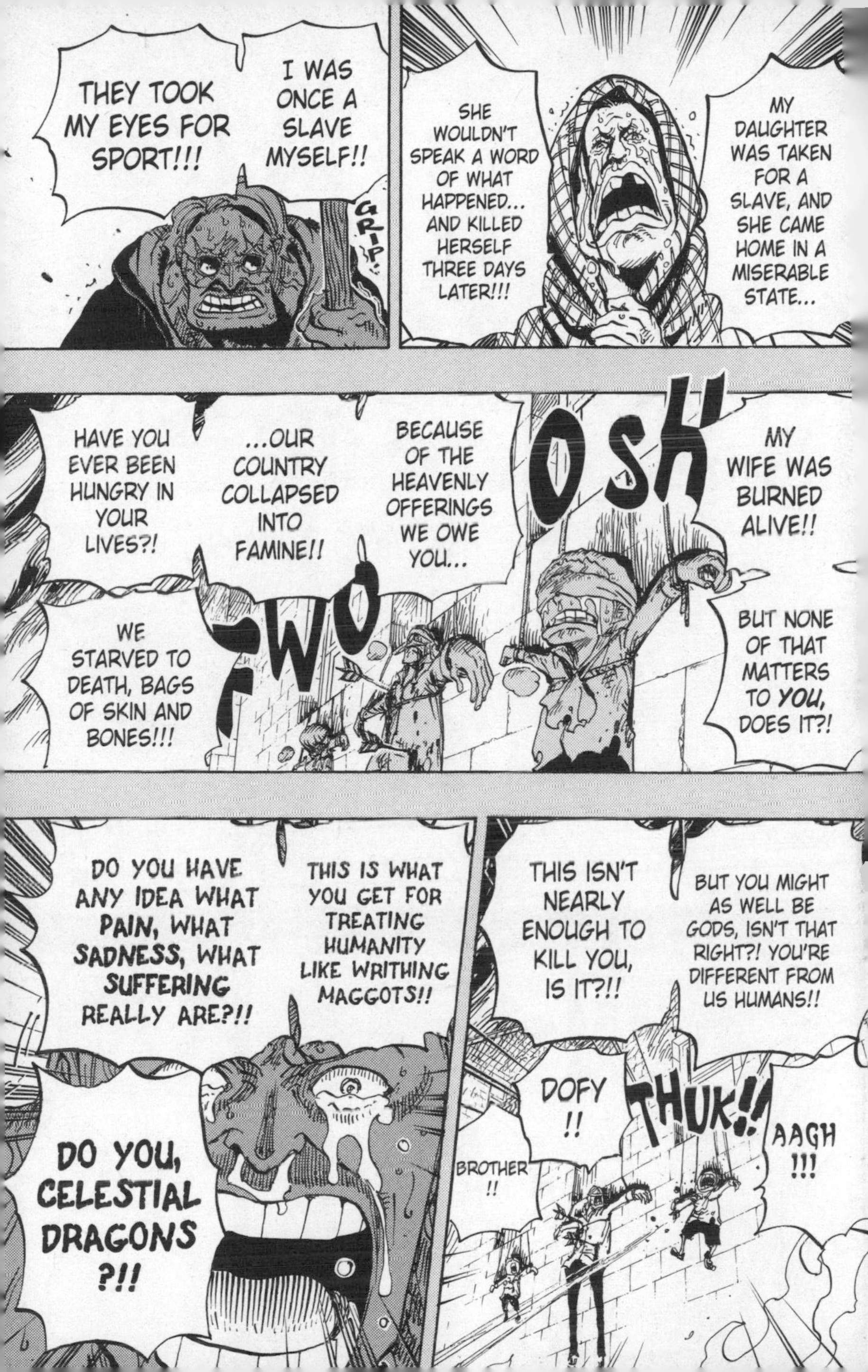
MY DAUGHTER WAS TAKEN FOR A SLAVE, AND SHE CAME HOME IN A MISERABLE STATE...
SHE WOULDN'T SPEAK A WORD OF WHAT HAPPENED... AND KILLED HERSELF THREE DAYS LATER!!!
I WAS ONCE A SLAVE MYSELF!!
THEY TOOK MY EYES FOR SPORT!!!
GRIP
MY WIFE WAS BURNED ALIVE!!
BUT NONE OF THAT MATTERS TO YOU, DOES IT?!
WO OSH
BECAUSE OF THE HEAVENLY OFFERINGS WE OWE YOU...
...OUR COUNTRY COLLAPSED INTO FAMINE!!
HAVE YOU EVER BEEN HUNGRY IN YOUR LIVES?!
WE STARVED TO DEATH, BAGS OF SKIN AND BONES!!!
BUT YOU MIGHT AS WELL BE GODS, ISN'T THAT RIGHT?! YOU'RE DIFFERENT FROM US HUMANS!!
THIS ISN'T NEARLY ENOUGH TO KILL YOU, IS IT?!!
AAGH!!!
THUK!!
DOFY!!
BROTHER!!
THIS IS WHAT YOU GET FOR TREATING HUMANITY LIKE WRITHING MAGGOTS!!
DO YOU HAVE ANY IDEA WHAT PAIN, WHAT SADNESS, WHAT SUFFERING REALLY ARE?!!
DO YOU, CELESTIAL DRAGONS?!!

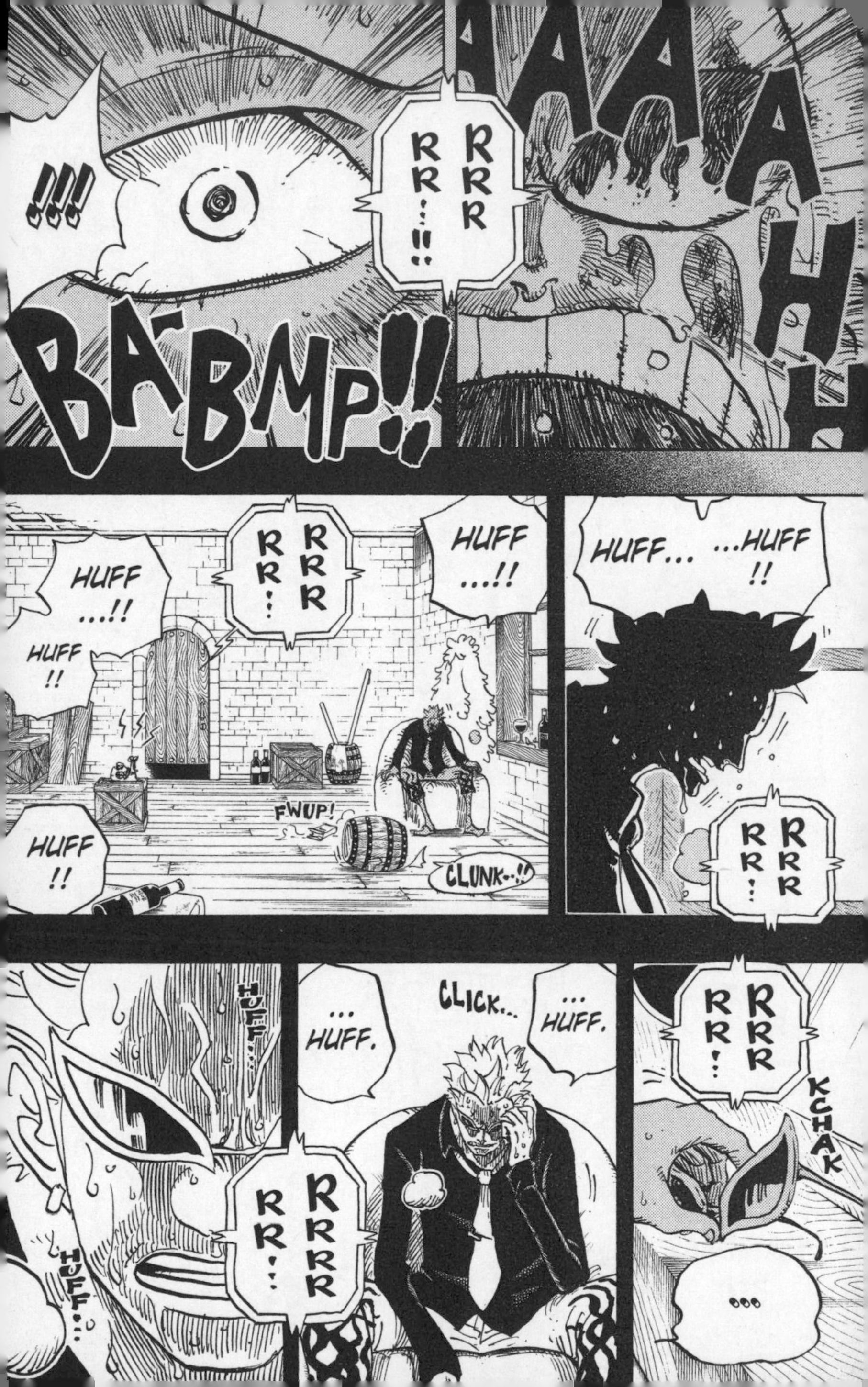
AAAAHH
RRR RRR...!!
!!!
BA-BMP!!
HUFF... ...HUFF!!
RRR RRR...
HUFF...!!
RRR RRR...
HUFF...!!
HUFF!!
FWUP!
CLUNK...!!
HUFF!!
RRR RRR...
KCHAK
...
...HUFF.
CLICK...
...HUFF.
RRRR RRR...
HUFF...
HUFF...

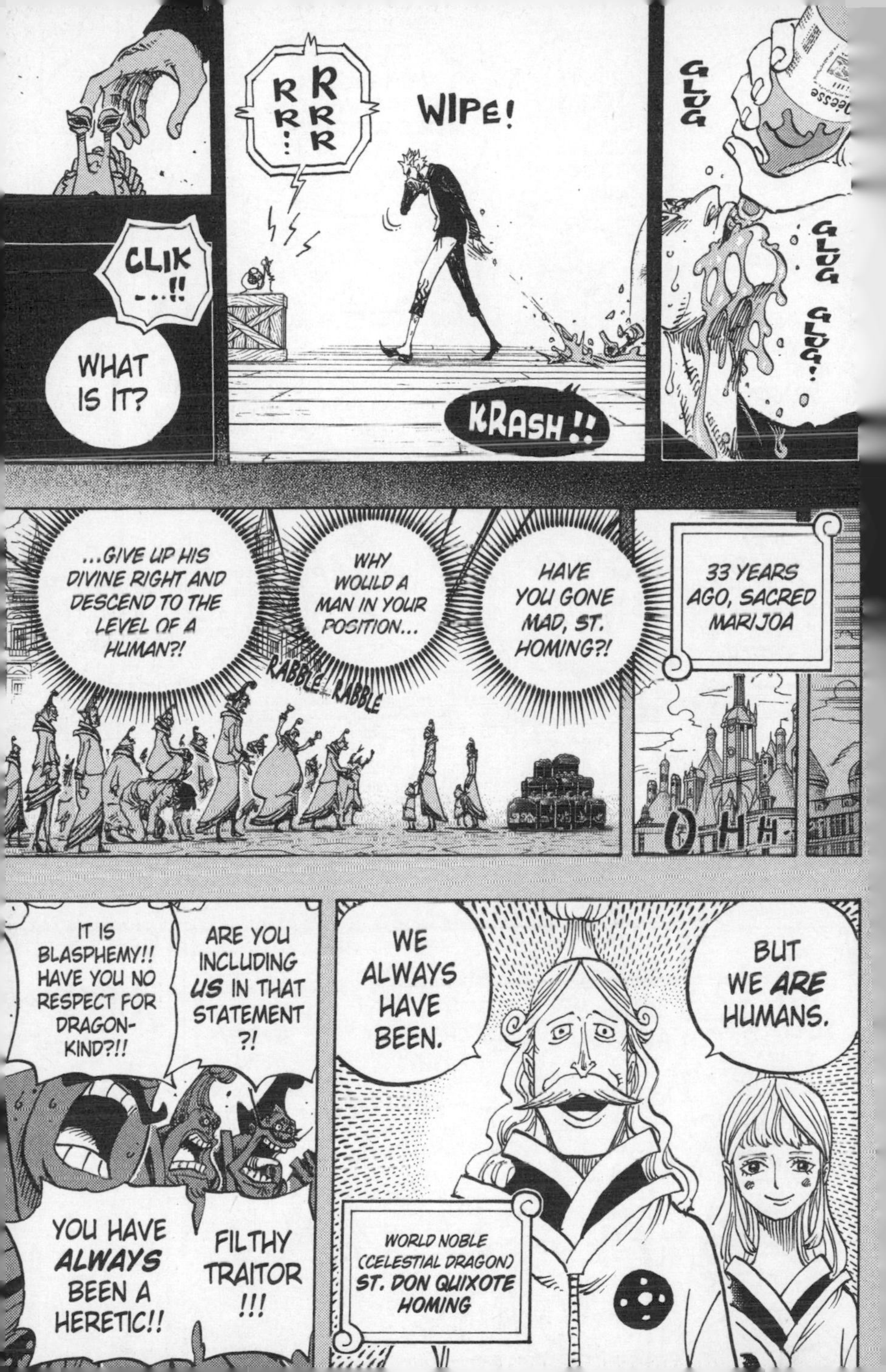
GLUG
GLUG
GLUG GLUG!
RRRRR!
WIPE!
KRASH!!
CLIK...!!
WHAT IS IT?
33 YEARS AGO, SACRED MARIJOA
OHH
HAVE YOU GONE MAD, ST. HOMING?!
WHY WOULD A MAN IN YOUR POSITION...
...GIVE UP HIS DIVINE RIGHT AND DESCEND TO THE LEVEL OF A HUMAN?!
RABBLE RABBLE
BUT WE ARE HUMANS.
WE ALWAYS HAVE BEEN.
WORLD NOBLE (CELESTIAL DRAGON) ST. DON QUIXOTE HOMING
ARE YOU INCLUDING US IN THAT STATEMENT?!
IT IS BLASPHEMY!! HAVE YOU NO RESPECT FOR DRAGON-KIND?!!
FILTHY TRAITOR!!!
YOU HAVE ALWAYS BEEN A HERETIC!!

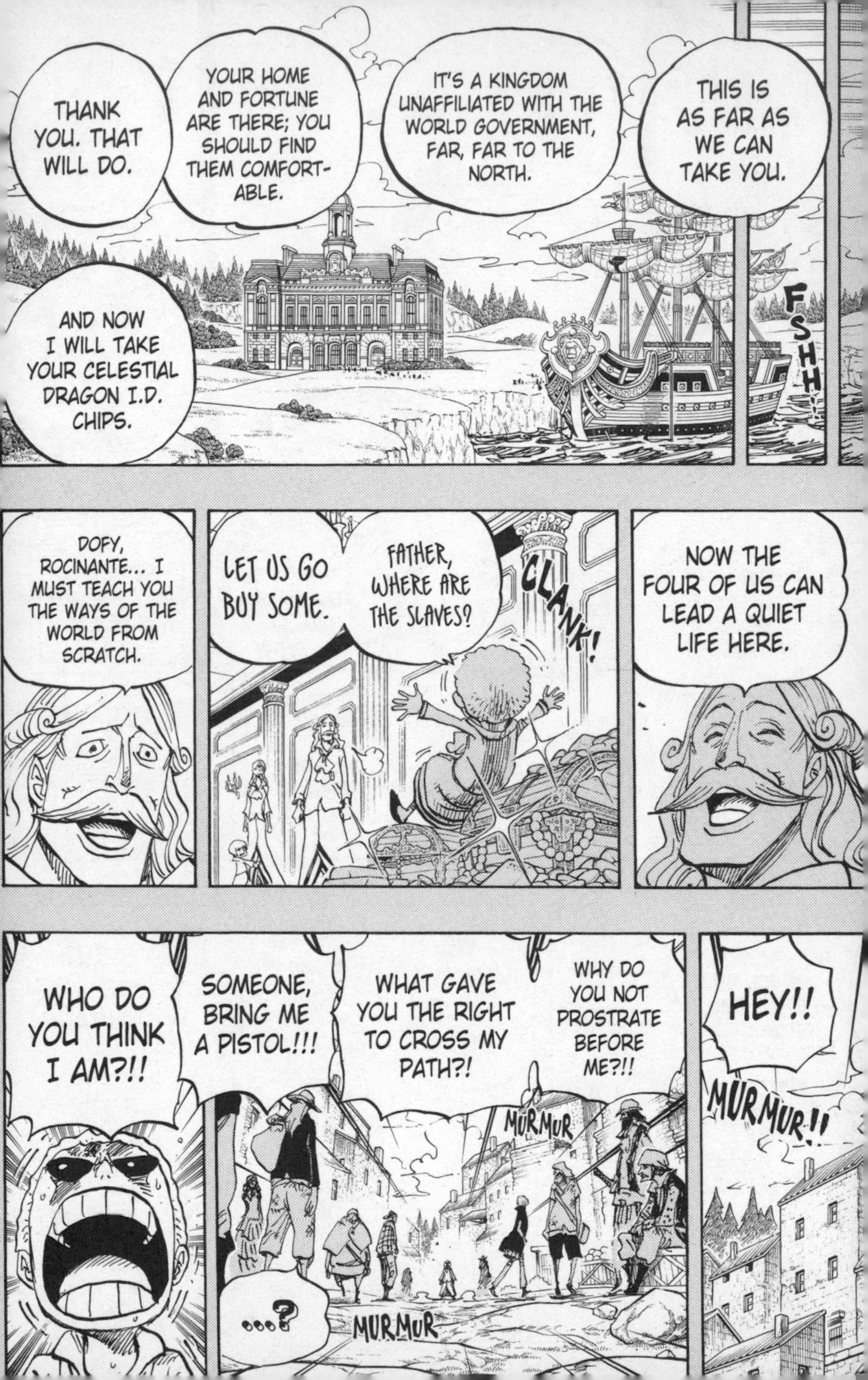
THIS IS AS FAR AS WE CAN TAKE YOU.
IT'S A KINGDOM UNAFFILIATED WITH THE WORLD GOVERNMENT, FAR, FAR TO THE NORTH.
YOUR HOME AND FORTUNE ARE THERE; YOU SHOULD FIND THEM COMFORT-ABLE.
THANK YOU. THAT WILL DO.
FSHH
AND NOW I WILL TAKE YOUR CELESTIAL DRAGON I.D. CHIPS.
NOW THE FOUR OF US CAN LEAD A QUIET LIFE HERE.
CLANK!
FATHER, WHERE ARE THE SLAVES?
LET US GO BUY SOME.
DOFY, ROCINANTE... I MUST TEACH YOU THE WAYS OF THE WORLD FROM SCRATCH.
HEY!!
MURMUR!!
WHY DO YOU NOT PROSTRATE BEFORE ME?!!
WHAT GAVE YOU THE RIGHT TO CROSS MY PATH?!
SOMEONE, BRING ME A PISTOL!!!
WHO DO YOU THINK I AM?!!
MURMUR
...?
MURMUR

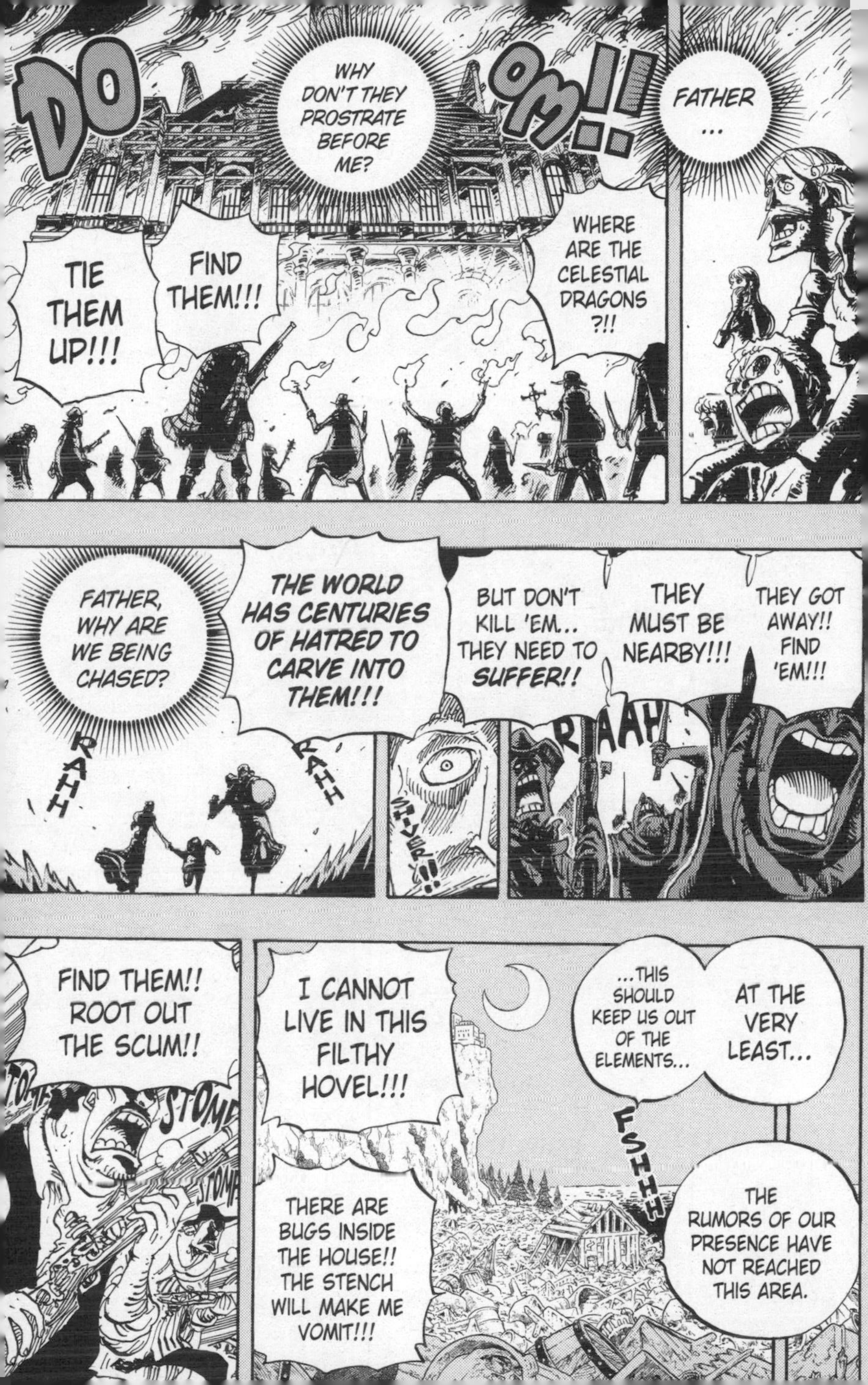
FATHER ...
DOOM!!
WHY DON'T THEY PROSTRATE BEFORE ME?
WHERE ARE THE CELESTIAL DRAGONS ?!!
FIND THEM!!!
TIE THEM UP!!!
THEY GOT AWAY!! FIND 'EM!!!
THEY MUST BE NEARBY!!!
BUT DON'T KILL 'EM... THEY NEED TO SUFFER!!
RAAAH
SHIVER!!
THE WORLD HAS CENTURIES OF HATRED TO CARVE INTO THEM!!!
RAHH
FATHER, WHY ARE WE BEING CHASED?
RAHH
AT THE VERY LEAST...
...THIS SHOULD KEEP US OUT OF THE ELEMENTS...
I CANNOT LIVE IN THIS FILTHY HOVEL!!!
FSHHH
THE RUMORS OF OUR PRESENCE HAVE NOT REACHED THIS AREA.
THERE ARE BUGS INSIDE THE HOUSE!! THE STENCH WILL MAKE ME VOMIT!!!
FIND THEM!! ROOT OUT THE SCUM!!
STOMP
STOMP
STOMP

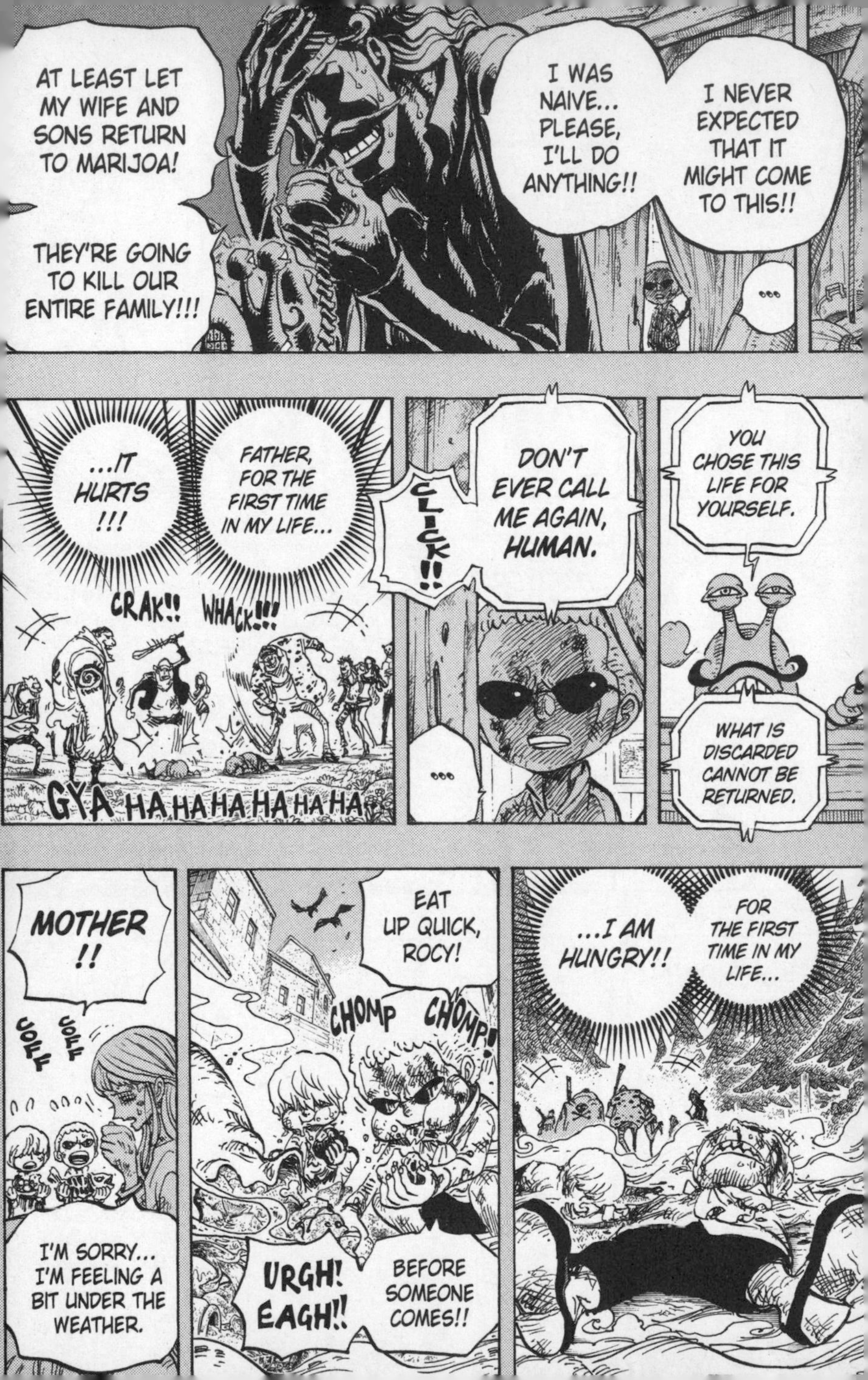
I NEVER EXPECTED THAT IT MIGHT COME TO THIS!!
I WAS NAIVE... PLEASE, I'LL DO ANYTHING!!
AT LEAST LET MY WIFE AND SONS RETURN TO MARIJOA!
...
THEY'RE GOING TO KILL OUR ENTIRE FAMILY!!!
YOU CHOSE THIS LIFE FOR YOURSELF.
WHAT IS DISCARDED CANNOT BE RETURNED.
DON'T EVER CALL ME AGAIN, HUMAN.
CLICK!!
...
FATHER, FOR THE FIRST TIME IN MY LIFE...
...IT HURTS!!!
WHACK!!!
CRAK!!
GYA HA HA HA HA HA HA HA
FOR THE FIRST TIME IN MY LIFE...
...I AM HUNGRY!!
EAT UP QUICK, ROCY!
CHOMP!
CHOMP
BEFORE SOMEONE COMES!!
URGH! EAGH!!
MOTHER!!
JOLT
JOLT
I'M SORRY... I'M FEELING A BIT UNDER THE WEATHER.

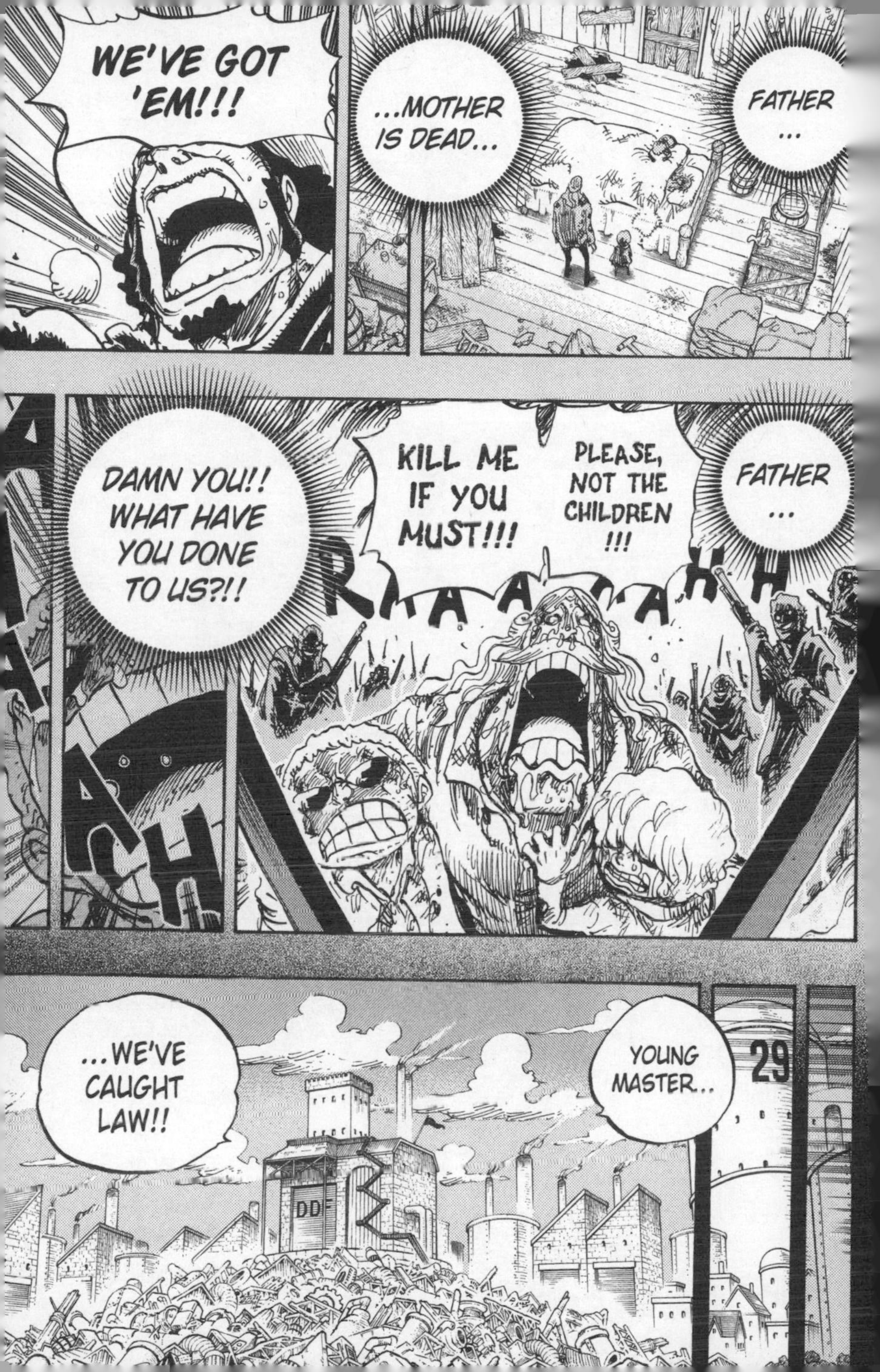
FATHER ...
...MOTHER IS DEAD...
WE'VE GOT 'EM!!!
FATHER ...
PLEASE, NOT THE CHILDREN !!!
KILL ME IF YOU MUST!!!
DAMN YOU!! WHAT HAVE YOU DONE TO US?!!
29
YOUNG MASTER...
...WE'VE CAUGHT LAW!!
DDF

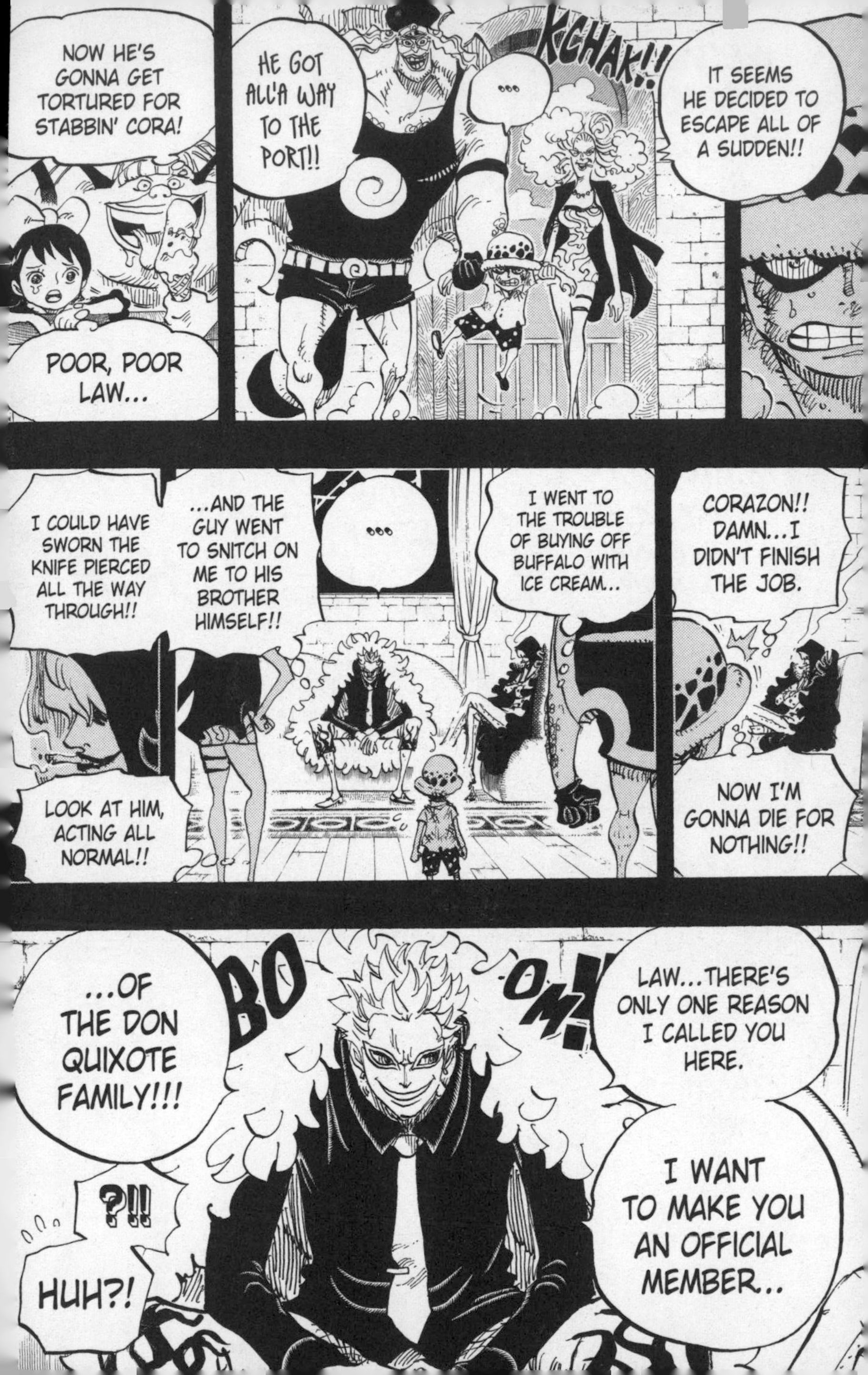

IT SEEMS HE DECIDED TO ESCAPE ALL OF A SUDDEN!!
KCHAK!!
...
HE GOT ALL'A WAY TO THE PORT!!
NOW HE'S GONNA GET TORTURED FOR STABBIN' CORA!
POOR, POOR LAW...
CORAZON!! DAMN...I DIDN'T FINISH THE JOB.
NOW I'M GONNA DIE FOR NOTHING!!
I WENT TO THE TROUBLE OF BUYING OFF BUFFALO WITH ICE CREAM...
...
...AND THE GUY WENT TO SNITCH ON ME TO HIS BROTHER HIMSELF!!
I COULD HAVE SWORN THE KNIFE PIERCED ALL THE WAY THROUGH!!
LOOK AT HIM, ACTING ALL NORMAL!!
LAW...THERE'S ONLY ONE REASON I CALLED YOU HERE.
BO-OM!!
I WANT TO MAKE YOU AN OFFICIAL MEMBER..
...OF THE DON QUIXOTE FAMILY!!!
?!!
HUH?!

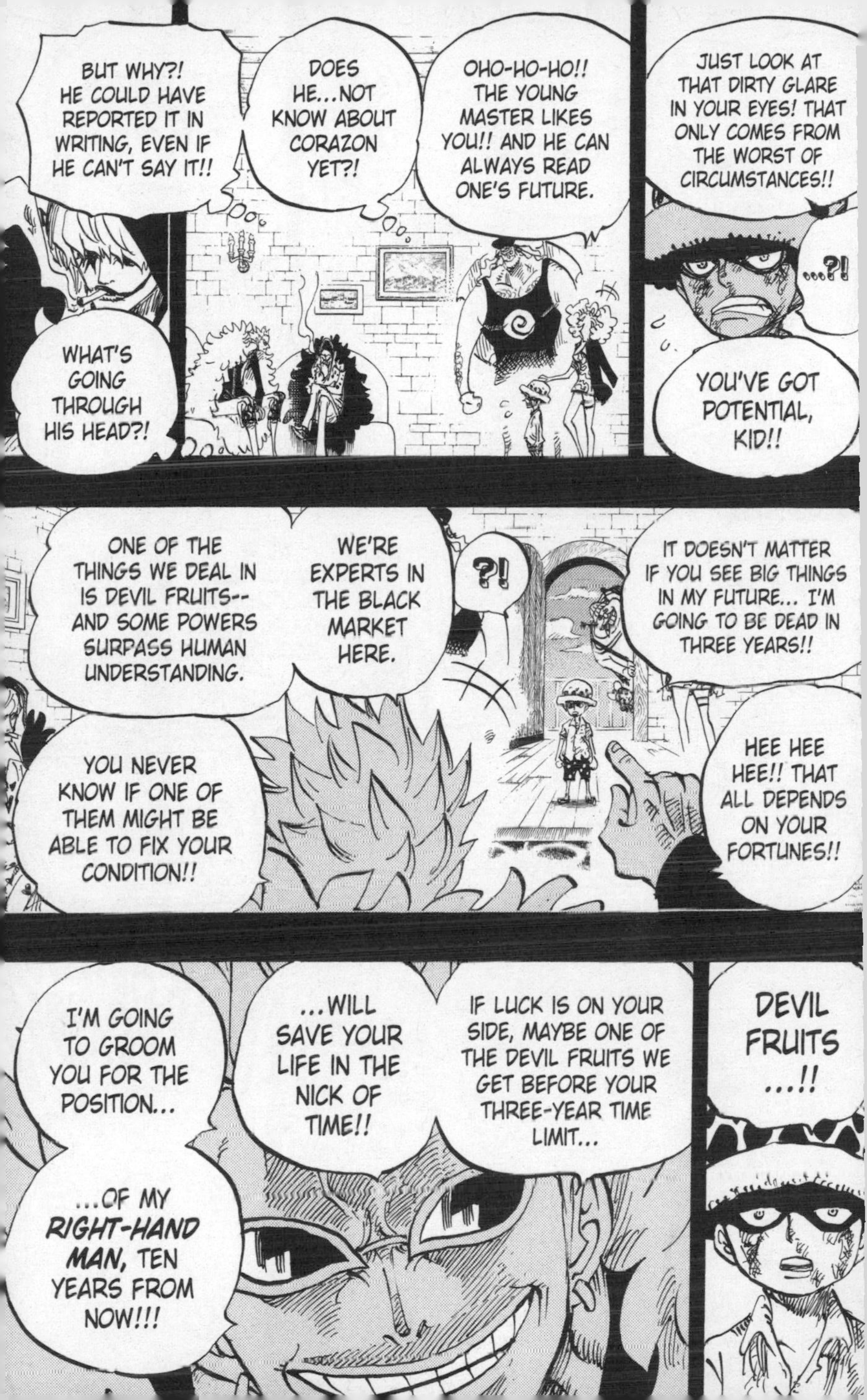
JUST LOOK AT THAT DIRTY GLARE IN YOUR EYES! THAT ONLY COMES FROM THE WORST OF CIRCUMSTANCES!!
...?!
YOU'VE GOT POTENTIAL, KID!!
OHO-HO-HO!! THE YOUNG MASTER LIKES YOU!! AND HE CAN ALWAYS READ ONE'S FUTURE.
DOES HE...NOT KNOW ABOUT CORAZON YET?!
BUT WHY?! HE COULD HAVE REPORTED IT IN WRITING, EVEN IF HE CAN'T SAY IT!!
WHAT'S GOING THROUGH HIS HEAD?!
IT DOESN'T MATTER IF YOU SEE BIG THINGS IN MY FUTURE... I'M GOING TO BE DEAD IN THREE YEARS!!
HEE HEE HEE!! THAT ALL DEPENDS ON YOUR FORTUNES!!
?!
WE'RE EXPERTS IN THE BLACK MARKET HERE.
ONE OF THE THINGS WE DEAL IN IS DEVIL FRUITS-- AND SOME POWERS SURPASS HUMAN UNDERSTANDING.
YOU NEVER KNOW IF ONE OF THEM MIGHT BE ABLE TO FIX YOUR CONDITION!!
DEVIL FRUITS ...!!
IF LUCK IS ON YOUR SIDE, MAYBE ONE OF THE DEVIL FRUITS WE GET BEFORE YOUR THREE-YEAR TIME LIMIT...
...WILL SAVE YOUR LIFE IN THE NICK OF TIME!!
I'M GOING TO GROOM YOU FOR THE POSITION...
...OF MY *RIGHT-HAND MAN*, TEN YEARS FROM NOW!!!

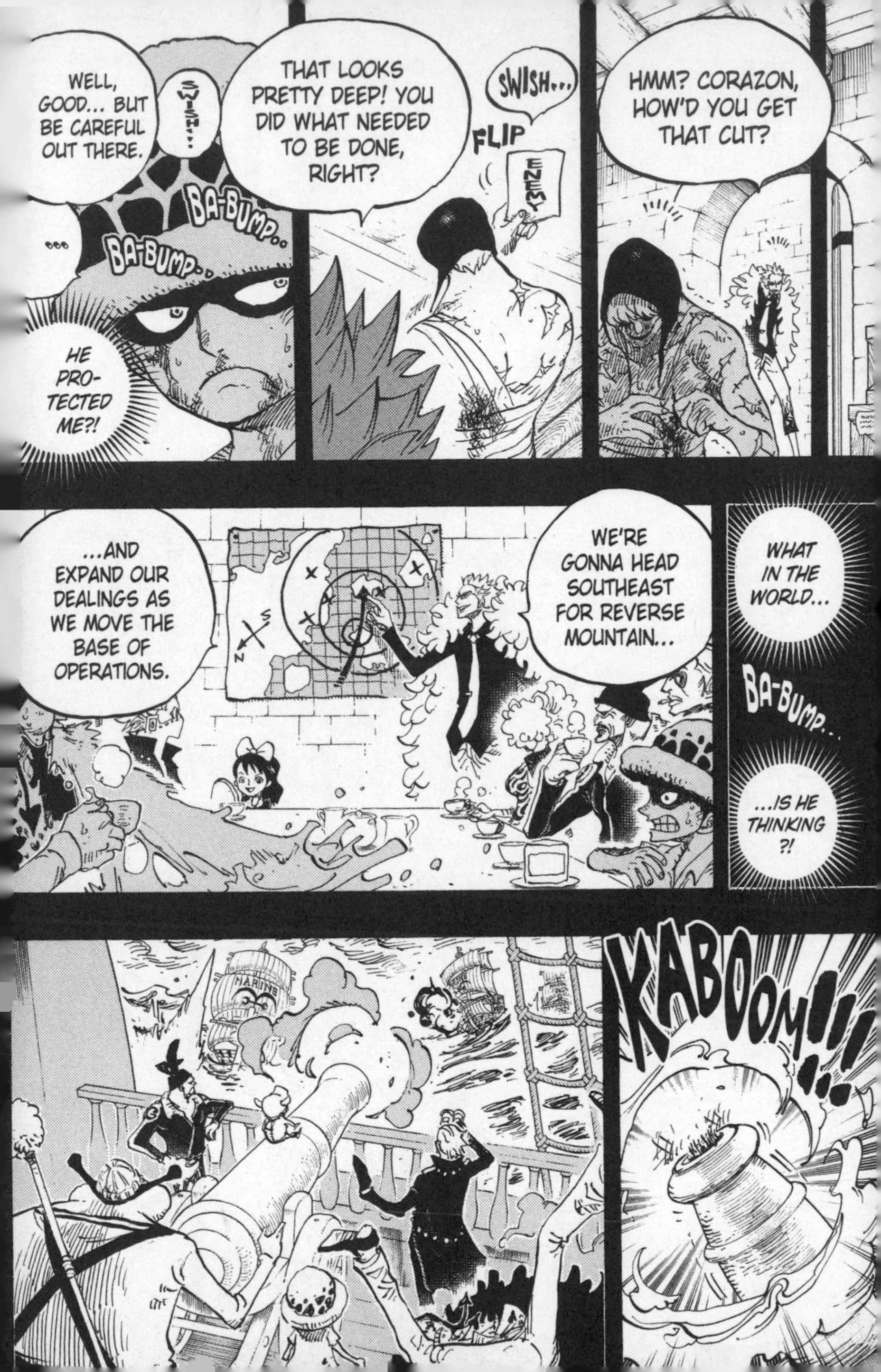
HMM? CORAZON, HOW'D YOU GET THAT CUT?
SWISH...
THAT LOOKS PRETTY DEEP! YOU DID WHAT NEEDED TO BE DONE, RIGHT?
FLIP
ENEMY
SWISH...
WELL, GOOD... BUT BE CAREFUL OUT THERE.
BA-BUMP..
BA-BUMP..
...
HE PRO-TECTED ME?!
WHAT IN THE WORLD...
BA-BUMP...
...IS HE THINKING?!
WE'RE GONNA HEAD SOUTHEAST FOR REVERSE MOUNTAIN...
...AND EXPAND OUR DEALINGS AS WE MOVE THE BASE OF OPERATIONS.
S
N
KABOOM!!!
MARINE

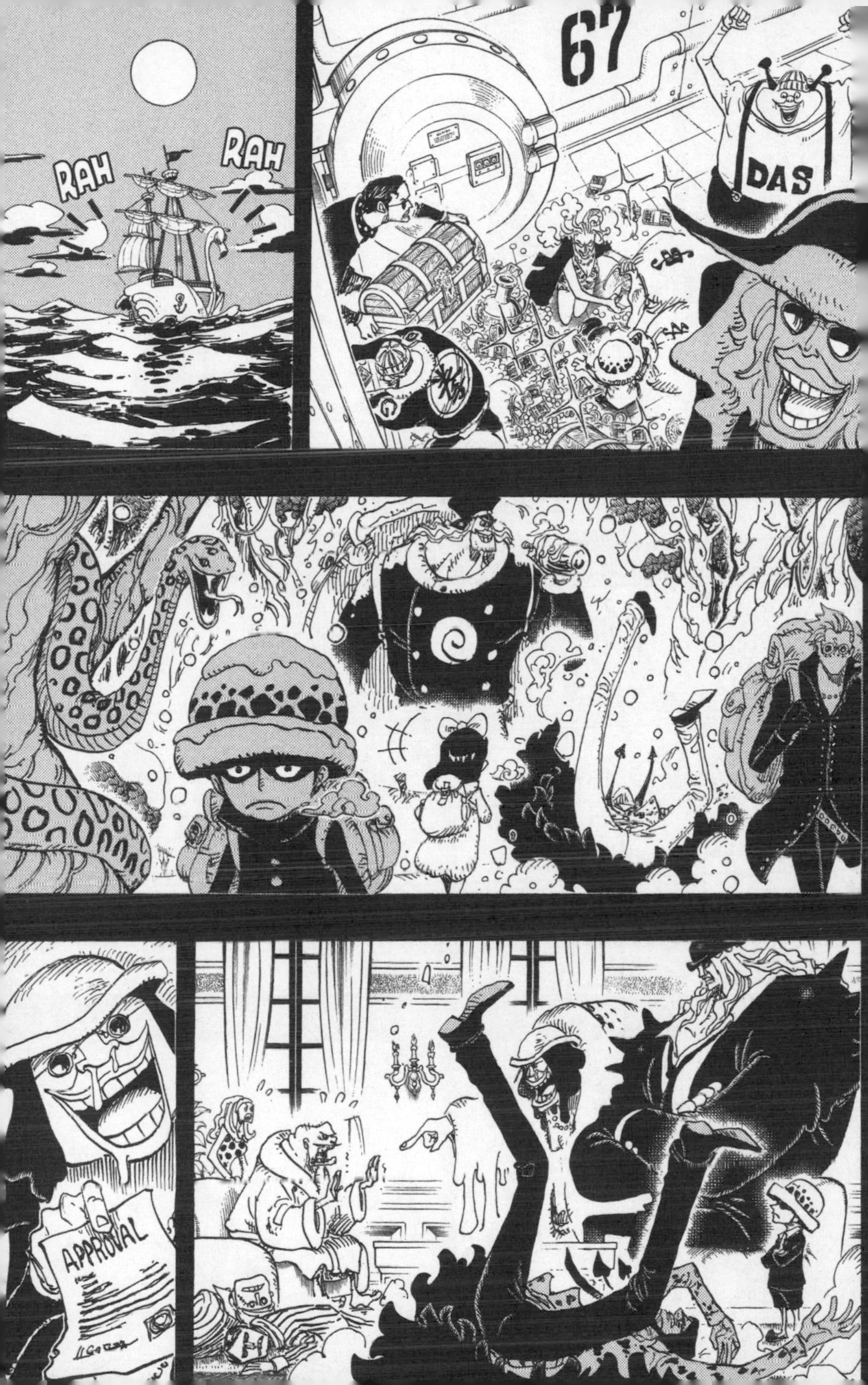
67
DAS
RAH
RAH
APPROVAL

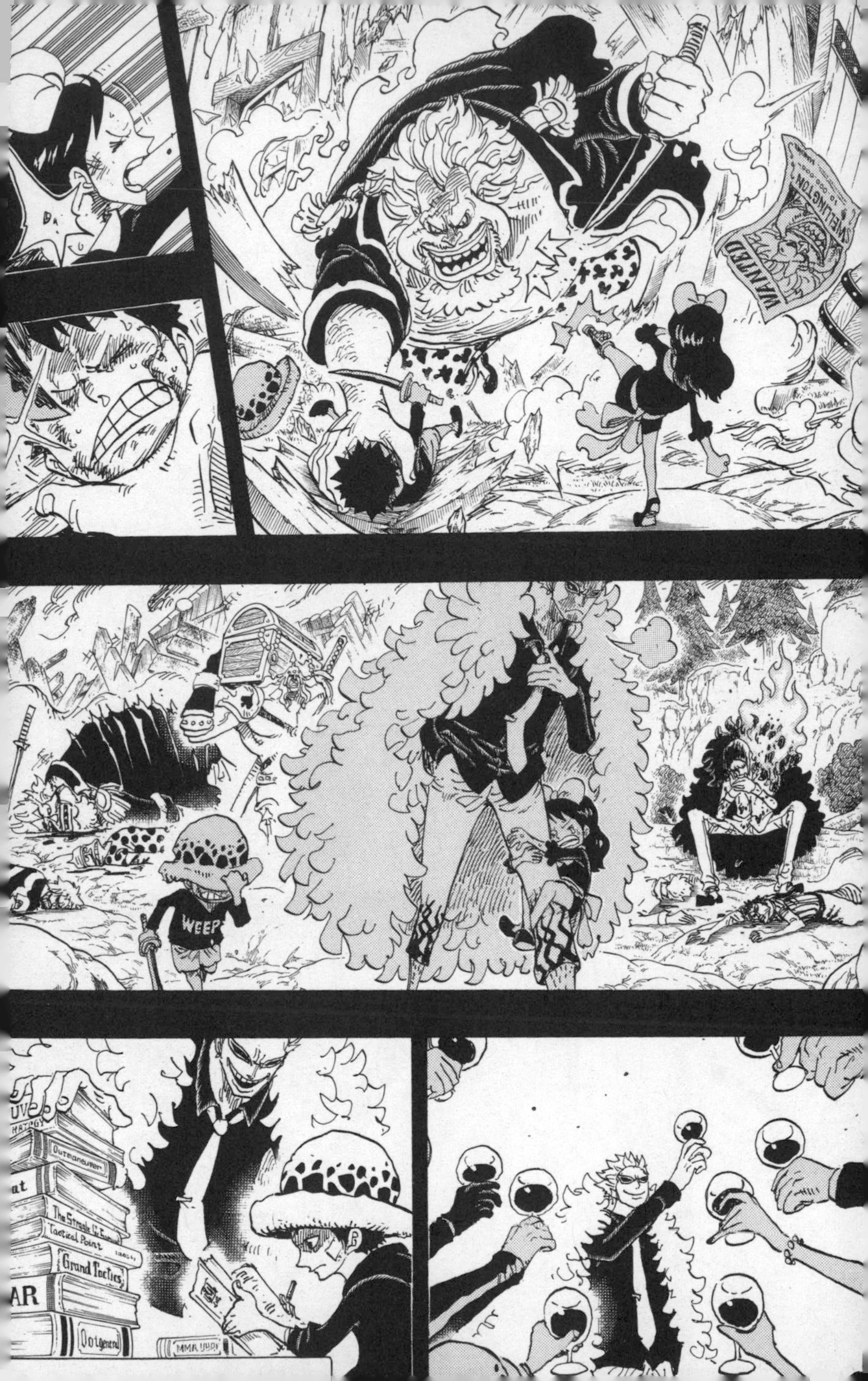
WANTED
WELLINGTON
WEEP
Outmaneuver
Tactical Point
Grand Tactics

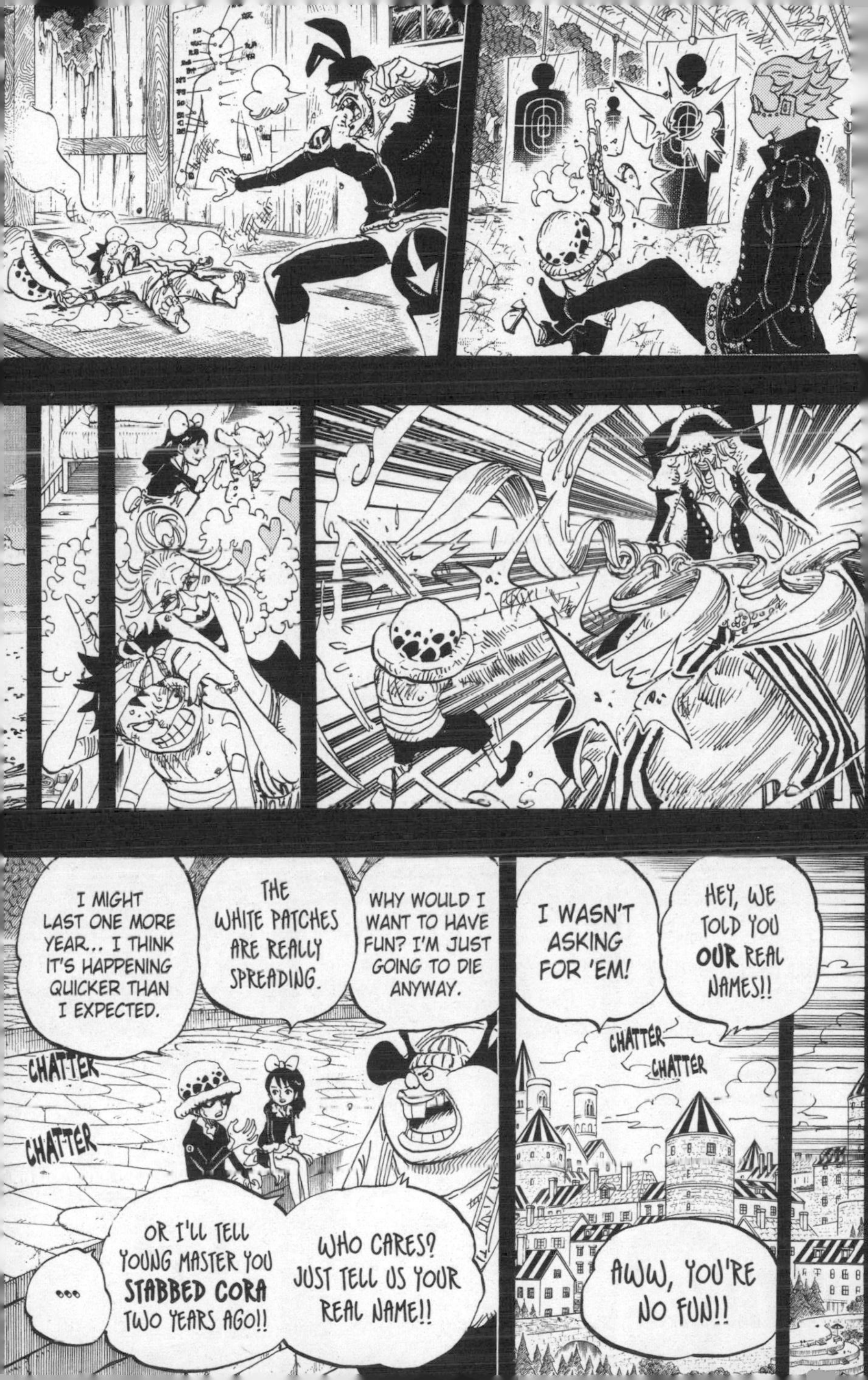
HEY, WE TOLD YOU **OUR** REAL NAMES!!
I WASN'T ASKING FOR 'EM!
CHATTER
CHATTER
AWW, YOU'RE NO FUN!!
WHY WOULD I WANT TO HAVE FUN? I'M JUST GOING TO DIE ANYWAY.
THE WHITE PATCHES ARE REALLY SPREADING.
I MIGHT LAST ONE MORE YEAR... I THINK IT'S HAPPENING QUICKER THAN I EXPECTED.
CHATTER
CHATTER
WHO CARES? JUST TELL US YOUR REAL NAME!!
OR I'LL TELL YOUNG MASTER YOU **STABBED CORA** TWO YEARS AGO!!
...

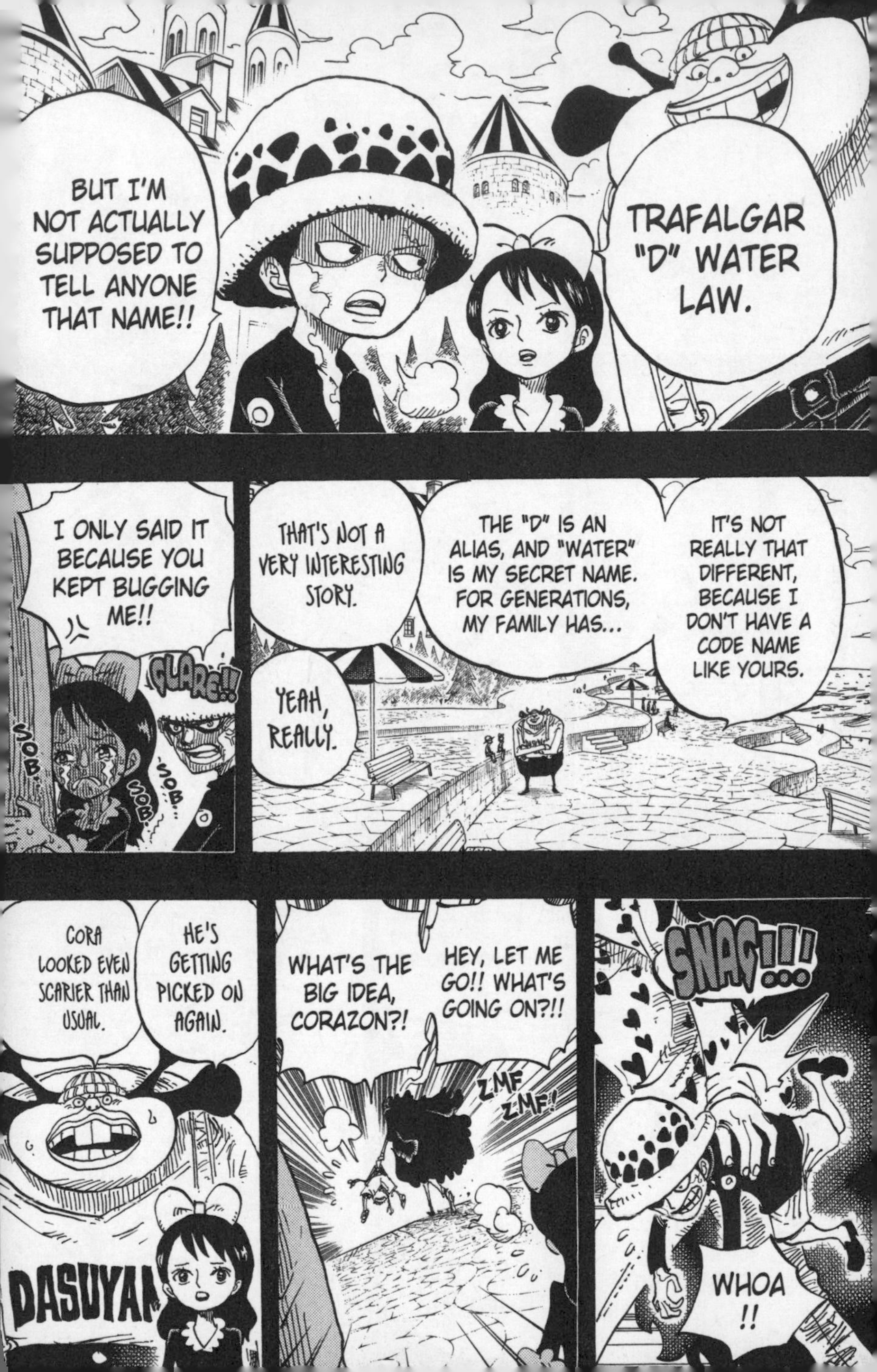
TRAFALGAR "D" WATER LAW.
BUT I'M NOT ACTUALLY SUPPOSED TO TELL ANYONE THAT NAME!!
IT'S NOT REALLY THAT DIFFERENT, BECAUSE I DON'T HAVE A CODE NAME LIKE YOURS.
THE "D" IS AN ALIAS, AND "WATER" IS MY SECRET NAME. FOR GENERATIONS, MY FAMILY HAS...
THAT'S NOT A VERY INTERESTING STORY.
YEAH, REALLY.
I ONLY SAID IT BECAUSE YOU KEPT BUGGING ME!!
GLARE!!
SOB
SOB...
SNAG!!!...
WHOA!!
HEY, LET ME GO!! WHAT'S GOING ON?!!
WHAT'S THE BIG IDEA, CORAZON?!
ZMF
ZMF!
HE'S GETTING PICKED ON AGAIN.
CORA LOOKED EVEN SCARIER THAN USUAL.
DASUYA

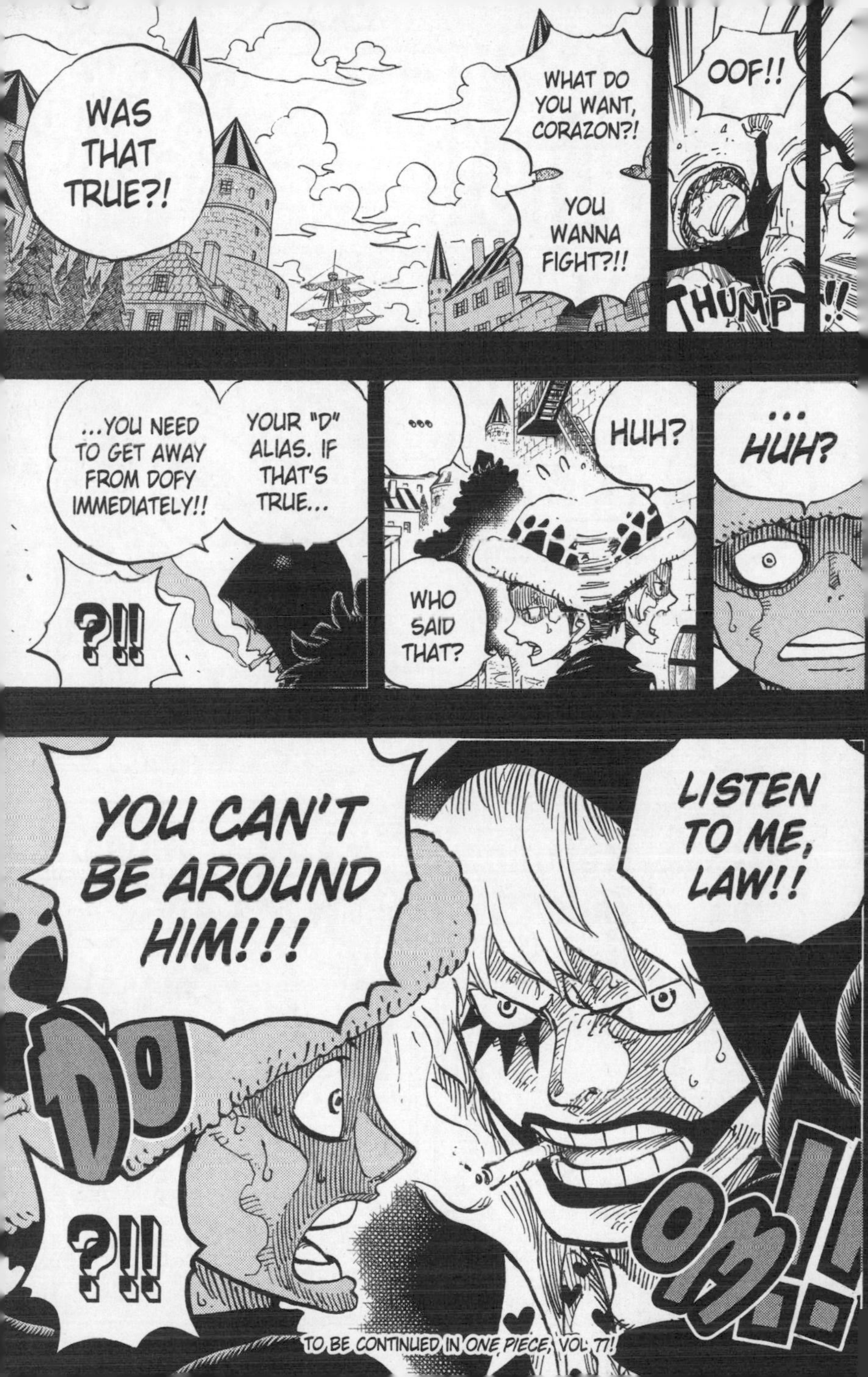
OOF!!
THUMP!!
WHAT DO YOU WANT, CORAZON?!
YOU WANNA FIGHT?!!
WAS THAT TRUE?!
... HUH?
HUH?
...
WHO SAID THAT?
YOUR "D" ALIAS. IF THAT'S TRUE...
...YOU NEED TO GET AWAY FROM DOFY IMMEDIATELY!!
?!!
LISTEN TO ME, LAW!!
YOU CAN'T BE AROUND HIM!!!
DO
OM!!
?!!
TO BE CONTINUED IN ONE PIECE, VOL. 71!

CHARACTER RESULTS!!

The New World is brimming with fascinating characters! The voting was wild and unpredictable!!

69,472 votes in total!!

#1 Monkey D. Luffy (including Lucy)

(1) →

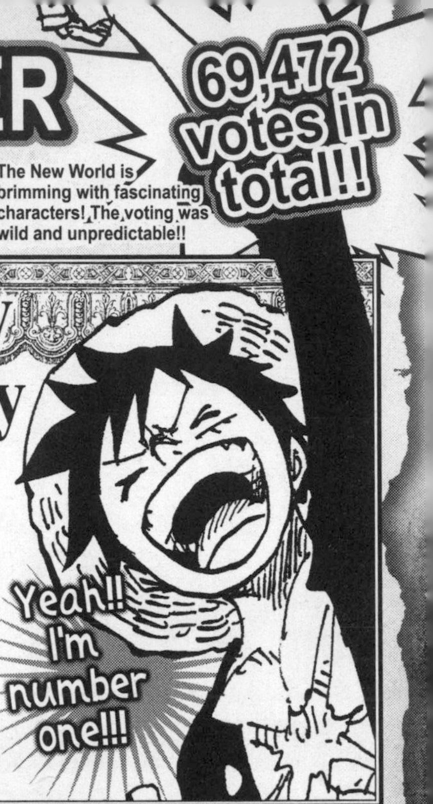

Yeah!! I'm number one!!!

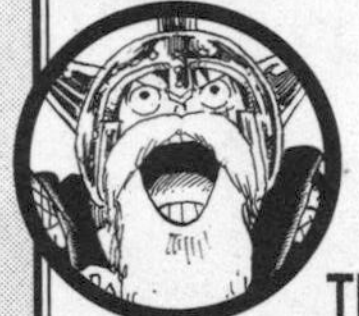

9,183 votes

The five-time champion!!

Message from God Usopp

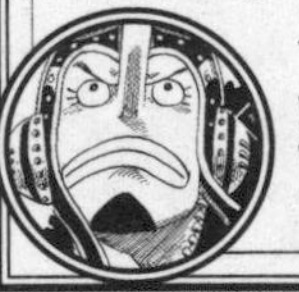

That's my pal! Good job! As your boss, my nose is held high with pride! I will humbly accept 13th place--no, I insist!

* Number in parentheses indicates previous rank.

#2 Trafalgar Law

(10) ↑

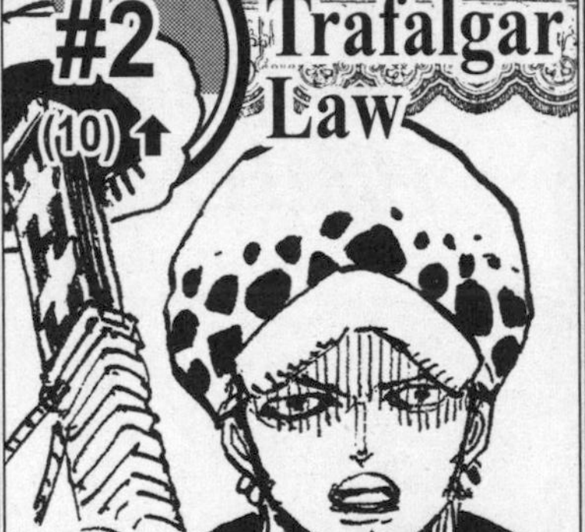

Why me ...?

8,794 votes

A huge rise from the last time!!

#3 Roronoa Zolo

(2) ↓

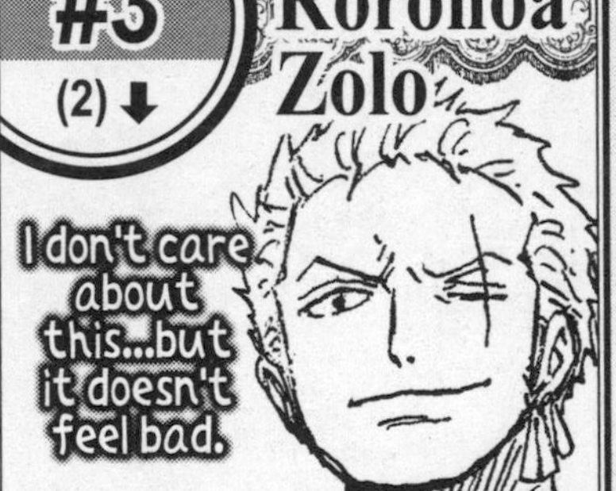

I don't care about this...but it doesn't feel bad.

7,997 votes

His manliness charms all, regardless of age or gender!!

For the first time, voting through both *Weekly Jump* and the graphic novels!!

The 5th ONE PIECE POPULARITY POLL

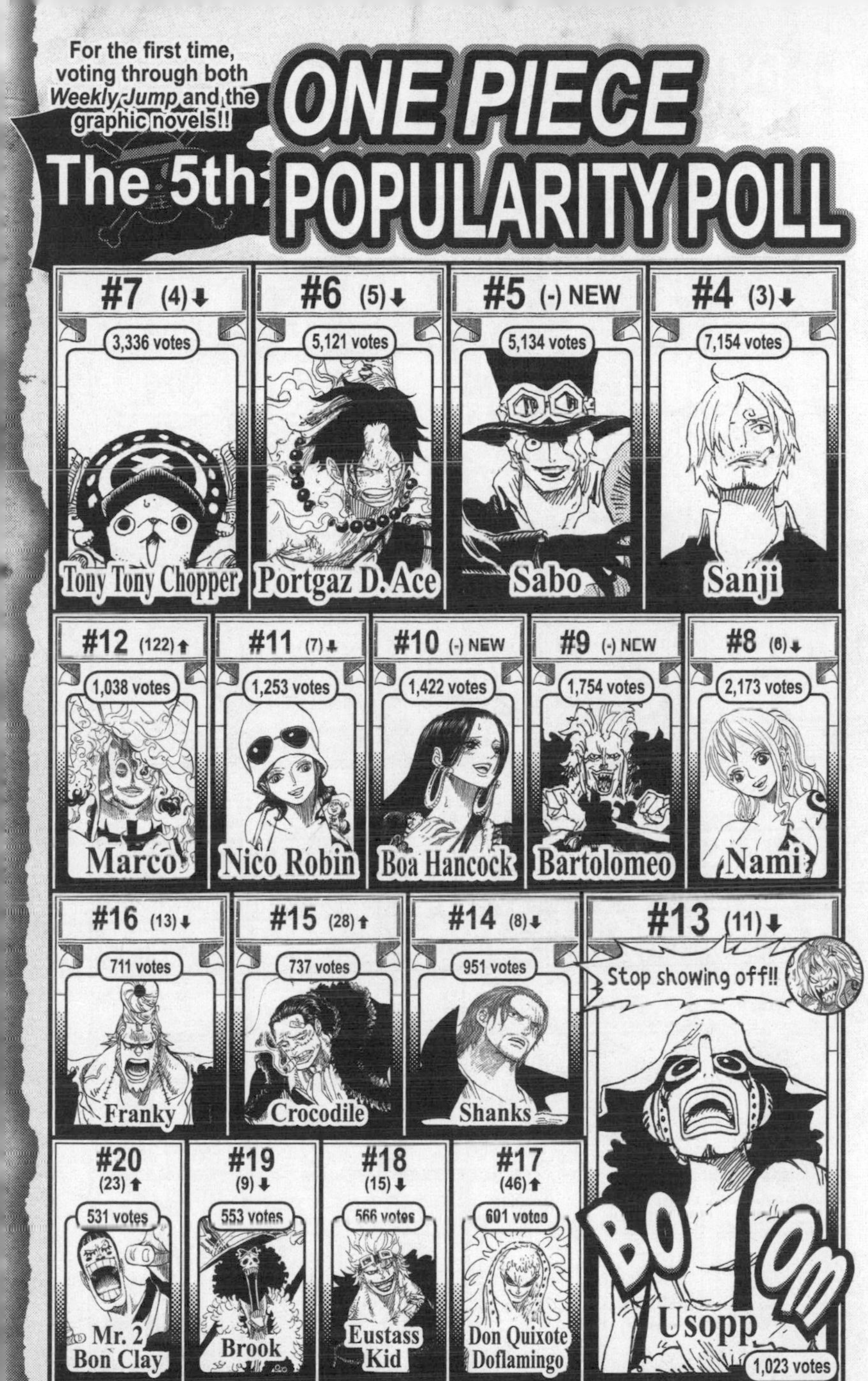
#4 (3)
7,154 votes
Sanji
#5 (-) NEW
5,134 votes
Sabo
#6 (5)
5,121 votes
Portgaz D. Ace
#7 (4)
3,336 votes
Tony Tony Chopper
#8 (6)
2,173 votes
Nami
#9 (-) NEW
1,754 votes
Bartolomeo
#10 (-) NEW
1,422 votes
Boa Hancock
#11 (7)
1,253 votes
Nico Robin
#12 (122)
1,038 votes
Marco
#13 (11)
Stop showing off!!
BOOM
Usopp
1,023 votes
#14 (8)
951 votes
Shanks
#15 (28)
737 votes
Crocodile
#16 (13)
711 votes
Franky
#17 (46)
601 votes
Don Quixote Doflamingo
#18 (15)
566 votes
Eustass Kid
#19 (9)
553 votes
Brook
#20 (23)
531 votes
Mr. 2 Bon Clay

← Spots 21 and lower are on the next page!!!

POPULARITY POLL RESULTS!! Part 2

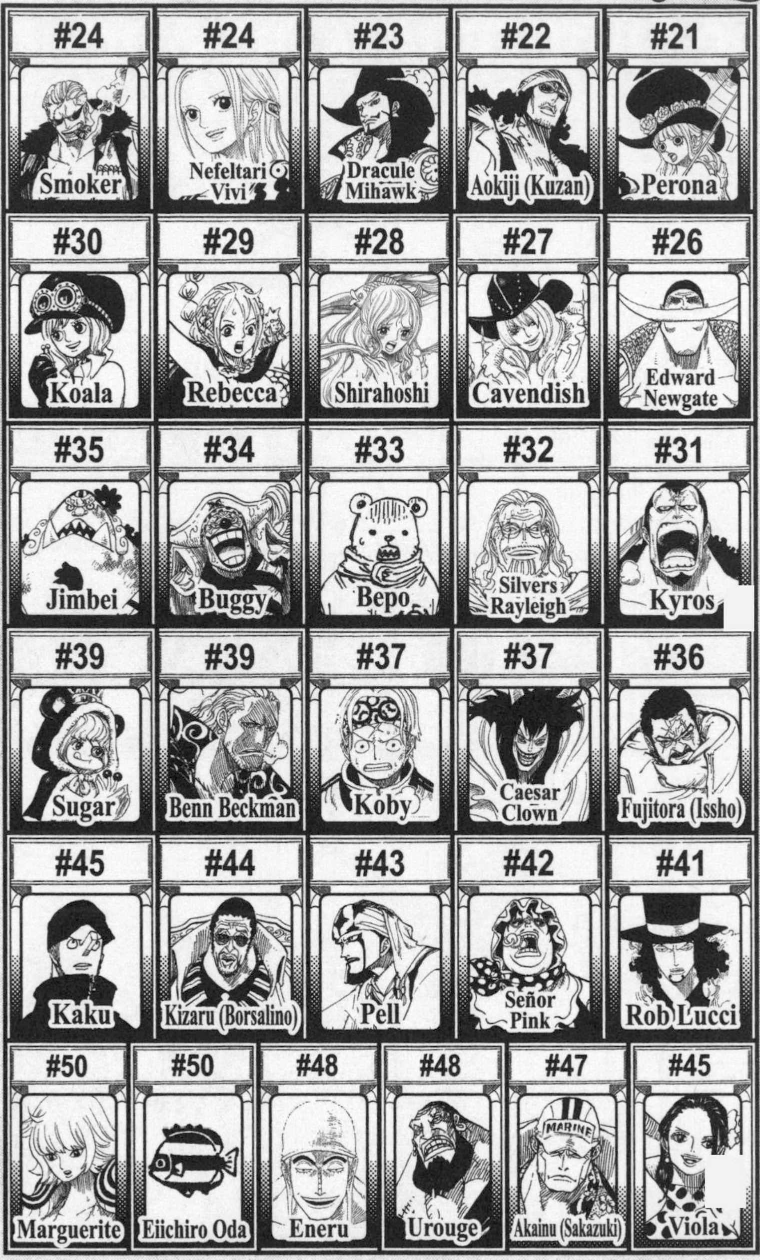
#21
Perona
#22
Aokiji (Kuzan)
#23
Dracule Mihawk
#24
Nefeltari Vivi
#24
Smoker
#26
Edward Newgate
#27
Cavendish
#28
Shirahoshi
#29
Rebecca
#30
Koala
#31
Kyros
#32
Silvers Rayleigh
#33
Bepo
#34
Buggy
#35
Jimbei
#36
Fujitora (Issho)
#37
Caesar Clown
#37
Koby
#39
Benn Beckman
#39
Sugar
#41
Rob Lucci
#42
Señor Pink
#43
Pell
#44
Kizaru (Borsalino)
#45
Kaku
#45
Viola
#47
Akainu (Sakazuki)
MARINE
#48
Urouge
#48
Eneru
#50
Eiichiro Oda
#50
Marguerite

The 5th ONE PIECE CHARACTER

#105: Black Cage Hina
Jaguar D. Saul
Kin'emon
Mr. 9
#109: Dalton
Django
Miss Goldenweek
Sadie
Lucky Roux
Iceberg
Inazuma
Jabra
Zeff
#118: T-Bone
Heracles
#120: Momonga
Bogard
(Garp's Assistant)
Dr. Kureha (Doctorine)
Chouchou
#124: Pappagu
Don Krieg
Gonbe
Wanze
Salome
Suleiman
Tom
Ripper
Trebol
Hikoichi
Schrier Bascude (Movie 4)
Momonosuke
Commodore Yarisugi
#137: Momousagi
Nola
Terracotta
Golden Lion Shiki (Strong World)
Itomimizu
Camie
Kalifa
Ein
Baratie Naval Weapon
Mackerel Head I
Nefeltari Cobra
Kalgara
Ryokugyu
Laboon
Accelegator
Mawaritosky Mizuuta

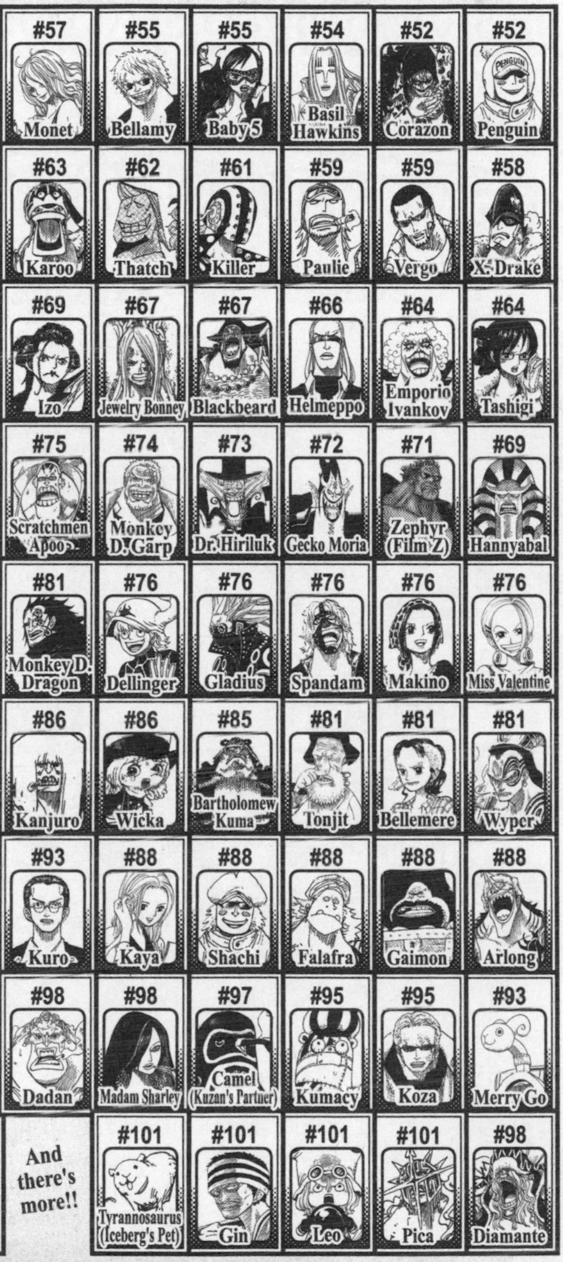

#52 Penguin
#52 Corazon
#54 Basil Hawkins
#55 Baby 5
#55 Bellamy
#57 Monet
#58 X. Drake
#59 Vergo
#59 Paulie
#61 Killer
#62 Thatch
#63 Karoo
#64 Tashigi
#64 Emporio Ivankov
#66 Helmeppo
#67 Blackbeard
#67 Jewelry Bonney
#69 Izo
#69 Hannyabal
#71 Zephyr (Film Z)
#72 Gecko Moria
#73 Dr. Hiriluk
#74 Monkey D. Garp
#75 Scratchmen Apoo
#76 Miss Valentine
#76 Makino
#76 Spandam
#76 Gladius
#76 Dellinger
#81 Monkey D. Dragon
#81 Wyper
#81 Bellemere
#81 Tonjit
#85 Bartholomew Kuma
#86 Wicka
#86 Kanjuro
#88 Arlong
#88 Gaimon
#88 Falafra
#88 Shachi
#88 Kaya
#93 Kuro
#93 Merry Go
#95 Koza
#95 Kumacy
#97 Camel (Kuzan's Partner)
#98 Madam Sharley
#98 Dadan
#98 Diamante
#101 Pica
#101 Leo
#101 Gin
#101 Tyrannosaurus (Iceberg's Pet)
And there's more!!

See next page for extra tidbits!!!

ONE PIECE CHARACTER POPULARITY POLL RESULTS!!!

EXTRA EDITION

Let's try breaking down the results into different subgenres!!You might see a few surprises pop up!!

POPULARITY RANKING BY GENRE!!!

BEST 5 OLDIES
#1 WHITEBEARD (EDWARD NEWGATE)
#2 SILVERS RAYLEIGH
#3 MONKEY D. GARP
#4 TONJIT
#5 ZEFF
BEST 5 WARLORDS (OLD AND NEW)
#1 TRAFALGAR LAW
#2 BOA HANCOCK
#3 CROCODILE
#4 DON QUIXOTE DOFLAMINGO
#5 DRACULE MIHAWK
BEST 5 LADIES
#1 NAMI
#2 BOA HANCOCK
#3 NICO ROBIN
#4 PERONA
#5 NEFELTARI VIVI
BEST 5 ANIMALS
#1 TONY TONY CHOPPER
#2 BEPO
#3 KAROO
#4 CAMEL
#5 TYRANNOSAURUS

A few more who actually got votes!

#152: Sawyer Wayback

#195: Sarfunkel
Kankichi Ryotsu

#261: Kuma-A
Stefan
Mikio Itoo
Pandawoman
Minatomo the Carpenter
Peekatha Krotch

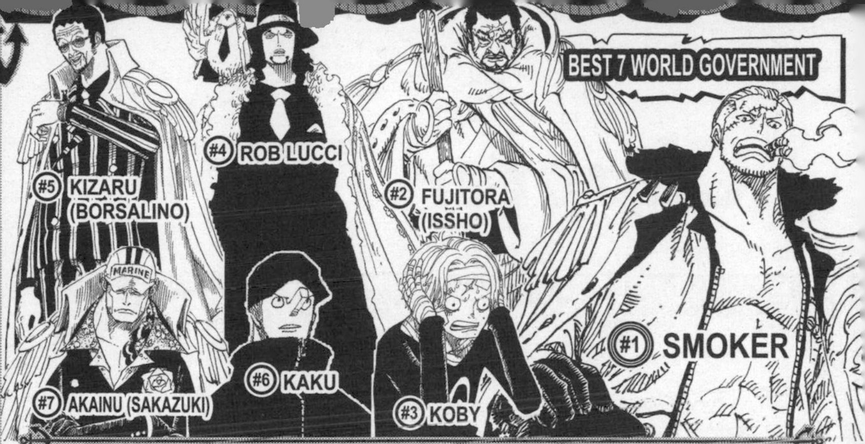
BEST 7 WORLD GOVERNMENT
#1 SMOKER
#2 FUJITORA (ISSHO)
#3 KOBY
#4 ROB LUCCI
#5 KIZARU (BORSALINO)
#6 KAKU
#7 AKAINU (SAKAZUKI)

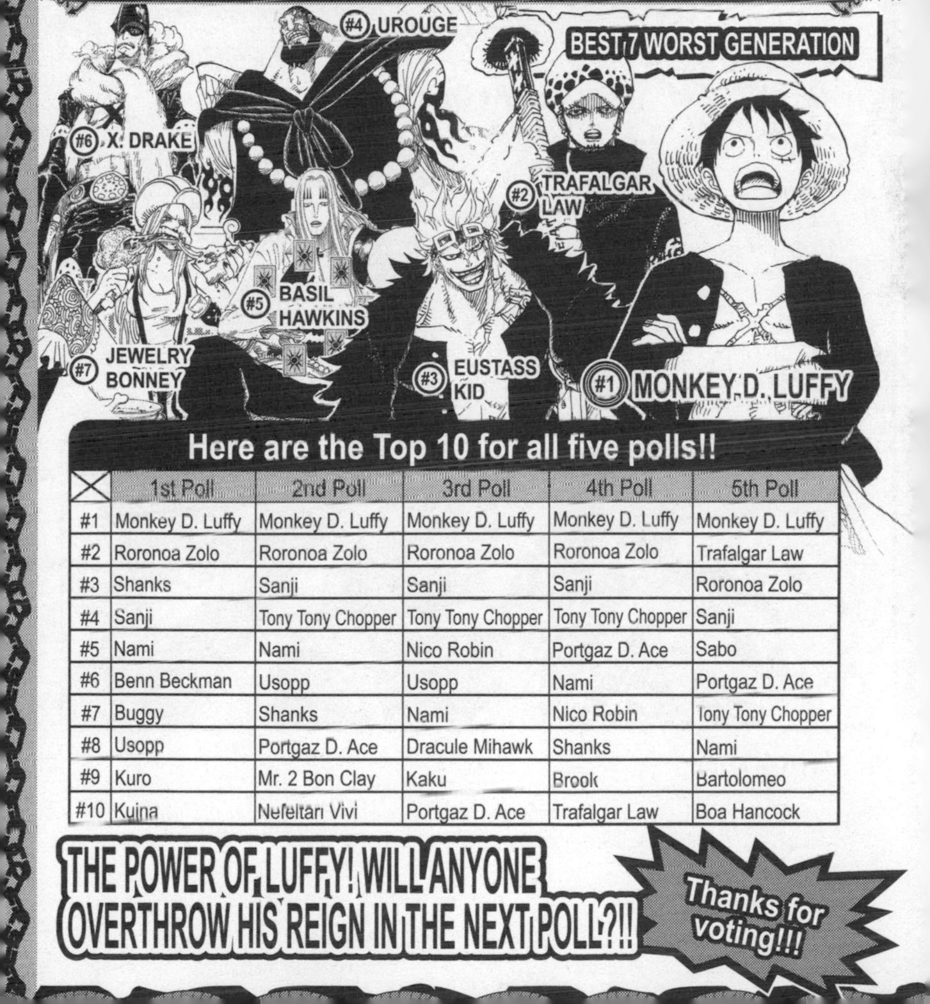
BEST 7 WORST GENERATION
#1 MONKEY D. LUFFY
#2 TRAFALGAR LAW
#3 EUSTASS KID
#4 UROUGE
#5 BASIL HAWKINS
#6 X. DRAKE
#7 JEWELRY BONNEY

Here are the Top 10 for all five polls!!

	1st Poll	2nd Poll	3rd Poll	4th Poll	5th Poll
#1	Monkey D. Luffy	Monkey D. Luffy	Monkey D. Luffy	Monkey D. Luffy	Monkey D. Luffy
#2	Roronoa Zolo	Roronoa Zolo	Roronoa Zolo	Roronoa Zolo	Trafalgar Law
#3	Shanks	Sanji	Sanji	Sanji	Roronoa Zolo
#4	Sanji	Tony Tony Chopper	Tony Tony Chopper	Tony Tony Chopper	Sanji
#5	Nami	Nami	Nico Robin	Portgaz D. Ace	Sabo
#6	Benn Beckman	Usopp	Usopp	Nami	Portgaz D. Ace
#7	Buggy	Shanks	Nami	Nico Robin	Tony Tony Chopper
#8	Usopp	Portgaz D. Ace	Dracule Mihawk	Shanks	Nami
#9	Kuro	Mr. 2 Bon Clay	Kaku	Brook	Bartolomeo
#10	Kuina	Nefeltari Vivi	Portgaz D. Ace	Trafalgar Law	Boa Hancock

THE POWER OF LUFFY! WILL ANYONE OVERTHROW HIS REIGN IN THE NEXT POLL?!!

Thanks for voting!!!

Chapter 759+

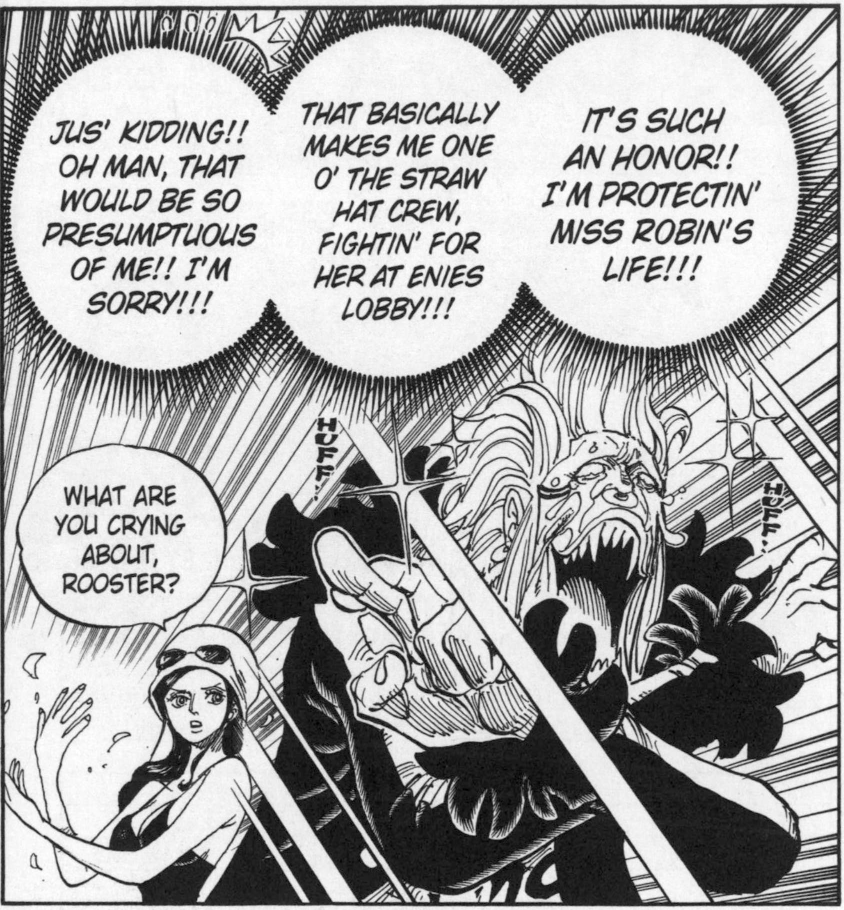
IT'S SUCH AN HONOR!! I'M PROTECTIN' MISS ROBIN'S LIFE!!!
THAT BASICALLY MAKES ME ONE O' THE STRAW HAT CREW, FIGHTIN' FOR HER AT ENIES LOBBY!!!
JUS' KIDDING!! OH MAN, THAT WOULD BE SO PRESUMPTUOUS OF ME!! I'M SORRY!!!
HUFF!!
HUFF!!
WHAT ARE YOU CRYING ABOUT, ROOSTER?

COMING NEXT VOLUME:

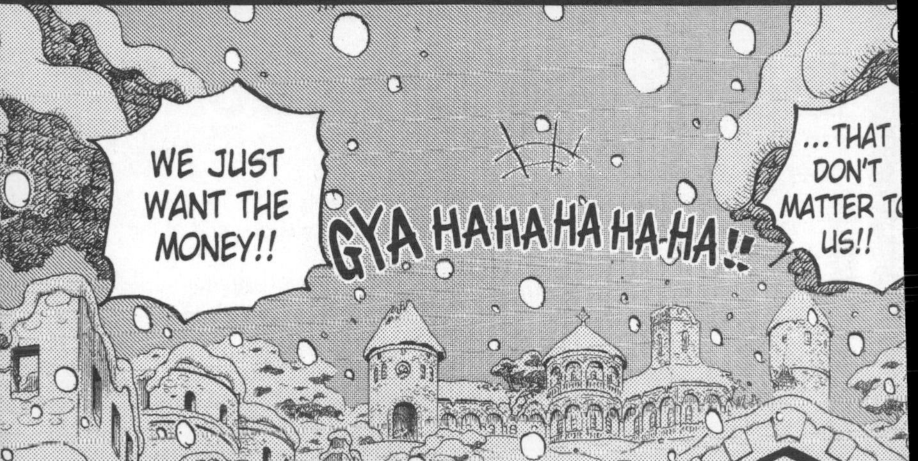
...THAT DON'T MATTER T US!!
GYA HAHAHA HA HA-HA!!
WE JUST WANT THE MONEY!!
...

As the story of Trafalgar Law's past continues, Corazon's secrets are revealed. Just how did these two come to be such close friends? And how was Law's fatal disease cured? And what will it all mean in the present time as Law confronts Doflamingo?

ON SALE NOW!

You're Reading in the Wrong Direction!!

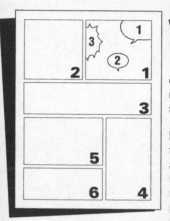

Whoops! Guess what? You're starting at the wrong end of the comic!

...It's true! In keeping with the original Japanese format, **One Piece** is meant to be read from right to left, starting in the upper-right corner.

Unlike English, which is read from left to right, Japanese is read from right to left, meaning that action, sound effects and word-balloon order are completely reversed...something which can make readers unfamiliar with Japanese feel pretty backwards themselves. For this reason, manga or Japanese comics published in the U.S. in English have sometimes been published "flopped"— that is, printed in exact reverse order, as though seen from the other side of a mirror.

By flopping pages, U.S. publishers can avoid confusing readers, but the compromise is not without its downside. For one thing, a character in a flopped manga series who once wore in the original Japanese version a T-shirt emblazoned with "M A Y" (as in "the merry month of") now wears one which reads "Y A M"! Additionally, many manga creators in Japan are themselves unhappy with the process, as some feel the mirror-imaging of their art skews their original intentions.

We are proud to bring you Eiichiro Oda's **One Piece** in the original unflopped format. For now, though, turn to the other side of the book and let the journey begin...!

—Editor